THE LEARNING GRID HANDBOOK

The Future of Learning

Learning is becoming more and more important as one of the indispensable tools to ensure future prosperity and well-being. This is the case not only for the individual, alone or as a member of a group, but also for organisational structures of all kinds. New learning paradigms and pedagogic principles, new learning environments and conditions, and new learning technologies are being tested in order to find the right combination of parameters that can optimise the outcome of the learning process in a given situation.

This book series presents to all stakeholders the latest advances in this important area, based on a sound foundation. Schools, higher education, industrial companies, public administrations and other organisational structures, including providers of learning and training services, including life-long learning, plus all the individuals involved, researchers, students, pupils, citizens, teachers, professors, instructors, politicians, decision makers etc., contribute to and benefit from this series. Pedagogic, economic, structural and organisational aspects, the latest technologies, and the influence from changing attitudes and globalisation are treated in this series, providing sound and updated information, which can be used to further improve the learning process in both formal and informal contexts.

Volume 2

Recently published in this series

Vol. 1. M. Pivec (Ed.), Affective and Emotional Aspects of Human-Computer Interaction – Game-Based and Innovative Learning Approaches

Related publications by IOS Press:

M. Tokoro and L. Steels (Eds.), The Future of Learning: Issues and Prospects
M. Tokoro and L. Steels (Eds.), A Learning Zone of One's Own: Sharing Representations and Flow in Collaborative Learning Environments
P. Kommers (Ed.), Cognitive Support for Learning: Imagining the Unknown
T. Hirashima, U. Hoppe and S. Shwu-Ching Young (Eds.), Supporting Learning Flow through Integrative Technologies
R. Mizoguchi, P. Dillenbourg and Z. Zhu (Eds.), Learning by Effective Utilization of Technologies: Facilitating Intercultural Understanding
P. Ritrovato, C. Allison, S.A. Cerri, T. Dimitrakos, M. Gaeta and S. Salerno (Eds.), Towards the Learning Grid: Advances in Human Learning Services

ISSN 1572-4794

The Learning Grid Handbook

Concepts, Technologies and Applications

Edited by

Saverio Salerno

Matteo Gaeta

Pierluigi Ritrovato

Nicola Capuano

Francesco Orciuoli

Sergio Miranda

and

Anna Pierri

DIIMA, Dipartimento di Ingegneria dell'Informazione e Matematica Applicata, Università degli Studi di Salerno, Italy

CRMPA, Centro di Ricerca in Matematica Pura ed Applicata, Italy

IOS Press

Amsterdam • Berlin • Oxford • Tokyo • Washington, DC

ISBN 978-1-58603-829-8
Library of Congress Control Number: 2007943827

Publisher
IOS Press
Nieuwe Hemweg 6B
1013 BG Amsterdam
Netherlands
fax: +31 20 687 0019
e-mail: order@iospress.nl

Distributor in the UK and Ireland
Gazelle Books Services Ltd.
White Cross Mills
Hightown
Lancaster LA1 4XS
United Kingdom
fax: +44 1524 63232
e-mail: sales@gazellebooks.co.uk

Distributor in the USA and Canada
IOS Press, Inc.
4502 Rachael Manor Drive
Fairfax, VA 22032
USA
fax: +1 703 323 3668
e-mail: iosbooks@iospress.com

PRINTED IN THE NETHERLANDS

*A book from the **Learning Grid** Special Interest Group of the Network of Excellence "**Kaleidoscope**: Shaping the Scientific Evolution of Technology Enhanced Learning"*

SIG Learning GRID

grid.noe-kaleidoscope.org

kaleidoscope
shaping the scientific evolution of Technology Enhanced Learning

www.noe-kaleidoscope.org

The Learning Grid Handbook
S. Salerno et al. (Eds.)
IOS Press, 2008

Preface

Grid technologies are rising as the next generation of Internet by defining a powerful computing paradigm by analogy with the electric Power Grid. A Grid user is able to use his private workplace to invoke applications from a remote system, use the system best suited for executing that application, access data securely and consistently from remote sites, exploit multiple systems to complete economically complex tasks or to solve large problems that exceed the capacity of a single system.

Grid could be used as a technology "glue" providing users with a uniform way to access resources by means of several devices. These technologies can provide, in a natural way, a support for Technology Enhanced Learning (TEL) by enabling new learning environments based on collaboration, real direct experience, personalisation, ubiquity, accessibility and contextualisation.

Nevertheless, to be effectively used in TEL, Grid must be complemented with other elements like semantics and educational modelling leading to the concept of "Learning Grid" as defined in the homonymous Special Interest Group (SIG) of the European Network of Excellence "**Kaleidoscope**: Shaping the Scientific Evolution of Technology Enhanced Learning".

The key challenge that Kaleidoscope is facing is the scientific and structural integration of the European TEL research. In this context, the **Learning Grid SIG** aims at contributing to the achievement of an improvement in TEL practices through the definition of open, distributed and pervasive environments for effective human learning, taking into account that effective learning requires an active attitude from learners and that learning is a social and collaborative activity requiring a technology that allows for active and realistic experiments, personalization, knowledge creation and evolution, as well as autonomous and dynamic creation of communities.

The research program of the Learning Grid SIG encompasses the definition of challenging scenarios for distributed service-oriented TEL, the analysis of technologies for creating distributed service-oriented TEL environments as well as the analysis of languages and frameworks for the dynamic composition of distributed TEL resources and services. Starting from that, the purpose of this book is to update, harmonize and consolidate obtained research results.

The **first section** of the book is about the concept of Learning Grid and related technologies. The first chapter gives a formal definition of the Learning Grid as an enabling architecture based on Grid, Semantics and Educational Modelling allowing the definition and the execution of TEL experiences obtained as cooperation and composition of distributed heterogeneous actors, resources and services. This chapter also presents an abstract architecture for the Learning Grid, a set of suitable learning approaches and some related research work.

The second chapter analyses and compares existing languages for the dynamic composition of distributed learning resources and services in a Learning Grid. It is worth noting that the application of such languages is important where heterogeneous services have to be dynamically composed according to learners' needs and preferences and to teacher defined learning methods and strategies. Based on that, the third chapter gives an overview of the main approaches to tackle the problems of semantic description and matchmaking of Learning Grid Services.

The fourth chapter concludes the first section with the definition of challenging application scenarios in the TEL domain that can be approached with a Learning Grid. The purpose is to understand and argue about the potential advantages of adopting a Learning Grid and to show why its features are paramount to improve personalisation and knowledge construction in the learning process as well as communication and collaboration inside learning groups.

The **second section** of the book is purposed to share research results obtained by European research groups connected with the Learning Grid SIG in their own projects on the field.

Chapter 5 is centred on some of the results of the ELeGI project: after having presented a theoretical learning model which allows to generate personalised learning experiences and to dynamically adapt them during the learning process, a Learning Grid software architecture created modifying the Intelligent Web Teacher (IWT) innovative learning platform and conceived for supporting the execution of the processes defined in the learning model, is described.

Chapter 6 presents an overview of Gridcole, a grid service-based tailorable collaborative TEL system enabling the integration of tools requiring supercomputing capabilities or specific hardware resources in order to support collaborative learning situations in which these types of tools are required and, at the same time, able to interpret collaboration scripts created by educators in order to guide participants during the realization of collaborative learning situations.

Chapter 7 presents a grid-based Virtual Observatory built in the AstroGrid project and explores how such a grid can be used as an e-learning platform for a wider audience. Moreover, in order to facilitate teacher interaction with remote students and to increase the interactivity level of the virtual classroom, the integration of Augmented Reality applications is also discussed.

Chapter 8, starting from the consideration that mobile and grid technologies provide complementary features that can address the requirements of next generation e-learning applications, presents some of the results of the Akogrimo project designed to build a platform based on both mobile and grid technologies and, in particular, discusses an m-learning scenario built on such platform.

Chapter 9 presents L4All: a system, coming from the homonymous project, able to record and share learning trails through educational offerings with the aim of facilitating progression of lifelong learners from Secondary Education, through to Further Education and on to Higher Education. The focus of the chapter is on the description of the service-oriented architecture of the system enabling a comprehensive set of educational activities.

Chapter 10 presents some results of the SeLeNe project which investigated the feasibility and designed tools to support learning communities (self e-learning networks) by matching learners' needs with educational resources potentially available on the Web. The focus is on the description of the personalisation services designed and developed using a combination of Web Service and Semantic Web technologies.

Chapter 11 presents a grid-based approach to capture and structure the information generated by collaborative learning activities in order to extract relevant knowledge and to provide learners and tutors with efficient awareness and feedback as regards group performance and collaboration. The authors demonstrate how a grid-based approach can considerably decrease the time of processing group activity log files and thus allow group learners to receive selected knowledge even in real time.

Chapter 12 presents a Virtual Scientific Experiment framework designed and developed on top of a grid infrastructure for running interactive virtual laboratory experiments for distributed student communities with visualization capabilities. The architecture is based on Web Services standard protocols such as WSDL and WS-Notification as implemented in the WSRF specification. The chapter also presents system evaluation results from a distributed pool of students showing the added value of the framework in enhancing distance-learning programs and Virtual Classes with extensible collaborative and interactive Virtual Laboratories sessions.

Chapter 13 presents ActiveMath, a Web-based TEL environment for mathematics, and discusses it from service and semantics perspectives. The service-oriented architecture of the system is described and how component services interplay with the domain and the pedagogical semantics used is shown. Details on the knowledge representation for mathematics are provided and how it is used to represent learning material and learning goals is explained as well as how a course generator assembles sequences of learning objects to fulfil these goals.

Saverio Salerno
Dept. of Information Engineering and Applied Mathematics
University of Salerno

Contents

Section I

Concept and Technologies

The Learning Grid Handbook
S. Salerno et al. (Eds.)
IOS Press, 2008

The Anatomy of the Learning Grid

Nicola CAPUANO [1,a,b], Matteo GAETA [a,b], Pierluigi RITROVATO [a,b]
[a] *CRMPA, Centro di Ricerca in Matematica Pura ed Applicata, Italy*
[b] *DIIMA, Università di Salerno, Italy*

Abstract. Over the last few years, Technology Enhanced Learning (TEL) needs have been changing in accordance with ever more complex pedagogical models as well as with technological evolution, demanding for high dynamic and configurable environments for running multiple teaching and learning scenarios.. Grid technologies have started to be very popular even in education due to the advantages that they offer being based on a secure, flexible and coordinated way of sharing resources over Internet as well as on its enormous capability of information processing. A Grid may facilitate learning processes in allowing each learner to collaboratively use the resources already existing online, by facilitating and managing dynamic communication with other people and agents, through the implementation of dynamic Virtual Organizations allowing to share learning resources. Nevertheless, in order to be effectively used in TEL, Grid must be complemented with other technologies bringing to the concept of "Learning Grid" whose description is the object of this chapter.

Keywords. Technology Enhanced Learning, Grid, Semantic Web, Semantic Grid, Learning Design.

Introduction

Grid technologies are rising as the next generation of Internet by defining a powerful computing paradigm by analogy with the electric Power Grid. A Grid user is able to use his private workplace to invoke any application from a remote system, use the system best suited for executing that application, access data securely and consistently from remote sites, exploit multiple systems to complete economically complex tasks or to solve large problems that exceed the capacity of a single system.

Grid could be used as a technology "glue" providing users with a uniform way to access resources by means of several devices. These technologies can provide, in a natural way, a support for Technology Enhanced Learning (TEL) by enabling new learning environments based on collaboration, social interaction, experience, realism, personalization, ubiquity, accessibility and contextualization.

Nevertheless, to be effectively used in TEL, Grid must be complemented with other elements like semantics and educational modeling so bringing to the concept of "Learning Grid" whose description is the object of this chapter. In particular the first paragraph of this chapter gives some more details on enabling technologies making the Learning Grid vision possible while the second paragraph gives a formal definition of the Learning Grid concept also presenting an abstract architecture. Paragraph 3 moves

---

[1] Corresponding Author: CRMPA, Centro di Ricerca in Matematica Pura ed Applicata, via Ponte Don Melillo, 84084 Fisciano (SA), Italy; E-mail: capuano@crmpa.unisa.it.

the focus to learning approaches that are more suitable for a Learning Grid while paragraph 4 summarizes some related research work.

Following this trend, a Special Interest Group (SIG) of the European Network of Excellence Kaleidoscope [28] have committed itself to establish an observatory on Grid applications to TEL in order to study the field and to foster discussion among several research groups on the theme spread in Europe. Main results coming from this SIG (including this book) have been summarised in paragraph 4 too. The last paragraph presents concluding remarks.

1. The Enabling Technologies

As detailed in this paragraph, the three Enabling technologies that, duly integrated, constitute a comprehensive technological platform able to support the implementation of a Learning Grid are:

- Grid technologies,
- Semantics,
- Educational Modelling.

As shown in Figure 1, if we refer to the well known two axis diagram that places the Semantic Grid in a two dimensional spaces (the scale of interoperability and the scale of data/computation), the Learning Grid can be seen as a projection of the Semantic Grid on a third axis measuring the supported scale of pedagogies.

In the next three sub-paragraphs we provide more details about these three pillars referencing relevant scientific literature where needed. The next paragraph focuses instead on how such technologies can be put together and exploited as a basis to build pervasive and challenging TEL environments.

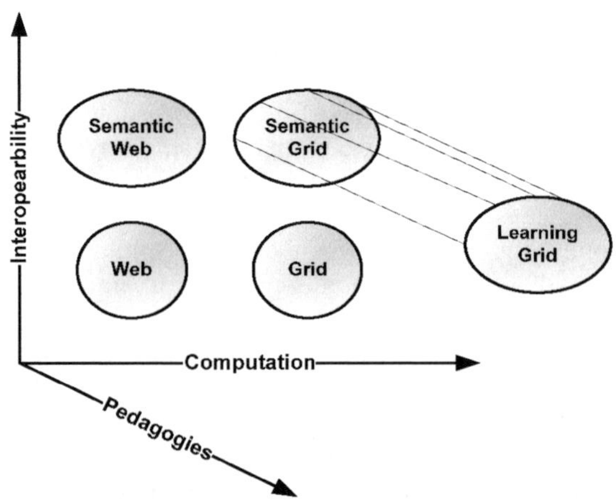

Figure 1. The Learning Grid with respect to Grid and Semantic Grid.

1.1. Grid Technologies

In the beginning, **Grid** was synonym of meta-computing and according to this first vision, Kesselman and Foster attempted a first definition of the Grid as “a hardware and software infrastructure that provides dependable, consistent, pervasive, and inexpensive access to high-end computational capabilities” [14]. Research has brought to a new vision of Grid that became synonym of infrastructure to “coordinate resource sharing and problem solving in dynamic, multi-institutional virtual organizations” [14] where the focus is on the concept of Virtual Organization (VO).

Currently, the evolution of Grid is marked by the adoption of a service oriented approach in designing Grid architectures. The Open Grid Services Architecture (OGSA) integrates key Grid technologies with Web Services mechanisms to create a distributed system framework for integrating, virtualizing and managing resources and services within distributed, heterogeneous and dynamic VOs [18]. In addition, by adopting the Web Services Resource Framework (WSRF) [13] it is possible to define a Grid resource as a “stateless service acting upon a stateful resource” so applying a service model of an intermediate complexity between pure stateless services and pure conversational ones, thus allowing a simple way to compose services without loosing the advantages of state management.

Upon the OGSA model, different kinds of Grids have been raised like Computation, Data or Information Grid. Apart from the specific term, the key features of all these Grids are virtualization in term of services and dynamic policy-based provision of what is virtualized. Some of them deal with well known issues, like Computational Grid that provides the access to a large virtual computer and Information Grid permitting the access to a large virtual information source.

1.2. Semantics

Among them a key role for TEL is played by the **Semantic Grid** that was defined by De Roure and other researchers as: “an extension of the current Grid in which information and services are given well-defined meaning, better enabling computers and people to work in cooperation” [11], [22]. In other words a Semantic Grid is a Grid improved through standards and technologies of the Semantic Web [5] community, to make explicit and machine understandable the knowledge about resources and services as well as communities and individuals of communities.

A Semantic Grid relies on specifications like OWL-S [46] and WSMO [42] in order to semantically enrich resources virtualised through a service to let software agents compare the requirements of a service against its description to find the service that best satisfy the requirements. In this way it supports the automatic negotiation, discovery and composition of services.

Following this trend, the Service Oriented Knowledge Utility (SOKU) vision, as elaborated in [38], builds on a natural evolution and combination of concepts from Web Services, Grid technologies, the Semantic Web, distributed analytics and self-organising systems that have broad international industry acceptance. SOKU presents at the core of its vision the concept of service that is semantically described and can be dynamically composed, adapted and configured.

The Semantic Grid is a good enabling infrastructure for Technology Enhanced Learning (TEL) by itself being it able to fulfil many of the new needs coming from ever more complex pedagogical models [41] including:

- wide geographical distribution of learners and tutors who can potentially belong to many different educational institutions;
- multiple administrations from different organisations with specific educational policies;
- access from anywhere, on any learners' computer platform and any software;
- support for a growing load of learning resources, services and users who access resources and services;
- transparent access and share of an huge variety of such software and hardware learning resources and services in dynamic environments;
- flexibility to reuse pieces of learning resources and services of different granularity according to specific needs;
- support to the autonomous and dynamic creation of communities through the VO paradigm;
- learning personalization and knowledge creation, acquisition and evolution.

1.3. Educational Modelling

Nevertheless, in order to be fully exploited in the TEL domain, the Semantic Grid should be enriched with **Educational Modelling** capabilities through the integration of feasible Education Modelling Languages (EMLs) and the provisioning of services discovery and composition capabilities driven by such languages. An EML can be defined as a semantic notation for units of learning to be used in TEL to support the reuse of pedagogical entities like learning designs, objectives, activities, etc. EMLs involves the description of learning processes and methods from a pedagogical and instructional rather then content-driven perspective.

IMS Learning Design (IMS-LD) [26] is currently the widest diffused EML and, according to the next chapter of this book, the one more feasible to be used as the basis in a Learning Grid environment. Through IMS-LD it is possible to describe a wide variety of pedagogical models, including group work and collaborative learning. It does not define individual pedagogical models but provides an high-level language that can describe many different models. The language describes how people perform activities using resources and services, and how to coordinate them into a learning flow.

2. The Learning Grid

The integration of the above mentioned technologies bring us to the following definition of the **Learning Grid**:

A Learning Grid is an enabling architecture based on three pillars: Grid, Semantics and Educational Modelling allowing the definition and the execution of learning experiences obtained as cooperation and composition of distributed heterogeneous actors, resources and services.

This definition, coming from the Learning Grid Special Interest Group of Kaleidoscope can be seen as a generalisation of the "Semantic Grid for Human

Learning" defined by Gaeta et al. in [19] where the focus was on complex learning experiences based on experiential-based conversational processes.

Basing on such definition the next sub-paragraphs define a layered architecture for the Learning Grid and explain how it can be used as a basis to provide Learning Services and Applications.

2.1. Learning Grid Architecture

According to the given definition, a Learning Grid architecture is composed by the following set of services organised in three layers (see Figure 2):

1. the **Infrastructure Services** provide an implementation of the Web Service Resource Framework (WSRF) specifications in order to define the underlying service model;
2. the **Grid Middleware for VO Management** provides an implementation of the services identified by the Open Grid Services Architecture (OGSA) allowing to create and manage a distributed VO and integrate, virtualize and manage resources and services upon it;
3. the **Semantic Annotation, Discovery and Composition Services** provide learning independent functionalities based on specifications and languages for the semantic description of Web services (e.g. OWL-S) to allow the automatic negotiation, discovery and composition of Grid Services;
4. the **Educational Modelling and Execution Services** provide contextualised features related to the formal description of learning experiences basing on Education Modelling Languages (e.g. IMS-LD) and the automatic discovery, composition and execution of learning resources and services available on the Grid basing on such descriptions.

With respect to Educational Modelling and Execution Services it is important to note that languages such as IMS-LD are currently hardly exploitable in Semantic Grid

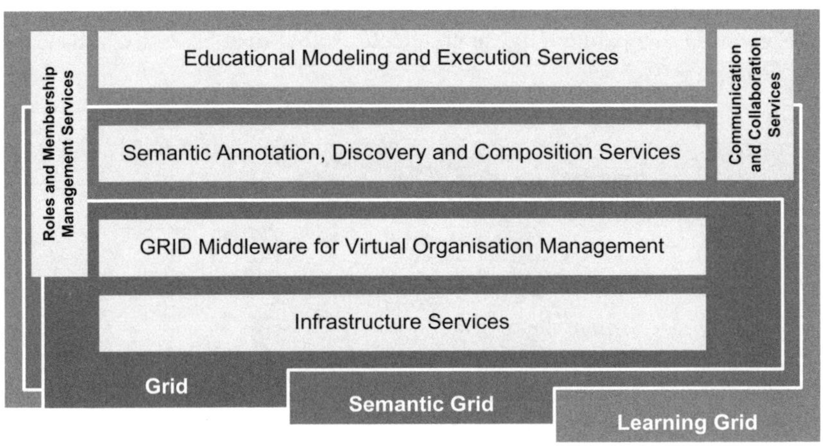

Figure 2. Architecture of a Learning Grid.

environments due to several limitations coming from design-time resource binding. This imply a lacks of dynamicity i.e. Learning Grid Services must be bind at design time rather that at execution time so hindering to fully exploit dynamic discovery and composition of learning services. To solve this problem [8] proposes semantic extensions to IMS-LD as we will further detail in the next chapter of this book.

The Figure 2 shows a layered architecture based on the above described services. As it can be seen, a Grid is composed by Infrastructure Services plus a Grid Middleware for VO Management; a Semantic Grid is composed by a Grid plus Semantic Annotation, Discovery and Composition Services; a Learning Grid is composed by a Semantic Grid plus Educational Modelling and Execution Services plus a set of "environment" services described below to support the creation, the operation, the evolution and the maintenance of a learning community:

- the **Role and Membership Management Services** manage users, groups, roles and membership inside VOs on the Learning Grid by supporting the Grid Middleware for VO Management as well as Semantic Annotation, Discovery and Composition Services and Educational Modelling and Execution Services;
- the **Communication and Collaboration Services** provide tools to support communication and collaboration among participants in groups, communities and actors involved in learning experiences by supporting Semantic Annotation, Discovery and Composition Services and Educational Modelling and Execution Services.

2.2. Learning Services and Applications

As summarised in Figure 3, the Learning Grid has to be seen as an enabling infrastructure able to be exploited for the implementation of several specific learning scenarios. In particular, several further learning services may be built on the basis of services provided by the Learning Grid, and several different learning applications may be built by leveraging on such services.

The fourth chapter of this book deals with different scenarios that may be built upon a Learning Grid while in the second section several systems based or inspired to this architecture are presented. Such systems, tough they aren't directly based on the definition given in this paragraph, use architectures that may be easily transposed on a Learning Grid.

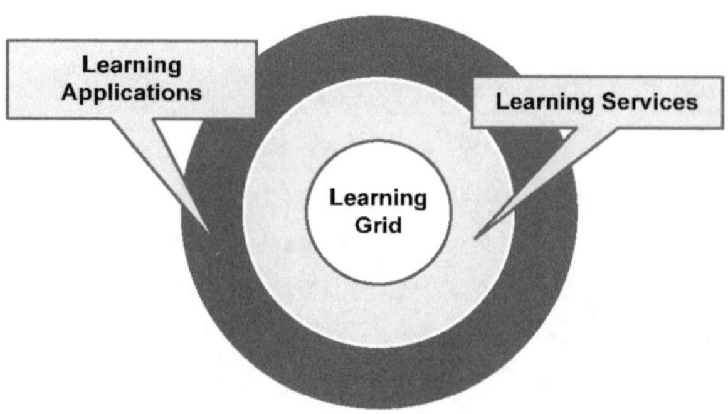

Figure 3. The Learning Grid as an enabling architecture to build learning applications.

3. Pedagogies and Learning Grid

This paragraph moves the focus from technology to pedagogy linked with the Learning Grid. It tries to show which kind of learning approaches are more suitable to be exploited in a Learning Grid environment in comparison with traditional e-Learning settings. Particular emphasis is given to learning approaches based on orchestrated learning activities and on communication and cooperation processes.

The dominant learning approach in TEL has been for many years the Information Transfer, based on the central figure of the teacher whose primary activity is the provisioning of educational contents to be transferred to learners that passively consume them. Consequently many e-Learning solutions provide a "digitized" version of this approach so, in most cases, distance learning platforms focus on educational resources and on their delivery.

This aspect, together with other relevant lacks, as the support for pedagogies, the contextualization of the learning experience and the centrality of the learner, lowers the effectiveness of the above learning solutions.

Nowadays, the need for e-learning systems supporting a rich set of pedagogical requirements (as those summarized in the first paragraph) has been identified as an issue of paramount importance. In this context, a Learning Grid allows the design, the implementation and the deployment of learning experiences based on the selection and the orchestration of different learning activities.

In the next sub-paragraph we try to demonstrate why Learning Grid is particularly suitable for the implementation and the deployment of such kind of learning experiences while in the second sub-paragraph we focus instead on a subset of pedagogical approaches based on Communication and Cooperation processes seeing, also in this case, the added value of the Learning Grid.

3.1. Learning Approaches based on Orchestrated Learning Activities

The Grid allows the deployment of complex learning processes based on knowledge, like the ones provided by IMS-LD scenarios. IMS-LD is used to model teaching and learning practices that go beyond simple traditional Web-based educational contents delivery. In [4] it is emphasized how IMS-LD adopts a two levels approach to fulfil this task, modelling both:

- the learning activities, to be defined as interactions between a learner and an environment, having the objective to achieve a planned learning outcome;
- the learning approaches, involving the selection and orchestration of the activities on the basis of the pedagogies ensuring, among other things, the reuse of their components.

As outlined also in [2], reuse and re-purposing is somewhat difficult to obtain by means of traditional technologies that are generally information oriented and URL based. Dynamicity and adaptivity features of (service oriented) Grid technologies can be so exploited to provide actual benefits from the viewpoint of reuse and repurposing of learning activities.

Indeed, to reuse learning activities in different contexts and to obtain different outcomes requires mechanisms for automatic discovery and binding of new suitable educational contents and services as well as self-adaptive mechanisms when deploying the learning activities composing a scenario, which are distinctive features of Grid. Work that investigates advantages and drawbacks of the integration between IMS-LD and Grid are presented in [6], [37] and [21].

- In [6] the authors propose and justify the adoption of IMS-LD for Computer Supported Collaborative Learning (CSCL), and the advantages of Grid technology to support CSCL. The main result of their work converges in a distributed system that can select and integrate Grid Services according to the prescriptions of IMS-LD documents.
- In [37], instead, the authors propose the Grid enabled Learning Object (GLOB) to allow the execution of learning activities exploiting mainly computational capabilities of a Grid.
- In [21] learning activities are bound to educational resources and services using semantic capabilities at learners' fruition time, in order to best fit their preferences and networked resources availability. They do not define a specific structure acting as interface to the Grid and, furthermore, they rely on semantic enrichment of IMS-LD documents in order to retrieve at run time educational resources through the Grid.

The need of a Grid-based approach in the creation of learning scenarios based on the IMS-LD specifications can be supported, moreover, by the Service Orientation and the Virtualization paradigms that are at the basis of the OGSA model. They are clearly useful in a learning approach that strongly relies on a composition paradigm allowing the creation of personalized learning experiences (re-)using data, educational contents, knowledge and tools virtualized as services and distributed across several organizations.

In addition, with respect to the other Service Oriented Computing approaches, the Grid approach provides a well defined taxonomy [17] able to solve many issues connected to the creation and management of a VO and, in accordance with this taxonomy, a set of capabilities have been already defined. This is a key factor in collaborative and community-based processes by supporting the dynamic creation of communities and their management as deepened in the next sub-paragraph.

3.2. Didactic Methods Based on Communication and Cooperation Processes.

Learning approaches based on Communication and Cooperation (C&C) processes generally bring to the creation and execution of learning experiences in which collaboration and communication among participants play a key role. There are several didactic methods based on C&C processes such as:

- Virtual Classroom that simulates on-line the characteristics of a real classroom;
- Synchronous Instant Communication relying on several means of synchronous communication among the involved actors;
- Problem-Based Learning in which students are engaged in the resolution of a problem related to learning objectives;
- Collaborative Apprenticeship based on the prior observation of a given task;
- Jigsaw method where each student's part is essential for the completion and full understanding of the final product.

In this context the Learning Grid is not only useful to reach the desired level of dynamicity and scalability for a group or a community and to manage its heterogeneity but also for transparent ubiquitous resource sharing. In fact through the virtualisation paradigm, traditional collaborative tools can be virtualised as services. This allows to add dynamicity since they can be provided on demand and it is possible to search and retrieve the most suitable tool on the basis of some parameters like, for instance, preferences of the group of learners and/or QoS.

Exploiting the distinctive features of Grid services (mainly lifecycle management and statefulness, but also manageability) it is possible to increase scalability and support management of interactions respectively. It is possible to create more instances of services to support the collaboration. Furthermore, the state management capabilities of Grid services allow to define and associate a state to each service (following the WSRF specification, the related stateful resource concept and implied resource pattern). This is an useful feature if we want to track data/information during cooperation and conversation among the learners.

As enabling technologies for learning-purposed VO, Grid provides support for geographically distributed community creation and management, logically defined as Virtual Learning Communities addressing issues like heterogeneity, single sign-on, group and community lifecycle management, localization and instantiation of tools and services, transparent resource sharing.

Table 1. Added value of the Learning Grid in C&C processes.

Needs	Traditional approaches	Learning Grid added value
Resources/Document sharing	Adoption of a centralised shared workspaces systems (e.g. BSCW)	Exploitation of VO functionalities for resources sharing (including tools) and management. Semantic capabilities to allow automatic search and retrieve of resources matching user needs and preferences
Awareness of the group members	Traditional tools for collaboration generally provide information on the availability on-line of members of a group.	Enhanced presence allowing to search and find peers/tutors with specific profiles, with specific interests, etc. To this purpose semantic capabilities and ontologies (like the Learner profile ontology, extending the W3C FOAF)
Creation and management of collaborative sessions inside a group	Traditional systems provide low support for this feature. For instance, the session has to be scheduled, participants have to join, the documents and materials for the collaborative session have to be uploaded in a shared workspace, etc.	Grid technologies and the Grid service container concepts allow to improve the creation and management of collaborative session allowing a dynamic adding/removing of services, resources and participants in the collaborative session. Semantic capabilities allows for automatic discovery of services and resources matching the specific needs of the group and/or the collaboration session.
Integration of different heterogeneous tools	Currently, many functionalities for C&C are provided by different tools that are difficult to integrate together in order to create a environment supporting C&C	The virtualisation paradigm and SOA (e.g. OGSA) approach allow to simplify the integration issue. Different tools can be virtualised and managed as services. Furthermore, they can rely upon functionalities of the Grid middleware to improve.

Dynamicity and adaptiveness of Grid technologies are key features in order to provide advanced mechanism for service discovery and instantiation on the basis of service-level agreements (SLA) documents and self-management, self-monitoring, etc. This allows, for instance, to deploy and execute a service on the most suitable host of a VO and to monitor at-run-time its SLA, control the resources access through policy based mechanisms, etc.

By exploiting flexible and standard based mechanisms for transparent resources reservation, sharing and accessibility, Grid also improves ubiquity and accessibility. Semantic Grid capabilities also allow semantic annotation of educational resources and services for automatic discovery and late binding of educational resources and services in the learning environment, improving the capability to support learning community creation and management.

The usefulness of these capabilities for learning is also supported by several research papers as summarised in [36] where a Semantic Web/e-Learning research issue correspondence map is provided. It is worth mentioning that in the case of creation of formal learning experiences based on the C&C approach, all the benefits that we have emphasised for the creation and execution of learning experiences based on other approaches apply as well.

In addition to what highlighted above, the table 1 summarises some needs of the C&C processes pointing out the benefits coming from the adoption of a Learning Grid with respect to traditional approaches.

4. Related Work

The concept of "Learning Grid" is defined as a synthesis of several, sometimes implicit, definitions coming from the most recent and significant scientific work on related topics. In the next sub-paragraph, according to [9], we will summarize some of these research works. In the second section of this book specific chapters are provided in order to give more details about some of the most relevant projects connected with the Learning Grid concept.

As already anticipated, a Special Interest Group (SIG) of the European Network of Excellence Kaleidoscope, following this research strand, have committed itself to studying the field and to fostering discussion among related research groups spread in Europe. More detail about the SIG are given in the second sub-paragraph.

4.1. Projects Connected with the Learning Grid

The Grid Service Based Portal for Virtual Learning Campus [45] developed an environment which makes use of the Grid capabilities so that to make possible the dynamic sharing and coordination of heterogeneous resources which are found dispersed in the network. The project focuses on the development of a video digital library based on Grid for a Virtual Campus that allows an easy access and implementation of several services. In spite of being a project that aimed to take advantage of the capabilities that Grid technology provides, it is limited on a unique type of educative resources, like video, which a structure of services is developed for.

In [33] it is described a TEL platform based on Grid service technologies. In this platform the supply of virtual learning services designed for students, instructors and course suppliers is based on the resource administration for group collaboration based on Grid, allowing ubiquitous access to information and taking advantage of the potentiality of the computer systems. On the one hand, the advantage of this proposal is that it is the first one that elaborates on the use of Grid resources and their description through Grid technologies, in particular WSDL. On the other hand, it dictates the need for the development of a semantic model description that enables a more complete description of learning resources.

ULabGrid, an Infrastructure to Develop Distant Laboratories for Undergrad Students over a Grid, [3] proposes a new architecture that allows the educators to design remote collaborative laboratories for university students using the Grid infrastructure. This project is one of the first in its type in trying to combine the facilities that Grid provides in a practical scenario in order to achieve resource sharing and motivate collaborative work. In this sense the design of Grid-based collaborative learning scenarios should be supported by semantic descriptions that allow the best tracking of resources available in the network.

Another work that aims at developing a Generic Engineering Framework for TEL Embracing the Semantic Web [32] proposes the convergence of TEL, Web semantics and e-business by introducing a generic engineering approach that labels learning objects with RDF for semantic e-learning and integrating it with a process oriented paradigm. This work can serve as one of the first approaches as regards the use of information modelling and RDF to label learning scenarios resources, making use of a process management approach, which if adapted to the Learning Grid will provide a new generation of applications.

A further work proposes an Agent-Based Collaborative Virtual Environment for TEL in the Service Grid [25]. In this virtual environment, all Web resources and services are accessed via service encapsulation, which may result in a more scalable and robust collaborative learning architecture. A very remarkable aspect of this work is the way it uses to implement complex services from more basic ones, though no use of semantic description is made to allow the automatic composition of complex services from lower level ones.

KGTutor, a Knowledge Grid Based Intelligent Tutoring System [48], proposes a model for the construction of intelligent tutoring in a more pleasant and effective way. The KGTutor is designed to provide better support to student cantered distributed learning. Students' characteristics, such as previous knowledge and learning styles, are used to choose, organize, and deliver the learning materials to individual students. During learning progress, the system can also provide objective evaluations and customized suggestions for each student according to their learning performance. This system provides a very important work as far as student centred learning concerns, though it could be further strengthened through the use of aspects of semantic description of learning services.

The Knowledge-Grid-Based Cooperative Learning Environment [49], supports the cooperation between a person and the computer at a knowledge level, and allows the enrichment not only of the resources in the Knowledge Grid but also of the users' knowledge by means of knowledge refinement, knowledge reuse and the online meeting of participants. The KGCL prototype has been currently applied and is available for online use. Experiments have shown that the environment can promote the effectiveness of group work. This system has also shown the great impact that Grid technologies can have even though no model of semantic description was implemented that could improve its performance.

The SELF project [1] proposes a learning environment that results from the integration of several technologies, specially the semantic Web, Grid technology, collaborative tools as well as customized tools and knowledge management techniques. SELF provides a mechanism for the intelligent search of services making use of semantic description tools. This project presents an important reference of the use of different technologies for the development of Grid-based learning scenarios, even though it is not based on semantic description models for the definition of its tools.

OntoEdu [24] is a flexible platform for online learning which is based on diverse technologies like ubiquitous computing, ontology engineering, Web semantics and computational Grid. It is compound of five parts: user adaptation, automatic composition, educative ontologies, a module of services and a module of contents; among these parts the educative ontology is the main one. The main objectives of OntoEdu are to obtain reusability of concepts, adaptability for users and devices, automatic composition, as well as scalability in functionality and performance.

The work developed in [31] presents a workflow framework for pervasive learning objects composition by employing a Grid services flow language. Learning objects are distributed in heterogeneous environments which have been used in order to allow effective collaboration and the reuse of learning objects; this fact can help users to learn with no limitations of time and space. This work shows the great opportunities that exist in those research groups which make use of Grid technology to develop innovative, pervasive and ubiquitous learning scenarios.

ELeGI (European Learning Grid Infrastructure) [40] aims to define and implement a software architecture able to unify the semantic Grid and information technologies in order to promote and give support to the definition and adoption of learning paradigms for the construction of knowledge that combines customized and ubiquitous techniques based on experiential, collaborative and contextualized learning. In this line, [23] presents a work about ontology based user modelling for personalization of Grid learning services. This work describes how the learning services of the Grid should support a user-centred, customized, contextualized, experiential and ubiquitous based learning approach. More details about ELeGI are given in the chapter 5 of this book.

In the work referenced as "Semantic Search of Learning Services in a Grid-Based Collaborative System" [47], the authors have constructed an ontological description for collaborative work tools that allow one to make a manual search of the diverse resources that these tools provide within a Grid environment with the minimum of technical knowledge. This work proposes a Grid-based tool called Gridcole, which can serve as a basis to implement different conceptual approaches of Grid-based semantic description of learning services, thus extending and endowing it with an innovative, pervasive and ubiquitous projection. More details about Gridcole are given in the chapter 6 of this book.

Akogrimo [27] is an FP6 project whose purpose is to obtain a convergence between grid and mobile technologies in order to provide dynamically concerted use of resources and services including e-learning services. In this context, grid services, comprising personalized knowledge and semantics, are allowing for ad-hoc, dynamic, and possibly federated formation of complex problem solving scenarios in everyday life, in business, science and learning to fixed, nomadic and mobile citizens. More details about the e-learning strand of Akogrimo are given in the chapter 8 of this book.

Finally, in [43], a Grid Service Framework for Metadata Management in Self-e-Learning Networks focuses on how the use of metadata can be critical for Grid systems. More specifically, the semantic description constitutes a very beneficial extension of

Grid environments. The Self e-Learning Network (SeLeNe) is used as a test application while a set of services is proposed which are implemented with OGSA. The project focuses on providing services that use learning objects metadata, based on a sufficiently generic approach so that they can be used by other Grid-based systems which need to make use of semantic descriptions. More details about SeLeNe are given in the chapter 10 of this book.

4.2. The "Learning Grid" Special Interest Group

Kaleidoscope [29] is a Network of Excellence funded by the European Commission which brings together European research teams in TEL. The key challenge that Kaleidoscope is facing is the scientific and structural integration of European TEL research. The challenge lies in the topic itself which is multi-disciplinary. Therefore, Kaleidoscope gathers researchers coming from various disciplines, from learning sciences to computational technology, which is critical since knowledge and meaning making are key to learning. The challenge lies also in the European dimension of the network, since European countries have different educational systems.

"Learning Grid" SIG [28] is a Special Interest Group of Kaleidoscope aiming at contributing to the achievement of an improvement in e-learning and training practices through the definition of open, distributed and pervasive environments for effective human learning. This view takes into account that effective learning requires an active attitude of learners and that learning is a social activity. Therefore, future learning scenarios require a technology that allows for active and realistic experiments, personalization, knowledge creation and evolution, as well as autonomous and dynamic creation of communities.

The Learning Grid SIG investigates on how Grid technologies can be exploited in future learning scenarios to support the learning processes by allowing learners to collaboratively use online resources, by facilitating dynamic communication with other people and agents on the Grid and by designing and implementing dynamic learning virtual organizations. The SIG also works on the concept of learning services and their deployment through Grid technologies.

SIG researchers cooperate to give a common answer on open issues about Learning Grid including the definition of new learning paradigms based on experiential, collaborative and contextualized approaches to exploit Grid technologies for addressing heterogeneous interoperability issues; the use and the extension of Grid technology for implementing Virtual Organizations to support the new emerging learning scenarios (collaborative virtual learning communities); the definition of evaluation models and strategies able to assess the efficacy and the effectiveness of Grid based learning models and systems.

SIG activities started in January 2004 on two main lines, the first one related to research, the second one to networking and dissemination activities:

1. the main aim of the research line is to pursue a common research program aimed to the resolution of the above mentioned issues allowing the full exploitation of grid technologies for effective human learning;
2. the main aim of the networking and dissemination line is to share SIG findings inside and outside Kaleidoscope boundaries in order to favour an in-depth understanding of the advantages offered by distributed and grid environments

in applying innovative learning paradigms and as enabling technology for creating dynamic Virtual Learning Communities.

From the **research** point of view, main SIG achievements can be summarized as follows. Several futuristic learning scenarios that aren't realizable with the current platforms/tools for distance learning have been defined, advantages introduced from a pedagogical viewpoint have been described, necessary features/services have been scratched, business benefits/drivers/needs have been emphasized.

A common set of concepts and terms related to e-learning infrastructures were defined; the need for a service-oriented approach in the context of e-Learning was justified; the nature of a service-oriented framework and its benefits for education was clarified; a methodology for constructing service-oriented e-Learning frameworks was defined; services to address the most pervasive challenges existing in education as a requirement to exploit the benefits of a service-oriented framework was defined; possibilities in developing an international service-oriented e-learning framework to extend the scope of the existing needs in education was explored.

A survey of existing languages and frameworks for the dynamic composition of distributed resources and services with particular regard to e-learning resources and services was performed and extension needed to use such languages in the context of a Learning Grid were defined.

From the **networking and dissemination** points of view, main SIG achievements can be summarized as follows. An observatory on Grid technologies for learning purposed to survey the field and report to the scientific community through a Web site and a quarterly newsletter have been established. The observatory also have in charge of disseminating main technological and methodological findings of related projects and advancements in standardization activities carried out by international bodies.

An yearly workshop connected with main events in the GRID and TEL fields collecting and publishing reviewed papers on SIG topics coming from inside and outside SIG boundaries is organized. Several dissemination activities are performed in conjunction with conferences and events.

5. Conclusions

This chapter described the concept of Learning Grid as defined in the homonymous Special Interest Group of Kaleidoscope (whose activities and main results have been also presented) and have contextualised it with respect to the relevant literature in the field. A formal definition of the concept was given as well as a reference architecture based on three overlying layers. Educational needs fulfilled by the learning grid have been presented and feasible pedagogical models have been introduced.

This chapter was a necessary introduction to the whole book and concepts here introduced will be detailed in the remaining chapters of this first section. The second section of the book will present instead some available prototype implementing or inspired to a Learning Grid.

Acknowledgements

This research was supported by the Network of Excellence Kaleidoscope "Shaping the scientific evolution of Technology Enhanced Learning" [28] in the context of the above mentioned "Learning Grid" Special Interest Group as well as research results presented in all paragraphs of the first section of this book.

References

[1] Abbas Z., M. Umer, M. Odeh, R. McClatchey, A. Ali, F. Ahmad "A Semantic Grid-based E-Learning Framework (SELF)" in Collaborative and Learning Applications on Grid Technology (CLAG), 5th International Symposium on Cluster Computing and Grid Cardiff, Wales, UK, May 2005.

[2] Allison C., S. Cerri, A. Gaeta, M. Gaeta and P. Ritrovato "Services, Semantics and Standards: elements of a Learning Grid Infrastructure" in Applied Artificial Intelligence Journal – Taylor & Francis, vol. 19, n. 9-10, November-December 2005, pp. 861 – 879.

[3] Ardaiz O., P. Artigas, L. Diaz de Cerio, F. Freitag, A. Gallardo, R. Messeguer, L. Navarro, D. Royo, and K. Sanjeevan "ULabGrid, an Infrastructure to Develop Distant Laboratories for Undergrad Students over a Grid" in Lecture Notes in Computer Science, n. 2970, pp. 265-272.

[4] Beetham H., JISC e-learning and Pedagogy Programme "Review: developing e-Learning Models for the JISC Practitioner Communities" Version 2.1, February 2004

[5] Berners-Lee T., J. Hendler and O. Lassila "The Semantic Web" in Scientific American, May 2001.

[6] Bote-Lorenzo M.L., D. Hernandez-Leo et al. "Toward Reusability and Tailorability in Collaborative Learning systems using IMS-LD and Grid Services", Special Issue of Advanced Technology for Learning International Journal on Web-Based Collaborative Learning, Vol. 1, N° 3, 2004

[7] Caballe S., T. Daradoumis, C. Paniagua and F. Xhafa "A Grid Approach to Provide Effective Awareness to On-line Collaborative Learning Teams" in Proceedings of the 1st International Kaleidoscope Learning Grid SIG Workshop on Distributed e-Learning Environments, Vico Equense (Naples), Italy, 2005.

[8] Capuano N., M. Gaeta, R. Iannone, F. Orciuoli "Learning Design and run-time resource binding in a distributed e-learning environment" in Proceedings of the 1st International Kaleidoscope Learning GRID SIG Workshop on Distributed e-Learning Environments, March 14 2005, Vico Equense (NA), Italy. N. Capuano, P. Ritrovato, F. Murtag eds., Electronic Workshops in Computing, British Computer Society.

[9] Daradoumis A. "State of the Art on Learning Grid: Technological Perspective" in Learning Grid: a newsletter from the Kaleidoscope Learning Grid SIG, N. Capuano ed., n. 10, pp. 4-6, December 2006.

[10] Daradoumis T., A. Gonzalez, P. Milligan, F. Murtagh and P. Sage "Learning Grid Scenarios" in Learning Grid: a newsletter from the Kaleidoscope Learning Grid SIG, N. Capuano ed., n. 2, pp. 8-12, October 2004.

[11] De Roure D., N.R. Jennings, N.R. Shadbolt "The Semantic Grid: Past, Present, and Future" in Proceedings of the IEEE, vol. 93, n. 3, March 2005, pp. 669-681.

[12] Duval P., A. Merceron, M. Scholl, L. Wargon "Empowering Learning Objects: an experiment with the Ganesha platform" in Proceedings of the World Conference on Educational Multimedia, Hypermedia and Telecommunications ED-MEDIA 2005, Montreal, Canada, Volume 2005, Number 1, pp. 4592-4599, 2005.

[13] Foster I, J. Frey, S. Tuecke et al. "The WS-Resource Framework", 2004.

[14] Foster I. and C. Kesselman "The Grid: Blueprint for a New Computing Infrastructure", Morgan Kaufmann, 1999.

[15] Foster I. et al. "OGSA WSRF Basic Profile 1.0", Recommendation GWD-R GGF, OGSA WG, September 7, 2005.

[16] Foster I. et al.: "The Open Grid Services Architecture, Version 1.0", Report GFD-I.030. GGF, OGSA WG, January 25, 2005.

[17] Foster I., C. Kesselman and S. Tuecke "The Anatomy of the Grid: Enabling Scalable Virtual Organizations" in Intern. Journal of Supercomputer Applications, vol. 15, 2001.

[18] Foster I., C. Kesselman, J. Nick and S. Tuecke "The Physiology of the Grid: An Open Grid Service Architecture for Distributed System Integration", 2002.

[19] Gaeta A., M. Gaeta, F. Orciuoli and P. Ritrovato "Enabling Technologies for future learning scenarios: The Semantic Grid for Human Learning" in Proceeding of the IEEE International Symposium on Cluster Computing and the Grid (CCGrid 2005), May 9-12 2005, Cardiff (UK).

[20] Gaeta A., M. Gaeta, P. Ritrovato "A Grid based architecture for delivery of adaptive and personalised learning experiences" submitted to a special issue of Personal and Ubiquitous Computing of ACM.

[21] Gaeta M., P. Ritrovato and S. Salerno "Making e- Learning a Service Oriented Utility: The European Learning Grid Infrastructure Project". Towards the Learning Grid, Advances in Human Learning Services. Frontiers in Artificial Intelligence and Applications, vol. 127, P. Ritrovato, C. Allison, S.A. Cerri, T. Dimitrakos, M. Gaeta and S. Salerno eds. IOS Press. November 2005.

[22] Goble C. and D. De Roure "The Semantic Grid: Myth Busting and Bridge Building" in Proc. of the 16th European Conference on Artificial Intelligence, Valencia, 2004.

[23] Gouardères G., E. Conté, S. Mansour, L. Razmerita "Ontology based user modelling for personalization of Grid learning services" in Electronic Workshops in Computing (eWiC) series, British Computer Society.

[24] Guangzuo C., C. Fei, C. Hu, L. Shufang "OntoEdu: A Case Study of Ontology-based Education Grid System for E-Learning", GCCCE2004 International Conference, Hong Kong. 2004.

[25] Huang C., F. Xu, X. Xu, and X. Zheng, "Towards an Agent-Based Robust Collaborative Virtual Environment for E-Learning in the Service Grid" in Lecture Notes in Computer Science, n. 4088, pp. 702-707, Springer 2006.

[26] IMS Learning Design Information Model (Version 1.0 Final Specification). Available at: www.imsglobal.org/learningdesign/index.html;

[27] Jähnert J., A. Cuevas, J. Moreno, V. Villagrá, S. Wesner, V. Olmedo, H. Einsiedler "The Akogrimo way towards an extended IMS architecture" in proceedings of ICIN 2007, 8-11 October 2007.

[28] Kaleidoscope Learning Grid SIG Web site at: http://grid.noe-kaleidoscope.org.

[29] Kaleidoscope Web site at: http://www.noe-kaleidoscope.org.

[30] Laria G. "Learning Grid Scenarios" in Learning Grid: a newsletter from the Kaleidoscope Learning Grid SIG, N. Capuano ed., n. 4, pp. 7-11, April 2005.

[31] Liao C., F. Ou Yang "A Workflow Framework for Pervasive Learning Objects Composition by Employing Grid Services Flow Language" in Proceedings of the IEEE International Conference on Advanced Learning Technologies (ICALT'04), pp: 840-841, 2004.

[32] Lischka J., D. Karagiannis "A Generic E-learning Engineering Framework Embracing the Semantic Web" in Lecture Notes in Computer Science, n. 3192, pp. 341-350, Springer 2004.

[33] Luo Z., Y. Fei and J. Liang "On Demand E-Learning with Service Grid Technologies" in Edutainment 2006: 60-69.

[34] Mac Randal D., T. Dimitrakos "A Vision about the Learning Grid" in Learning Grid: a newsletter from the Kaleidoscope Learning Grid SIG, N. Capuano ed., n. 2, pp. 2-8, October 2004.

[35] Merceron A., N. Capuano, F. Orciuoli, P. Ritrovato "Scenarios for a Learning GRID" in Proceedings of SWEL'07: Ontologies and Semantic Web Services for Intelligent Distributed Educational Systems, pp. 74-79, held in conjunction with AIED 2007, July 9 2007, Marina del Rey, USA.

[36] Naeve, A, Lytras, M., Nejdl, W., Balacheff, N., Hardin, J., "Editorial" of Advances of the Semantic Web for E-learning: Expanding Learning Frontiers, Naeve, A, Lytras, M., Nejdl, W., Balacheff, N., Hardin, J (Eds.), Special Issue of the British Journal of Educational Technology, Vol 37, No 3, 2006, pp. 321-330.

[37] Navarr L.I., A.S. Diaz, M.M. Such, D.M. Martin, P.P. Peco "Learning Unit Design based in Grid Computing" in Journal of Interactive Media in Education - Special Issue on Advances in Learning Design August 2005.

[38] Next Generation GRIDs Expert Group, "Future for European Grids: GRIDs and Service Oriented Knowledge Utilities, Vision and Research Directions 2010 and Beyond", Next Generation GRIDs Expert Group Report 3, January 2006.

[39] Ritrovato P. "Research Projects Focus: ELeGI" in Learning Grid: a newsletter from the Kaleidoscope Learning Grid SIG, N. Capuano ed., n. 1, pp. 4-8, July 2004,

[40] Ritrovato P. and M. Gaeta "Towards a Semantic Grid for Human Learning", IOS Press, 2005, ISBN: 1586035347.

[41] Ritrovato P., G. Albano, A. Daradoumis, A. Merceron, L. Montandon, F. Murtagh and A. Poulovassilis "Survey on Service Oriented Frameworks for e-Learning" in D12.1.6 of Kaleidoscope (NoE IST-507838), September 2005.

[42] Roman D., U. Keller, H. Lausen, J. de Bruijn, R. Lara, M. Stollberg, A. Polleres, C. Feier, C. Bussler and D. Fensel "Web Service Modeling Ontology", Applied Ontology, 1(1): 77-106, 2005.

[43] Samaras G., K. Karenos, E. Christodoulou "A Grid Service Framework for Metadata Management in Self-e-Learning Networks" in Proc. Of the 2nd European Across Grids Conference (AxGrid), Jan 2004, Nicosia, Cyprus.

[44] Schaeck T. and R. Thompson "Web Services for Remote Portlets (WSRP) Whitepaper", May 28, 2003.

[45] Sherly E., G. Bindya, L. Deepa and K. S. Resmy "A Grid Service Based Portal for Virtual Learning Campus" in K. Liew, H. Shen, S. See, W. Cai, P. Fan, S. Horiguchi eds. Parallel and Distributed Computing: Applications and Technologies, 5th Int. Conference, PDCAT 2004, Singapore, December 8-10, 2004, Proceedings. Lecture Notes in Computer Science 3320 Springer 2004, ISBN 3-540-24013-6, 86-89.

[46] The OWL Service Coalition "OWL-S: Semantic Markup for Web Services", 2003.

[47] Vega-Gorgojo G., M. L. Bote-Lorenzo, E. Gómez-Sánchez, Y. A. Dimitriadis, J. I. Asensio-Pérez "Semantic Search of Learning Services in a Grid-Based Collaborative System" in Proceedings of the 5th IEEE/ACM Int. Symposium on Cluster Computing and the Grid (CCGrid 2005), Workshop on Collaborative and Learning Applications of Grid Technology and Grid Education (CLAG) 2005, 19-26, Cardiff, UK, May 2005.

[48] Zhuge H. , Y. Li "KGTutor: A Knowledge Grid Based Intelligent Tutoring System" in Lecture Notes in Computer Science, n. 3007, pp. 473-478, Springer 2004.

[49] Zhuge H., Y. Li, J. Bi and T. Cheung "KGCL: A Knowledge-Grid-Based Cooperative Learning Environment" Lecture Notes in Computer Science, n. 2436, Proceedings of the 1st International Conference on Advances in Web-Based Learning table of contents, pp: 192-202, 2002.

The Learning Grid Handbook
S. Salerno et al. (Eds.)
IOS Press, 2008

Educational Modelling and Service Composition on the Learning Grid

Angelo GAETA [a b,1], Sergio MIRANDA [b], Francesco ORCIUOLI [b]
[a] *CRMPA, Centro di Ricerca in Matematica Pura ed Applicata, Italy*
[b] *DIIMA, Università di Salerno, Italy*

Abstract. This chapter analyses existing languages for the dynamic composition of distributed resources with particular emphasis on e-learning objects and services that may be exploited in a Learning Grid. The application of such languages has a paramount importance where heterogeneous services are distributed on the Grid and have to be dynamically composed according to learners needs and preferences and to teacher defined learning methods and strategies. The paper first explores education modelling languages, i.e. languages thought to manage workflows of learning activities (so learning-oriented but not specifically service-oriented); then it deepens services composition languages, i.e. languages thought for static or dynamic composition of Web Services of any nature (so service-oriented but not specifically learning-oriented). In both cases, the description of languages and related tools is followed by a comparison and by the definition of extensions needed in order to be fully exploitable in a Learning Grid environment.

Keywords. Education Modelling Languages, Web Services, Service Composition Languages, Learning Grid.

Introduction

The dynamic composition of learning objects and services on the basis of teacher-specified pedagogies taking into account learner needs and preferences is one of the main features that a Grid for Learning should provide. To design workflows of learning activities able to exploit distributed learning resources, specific languages and editors are needed and specific players are required to execute defined workflows.

To define such languages two opposite paths are possible: the first is to start from existing education modelling languages and improve them with service-orientation capabilities; the second is to start from existing services composition languages and improve them with specific learning-oriented constructs.

The purpose of this chapter is to explore both possibilities by describing main education modelling and service composition languages, by comparing them and by suggesting possible improvements in order to be exploited in a Learning Grid.

Among available education modelling languages we have deepened (in the first section) IMS Learning Design and UNED Palo. A brief description of EML, TML, CDF, LMML and Targeteam have been also provided mainly for historical reasons. Among service composition languages we will focus instead (in the second section) on

[1] Corresponding Author: CRMPA, Centro di Ricerca in Matematica Pura ed Applicata, via Ponte Don Melillo, 84084 Fisciano (SA), Italy; E-mail: agaeta@crmpa.unisa.it.

the most diffused BPEL4WS, WS-CDL and OWL-S while briefly describing also BPML, XPDL, WSCI and CCML.

The third section is instead dedicated to languages comparison and to the definition of extensions needed to such languages in order to be fully exploitable in a Learning Grid environment. Conclusions and references will follow.

1. Education Modelling Languages

An Education Modelling Language (EML) is a semantic notation for units of learning to be used in e-learning to support the reuse of pedagogical entities like learning designs, learning objectives, learning activities, etc. [1]. EMLs constitute an evolution of content-centred specifications of learning objects, involving the description of learning processes and methods from a pedagogical and instructional perspective. In other words, an Educational Modelling Language is a modus operandi that describes “units of learning” in a pedagogical way.

EMLs and Learning Objects (LOs) currently represent opposite approaches to the interoperability question. As far as the LOs approach is concerned, interoperability for content is hampered by the contextual “baggage” of the object; an object can only truly be reusable by stripping the content of all its external referents such as teaching methods, student roles, and activities. EMLs take an opposite approach: they conclude that components are truly shareable and reusable if all units include complete lessons, hands on work, or entire courses and all contextual information. Moreover EMLs incorporate the definition of pedagogical aspects and learning processes that make interoperable courses or units of study, so they provide appropriate instructional elements at its adequate abstraction level.

Several EMLs have been defined till now. Next sub-sections will deal with the description of the two most diffused: IMS Learning Design and UNED Palo. A subsequent sub-section will deal with less diffused languages like EML, TML, CDF, LMML and Targeteam. A comparison of such languages taking in mind the Learning Grid as their application environment is finally provided in section 3.

1.1. IMS Learning Design

IMS Learning Design (LD) [2] is a LMS developed by the IMS Working Group on Learning Design. Through LD it is possible to describe a wide variety of pedagogical models, or approaches to learning, including group work and collaborative learning. It does not define individual pedagogical models but provides a high level language that can describe many different models. The language describes how people perform activities using resources, and how these things are coordinated into a learning flow.

LD describes how a learning design scenario unfolds through the analogy of a theatrical play. The core concept of the LD specification is that a person gets a role in the learning process (i.e. student, teacher, tutor, etc.). The environment where the process takes place consists of the appropriate LOs and services to be used during the performance of process activities. Which role gets which activities at what moment in the process, is determined by the method or by a notification.

LD provides a level of abstraction in the learning process, offering constructs capable of building different pedagogical approaches. LD specification is sometimes discussed in terms of pedagogical neutrality, since no single pedagogy is inherent in, or implied by, the specification. However, using the specification requires a designer to think which objectives a learning process is designed to achieve and which pre-requisites are involved, to identify the activities learners and staff should undertake and which tools should be used in the process.

LD has been divided into three parts, known as Level A, Level B, and Level C. Separate XML schemas are provided for each level, each integrating with and extending the previous Level.

- The **level A** contains the core of LD: people, activities and resources, and their coordination through method, play, act and role-parts elements. This simply allows a series of time ordered learning activities to be performed by learners and teachers, using LOs and services. Activities and roles are defined as reusable components that can be designed into a workflow using the method element. Services such as e-mail and conferencing may be also specified at design time as placeholders within the design that will be instantiated by the run-time system.
- The **level B** allows the inclusion of properties and conditions. Properties are used to store information about a person (e.g. learner preferences of test results), a role (e.g. whether the role is for a full-time or part-time learner) or a learning design itself. Internal properties persist only during a single run of a learning design, while external properties retain their values beyond the end of a run, and can be accessed from different runs and different learning designs. Conditions allow the learning flow to be constrained according to specific circumstances, preferences or learner characteristics. For instance, a particular learner may be presented with resources in random order, if their learning style or preference requires this.
- The **level C** provides a notification capability that allows messaging between system components and means the flow of events could be adapted at run-time based on event triggers such as completion of earlier tasks. This paves the way for adaptive sequencing capabilities as well as role-play and event-driven simulations.

LD orchestrates e-learning scenarios by describing and implementing learning activities based on different pedagogies (including group work and collaborative learning), by coordinating multiple learners and multiple roles within a multi-learner model or, alternatively, by supporting single learner activities, by coordinating the use of learning contents with collaborative services and by supporting multiple delivery models (including mixed-mode learning).

Several tools are available to design and execute LD learning experiences. In [3] 23 software tools supporting LD specifications at different levels are listed. Among the others there are available several editors (e.g. the Reload LD Editor [4]), players (e.g. the Reload Learning Design Player [4]) and execution engines (e.g. the CopperCore LD Engine [5] and the SLED Player [6]).

1.2. UNED PALO

PALO [7] is a proposal of EML developed by the Universidad Nacional de Educación a Distancia (UNED) of Madrid since 1988 to describe and design learning content and learning environments at a high abstraction level.

PALO allows the definitions of courses or units of study structured in modules where each module includes a declaration of the structure, activities to be undertaken by students and tutors and the schedule of activities and content. The sequencing of modules is scheduled through deadlines and dependence between modules, based on different types of prerequisites.

PALO also provides a layer of abstraction for the description of learning material, including the description of learning activities, structure and scheduling. In particular the language provides mechanism to express the following aspects: contents and references to the domain model; structure and navigational model including style and presentation; degree of interactivity for a remote o local usage; user access and tracing.

The PALO description language is composed by a group of structure dependant tags and a group of domain model related tags. Tag attributes also play an important role on defining some other aspects of the final environment. The system includes also an editor to create a document from a template and a PALO compiler able to process an instantiated template and build a Web environment with the structure.

In PALO, activity scheduling is done using language attributes. These attributes define deadlines and dependencies between activities (or modules) based on different prerequisite types. PALO defines learning strategies with instructional templates which are some scenario models with particular pedagogical properties (e.g. a constructive approach or a behavioural one). Thus PALO can be extended each time there is a need for a certain pedagogical functionality.

PALO defines learning scenarios by means of instructional templates that define types of learning scenario with certain pedagogical properties. Pedagogical domains are defined by means of elements of the language that provides different functionality. Instructional templates, however, do not define different "languages" by themselves, but a subset of the element of the language that provides a certain type of pedagogical functionality. A group of consistent elements of PALO that provide an instructional or pedagogical purpose constitute a template.

The Palo description language consists of five layers where each layer, for a given template, will contain a selection of elements from the information model. Whether to create elements of the information model for all these categories or not, depends on the template. The five layers are:

- layer 1 – educational or content layer;
- layer 2 – activity and cooperative model;
- layer 3 – structure;
- layer 4 – sequencing and scheduling;
- layer 5 – management.

Differently from IMS LD, PALO tools are very few and only available as academic prototypes. The only tool available online is a PALO compiler (paloc) able to process an instantiated template and build a Web environment with the structure, content and features described in the document. No authoring tools have been developed till now and documents are written using SGML and XML editors.

1.3. Life-long Education Modelling Languages

Apart the most diffused IMS Learning Design and UNED PALO, several other Educational Modelling Languages have been proposed in literature. Some of these languages have had a very limited diffusion, some others have stopped their evolution given the wide diffusion of IMS Learning Design.

EML (Education Modelling Language) [8] was developed by the Open University of the Netherlands (OUNL) and was elected as the basis to develop the IMS LD specification. EML tries to capture the pedagogical diversity so designs might involve a single user or multiple users. The rationale of this specification is that, regardless of the pedagogy involved, in practice a learning design specification comes down to a method prescribing various activities for learner and staff roles in a certain order. Each activity refers to a collection of specific objects and services needed to perform the activity. Previous learning technology specifications allowed only for some simple ordering and sequencing of resources used in e-learning. EML added to this the ability to integrate instructional designs to enable more advanced e-learning applications.

TML (Tutorial Markup Language) [9] is an interchange framework designed to separate the semantic content of a question from its screen layout or formatting developed in the context of NetQuest, a project of the ILRT, University of Bristol (UK). The language is designed to support several different types of question within the same content model. TML is essentially a super-set of HTML, with new elements added to describe question information. The TML software distribution is freely available as an example implementation of the language specification. Its main features include: standards-based content interchange formats, integration with digital library resource banks, availability of open source software for Unix and Windows.

CDF (Curriculum Description Format) [10] is implemented as an editor tool and provides a powerful design framework for pedagogical engineers and ODL trainers, for many kind of technology-supported learning processes. CDF comprises seven elements categories that enable the description of general characteristics of the curriculum at design and execution time; information on the target learner population; list of session types defined for and used in this course; list of actual sessions defined for this course; list of communication resources needed for this course; list of teaching staff members involved in this course; list of generic or actual physical locations needed for all kinds of learning activities included in this course.

LMML (Learning Material Markup Language) [11] was defined by the University of Passau, Germany as an adaptable and extensible family of XML markup languages for learning and teaching material. It provides sub-languages for several educational fields and is currently used in university education, life-long education as well as company training. The structure of LMML-documents, and therefore the form of the resulting learning material, is defined by DTD modules. Modules contain Media Objects, for instance pictures, animations or text that can be structured as lists or tables. Because of this, learning material reveals a hierarchical structure.

Targeteam [12] was defiled by the Universitet der Bundeswehr, Munchen. It is a system for supporting the preparation, use, and reuse of teaching materials centred around the XML based language TeachML. Targeteam does not actively support the learning process itself. The information model consists of a homogeneous hierarchy of neutral issues containing text or media objects such as images, animations or applets. Additional metadata can be attached on all levels to identify the educational purpose of the issue, such as illustration, exercise, explanation, motivation etc. Targeteam is based on the assumption that this structure is crucial for providing an understanding for the learners. A simple linear sequence of standalone "learning modules" is not sufficient.

2. Service Composition Languages

Web Services (WSs) are defined as self-contained, modular units of application logic which provide business functionality to other applications via an Internet connection. WSs support the interaction of business partners and their processes by providing a stateless model of atomic synchronous or asynchronous message exchanges. A relevant feature for WSs is the mechanism for their reuse when complex tasks are carried out. It is often the case, to define new processes out of finer-grained subtasks that are likely available as WSs. To this aim, extensions of the WSs technology are considered which support the definition of complex services out of simpler ones.

Composition rules deal with how different services are composed into a coherent global service. In particular, they specify the order in which services are invoked, and the conditions under which a certain service may or may not be invoked. Two possible approaches are currently investigated for the static service composition.

- The first approach, referred to as WSs **orchestration**, combines available services adding a central coordinator (the "orchestrator") which is responsible for invoking and combining the single sub-activities.
- The second approach, referred to as WSs **choreography**, does not assume the exploitation of a central coordinator but it defines complex tasks via the definition of the conversation that should be undertaken by each participant. Following this approach, the overall activity is achieved as the composition of peer-to-peer interactions among the collaborating services.

Several proposal already exist for orchestration languages, among the others the first sub-section will describe BPEL4WS. On the contrary, choreography languages are still at a preliminary stage of definition. A proposal, named WS-CDL (described in the second sub-section) has been issued from W3C. Unfortunately, neither current orchestration and choreography languages nor WS description standards (like WSDL) deal with the dynamic composition of services. They in fact conversely focus on representing composition where the information flow and the binding between services are known a priori.

A more challenging problem is to compose services dynamically (e.g. when a functionality that cannot be provided by the existing services is required, the existing services can combined together to fulfil the request). The dynamic composition of services requires the location of services based on their capabilities and the recognition of those services that can be matched together to create a composition. The full automation of this process is still the object of ongoing research activity, but the right path seems that given by Semantic Web languages like OWL-S (described un the third sub-section).

While WSDL provides a function-centric description of WSs covering inputs, outputs and exception handling, on the other side, OWL-S provides a process level description of the service which, in addition to functional information, models the preconditions and postconditions of the process so that the evolution of the domain can be logically inferred. It relies on ontologies to formalize domain concepts which are shared among services. OWL-S efforts aim at fully automating all the stages of the WSs lifecycle. With the Semantic Web infrastructure in place, practical and powerful applications can be written that use annotations and suitable inference engines to automatically discover, execute, compose, and interoperate WSs.

Figure 1 summarises the different approaches available for service composition. The next three sub-sections will deal with the description of the three most diffused service composition languages from three different groups: BPEL4WS for the orchestration model, WS-CDL for the choreography model and OWL-S for the semantic composition model. A further sub-section will briefly describe more, less used, languages for services composition.

2.1. BPEL4WS

The Business Process Execution Language for Web Services (BPEL4WS) [13] is an initiative of the industry leaders BEA, IBM, Microsoft, SAP, Siebel to drive and ensure interoperability for the description and communication of business processes based on WSs. Particularly BPEL4WS builds on IBM's WSFL and Microsoft's XLANG. Accordingly, it combines the features of a block structured process language like XLANG with those of a graph-based process language like WSFL.

Processes in BPEL4WS export and import functionality by using WS interfaces exclusively. It provides a language for the formal specification of business processes and business interaction protocols. By doing so, it extends the WS interaction model and enables it to support business transactions. BPEL4WS defines an interoperable integration model that should facilitate the expansion of automated process integration in both the intra-corporate and the business-to-business spaces. BPEL4WS represents a convergence of the ideas in the XLANG and WSFL specifications. Both XLANG and WSFL are superseded by the BPEL4WS specification.

In BPEL4WS, processes can be described in two ways. Executable business processes model actual behaviour of a participant in a business interaction. Business protocols, in contrast, use process descriptions that specify the mutually visible message exchange behaviour of each of the parties involved in the protocol, without revealing their internal behaviour. The process descriptions for business protocols are called

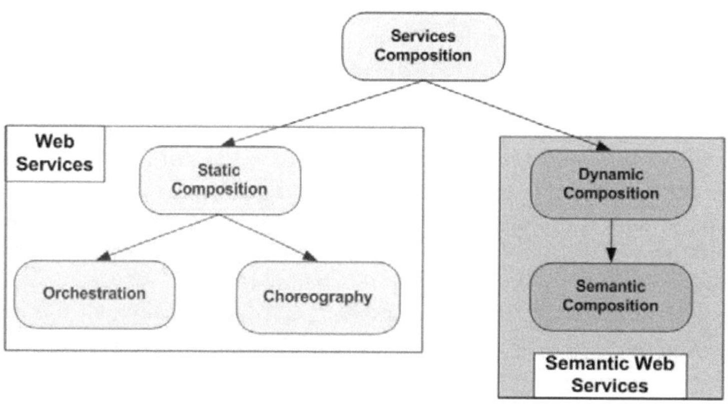

Figure 1. Different approaches available for Web Services composition.

abstract processes. Essentially, executable processes provide the orchestration support while the business protocols focus more on the choreography of the services.

At the core of the BPEL4WS process model is the notion of peer-to-peer interaction between services described in WSDL; both the process and its partners are modelled as WSDL services. A business process defines how to coordinate the interactions between a process instance and its partners. In this sense, a BPEL4WS process definition provides and/or uses one or more WSDL services, and provides the description of the behaviour and interactions of a process instance relative to its partners and resources through WS interfaces.

BPEL4WS defines the message exchange protocols followed by the business process of a specific role in the interaction. The definition of a BPEL4WS business process also follows the WSDL model of separation between the abstract message contents used by the business process and deployment information.

Among BPELWS implementations currently exist there are: Microsoft BizTalk, IBM BPWS4J, Active BPEL, Oracle BPEL Process Manager, Agila BPEL, Digité Process Composer, WebSphere Process Server, OpenLink Virtuoso Universal Server, Parasoft BPEL Maestro, SAP NetWeaver Exchange Infrastructure, Sun Microsystems eInsight BPM, Bexee, BPEL Process eXecution Engine.

2.2. WS-CDL

The Web Services Choreography Description Language [14] is a choreography model that describes a collaboration between a collection of services in order to achieve a common goal. It captures the interactions in which the participating services engage to achieve this goal and the dependencies between these interactions, including control-flow dependencies, data-flow dependencies, message correlations, time constraints, transactional dependencies, etc.

A choreography does not describe any internal action that occurs within a participating service that does not directly result in an externally visible effect, such as an internal computation or data transformation. A choreography captures interactions from a global perspective, meaning that all participating services are treated equally. In other words, a choreography encompasses all the interactions between the participating services that are relevant with respect to the choreography's goal.

WS-CDL is an XML-based language that describes peer-to-peer collaborations of participants by defining, from a global viewpoint, their common and complementary observable behaviour; where ordered message exchanges result in accomplishing a common business goal. It is a layered language providing different levels of expression ability to describe a choreography.

The substrate of the choreography are abstract request/response operations that are referenced by interactions. An interaction is the realization of a collaboration between roles. Roles are grouped into participants. Roles are analogous to the entities at the top of our UML sequence diagrams and participants group these roles into domains of control which can be said to be the location the behaviours defined by the roles. An interaction must specify what relationship it is bound too.

In WS-CDL each role defined has a behaviour. A behaviour in this sense is the binding point for a WSDL description i.e. the interface which normally references a WSDL description but this is optional in WS-CDL. Because it is optional we can use this as a binding point to different service descriptions. The WS-CDL choreography definition is relatively classic: it has the *sequence* / *parallel* / *choice* construct, along with *assign*. Recursive composition is achieved with the *perform* element.

In terms of messaging quality of service, WS-CDL relies on WS-Reliable-Messaging principally. The extent of quality of service messaging on which WS-CDL depends is not fully established, and the mapping for reliable messaging at the very least remains open. In general, no a priori configurability of WS-CDL specifications for different quality of messaging service is in place. This limits the layering and exploitation of choreography for lower level services from current and oncoming messaging standards.

Among the more main tools, systems and frameworks needed to support WS-CDL specifications there are: Pi4SOA CDL Editor and WS-CDL Eclipse.

2.3. OWL-S

One of the barriers to a wider adoption of WS technology is the lack of tools for creating WS specifications. OWL-S [15] tries to overcome this barrier by supplying a WS designer with a set of markup language constructs for describing the properties and capabilities of a WS in unambiguous, computer-interpretable form. OWL-S markup of WSs facilitates the automation of WS tasks including automated discovery, execution, interoperation, composition and execution monitoring.

Following the layered approach to markup language development, the current version of OWL-S builds on top of OWL. OWL-S introduces ontologies to describe, on the one hand, the concepts in the services' domain and, on the other hand, generic concepts to describe the services themselves and how they relate to the domain ontologies. These semantically rich descriptions enable automated machine reasoning over service and domain descriptions and allow to perform the following tasks.

- Automatic **WS discovery**: it is an automated process for location of WS that can provide a particular class of service capabilities, while adhering to some client-specified constraints.
- Automatic **WS invocation**: it is the automatic invocation of a WS by a computer program or agent, given only a declarative description of that WS, as opposed to when the agent has been pre-programmed to be able to call that particular service.
- Automatic **WS composition and interoperation**: it involves the automatic selection, composition and interoperation of WSs to perform some complex task, given a high-level description of an objective.

With OWL-S, the information necessary to select and compose services is encoded at the service Web sites. Software can be written to manipulate these representations, together with a specification of the objectives of the task, to achieve the task automatically. To support this, OWL-S provides declarative specifications of the prerequisites and consequences of application of individual services, and a language for describing service compositions and data flow interactions.

The overall structure of the ontology is composed by three main parts: the service profile for advertising and discovering services; the process model that describes how a service performs its tasks; the grounding, which provides details on how to interoperate with a service, via messages.

A set of OWL-S tools exists but a complete execution environment based on OWL-S concepts is still lacking. For example, OWL-S Editors allow the maintaining of OWL-S service descriptions, OWL-S Composer provides an algorithm for different degrees of matching for individual elements of OWL-S, OWL-S Axis plug-in advices service providers on how to provide service description using OWL Services, etc.

2.4. Further Services Composition Languages

An overview of further Services composition languages and frameworks, namely BPML, XPDL, WSCI and CCML, is presented below.

BPML (Business Process Management Language) [16] is a standard proposed by the Business Process Management Initiative (BPMI) and was originally developed to enable the standard-based management of e-business processes used with Business Process Management System (BPMS) technology. BPML is able to express abstract and executable processes that address enterprise business processes, including WSs. It includes support on control flow, data flow and event flow with structures of sending, receiving and invoking services, and control structures of conditional choice, sequential, iteration and parallel execution with synchronization. BPML provides an abstract model and an XML-based syntax.

XPDL (XML Process Definition Language) [17] is a graph-structured language for business processes modelling. In XPDL, the activities in a process can be thought of as the nodes of a directed graph, with the transitions being the edges. Conditions associated with the transitions determine at execution time which activity or activities should be executed next. XPDL focuses on issues relevant to the distribution of work in fact activity attributes specify the resources required to perform an activity. This is an expression, evaluated at execution time, which determines the resource required. Activity attributes also specify applications required to implement an activity. These concepts together support the notion of a resource (e.g. participant), in conjunction with an application, performing the activity.

WSCI (Web Service Choreography Interface) [18] was the first XML-based language aiming to provide a standard for specifying the overall collaboration between WSs providers and services users by describing messages exchanges among the involving parties. WSCI was built on top of WSDL. It is developed and maintained by the W3C. WSCI describes the flow of messages exchanged by a WS participating in choreographed interactions with other services, describing the dynamic interface of the WS participating in a given message exchange. WSCI describes how WS operations, e.g. defined in WSDL, can be choreographed in the context of a message exchange in which the WS participates. WSCI can be employed for describing both intra and inter organisational components and applications.

CCML (Component Compatibility Markup Language) [19] has been developed to support a particular application (i.e. application level active networking), but a general purpose for it has been recognized. CCML allows systems of various kinds to obtain the various components of a facility that are compatible with those systems, even when different kinds of systems need variations of the same component. A system requiring a facility requests it through its URI, and receives a URC describing the components of the facility. The system then compare these descriptions with its own characteristics, eliminate components which would not be compatible, and download and install the remaining ones on the system: the amount downloaded is minimized, while being sufficient to provide the facility.

3. Comparison and Applicability on a Grid for Learning

The purpose of this chapter is to compare the above-mentioned languages in order to evaluate their applicability in the context of a Grid for Learning as defined in the first chapter of this book. The first sub-section will focus on the comparison of Education Modelling Languages (EMLs) described in section 1 followed by a sub-section about possible improvements needed for a better fitting of compared languages on a Learning Grid infrastructure. The third sub-section will focus instead on comparison of Web Services (WS) composition languages described in section 2 followed by a further sub-section about improvements related to their applications on a Learning Grid.

3.1. Comparison of Education Modelling Languages

To give an overview and to facilitate a comparison of studied EMLs, this section puts together in a couple of tables their main features. Tables are presented below.

Table 1. Comparison between IMS-LD, EML, PALO and TML.

Features	IMS-LD and EML	PALO	TML
Semantic information model available	Y	Y	Y
Models a 'unit of learning'	Y	Y	N/A
Language of binding	XML, SGML	XML, SGML	XML, SGML
One generic model and binding?	Y	N	Y
Includes complete process description	Y	Y	N
Pedagogical perspective	Pedagogical meta-language to express all types of pedagogical models	It can be extended to support new pedagogical functionalities	Restricted to tutorial models and assessment
Re-usability	Y	Y	Y
Integration of other Standards	LOM, IMS CP, IMS SS, WfMC, XHTML	Dublin Core, HTML, LaTeX	HTML
Main scope of the entities in the information model.	Content and process	Content and process	Limited to questions
Main semantic entities in the information model.	objective; prerequisite; role; activity; environment; object; method	course; module; activity; LO; learning content	question type; choice; hint; response; score
Do academics use the system operationally	Y	Y	N
Was the language developed within a partnership?	Companies, institutes and standard bodies	In-house	Open source

Features	IMS-LD and EML	PALO	TML
What are the authoring tools like? Are they user friendly or low-level	About 20 tools currently available. Several are user-friendly.	Standard SGML and XML editors; XEmacs.	Text-based mark up.

Table 2. Comparison between CDF, LMML and Targeteam.

Features	CDF	LMML	Targeteam
Semantic information model available	Y	Y	N
Models a 'unit of learning'	Y	Y	Y
Language of binding	XML	XML	XML
One generic model and binding?	Y	Y	Y
Includes complete process description	Y	Y	Y
Pedagogical perspective	It is not possible to actually express a pedagogical model	It is possible to express pedagogical models using sub-typing	It is not possible to actually express a pedagogical model
Re-usability	Y	Y	Y
Integration of other Standards	LOM	Extension mechanism for standard supp.	N
Main scope of the entities in the information model.	Limited to content and resources	Limited to content and domain specific	Limited to content
Main semantic entities in the information model.	general; target learner; sessions type; sessions; teachers; locations	module; structure model; content module; structure object	hierarchy of section sized issues
Do academics use the system operationally	Y	Y	Y
Was the language developed within a partnership?	Academic and no-profit associations	Academic	Academic
What are the authoring tools like? Are they user friendly or low-level	Any authoring tool can be used.	Standard XML tools and some specialized tools.	Standard XML editors and some system specific tools.

The outcome of this comparison makes clear that the scope of the above-mentioned languages differs very much. There appear to be two groups: the first group, consisting of CDF, LMML, TML and Targeteam, seems to be "ignorant" in expressing pedagogical models. The second group consisting of IMS-LD/EML and PALO are semantic rich information models able to describe the content and process within 'units of learning' from a pedagogical perspective.

From the last two, moreover, while IMS-LD fully lives up to this definition, PALO is limited to the definition of individual tasks. Nevertheless at this stage it is already clear that the expressive power of the current version of IMS-LD, by simply studying and looking at the number of defined elements and attributes, exceeds the expressive power of PALO.

It is important to note, moreover, that currently IMS-LD is the only language which both is compatible with various international standards and follows the process and procedures to be accepted as a standard. Moreover a lot of high-level user-friendly editing and executing tools are already available for IMS-LD. For this reason IMS-LD is currently the widest diffused education modelling language and the one more feasible to be used as the basis in a Learning Grid environment.

3.2. Possible Extensions to Education Modelling Languages

As we have seen in the previous sub-section, IMS-LD is the best choice for a Learning Grid. Nevertheless IMS Learning Design is currently hardly exploitable in distributed e-learning environments due to several limitations coming from design-time resource binding. Design-time resources binding in fact is affected by the following problems.

- Learning design scenarios implement **domain-dependent pedagogies**: the instructional designer is forced to establish “a priori” the didactic domain, building the environments tied to the scenario’s activities.
- Learning **processes cannot be really adaptive** (based on learner profiles): systems for learning material delivery cannot take into account learner preferences and cannot select, at run-time, learning objects that best fit learners characteristics.
- Learning **scenarios don’t exploit advantages of distributed infrastructures**: the early binding of resources at design-time thwarts the opportunity for dynamic selection of learning objects and services that best fits learning process needs. Of course, these needs can be better supplied if the source of resources is a whole virtual organization (on a networked infrastructure) than the environments linked to the learning design scenario.

In [20] a solution is proposed to overcome these issues. It consists in modifying the learning design scenario authoring process specified by IMS-LD in order to provide only requirements for a desired LO rather than a reference to a real LO. Requirements can be expressed using a subset of IMS Learning Resource Metadata (IMS-MD) specification. These requirements will be transformed in references to real LOs at learning design scenario execution-time.

Within this solution, a learning design scenario with pending references to LOs can be then considered a template learning design scenario [21]. The delivery of learning design scenario is then based on the definition of three types of distributed services:

- a **Delivery Service** that allows the playing of the learning design scenario for authorized users enrolled to the learning experience;
- a **Localization Service** that allows to localize needed resources e.g. it can be invoked in order to find available repositories storing correct (with respect to requirements in template learning design scenario) learning objects;

- several **Repositories**, that may be invoked to query the archive of learning objects and to obtain the GUI that renders a specific learning object delivery.

An experience in realising such an extension to IMS-LD was done in the context of the FP6 EC project ELeGI [22] [24][25].

3.3. Comparison of Services Composition Languages

To give an overview and to facilitate a comparison of studied WSs Composition Languages, this section puts together in the following tables their main features.

Table 3. Comparison between BPEL4WS, WS-CDL and OWL-S.

Features	**BPEL4WS**	**WS-CDL**	**OWL-S**
Abstraction level	Very high	High	High
Modeling the collaboration	Strong support	Strong support	Strong support
Modeling the execution	Strong support	No support	Strong support
Representation of the role	Weak support	Strong support	No support
Composability	Support	Strong support	Support
Event handling	Strong support	No support	Strong support
Semantics support	No support	No support	Strong support
Support for Automated Composition	N	N	Y
Expressiveness	High	High	High
Defined Level of Abstraction	Low	Low	High
Semantic Constraints	Low	High	High
Transaction and Compensation	Indirect support	Indirect support	Indirect support
Business agreement support	No support	No support	No support
Software vendor support	Many	No	Few
Tool support available	Low	Low	Low

Table 4. Comparison between BPML, XPDL, WSCI and CCML.

Features	**BPML**	**XPDL**	**WSCI**	**CCML**
Abstraction level	Low	Low	High	High
Modeling the collaboration	Indirect support	Indirect support	Strong support	Support

Features	BPML	XPDL	WSCI	CCML
Modeling the execution	Strong support	Strong support	No support	No support
Representation of the role	No support	No support	Strong support	No support
Composability	Strong support	Strong support	No support	Support
Event handling	Support	Support	Support	No support
Semantics support	No support	No support	No support	No support
Support for Automated Composition	N	N	N	N
Expressiveness	High	High	High	High
Defined Level of Abstraction	Low	Low	Low	Low
Semantic Constraints	Low	Low	Low	Low
Transaction and Compensation	Strong support	Strong support	Strong support	No support
Business agreement support	No support	No support	No support	No support
Software vendor support	Few	Few	Few	Few
Tool support available	Low	Low	Low	Low

From one side the best language able to describe e-learning processes seems to be OWL-S that is the only one able to support dynamic processes i.e. processes where actors are not defined a priori. From the other side the only language that can be extended to support people is BPEL4WS (see next sub-section).

These considerations lead to the conclusion that two partial solutions to describe e-learning processes on a Learning Grid are available starting from service composition languages, each one with some missing piece to cover all required functions:

- BPEL4WS extended with BPEL4People is useful to describe static e-learning processes but it lacks of dynamicity i.e. services must be bind at design time rather that at execution time so semantic extensions are needed to the language to overcome these limitations. It has a further lack with respect to learning modelling languages being not explicitly thought to support learning activities (so there are no specific constructs for e-learning modelling).
- OWL-S is the only available semantic service composition language that is also able to provide dynamic functionalities. Conversely it cannot be easily used in e-learning given that, as BPEL4WS, doesn't explicitly support people interactions inside process models.

The next sub-section explains how to improve BPEL4WS feasibility to act as a base language for a Grid for Learning by extending it with language constructs able to support people-driven activities.

3.4. Possible Extensions to Service Composition Languages

The main problem related to the exploitation of service composition languages to describe learning processes is related to the lack of expressiveness about people driven activities. Differently from automated business processes, e-learning processes are strongly based on interactions with users with different roles (learner, teachers, tutors, learning providers, content providers, etc.). So, to be actively exploited in learning processes, such languages have to be appropriately extended to involve people.

People can be involved in business processes as a special kind of implementation of an activity: a communication step which may be called people activity. From the user's perspective, the people activity is a task that is assigned to a user and requires the user to perform some action. Users are made aware of this assignment by a distribution mechanism that adds a work item to their task list.

A work item denotes an assignment of a task to a user. Work items specify that a certain user is eligible to perform specific actions on a task. As well as being involved in tasks, people may be involved in a more simple communication step called notification, which is simply the transmission of information to an interested party. The most important difference between tasks and notifications is that a task holds up the process until it is completed.

Among the surveyed languages, only BPEL4WS has a feasible extension to support such scenarios named "the BPEL4WS Extension for People" or BPEL4People [23] that is defined in a way that it is layered on top of the BPEL language so that its features can be composed with the BPEL core features whenever needed. Such extension describes how the BPEL language needs to be extended in principle to cover user interactions with business processes.

The value of the proposal is that it can be used as a basis for a solution that covers different flavours of processes ranging from fully automated processes to processes supporting different user interactions patterns, including ad-hoc collaborations. This extension, combined with the existing BPEL features, will allow designing business processes that range from fully automated processes to processes that support different user interactions patterns.

BPEL4People covers several relationship between people. Among the others it analyzes the different ways that people interact with processes ("generic human roles") and how the process identifies the people to interact with ("people links"). People activities and processes have well-defined generic human roles defining what a person or a group of people resulting from a people query can do with them. This perception is independent of the actual business scenario the activity is used in, and is orthogonal to the organizational roles mentioned earlier.

4. Conclusions

As resulting from the previous section, the best EML to be exploited in a Learning Grid seems to be IMS-LD while among service composition languages there isn't a real winner because, if from one side the best language seems to be OWL-S that is the only one able to support dynamic processes, from the other side the only language that can be extended to support people is BPEL4WS.

These considerations lead to the conclusion that three partial solutions to describe e-learning processes on a Learning Grid are available, each one with some missing piece to cover all required functions as described below.

- IMS-LD is useful to describe static e-learning processes but lacks of dynamicity i.e. services must be bind at design time rather that at execution time. Semantic extensions are needed to the language as those proposed in section 3 in order to overcome these limitations.
- BPEL4WS extended with BPEL4People is useful to describe static e-learning processes but it has the same limitations of IMS-LD having moreover a further lack in being not explicitly thought to support learning activities (so there are no specific constructs for e-learning modelling).
- OWL-S is the only available semantic service composition language that is also able to provide dynamic functionalities. Conversely it cannot be easily used in e-learning given that, as BPEL4WS, doesn't explicitly support people interactions inside process models.

Among the three feasible solutions the one chosen for the definition of the Learning Grid concept is the first one given that a solution for the reported problem is already available end experimented in the context of a prototype system [22].

Future works will involve a semantic layer for the description of resources and services, especially for learning activities, so to improve their selection, their composition to create best solutions respecting always growing user needs [26] [27].

References

[1] KOPER R. (2001), Modeling units of study from a pedagogical perspective : the pedagogical meta-model behind EML, 06/2001. (http://www.eml.ou.nl/introduction/articles.htm).
[2] IMS Learning Design Consortium web site (http://www.imsglobal.org/learningdesign).
[3] Unfold Project web site (http://www.unfold-project.net/).
[4] Reload editor web site (http://sourceforge.net/projects/x4l-reload/).
[5] CopperCore v3.0 we site (http://coppercore.sourceforge.net/).
[6] Service Based Learning Design Player web site (SleD – http://sled.open.ac.uk/sledweb/).
[7] Web site of Universidad Nacional de Educación a Distencia de Madrid (http://portal.uned.es).
[8] Website on Educational Modelling Language (EML – http://www.learningnetworks.org).
[9] NETQUEST Project web site (http://www.cti.ac.at/netquest).
[10] ARIADNE Foundation for the European Knowledge Pool (http://www.ariadne-eu.org).
[11] University of Passau web site (http://www.lmml.de/).
[12] Web site of Universit"t der Bundeswehr, Mnchen (http://www.unibw.de/startseite).
[13] Business Process Execution Language for Web Services version 1.1 (http://www-128.ibm.com/developerworks/library/specification/ws-bpel/).
[14] Web Services Choreography Description Language Version 1.0 (http://www.w3.org/TR/ws-cdl-10/).
[15] OWL-S web site (http://www.w3.org/Submission/OWL-S/).
[16] Business Process Management Initiative web site (http://www.bpmi.org/).
[17] XML Process Definition Language (http://www.wfmc.org/standards/XPDL.htm).
[18] Web Service Choreography Interface web site (http://www.w3.org/TR/wsci/).

[19] Steven Simpson, Paul Smith, Mark Banfield, David Hutchison. Component Compatibility for Heterogeneous active networking (IEEE Informatics – Application Level Active Networks: Techniques and Deployment, 1st November 2000, London, UK).

[20] N. Capuano, M. Gaeta, R. Iannone, F. Orciuoli. Learning Design and run-time resource binding in a distributed e-learning environment. Proceedings of the 1st International Kaleidoscope Learning GRID SIG Workshop on Distributed e-Learning Environments, March 14 2005, Vico Equense (NA), Italy.

[21] Pythagoras Karampiperis and Demetrios Sampson – Designing Learning Services for Open Learning Systems Utilizing IMS Learning Design (From Proceeding (461) Web-based Education – 2005).

[22] ELeGI: European Learning Grid Infrastructure web site (http://www.elegi.org/).

[23] BPEL4PEOPLE web site http://www-128.ibm.com/developerworks/webservices/library/specification/ws-bpel4people/.

[24] A.Gaeta, M.Gaeta, S.Miranda, F.Orciuoli and P.Ritrovato, "A preliminary investigations on how e-Learning 2.0 fits into the ELeGI vision", Proceedings of ELEGI Conference (Barcelona, October 2006).

[25] N.Capuano, R.Iannone, S.Miranda, M.Rosciano, "A Grid Based IMS Learning Design Player: the ELeGI Case Study", SWEL 2007: 3rd International Kaleidoscope Learning GRID Special Interest Group Workshop on Ontologies and Semantic Web Services for Intelligent Distributed Educational Systems (AIED 2007 July 9-13, 2007, Marina Del Rey, California, USA).

[26] Stefan Dietze, Alessio Gugliotta, John Domingue, "A Semantic Web Service oriented Framework for adaptive Learning Environments" ESWC 2007 (June 2007 Austria).

[27] Bailey, C. P., Fill, K., Zalfan, M. T., Davis, H. C. and Conole, G. C. (2006) Panning for Gold: Designing Pedagogically Inspired Learning Nuggets. Educational Technology & Society, 9 (1). pp. 113-122.

The Learning Grid Handbook
S. Salerno et al. (Eds.)
IOS Press, 2008

Semantic Description and Matchmaking of Learning Grid Services

Gustavo GUTIÉRREZ-CARREÓN [1], Thanasis DARADOUMIS and Josep JORBA
Open University of Catalonia, Spain

Abstract. Learning Grid services are the fundamental component of learning systems based on Grid Technology and represent functionalities that can be easily reused without knowing the details of how services have been implemented. Semantic Web Service technology promises to automate web service discovery, composition and integration, tasks that currently need to be performed manually despite the quickly increasing number of online service. A number of approaches have been proposed to tackle the problems of semantic description and matchmaking of Learning Grid Services. This article gives an overview of those recent research efforts.

Keywords: Learning Grid, Learning Services, Semantic Web.

Introduction

Distant e-learning emerges as one of promising means for people to learn online [1]. Although there is a substantial increase in computer and network performance in recent years, mainly as a result of faster hardware and more sophisticated software, there are still problems in the fields of integrating various resources towards enabling distant e-learning. The introduction of web services has fundamentally changed the way learning software is developed. A "service" is a network enabled component. Like components, services in general (and Learning services in particular) represent functionality that can be easily reused without knowing the details of how the service is implemented. And, since Web protocols are completely independent across vendor, platform, and language implementations, the result is an application that integrates well with the rest of the enterprise while being flexible enough to modify as learning needs change.

Service-based educational systems open new ways in the usability of the Grid as their primary requirements include the provision of adequate services for sharing, syndicating heterogeneous resources and relevant content discovery [2]. The Learning Grid paradigm aims at making use of the collective intelligence and the personalized use of a range of available and potential Grid Learning services. In that sense Grid Learning Services, taking advantage of technological support of Web services in general and Grid services in particular, have fundamentally changed the way that e-learning frameworks were developed. As a learning service example we could consider a Learning Object (LO) [3] from the point of view that a LO is any digital resource that

[1] Corresponding Author: Open University of Catalonia, Av. Tibidabo 39-43, 08035 Barcelona, Spain; E-mail: ggutierrezc@uoc.edu.

can be used, reused or referenced to support learning, but not in the sense that it is necessarily designed to explain a stand-alone learning objective.

In the field of Grid services, an important issue is how to achieve the correct integration of inter-organizational and heterogeneous services on the Web. If no single Grid service can satisfy the functionality required by the user, there should be a possibility to combine existing services together in order to fulfill the request. In that sense a lot of efforts have been made to develop techniques and methods for search [4,5], discovery [6] , matching [7] and composition [8, 9, 10, 11, 12] of grid and web services using semantic description, which showed that important advantages could be achieved if compared with syntactic search.

Section 1 of this chapter provides an overall review of Learning Services Infrastructure. After that we make a review of research works that mostly contribute to the semantic enrichment of Grid based learning services description and discovery (Section 2). Then, Section 3 goes further and describes technologies for web services matching and composition. Section 4 concludes the paper.

1. Learning Services Infrastructure

The design of the virtual university is based on several key characteristics. All other design de-tails follow from these.

- Distributed Services: The architecture of the virtual university is based on a collection of distributed services, with each service (be it a component or an information source) providing one or more separately identifiable features for the user. The architecture makes no assumptions about either logical or physical integration of services. Each service is considered to be independent and each could be provided by one or more service processors located anywhere on the internet.
- Open Communications: All components and services are interconnected via a messaging scheme. Messages (request and responses) are XML data, and the messaging scheme is based on XML message encapsulation (e.g., Soap, XML-RPC). All message formats and service protocols are published in an open directory, enabling any component to discover and communicate with any other component.
- Standards Based: Whenever possible, the services, protocols and data formats should rely on established or emerging standards. Standards for core infrastructure and internet protocols are well established. Various application level standards are under development. In all cases, approaches that are compatible with an overall web model of distributed services and XML-formatted information bindings are preferred.
- Web Interfaces: All components for use, operations, maintenance and content development must be accessible via web-enabled devices, using web (http) protocols for access.
- COTS Components: Core components, such as database management, directory services, mail services, web server and web application servers are assumed to be available for direct use. In addition, application level services with appropriate interfaces are available or can be adopted for core services

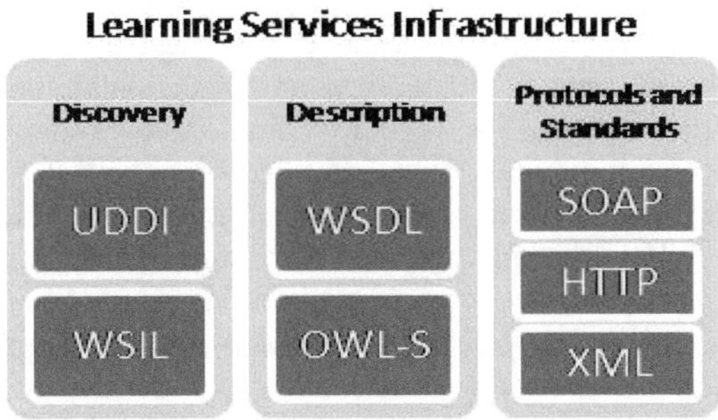

Figure 1. Learning Services Infrastructure

such as groupware, e-commerce, content management, news and event management.

The Learning Services approach is based on widely accepted technologies and commonly used standards. Standards for core infrastructure and internet protocols are well established. A variety of application level standards of the learning services infrastructure (Figure 1) are under development. In all cases, approaches that are compatible with an overall web model of distributed services and XML-formatted information bindings are preferred. Some of the core concepts of the Web services approach include:

- Accessible over the Internet, Web services communicate through platform-independent Web protocols, facilitating the integration of heterogeneous environments.
- Web services standards define an interface and communication protocol that can be invoked from an application client or provided through a server.
- The Web Services Description Language (WSDL) adds a layer of abstraction between implementation and interface, providing a loosely coupled application that results in future flexibility.

1.1. Protocols and Standards

In contrast to building large, closed, learning technology systems, the focus of the learning services architecture is on a flexible design that provides interoperability of components and learning content, and that relies on open standards (both learning technology standards and common web and network standards) for information exchange, behavior descriptions and component integration. Web services are built upon open, often already widely adopted standards.

Typically, these standards are maintained by independent, non-profit standards organizations composed of a diverse membership. Some of the protocols and standards related with learning services are:

- HTTP: The Hypertext Transfer Protocol (HTTP) [13] is an application-level protocol for distributed, collaborative, hypermedia information systems. HTTP has been in use by the World-Wide Web global information initiative since 1990. The HTTP protocol is a request/response proto-col. A client sends a request to the server in the form of a request method, URI, and protocol version, followed by a MIME-like message containing request modifiers, client information, and possible body content over a connection with a server. The server responds with a status line, including the message's protocol version and a success or error code, followed by a MIME-like message containing server information, entity metainformation, and possible entity-body content.

- XML: Extensible Markup Language (XML) [14] is a simple, very flexible text format derived from SGML (ISO 8879). Originally designed to meet the challenges of large-scale electronic publishing, XML is also playing an increasingly important role in the exchange of a wide variety of data on the Web and elsewhere. By offering a standard, flexible and inherently extensible data format, XML significantly reduces the burden of deploying the many technologies needed to ensure the success of Web services.
- SOAP: Simple Object Access Protocol (SOAP) [15] is a standard that represents a lightweight "envelope" containing the message payload as it moves between service producers and consumers. It is an XML-based standard that describes the contents of a message and how to process it, and offers a transport binding for exchanging messages.

1.2. Web Services Description Language (WSDL)

In the learning services architecture, it becomes increasingly possible and important to be able to describe the communications in some structured way. Web Services Description Language (WSDL) [16] is a new specification to describe networked XML-based services. It provides a simple way for service providers to describe the basic format of requests to their systems regardless of the underlying protocol (such as Simple Object Access Protocol) or encoding (such as Multipurpose Internet Messaging Extensions).

WSDL describes the functional information of services such as input parameters, output parameters, service providers and service locations. However, it is limited in supporting the discovery, execution, composition and interoperation of Web services.

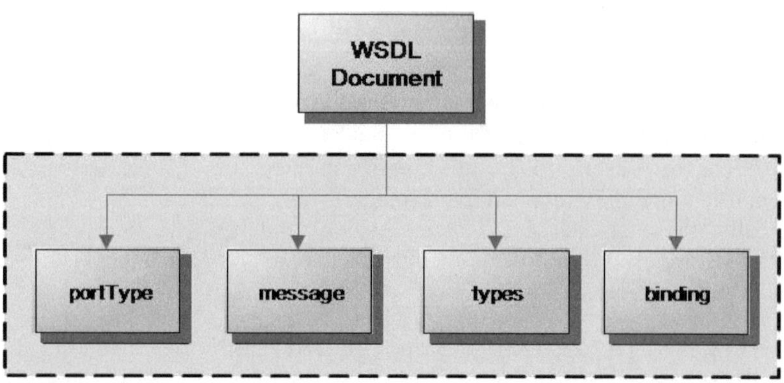

Figure 2. WSDL document

WSDL cannot provide semantic information of Web services that enable the semantic description of services capabilities.

A WSDL document defines services as collections of network endpoints, or ports. In WSDL, the abstract definition of endpoints and messages is separated from their concrete network deployment or data format bindings. It specifies the location of the service and the operations (or methods) the service exposes. WSDL document defines a web service using these major elements (Figure 2).

- The <portType> element is the most important WSDL element. It defines a web service, the operations that can be performed, and the messages that are involved. The port defines the connection point to a web service. It can be compared to a function library (or a module, or a class) in a traditional programming language. Each operation can be compared to a function in a traditional programming language.
- The <message> element defines the data elements of an operation. Each message can consist of one or more parts. The parts can be compared to the parameters of a function call in a traditional programming language.
- The <types> element defines the data type that are used by the web service. For maximum platform neutrality, WSDL uses XML Schema syntax to define data types.
- The <binding> element defines the message format and protocol details for each port. A WSDL port describes the interfaces (legal operations) exposed by a web service.

1.3. Semantic Web Services Description

Semantic Web Service technology promises to automate web service discovery, composition and integration, tasks that currently need to be performed manually despite the quickly increasing number of on-line services. The complexity of the reasoning tasks that can be performed with semantic web service descriptions is conditioned by several factors. First, all web services in a domain should use concepts from the same domain ontology in their descriptions. Otherwise the issue of ontology mapping has to be solved which is a very difficult problem in itself. This requires that domain ontologies should be generic enough to provide the needed concepts by any web service in a certain domain. Second, the richness of the available knowledge is crucial for performing complex reasoning. Therefore, the domain ontology should be rich in semantics. We conclude that such quality domain ontologies are at least as important as generic web service description ontologies. Despite their importance, few domain ontologies for web service descriptions exist and building them is a challenging task. A major impediment is the lack of guidelines on how to build such ontologies, what knowledge they should contain and what design principles they should follow. In the bioinformatics domain, for example, different communities used different approaches to build very different ontologies for semantically describing web services.

1.3.1 Semantic Markup for Web Services (OWL-S)

Semantic Web and Knowledge technologies provides an expressive and semantically enriched description of services, by the use of ontology description languages as

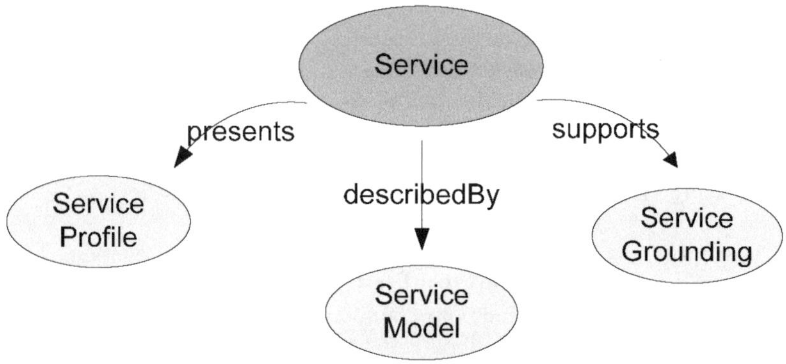

Figure 3. Semantic Web Services Description (OWL-S)

OWL-S [17], and allows for automatic selection, location and composition of services in order to achieve the required objectives. It is based on the Resource Description Framework (RDF), which integrates a variety of applications using XML for syntax and URIs for naming.

OWL-S is motivated by the need to provide three essential types of knowledge about a service, each characterized by the question it answers (Figure 3):

- What does the service provide for prospective clients? The Service Profile describes what the service does by specifying the input and output types, preconditions and effects.
- How is it used? The Process Model describes how the service works.
- How does one interact with it? The Grounding contains the details of how an agent can access a service by specifying a communications protocol, parameters to be used in the protocol and the serialization techniques to be employed for the communication.

1.3.2 Other Semantic Web Services Initiatives

The Web Service Modeling Ontology (WSMO) [18] provides ontological specifications for the core elements of Semantic Web services. In fact, Semantic Web services aim at an integrated technology for the next generation of the Web by combining Semantic Web technologies and Web services, thereby turning the Internet from a*n* information repository for human consumption into a world-wide system for distributed Web computing. Therefore, appropriate frameworks for Semantic Web services need to integrate the basic Web design principles, those defined for the Semantic Web, as well as design principles for distributed, service-orientated computing of the Web.

The Semantic Web Services Framework (SWSF) [19] is a relatively recent attempt towards a Semantic Web service annotation framework that greatly profits from previous work with its roots in OWL-S and the Process Specification Language (PSL). SWSF is based on two major components: an ontology (or conceptual model) and a language used to axiomatize it.

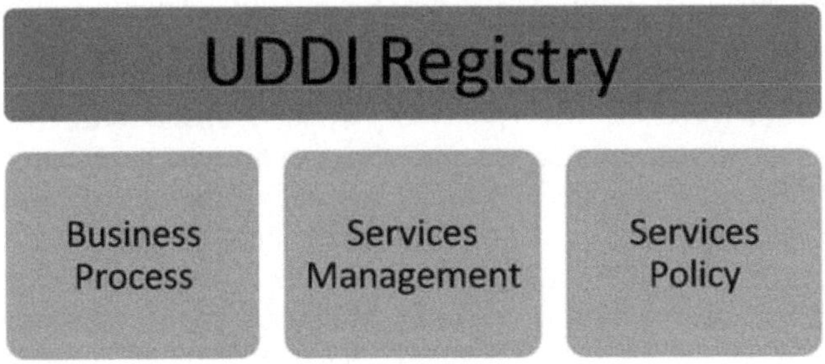

Figure 4. UDDI Registry [21]

Compared with WSMO, OWL-S, and SWSF, WSDL-S [20] is a rather minimalist approach which aims at a direct extension of the existing "traditional" Web service descriptions in WSDL with semantics. This approach offers multiple advantages over OWL-S. First, users can describe, in an upwardly compatible way, both the semantics and operation level details in WSDL- a language that the developer community is familiar with. Second, by externalizing the semantic domain models, we take an agnostic approach to ontology representation languages. This allows Web service developers to annotate their Web services with their choice of ontology language (such as UML or OWL) unlike in OWL-S. This is significant because the ability to reuse existing domain models expressed in modeling languages like UML can greatly alleviate the need to separately model semantics. Finally, it is relatively easy to update the existing tooling around the WSDL specification to accommodate our incremental approach.

1.4. Web Services Discovery

The Universal Description, Discovery, and Integration (UDDI) [21] protocol defines a standard method for publishing and discovering the network-based software components of a service-oriented architecture (SOA). UDDI is advanced by the OASIS UDDI Specification Technical Committee. The specification defines a group of Web services and programmatic interfaces for publishing, retrieving, and managing information about services (Figure 4).

Another Web Services Discovery specification is WSIL [22] that "*... provides an XML format for assisting in the inspection of a site for available services and a set of rules for how inspection related information should be made available for consumption. A WS-Inspection document provides a means for aggregating references to pre-existing service description documents which have been authored in any number of formats. These inspection documents are then made available at the point-of-offering for the service as well as through references which may be placed within a content medium such as HTML*".

1.5. IMS Abstract Framework

A grid learning service is a granular functional component accessible to other applications via standard interfaces.

The abstract learning framework proposes by IMS Global Learning Consortium can be represented as a layered model, as shown in Figure 5, consisting of four layers:

- Application layer - this is a tool, system, agent, etc. that presents the appropriate application services to the user i.e., an application manages the user interface. The application may use one or more application services but whenever possible the system composition should be hidden from the user;
- Application Services layer - a set of services that provide the required eLearning functionality to the applications. An application service may make use of one or more common services. Distributed application services communicate using via the Infrastructure Layer;
- Common Services layer - a set of services that are available to the application services. Common services may use other common services. Therefore, a common service is available to any other service;
- Infrastructure layer - this provides the end-to-end transaction and communications services for the application and common services.

One of the design principles for the abstract framework is the adoption of service abstraction to describe the appropriate e-Learning functionality (Figure 6).

Access to a service is through the appropriate Service Access Point (SAP). Each service has a single SAP. A Component may support one or more SAPs (in an object oriented representation, a SAP could be supported by one or more operators where the class is itself the definition of the service).

The SAP may consist of one or more objects and each object will, in general, will have more than one operator. Each object is defined using a class definition and consists of a group of attributes and operators. The operators describe how the state of the attributes may be changed. The set of behaviors permitted for each class must also be defined. These behavioral definitions ensure that any implementation of the class provides the same predicted behaviors for the same trigger events. Both the classes and

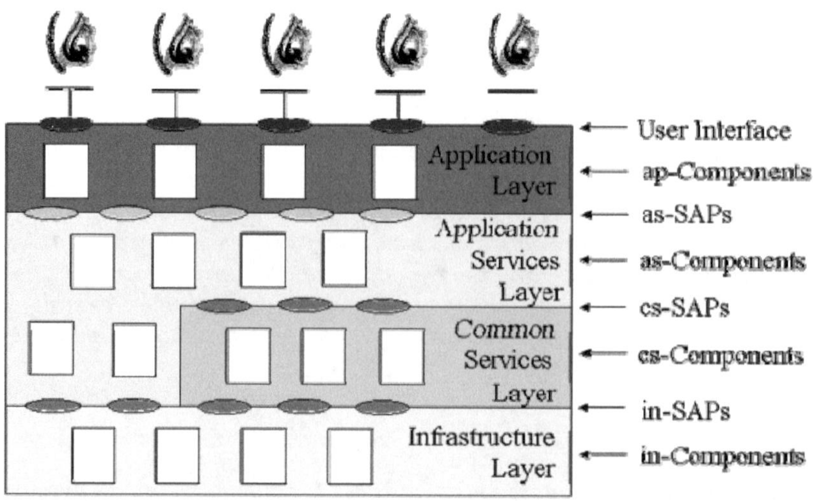

Figure 5. IMS Learning Abstract Framework [23]

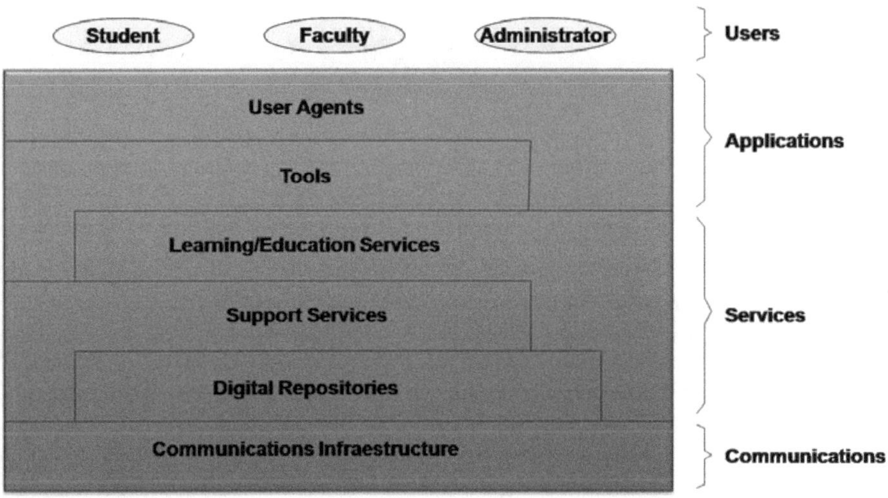

Figure 6. A logical architecture for an eLearning system .

their behaviors are defined in an implementation-independent manner;

This approach means that every service (application and common) must be defined using this form of abstraction. In many cases the services interact with each other e.g., an application service will use a common service. This interaction is reflected by the service invoking the SAP of the required service.

2. Grid Learning Services Semantic Description and Discovery

In the recent years, distributed Grid technologies have started to be very popular in education due to the advantages that Grid architecture offers being based on a secure, flexible and coordinated way of sharing resources in the Internet as well as on its enormous capabilities of information processing. This fact not only increased their demand but also generated new challenges in order to improve their functionality and decrease their limitations. For this reason, we proceed to outline the most recent and significant works that contributed to the development of technologies that make possible the vision of the Learning Grid.

2.1. Semantic Description of Grid Learning Services

There are some works related to the semantic description of Grid Learning Services. OntoEdu [24] is a flexible platform for online learning which is based on diverse technologies like ubiquous computing, ontology engineering, Web semantics and computational Grid. It is compound of five parts: user adaptation, automatic composition, educative ontologies, a module of services and a module of contents; among these parts the educative ontology is the main one. The main objectives of OntoEdu are to obtain reusability of concepts, adaptability for users and devices, automatic composition, as well as scalability in functionality and performance. In the

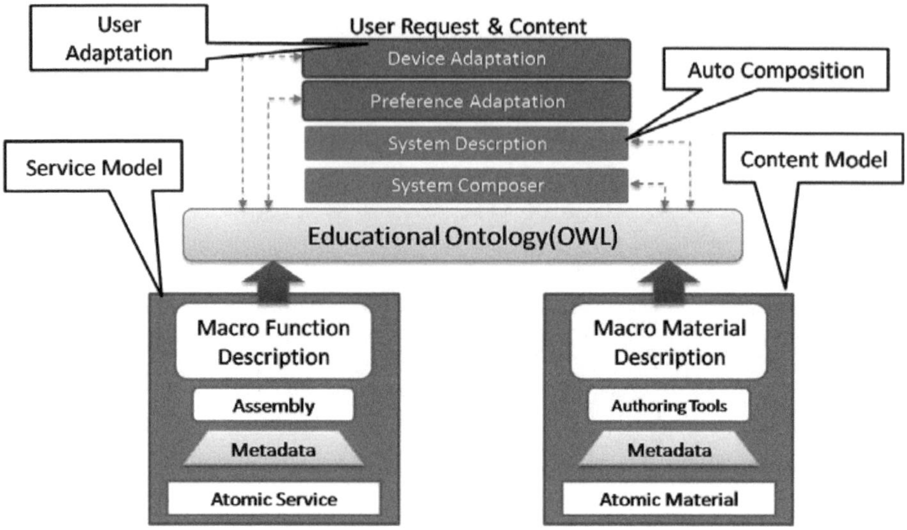

Figure 7. A logical architecture of OntoEdu.

near future, this platform aims to be adapted to a Grid environment so that it can carry out its activities based on distributed computing (Figure 7).

In [4], the authors have constructed an ontological description for collaborative work tools that allow one to make a manual search of the diverse resources that these tools provide within a Grid environment with the minimum of technical knowledge. About their model the authors said: "*...the ontology should allow to describe what types of activities does a particular tool support, either individual or collaborative. This issue is expressed independently of the type of learning tool, as shown pictorially in Figure...*" (Figure 8). This work proposes a Grid services-based tool, called Gridcole, which can serve for the support of collaborative learning, thus extending and endowing it with an innovative, pervasive and ubiquitous projection.

In [25] we propose a mechanism using OWL-S to describe semantically a Grid

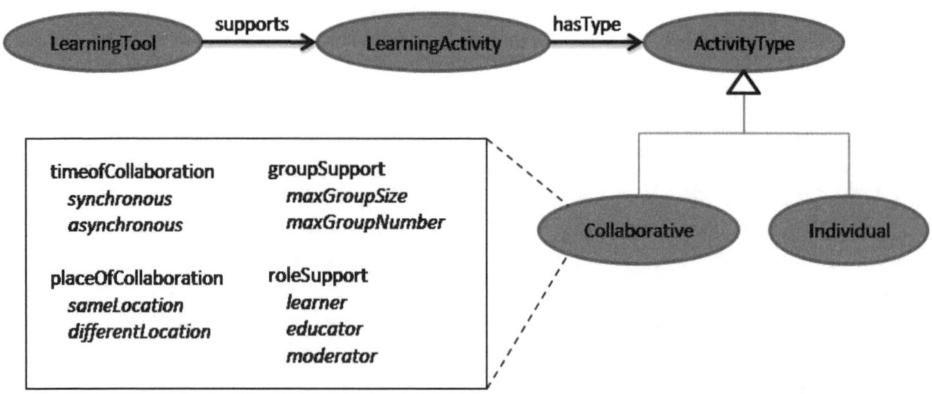

Figure 8. Information model of the ontology of learning tools.

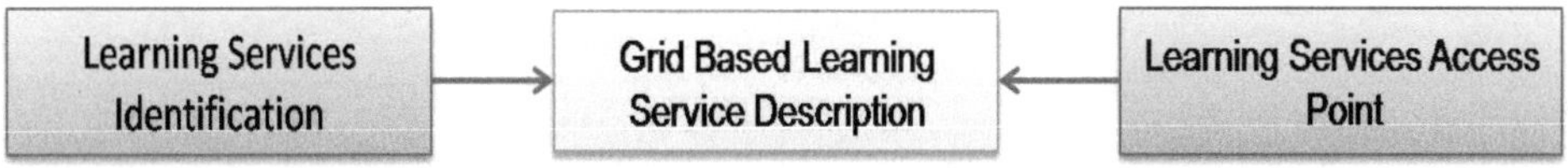

Figure 9. Parts of the conceptual model for a GBLS semantic description.

Based Learning Service (GBLS). One the one hand, we identify the principle characteristics of a GBLS related to an e-learning environment and the activities that support it. On the other hand, we consider a Grid Based Learning Service (GBLS) as a granular functional component with some input information, a functional activity and some output information. In this sense we form two conceptual groups of properties to achieve a complete description of a GBLS: the Learning Services Identification (LSI) and the Learning Services Access Point (LSAP) (Figure 9).

Table 1. LSI Elements.

Element	Description	OWL's Element	Parameter
Name	The name of a service	Service Profile	ServiceName
Category	Depending on the e-learning framework, services providers could construct the domain of categories for each group of learning services	Service Profile	ServiceCategory
Description	General description of a service	Service Profile	textDescription

The LSI element constitutes a set of parameters used to define the principle characteristics of a GBLS. Table 1 describes it in more detail. The LSAP element is characterized by the most important functional properties of a GBLS and is described in Table 2.

Table 2. Properties and resulting parameters of LSAP.

Element	Description	OWL's Element	Parameter
Activity	Activity in the e-learning framework supported by a service	Service Model	hasParameter
User	Defines the profile that makes use of a service (learner, teacher, another process, etc)	Service Model	hasParameter
Related Services	Specifies one or more services related to a service	Service Model	hasParticipant
Process	A service is described as a functional process	Service Model	Process
Errors	Specifies the errors resulting from the execution of a service	Service Model	hasParameter
Bindings	Definitions included in a WSDL description of a learning service	Service Grounding	WsdlAtomicProcessGrounding

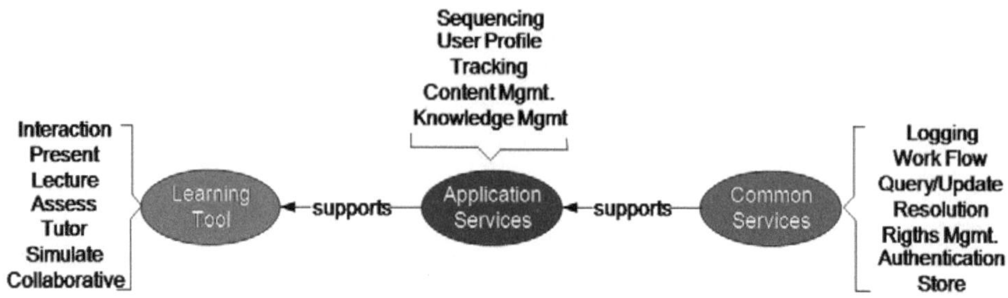

Figure 10. Service Categories for the IMS Abstract Framework.

On the one hand, the LSI contains basic information related to a learning service, allowing a user centric search. This model is generic enough to be implemented in any e-learning framework supported by GBLS and can be used for describing both low-level and composed services. In that sense, the domain of categories could be adapted to any ontology or taxonomy of services. For example, if we adopt the IMS Abstract Framework [23] Service's categories, we can obtain a taxonomy of learning tools supported by Common Services and they are in turn supported by Basic Services (Figure 10). On the other hand, LSAP allows the construction of an ontology domain for functional parameters related to the e-learning framework.

2.2. Semantic Discovery of Grid Learning Services

Discovery is the process of finding Web services with a given capability [24]. In general, discovery requires that Web services advertise their capabilities with a registry, and that requesting services query the registry for Web services with particular capabilities. The role of the registry is both to store the advertisements of capabilities and to perform a match between the request and the advertisements.

In general, a semantic discovery process relies on semantic annotations, containing high-level abstract descriptions of service requirements and behaviour. Metadata is an essential element in semantic discovery with the capability to expand service descriptions with additional information.

3. Grid Learning Services Matching and Composition

The achievement of dynamic composition and automation of services involves discovering new services at run time by software components without human interaction. SOAP provides a description of message transport mechanisms, whereas WSDL describes the interface used by each learning service. However, neither SOAP nor WSDL are of any help for the automatic location of learning services on the basis of their capabilities. Paolucci [27] comments that in order to enable the automation of this process we need a meaningful description of the service and its parameters that can be processed automatically by tools. This implies the possibility to process the context of description by discovery engines.

In this sense, there are some works that aim to improve the semantic services capability of matching. On the one hand, in [28] Paolucci focuses primarily on comparing inputs and outputs of a service as semantic concepts represented in OWL to improve UDDI. This work proposes a way of ranking semantic matching results. This ranking can be used in conjunction with other user-defined constraints to inform of an exact, or potentially useful web-service capability match. On the other hand, there are important lines of research that propose extensions to Web service description WSDL in two ways, annotated WSDL and WSDL-S files [6].

One of the most important contributions in this field is developed in [5] where the authors propose an integration of UDDI with OWL-S (Figure 11). They comment: *"In order to combine OWL-S and UDDI, we need embed an OWL-S profile description in a UDDI data structure, and we need to augment the UDDI registry with an OWL-S Matchmaking component, for processing OWL-S profile information. On receiving an advertisement through the publish port the UDDI component, in the OWL-S/UDDI matchmaker, processes it like any other UDDI advertisement. If the advertisement contains OWL-S Profile information, it forwards the advertisement to the matchmaking component. The matchmaker component classifies the advertisement based on the semantic information present in the advertisement. A client can use the UDDI's inquiry port to access the searching functionality provided by the UDDI registry, however these searches neither use the semantic information present in the advertisement nor the capability description provided by the OWLS Profile information. Hence we extended the UDDI registry by adding a capability port to solve the above problem. As a consequence, we also extended the UDDI API to access the capability search functionality of the OWL-S/UDDI matchmaker.*"

These approaches try to adhere to the current standards while trying to maximize semantic representations required for automation.

3.1. Semantically Matching Grid Learning Services

In [29] the authors have identified five matchmaking notions for functional discovery as shown in Figure 12. "*.. The important characteristic of these notions is that each one*

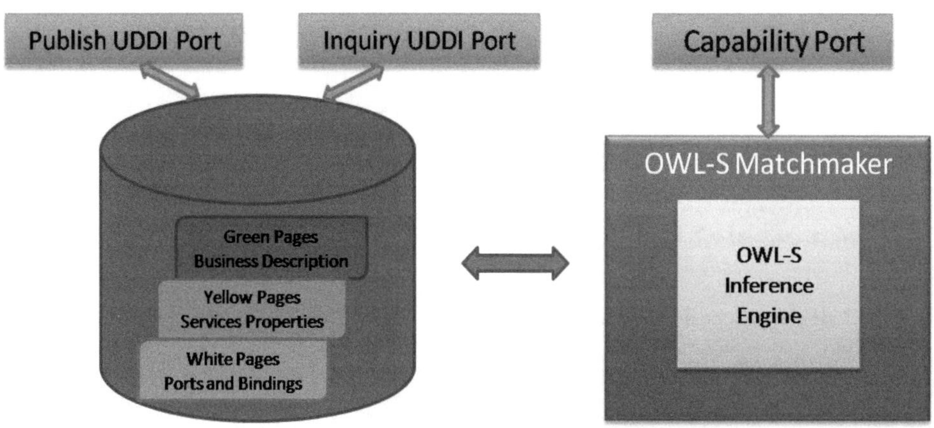

Figure 11. Architecture of UDDI/OWL-S Registry [5]

denotes a different logical relationship that must hold true when considering whether a Web service is suitable for achieving a given goal. For instance, an Exact Match holds if and only if each possible ontology instance that can satisfy the Web service also satisfies the goal, and there exists no possible ontology instance that satisfies only the goal or the Web service. In contrast, an Intersection Match holds if there exists one possible instance that can satisfy both the goal and the Web service…"

In that sense in [7] the author classifies the major approaches to schema matching:

- *Instance vs schema*: matching approaches can consider instance data (i.e., data contents) or only schema-level information.
- *Element vs structure matching*: match can be performed for individual schema elements, such as attributes, or for combinations of elements, such as complex schema structures.
- *Language vs constraint*: a matcher can use a linguistic based approach (e.g., based on names and textual descriptions of schema elements) or a constraint-based approach (e.g., based on keys and relationships).
- *Matching cardinality*: the overall match result may relate one or more elements of one schema to one or more elements of the other, yielding four cases: 1:1, 1:n, n:1, n:m. In addition, each mapping element may interrelate one or more elements of the two schemas. Furthermore, there may be different match cardinalities at the instance level.
- *Auxiliary information:* most matchers rely not only on the input schemas S1 and S2 but also on auxiliary information, such as dictionaries, global schemas, previous matching decisions, and user input.

In the same work, there is a detailed development of web services matching procedures for locating the most suitable Web Services, combining and integrating a number of matching algorithms, and adopting two principal approaches: the structural matching approach and the linguistic or syntactic approach. This work focuses on the issue of searching a Web Service with required functionalities and addressing a specific application domain, by means of an ontology-based semantic description.

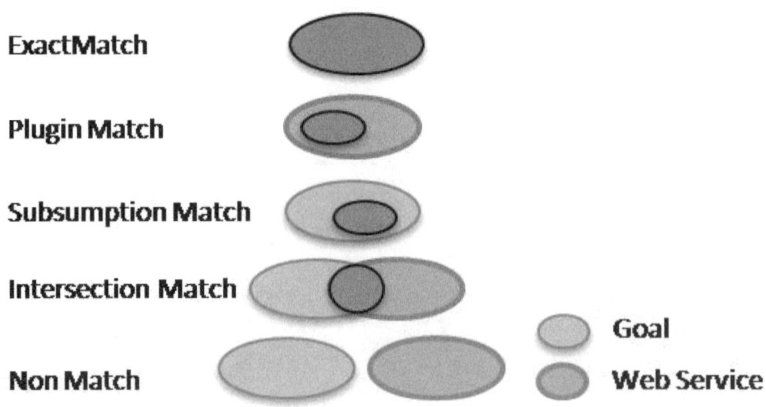

Figure 12. Matchmaking notions for semantically enabled discovery

3.2. Composition of Grid Learning Services

Web service composition originated from the necessity to achieve a predetermined goal that cannot be realized by a standalone service. Internally, in a composition, services can interact with each other to exchange parameters, for example a service's result could be another service's input parameter.

In general, a framework used for Web service composition [8] (Fig. 13) describes two kinds of participants, service provider and service requester. It contains the following components: a translator, a process generator, an evaluator, an execution engine and a service repository. The service providers propose Web services for use. The service requesters consume information or services offered by the service providers. The translator translates between the external languages used by the participants and the internal languages used by the process generator. For each request, the process generator tries to generate a plan that composes the available services in the service repository to fulfil the request. If more than one plan is found, the evaluator evaluates all plans and proposes the best one for execution. The execution engine executes the plan and returns the result to the service provide.

There are three principal motivations for Learning Grid Services Composition: build a more powerful service using basic existing services, fulfil service requester's requirement better, and enhance resource reuse while reducing the cost and time of a new service development.

The Learning Application composition process consists of identifying sub-tasks of the learning process, locating suitable Learning application Services to construct each process, locating suitable Common Services to construct each learning service, formatting the Learning and Common services into a service flow and executing the service flow to achieve a task which is the goal of the learning process.

The core stage is the composition of learning web services and their adaptation to the needs of a learner or group of learners [20]. Such a composition is carried out by retrieving previously registered objects. Once composed and packaged as learning objects, these composite processes can be executed and then instantiated and adapted to the learner's particular needs.

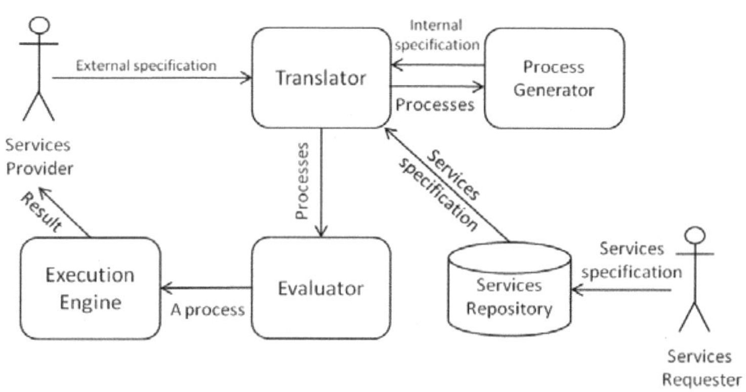

Figure 13. The framework of the service composition system [8]

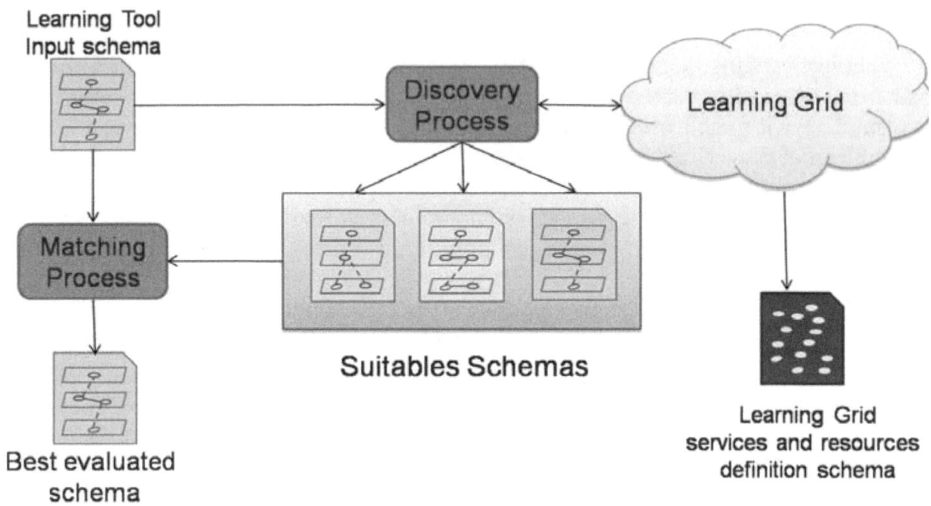

Figure 14. Grid Learning services automatic composition.

These adaptations can be realized, either by predefined rules implemented into the process description and driven by the learner behavior, or in a supervised manner. In the later case, the instructional designer can return to the composition tools to adapt the process.

Dealing with the specific problem of constructing a suitable workflow for a learning scenario, in [31] the authors propose a framework to facilitate automated composition of scientific workflows in Semantic Grids made up of a Manager Service and other supporting services, including an abstract and a concrete workflow generator. They described these components in detail and outlined their interactions. Finally, they described their implementation and its use within the physics domain. The important features of this approach are: an adaptive workflow generation algorithm and the distinction between different levels of abstraction of the workflow in order to allow reuse and sharing.

3.3. A Conceptual Model for Grid Learning Services automatic composition

In [32] we propose a model for the automatic composition of learning services (Fig. 14) that is based on the use of the defined syntactic and semantic characteristics for the different levels of services involved in the Learning Abstract Framework.

The first step to carry out the automatic composition is to generate a Semantic schema of the learning tool or learning services that will be composed. This schema will be able to be constructed using the different tools of descriptions at the "syntactic level" through WSDL, or at the semantic level, through service ontologies included in OWL-S, WSMO, SWSF and WSDL-S.

Once the semantic schema of the tool or learning service that we want to build is designed, we have to pass it to our discovery process that will locate a set of different level services in the Learning Grid. The operation of these services as a whole allows to carry out the processes defined in the schema. The result of the search will be a group of suitable schemas that conforms to the functional process described in our initial schema.

These resulting schemas will be compared to the initial schema through a Matching process that is based on a structural matching approach and on a linguistic or syntactic approach and whose result will be the best evaluated schema for our learning tool or services.

4. Conclusions

In this chapter on the one hand we review some technologies related with infrastructure and some methods for web services description and discovery and on the other hand we review some approaches related with Grid Learning Services semantic description, matchmaking and composition. In general we highlight the increasing importance of semantic description to support automatic matchmaking and composition of Grid Learning Services.

References

[1] Zongwei Luo, Yulian Fei, and Junyuan Liang, On Demand E-Learning with Service Grid Technologies. Edutainment 2006: 60-69.

[2] George Samaras, Kyriakos Karenos, Eleni Christodoulou. A Grid Service Framework for Metadata Management in Self-e-Learning Networks. Proc. 2nd European Across Grids Conf (AxGrid), Jan 2004, Nicosia, Cyprus.

[3] Wiley, D. A. (2000). "Connecting learning objects to instructional design theory: A definition, a metaphor, and a taxonomy," in D. A. Wiley, ed., The Instructional Use of Learning Objects: Online Version. Retrieved May 18, 2001, from the World Wide Web: http://reusability.org/read/chapters/wiley.doc.

[4] Guillermo Vega-Gorgojo, Miguel L. Bote-Lorenzo, Eduardo Gómez-Sánchez, Yannis A. Dimitriadis, Juan I. Asensio-Pérez, Semantic Search of Learning Services in a Grid- Based Collaborative System, Proc. of the Fifth IEEE/ACM Int. Symposium on Cluster Computing and the Grid (CCGrid 2005), Workshop on Collaborative and Learning Applications of Grid Technology and Grid Education (CLAG) 2005, 19-26, Cardiff, UK, May 2005.

[5] Naveen Srinivasan, Massimo Paolucci, and Katia Sycara, An Efficient Algorithm for OWL-S Based Semantic Search in UDDI, Book Series Lecture Notes in Computer Science, Springer Berlin / Heidelberg, ISSN 0302-9743, Volume 3387, 2005

[6] Preeda Rajasekaran, John Miller, Kunal Verma, Amit Sheth, Enhancing Web Services Description and Discovery to Facilitate Composition, International Workshop on Semantic Web Services and Web Process Composition, 2004 (Proceedings of SWSWPC 2004)

[7] Beniamino Di Martino, An Ontology Matching Approach to Semantic Web Services Discovery, Lecture Notes in Computer Science, Springer Berlin / Heidelberg, ISSN 0302-9743, Volume 4331, 2006

[8] Jinghai Rao and Xiaomeng Su, A Survey of Automated Web Service Composition Methods, Lecture Notes in Computer Science, Springer Berlin / Heidelberg, ISSN 0302-9743, Volume 3387, 2005

[9] Ching-Jung Liao, Fang-Chuan Ou Yang, A Workflow Framework for Pervasive Learning Objects Composition by Employing Grid Services Flow Language. Proceedings of the IEEE International Conference on Advanced Learning Technologies (ICALT'04), pp: 840 – 841, ISBN:0-7695-2181-9, 2004.

[10] Xiaofeng Du, William Song, Malcolm Munro, Service Composition in the Context of Grid, AHM2006, 2006

[11] Yang-Seung Jeon, Eun-Ha Song, Minyi Guo, Laurence T. Yang, Young-Sik Jeong, Jin-Tak Choi, Sung-Kook Han, Ontology-Based Composition of Web Services for Ubiquitous Computing, Lecture Notes in Computer Science, Springer Berlin / Heidelberg ISSN 0302-9743, Volume 4331, 2006

[12] F. Casati, S. Ilnicki, and L. Jin. Adaptive and dynamic service composition in EFlow. In Proceedings of 12th International Conference on Advanced Information Systems Engineering(CAiSE), Stockholm, Sweden, Springer Verlag, 2000

[13] Hypertext Transfer Protocol -- HTTP/1.1, http://www.w3.org/Protocols/rfc2616/rfc2616.html.

[14] Extensible Markup Language, http://www.w3.org/XML/.

[15] Simple Object Access Protocol, http://www.w3.org/TR/soap/.

[16] E.Christensen, F.Curbera, GMeredith, and S.Weerawarana. Web Service Description Language (WSDL) 1.1 http://www.w3.org/TR/2001/NOTE-wsdl20010315, 2001.

[17] OWL-S: Semantic Markup for Web Services, http://www.w3.org/Submission/OWL-S.

[18] WSMO Final Draft, http://www.wsmo.org/TR/d2/v1.2/

[19] Semantic Web Services Framework (SWSF). http://www.w3.org/Submission/SWSF/.

[20] Web Service Semantics: WSDL-S http://www.w3.org/Submission/WSDL-S/.

[21] Universal Description, Discovery, and Integration, http://uddi.xml.org/uddi-101.

[22] Web Services Inspection Language, http://www.ibm.com/developerworks/library/specification/ws-wsilspec/.

[23] IMS Global Learning Consortium, IMS Abstract Framework: White Paper, 2003

[24] Cui Guangzuo, Chen Fei, Chen Hu, Li Shufang, OntoEdu: A Case Study of Ontology-based Education Grid System for E-Learning, GCCCE2004 International conference, Hong Kong. 2004

[25] Gustavo Gutiérrez-Carreón, Thanasis Daradoumis y Josep Jorba, Semantic Description of Grid Based Learning Services, Lecture Notes in Computer Science, Springer Berlin / Heidelberg, ISSN 0302-9743, Volume 4331, 2006

[26] David Martin, Massimo Paolucci, Sheila McIlraith, Mark Burstein, Drew McDermott, Deborah McGuinness, Bijan Parsia, Terry Payne, Marta Sabou, Monika Solanki, Naveen Srinivasan, and Katia Sycara, Bringing Semantics to Web Services: The OWL-S Approach, Lecture Notes in Computer Science, Springer Berlin / Heidelberg, ISSN 0302-9743, Volume 3387, 2005

[27] Massimo Paolucci, Takahiro Kawamura, Rerry R. Payne, and Katia Sycara. Semantic matching of web services capabilities, The Semantic Web - ISWC 2002: First International Semantic Web Conference, Sardinia, Italy, June 9-12, 2002

[28] Massimo Paolucci, Takahiro Kawamura, Terry R. Payne, Katia Sycara, Importing the Semantic Web in UDDI, Robotics Institue, Carnegie-Mellon University, USA, 2002

[29] Dieter Fensel, Holger Lausen, Jos de Bruijn, Michael Stollberg, Dumitru Roman, Axel Polleres and John Domingue, Enabling Semantic Web Services The Web Service Modeling Ontology, Springer Berlin Heidelberg, ISBN 978-3-540-34519-0, 2007

[30] Jorge Torre, Juan Manuel Dodero, Carmen L. Padrón, A Framework Based on Web Services Composition for the Adaptability of Complex and Dynamic Learning Processes, Learning Technology newsletter, Vol. 6, Issue 1, January 2004

[31] Shalil Majithia, David W.Walker, W.A.Gray, Automated Composition of Semantic Grid Services, International Conference on Autonomic Computing (ICAC'04), May, 2004

[32] Gustavo Gutiérrez-Carreón, Thanasis Daradoumis y Josep Jorba, A Conceptual Model for Grid Learning Services Automatic Composition, Lecture Notes in Computer Science, Springer Berlin / Heidelberg, ISSN 0302-9743, Volume 4805, 2007

The Learning Grid Handbook
S. Salerno et al. (Eds.)
IOS Press, 2008

Application Scenarios for a Learning Grid

Nicola CAPUANO [1,a,b], Angelo GAETA [b], Stefano PAOLOZZI [c]
[a] *DIIMA, Università di Salerno, Italy*
[b] *CRMPA, Centro di Ricerca in Matematica Pura ed Applicata, Italy*
[c] *IRPPS-CNR, Consiglio Nazionale delle Ricerche, Italy*

Abstract. This chapter analyses the adoption of the Learning Grid for the development of challenging Application Scenarios in the eLearning domain. The Application Scenarios described in this chapter create a breakthrough in current learning practices. Instead of adopting a traditional information transfer paradigm, the proposed scenarios, in fact, promote and support a learning paradigm centred on the learner and focused on knowledge construction using experiential based and collaborative learning approaches in a contextualised, personalised and ubiquitous way. The purpose of our analysis is to understand and argue about the potential advantages of adopting the Learning Grid for the proposed scenarios. Preliminary findings show that Learning Grid can be considered an enabling technology for the presented scenarios since its features (e.g. dynamicity, adaptiveness, support for Virtual Organisation creation and management, advanced mechanisms for resources and services discovery on the basis of Quality of Services) are key to improve personalisation and knowledge construction in the learning process as well as communication and collaboration inside learning groups.

Keywords. Technology Enhanced Learning, Application Scenarios, Pedagogy, Learning Design.

Introduction

This chapter concludes the first section of this book. In the previous chapters, the authors have provided a detailed description of the Learning Grid and how it combines its three building blocks (Grid, Semantics and Educational Modelling Languages) in order to provide a reference Service Oriented Architecture (SOA) for human learning. In this chapter the reader will see what are the advantages of adopting the Learning Grid as enabling technology for the development of challenging Application Scenarios in different learning contexts.

The chapter is structured as follow. Paragraph 1 provides an overview of several Application Scenarios that can be developed taking advantages of the Learning Grid. The Application Scenarios presented are the ones proposed in the context of the Kaleidoscope Special Interest Group (SIG) for the Learning Grid. Paragraph 2 presents some common features of the proposed application scenarios. Paragraph 3 points out what are the main benefits of adopting the Learning Grid as a reference architecture for the development and deployment of the above scenarios.

Eventually, the main conclusions of our investigations are drawn in the section 4.

[1] Corresponding Author: CRMPA, Centro di Ricerca in Matematica Pura ed Applicata, via Ponte Don Melillo, 84084 Fisciano (SA), Italy; E-mail: capuano@crmpa.unisa.it.

1. Overview of the Application Scenarios

Several scenarios have been proposed inside the SIG for the Learning Grid. A complete description can be found in [1] and [2]. Scenarios presented in [1] are either already under implementation or are possible extensions of existing teaching and learning practices. Scenarios presented in [2], instead, are more futuristic and still to be implemented.

Next sub-paragraphs present a selection of application scenarios defined inside the SIG where paragraph 2 categorises defined scenarios on the basis of common features presented by each of them.

1.1. Distance Programming Course based on Practice

This scenario is based on an existing e-learning programming course running in the Engineering School Léonard de Vinci [3] and, indeed, among the scenarios presented it is the most traditional one.

In this course, students are provided with many programming exercises that are automatically corrected. Moreover, all their attempts are stored so that students can consult their history. Compilation and program execution are implemented as services, students do not need to worry about downloading themselves any programming environment.

As evidenced previously, this is a traditional distance learning scenario presenting functionalities needed for the execution of programming exercises (e.g. compilation) in a service oriented fashion. Anyway, we consider useful to describe the scenario in this paper since it presents some features that can be enhanced adopting Learning Grid. Learning Grid would in fact improve the existing system in the following ways:

- by allowing a distributed code compilation and execution as well as a distributed storage of students' answers, would make the current system scalable in terms of supported users;
- by providing functionalities in a service oriented way, exploiting the WS-* standards, would make the systems open and easy extensible in terms of supported functionalities. Furthermore, some complex functionalities (e.g. a software development environment) can be obtained by orchestrating atomic ones (e.g. a compiler, a debugger, and so);
- semantics would allow for better personalization and flexible course composition and, pragmatically, this would allow for selection of tools and instruments tailored on learner features (e.g. the selection of a C# compiler instead of a Java one).

The main benefits of this scenario are for students that will be able to learn computer programming not primarily by receiving information but by practicing a lot at their own place and at their own pace.

1.2. Enhanced Digital Library

This scenario takes its inspiration from Citeseer [4], a digital library which organizes scientific literature, allowing flexible searching and citation statistics.

The use of Grid technology makes it possible to extend the digital library with new forms of collaborative activities. Apart form papers, more resources can be shared such as formal or informal comments, reviews, summaries, videos, code, etc. in a Virtual Organisation (VO) [5], defined as a coordinated group of individuals and/or institutions that cooperate by sharing resources, according to predefined policies, to achieve a common goal.

Among the benefits of the Learning Grid and of the exploitation of the VO paradigm to achieve the enhanced digital library we point out:

- the capability to harmonise and interconnect several heterogeneous distributed digital repositories, thus creating a network of digital libraries having a single point of access (e.g. a VO portal);
- advanced mechanism to authenticate and authorise users to access digital libraries as well as other resources of the VO;
- advanced mechanism for annotation and search of contents in the repositories;
- notification mechanism allowing the VO users to be advised when new contents matching her/his interests, needs, preferences is uploaded.

Personalisation options could be specified at individual level or at VO level. The access to the environment could be done through a grid portal, which is a Web-based application that provides personalisation, single sign-on, content aggregation from different sources and hosts the presentation layer of information services.

Furthermore, the enhanced digital library can be considered as a base scenario for more complex collaborative research environment, user centred, allowing the researchers to learn with some hints (classification of documents) provided by his/her supervisor(s), by other people in the research group, and most importantly, by himself-herself. Thus, this scenario fosters the transition from a content-oriented learning solutions to a user-centred collaborative model.

1.3. Enhanced Virtual Laboratory

Virtual Laboratories are exploited by several eScience communities such as astronomy and earth science communities, bioinformatics, researchers and pharmaceutical companies, and so on.

Currently actual implementations of Virtual Laboratories are mainly in terms of problem solving environments providing functionalities to addresses key issues of the above communities, and they are mainly used for sharing and access to data and information, data mining purposes, to support data to information and information to knowledge processes, to execute simulations and experiments.

Rather than enumerate all the possible example of Virtual Laboratories in detail, we shall look at a future learning scenario, the Enhanced Virtual Laboratory, exploiting the learning Grid features to combine conventional data and computing technologies with technologies from the Semantic Web in order to allows the execution of collaboration activities inside the traditional Virtual Laboratory. Adopting a Learning Grid we can obtain the following advantages.

- To enhance the Virtual Laboratories allowing its customisation on the needs of a specific communities or group of communities. In fact, adopting the dynamicity features of the Learning Grid and its advanced mechanisms for location and discovery, we can build the laboratory on the basis of the real problem to solve by selecting and orchestrating the most appropriate tools, services, sensors and scientific instruments.

- To put the researchers at the centre of the experiments. Experiments often involve many processes or services that need to be orchestrated. Previous knowledge, know-how, and experiences can be taken into account by adopting the personalisation services of the Learning Grid.
- To tailor the scientific processes to the profiles of the researchers not just in terms of selection of more suitable tools/services but mainly in terms of a personalised path of activities of the workflow that are more "simple" to execute given the researchers background.
- To allow collaborative activities among the researchers.

1.4. Virtual Learning Community for Professionals

The following scenario relates to continuous education in medicine. A community of medical professional has to learn new medical techniques based on some innovative research results. They can exploit the Learning Grid to create a Virtual Learning community.

The virtual community behind this scenario consists of a high number of medical professional, a reduced number of professors being involved in the finding of the new knowledge to be learnt by the medical professional, an interactive simulation being developed by a specialised research centre available to the medical professional to simulate the new techniques.

The medical professionals are grouped on the basis of their skill and expertise and, also on this basis, they access personalised learning experience on the new techniques. Next, they are required to virtually apply the new techniques using the simulator service (part of the personalised learning experience). They can collaborate with the teacher either during the course or during the simulation.

The adoption of Learning Grid technologies make easy the implementation of this scenario highlighting two key aspects with respect to possible alternative solutions based on more traditional technologies:

- dynamicity versus static provisioning (i.e. the services are available on fixed servers);
- adaptivity versus pre-defined configuration (i.e. everything have to be pre-configured and installed).

Features of membership negotiation offered by a Grid can improve the dynamicity in the process of creation of groups with similar skills (without Grid facility this should be done statically with the support of tools). Furthermore, the same negotiation features allows to negotiate the terms for accessing the resources of the research centre providing the simulation (without a Grid, this should be done statically with the research centre that a-priori sets the access policy on the resources).

During the simulation execution, the research centre can scale the application to the number of medical professional interacting with it and/or to the status of the network and of resources requiring, if necessary, the provision of additional resources that can be taken also from other providers (without a Grid an adequate number of servers/clusters have to be provided in a physical place and properly managed).

1.5. Immersive Virtual Reality

In this scenario, a student is learning water and aquifer behaviour by using an e-Learning platform. S/he can access introductory books to gain initial knowledge on the topic. S/he can also use a dynamically generated set of services that, according to her user profile and current PC capabilities create an immersive virtual reality. The service also informs the student about immersion requiring special equipment like gloves and glasses and about the nearest locations where such immersions are possible.

Such immersions allow her to go deeper on the aquifer behaviour and characteristics of water. In these virtual sites, she also meets other students and interact with them. Learning occurs naturally as a result of experiments and interactions with other students.

Learning Grid technology (user profile, semantics, provision of Virtual Environments) is needed to make this scenario work.

1.6. Field Trip

Based on the traditional field trip and on the Immersive Virtual Reality previously presented, the proposed scenario illustrates experiential, contextualised, collaborative and active learning for knowledge creation and experience sharing in the context of a Mobile Dynamic Virtual Organization [6] based on a Learning Grid.

Two departments have a common goal: they are involved in a project related to the Evolution of Classical Greece Architectures. Department A decides to send a group of students in the archaeological site of Athens, while department B sends a group of researchers in the site of Paestum, in order to valuate the contamination of Greece style due to external influences.

Both the departments provides their human resources with mobile and wearable devices and they have their own resources in the departments. Furthermore, they have an agreement to use some resources of the computational centres in the archaeological sites and the two groups can rely upon local network providers and telco operators.

Both groups are equipped with mobile and wearable device enhanced with sensors to be geographically referenced. These sensors send, via the Wireless LAN of the site, information about the location and orientation of the user to a Service Centre that is able to provide notifications about the availability of important structures, facilities and so on. Group A and group B works for the same goal: to create knowledge about the evolution of Greece architectures.

During their activity they store information, experience, emotion, in terms of photos, video clips, text notes, audio comments, etc. Both the groups can collaborate among themselves and with remote experts using the Collaboration Services provided by their departments. The mobile devices indexed these contents using appropriate metadata standards.

The information collected by all students (group A) and researcher (group B) are send via the appropriate network (The device will negotiate with the network service provider (T) operative in that zone which kind of network communication will be used according to the bandwidth necessary, the price, etc.) to a Field Trip (FT) grid service

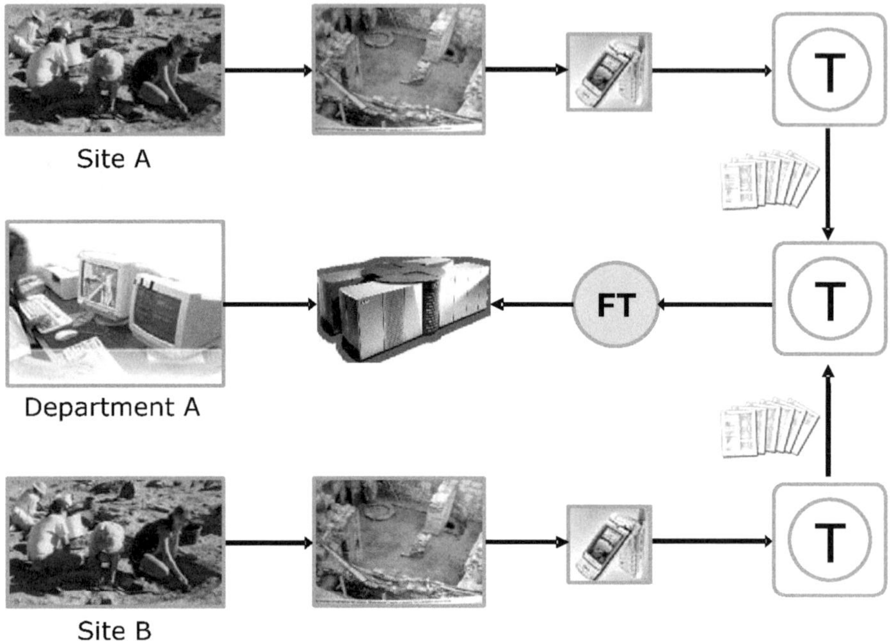

Figure 1. The Field Trip Scenario

created by a teacher of the Department A. The mobile devices will use user biometric data for secure access to Grid.

The FT grid service, orchestrating speech to text grid services, advanced semantic tool for text and images interpretation and other tools for knowledge management (virtualised as grid services) will analyse the information comparing content produced by group A and group B and formalise, in an ontology based knowledge representation, the knowledge about the evolution of Greece architectures.

The FT service stores all the information in a multimedia repository grid service. For the group A, since they are students, the student's information will be compared by their teachers with their learning objective. Furthermore, teachers of Department A can analyse the knowledge structure created and can require some remedial content. The Figure 1 summaries this workflow.

It is important to emphasize that both the groups are involved in a collaborative process by which they acquire and create knowledge. They are free to move and perform all actions they want during the exploration of sites in an independent way, but they are able to share contents that produce during the visit, to communicate and collaborate among themselves. Students of group A can also rely upon the experience of researchers of group B, that act as tutors for their experiential and active learning process. In this scenario:

- the learner is an active figure placed in a real world context allowing him to be part of a collaborative process aimed to knowledge creation and experience sharing;

- the real context, in which learner is immersed, is enhanced by services and tools to provide real-time collaboration, content management and provisioning, high performance 3d modelling and rendering;
- it relies on a Mobile Dynamic Virtual Organization based on the Learning Grid paradigm: during his learning process, a learner can be considered as a resource that can be accessed (also in terms of experiences) by other persons belonging to the VO.

As we have seen, this scenario uses the typical Grid approach in combination with mobility. Moreover semantics is required for knowledge based services. More details about this scenario are given in chapter 8 of this book.

2. Common features of the proposed application scenarios

The scenarios described in the previous section present some common characteristics. First and foremost, all the scenarios create a breakthrough in current learning practices. Instead of adopting a traditional information transfer paradigm, the proposed scenarios, in fact, promote and support a learning paradigm centred on knowledge construction using experiential based and collaborative learning approaches in a contextualised, personalised and ubiquitous way.

From the above statement, we can argue about the main features of the Application Scenarios that, in the follow, we are going to explain.

- ***Knowledge construction***. For many years, learning approaches and scenarios were based on traditional information transfer paradigm in which there is a central figure, the teacher, whose primary activity is the provisioning of educational contents in order to transmit information to learners. These approaches aim to monitor learner's progresses and to give him a score. In most of the Application Scenarios presented in the previous section, instead, the main goal is the Knowledge construction that occurs through forms of learning based on the understanding of concepts through direct experience of their manifestation in realistic contexts (i.e. providing access to real world data) which are constructed from sophisticated software interfaces and devices, and represented as services.
- ***Experiential based and collaborative approaches***. The Application scenarios presented foresee active collaboration with other students, teachers, tutors, experts or, in general, available human peers, by using different kinds of communication and collaboration technologies, including enhanced presence. The learning resources of the Application Scenarios, moreover, are interactive, engaging, and responsive – active learning and knowledge formation is emphasised above simple information transfer.
- ***Contextualised, personalised and ubiquitous***. In the Application scenarios the learners are themselves at the centre of their online environment, with their individual needs addressed and the quality of the learning experience continually validated and evaluated. Furthermore, a wider and more flexible access to educational resources is provided, including support to multiple different types of devices, interfaces, and network connection types.

Last but not the least, there is another important feature we point out. The Application Scenario proposed are ***learner centred*** meaning that the learner is in the centre of the learning process. The essence of the proposed scenarios is to create dynamic contexts providing suitable conditions for learners (taking into account their features and social context, providing tutoring and enhanced presence), supporting learners during their learning process (also by the use technologies for collaboration, highly realistic virtual scientific experiments, real time simulations, personalized learning path definitions, stateful message exchange sessions to support conversation) and, finally, that let them free to reason about their experience creating, in this way, the knowledge model suitable for them.

In those scenarios, there isn't more an overemphasize of the role of the teacher: she comes into this process as a domain expert whose purpose is to propose educational goals and topic of discussion, to moderate discussions inside a community, to give feedbacks to learners and to prepare educational contents.

The table 1 maps the presented Application Scenarios against the most relevant learning features they presents. It is worth to mention that the mapping evidences just the major features of each Application Scenario. This means that, for example, the *Distance Programming Course based on Practice* scenario presents as main features the Experiential and Active Learning and the Personalisation even if it is clear that in the scenario also Accessibility is a need.

The filed trip is, among the application scenarios of the SIG, the most complete one in terms of learning features. Even if, of course, they can not be considered as a statistical sample of the learning scenarios we can retrieve as useful information that the two most common features are the *personalisation* and the *communication & collaboration.* In the next sections we present the benefits of adopting the Learning Grid for the proposed scenario focalising our attention mainly on the above mentioned two features.

3. The Benefits of the Learning Grid for the Proposed Scenarios

This section gives an overview of the benefits of the Learning Grid for education, in general, and for the proposed scenarios. Then we will focalise our attention on two of the most important features of the scenarios, namely the personalisation form one side and the communication and collaboration from the other side.

Generally speaking, the importance of Grid in education has been emphasized by G. Fox in [7]. In [8] the impact that Semantic Web technologies can have in e-Learning is also evidenced. As described in the first chapter of this book, the Learning Grid combines Grid and Semantic Web technologies in defining an open and service oriented architecture to support human learning.

The Learning Grid is based on a Service Oriented Model, the Open Grid Services Architecture (OGSA) [9]. In general, Service Oriented Architectures (SOA) relies upon the service's concept and its technical implication (e.g. message based strategy with respect to method based one) and provide a suitable approach to implement a composition paradigm or building block approach, where a set of capabilities or functions is built or adapted as required, from a minimalist set of initial capabilities, to meet a need.

Table 1 - Mapping the Application Scenarios against common learning features

SIG Scenarios	Knowledge Construction	Experiential Active Learning	Communication and Collaboration	Personalisation	Contextualisation	Ubiquity and accessibility
	Main features of Application Learning Scenarios					
Distance Programming Course based on Practice		X		X		
Enhanced Digital Library	X	X	X	X		
Enhanced Virtual Laboratory	X		X		X	
Virtual Learning Communities for professionals	X	X	X	X		X
Immersive Virtual Reality	X		X	X	X	
Filed Trip	X	X	X	X	X	X

This is clearly useful in most of the presented Application scenarios that strongly relies upon a composition paradigm allowing the creation of (personalized) learning experiences (re-)using data, units of learning, knowledge, tools virtualized as services and distributed across different organizations.

In particular, the OGSA model is based on a stateful and dynamic service model based on a set of WS-Specification able to manage the state associated to a service/resource. Recognizing the need for state management in learning scenarios (e.g. knowledge acquisition in informal learning happens as results of a conversational process among peers actively involved in experiments), an underlying stateless service model would force the developer to manage the state at higher (e.g. Application) level. From a technical point of view, this is an additional effort that the adoption of Grid technologies can minimize and, in some case, can eliminate.

Another important reason is that the Learning Grid, bringing together Grid, Semantic Web and Web Service technologies, can be considered as glue among these different technologies that, taking them alone, can only provide partial benefits to our Application Scenarios. We do not see, in fact, an advantage to use only Semantic Web technologies (providing a very good support to Knowledge management, sharing and creation, resources annotation) and to spend effort to define advanced algorithm for resources reservation (to support efficient resources management allowing 3d simulations and immersive VR) or to use Semantic Web technologies (providing a good support for contextualization and personalization) if they have to be reinforced with mechanisms to discover, acquire, federate, and manage the capabilities, resources and contents needed to create/deliver the personalized learning experiences.

In the nest sub-paragraphs, we focus our attention on two of the common features of our application scenarios, such as the *personalisation* and the *communication & collaboration*, and present the added value of the Learning Grid.

3.1 Benefits of the Learning Grid for personalisation

Personalisation is one of the major trend in Technology Enhanced Learning and one of the common feature of the scenario presented in this chapter. The purpose of personalisation is to dynamically adapt and delivery educational contents and services matching the learner needs and preferences according to her/his profile.

Currently, personalisation is mainly addressed at the content level on the basis of simple information (traditional preferences such us age, language, school grade, ...) stored in a student profile and do not take sufficiently into account the characteristics of the users (especially regarding learning style preferences and her/his knowledge and skills). The Learning Grid provides several benefits for the personalisation coming from each one of its building blocks: Grid, Semantics and Educational Modelling Languages.

First of all, the adoption of a Service Oriented Grid, such as the OGSA one, allows for a seamless and ubiquitous access to heterogeneous and distributed repositories. This aspect, together with the availability of services for semantic annotation and advanced mechanisms for resources and services discovery, clearly helps in addressing one of the current issues of personalisation: the enormous number of items of the required quality. Quoting from [10]:

"Depending of the number of parameters taken up in the learners' profiles, an enormous amount of orchestrating decisions would have to be taken. In order to fulfil the individual needs properly, the availability of large amounts of learning related object would be needed in the reach of the orchestrating engine. If we go for a combinatorial simulation and assume, that our learner profile mirrors just five parameters, with the respective number of variables, e.g. (1) five languages, (2) three learning styles, (3) three degrees of difficulty,(4) three age ranges and (5) two genders, omitting so far elements like learner support services, or billing services, we would need a repository of nearly 300 items for just one learning object of one subject domain."

Furthermore, the adoption of Semantic technologies provides support for the various phases of the personalisation of learning experiences. First, authoring tools for the production of learning scenarios can make use of knowledge-based decision making systems to suggest the best pedagogical models and/or activities for a learning scenario, and also use knowledge (e.g. starting skills, personal pro-files, etc...) about the actors in the scenario. Next, in the delivery phase of a learning experience, semantic services can be used to bind at run-time a (learning) activity with an environment (that is a set of resources and services able to execute the activity).

In this binding phase, the semantics can provide some benefits. In fact, in order to find inside a Grid the resources and services that best match the requirements of an environment, the Learning Grid relies upon ontologies to index the core elements of the infrastructure, the educational resources and services.

In particular, to index services and resources of a Grid environment, it is a feature that can be used:

- by the Grid itself, in order to “know” its infrastructure and to provide machine understandable information about its resources and services,
- by knowledge tools, services or agents inside the Grid, in order to perform an automatic discovery of services and contents matching demand’s requirements vs. supply’s offers.

Eventually, it is worth to mention that Personalisation is also difficult to achieve exploiting the current learning standards/specifications (e.g. IMS Simple Sequencing and IMS-Learning Design).

Currently, in fact, exploiting these standards it is possible to sequence discrete learning activities in a consistent way. The created path, of course, can be personalized for a single learner (in the case of IMS Simple Sequencing) but this step is really difficult and it is performed manually by the teacher/instructional designer that has to rely upon her/his expertise and knowledge about the characteristics of the user. In many cases, anyway, the creation of a learning path on the basis of a specific pedagogical model is a joint effort of the designer (expert of the specifications) and of a teacher (expert of pedagogies).

Learning Grid services, by leveraging on semantic descriptions of didactical resources and services, allows to automatic personalise a learning experience first at the level of the knowledge to be created/transferred by/to a learner (e.g. the creation of a Specific Personalized Ontology), next at the level of the pedagogy (e.g. the selection of a suitable Didactic Method and preferred learning styles) and, finally, at the content level (e.g. the selection of suitable contents on the basis also of the Learner Profile that includes existing knowledge and learning style preferences).

The main advantages of the Learning Grid approach is that it is possible to personalise the educational objectives to reach, the suitable way to achieve them and, finally, the instruments by which it is possible to achieve the objectives shifting the complexity of personalisation from instructional designers to the process of creation and delivery of a learning experience.

3.2 Benefits of the Learning Grid for Communication and Collaboration

In the case of the collaborative scenarios (such as the Virtual Learning community for professionals, the Field Trip, etc.) the Learning Grid allows to reach the desired level of dynamicity and scalability for a group/community, to manage its heterogeneity and for transparent ubiquitous resource sharing.

In fact through the virtualisation paradigm, traditional collaborative tools can be virtualised as services (both Grid or Web). This allows to add dynamicity since they can be provided on demand and it is possible to search and retrieve the most suitable tool on the basis of some parameters like, for instance, preferences of the group of learners and/or QoS.

Moreover, exploiting the distinctive features of the Grid services (mainly lifecycle management and statefulness, but also manageability) it is possible to increase scalability and support management of interactions respectively. In fact, it is possible to create more instances of services to support collaboration. Furthermore, the state management capabilities of Grid services allow defining and associating a state to each service (following the WSRF specification, the related stateful resource concept and implied resource pattern). This is an useful feature if we want to maintain trace of some data/information during the cooperation/conversation among the learners.

As enabling technologies for VO, the Grid provides support for geographically distributed community creation and management addressing issues like heterogeneity, Single Sign On, group/community lifecycle management, localisation and instantiation of tools/services, transparent resource sharing.

In particular dynamicity and adaptiveness of Grid technologies are key features in order to provide advanced mechanism for service discovery and instantiation on the basis of Service Level Agreements (SLA) documents allowing, for instance, to deploy and execute a service on the most suitable host of a VO and to monitor at-run-time its SLA; by exploiting flexible and standard based mechanisms for transparent resources reservation, sharing and accessibility, Grid technologies aldo improve ubiquity and accessibility.

Last but not least, semantic capabilities allow semantic annotation of educational resources and services for automatic discovery, the late binding of educational resources and services in the learning environment, improving the capability to support learning community creation and management.

4. Conclusions

This chapter has provided an overview of the Application Scenarios that can be built adopting the Learning Grid as enabling technology. The scenarios presented demonstrate the suitability of an open services environment, such as the one supported by the Learning Grid, to foster a learning paradigm centered on the learner and focused on knowledge construction using experiential based and collaborative learning approaches in a contextualised, personalised and ubiquitous way.

It is worth to mention that the scenarios described in this chapter, coming from the research activities of the Kaleidoscope Learning Grid SIG, present characteristics such as personalisation, communication and collaboration, accessibility, that can be considered as common features of future learning scenarios and can be suitably addressed by the key capabilities of the Learning Grid.

Of course, a real validation and evaluation can happen only if one of the Application Scenario will be deployed and instantiated on top of an instance of the Learning Grid architecture. Some examples going in this direction are presented in the second section of this book. Anyway, starting from the scenarios here described we can affirm the following things.

- Future learning scenarios will be more and more based on a compositional approach in which a learning experience consists of several building blocks (e.g. learning activities, contents, educational services) to be discovered on the basis of learning needs and preferences. The service orientation of the Learning Grid is a key to support this approach and the adoption of semantic technologies simplifies the processes of selection and matchmaking of contents, services and other building blocks of a learning experiences.
- Communication and collaboration will be central in future learning scenarios that will be more and more based on the concepts of *community* or *network*. This trend is evident also in other researches such as the eLearning 2.0 [11] or the Learning Networks [12]. The Learning Grid is so a key technology in supporting the lifecycle management of learning communities. The Learning Grid, in fact, strongly relies on the capability of Grid technologies to manage

VOs and it is enhanced with specific features, standards and Educational Modelling Languages to support learning.
- Personalisation is going to happen at several level. In addition to the personalisation at the content level, future learning scenarios foresee the personalisation at the level of the knowledge to be created/transferred by/to a learner as well as at the level of the pedagogy. To support this multi-level of personalisation, knowledge and semantics technologies are key in order to create and manage ontologies, annotate educational contents and services, perform matchmaking. Educational Modelling Languages, instead, are key to create learning experiences based on several pedagogical models.

Eventually, it is worth to evidence that the Learning Grid is not, of course, the only one technology enabling the creation of those future learning scenarios. Web Services, Agent, Semantic Web or Web 2.0 are all available technologies that can address one or more of the needs and requirements of the future learning scenarios.

The added value of the Learning Grid lies in the "glue" role that this technology has among Web Services, Semantics and Grid. Furthermore, we take advantages also from similar experiences in other scientific fields. The Learning Grid can be so considered as a particular instance of the Semantic Grid improved with tools, services, standards and technologies for the education.

The Semantic Grid aims at reaching the e-Research vision [13]. The e-Education is a specific domain of the e-Research and both have to deal with some common scientific and technological issues (e.g. collaboration between researcher/learners, knowledge management and sharing between researchers/learners, discovery, description and reuse of Scientific Object/Learning Object).

So, it seems a natural choice to leverage on the Semantic Grid technologies and it appear an useful choice also to rely upon a well defined set of services, specification, best-practices and standards developed by the scientific community involved in the Semantic Grid: we do not aim at reinventing the wheel, but contributing to make it smooth and easy to use.

References

[1] T. Daradoumis, A. Gonzalez, P. Milligan, F. Murtagh, P. Sage. Learning Grid Scenarios. Learning Grid SIG Newsletter n. 2, 2004, http://grid.noe-kaleidoscope.org/.

[2] C. Allison, S. A Cerri, A. Gaeta, M. Gaeta and P. Ritrovato "Services, Semantics and Standards: elements of a Learning Grid Infrastructure" in a Special Issues on Learning Grid Services of Applied Artificial Intelligence Journal – Taylor & Francis, ISSN: 0883-9514 print/1087-6545 online, Volume 19, Number 9-10 / November-December 2005, pp. 861 – 879.

[3] P. Duval, A. Merceron, M. Scholl, L. Wargon. Empowering Learning Objects: an experiment with the Ganesha platform. Proceedings of the World Conference on Educational Multimedia, Hypermedia and Telecommunications ED-MEDIA 2005, Montreal, Canada, Volume 2005, Number 1, pages 4592-4599, 2005.

[4] S. Lawrence, C. L. Giles, and K. Bollacker, Citeseer. http://citeseer.ist.psu.edu.

[5] I. Foster, C. Kesselman and S. Tuecke, "The Anatomy of the Grid: Enabling Scalable Virtual Organizations", Intern. Journal of Supercomputer Applications, vol. 15, 2001

[6] Jähnert J., A. Cuevas, J. Moreno, V. Villagrá, S. Wesner, V. Olmedo, H. Einsiedler "The Akogrimo way towards an extended IMS architecture" in proceedings of ICIN 2007, 8-11 October 2007.

[7] G. Fox, "Education and the Enterprise with the Grid" in Grid Computing: Making the Global Infrastructure a Reality, F. Berman, G. Fox, and A. J. G. Hey, Eds.: John Wiley and Sons Ltd., 2003, pp. 963-976

[8] T. Anderson and D. Whitelock: The Educational Semantic Web: Visioning and Practicing the Future of Education. (Special Issue on) Journal of Interactive Media in Education, 2004 (1) ISSN: 1365-893X. [www-jime.open.ac.uk/2004/1]

[9] I. Foster, C. Kesselman; J. Nick and S. Tuecke, "The physiology of the Grid: An Open Grid Services Architecture for distributed systems integration" (extended version of I. Foster, C. Kesselman, J. Nick, and S. Tuecke, "Grid Services for Distributed System Integration," Computer, vol. 35, 2002), available at http://www.globus.org/alliance/publications/papers.php

[10] P. Held: The personalisation trap. Proceeding of the 2nd ELeGI conference, October 24, 2006, Barcelona, Spain.

[11] E-Learning 2.0 - By Stephen Downes, National Research Council of Canada. Available on the Web at: http://www.elearnmag.org/subpage.cfm?section=articles&article=29-1.

[12] E. J. R. Koper and P. Sloep, "Learning Networks: connecting people, organizations, autonomous agents and learning resources to establish the emergence of effective lifelong learning" (OTEC RTD Programme Plan 2003-2008). Heerlen: Open University of the Netherlands – 2003

[13] D. De Roure, N. R. Jennings and N.R. Shadbolt: The Semantic Grid: Past, Present and Future, March 2005 issue of IEEE Proc

Section II

Applications

ELeGI: a European Grid Infrastructure for Formal Learning

Matteo GAETA [a], Francesco ORCIUOLI [b], Anna PIERRI [b], Pierluigi RITROVATO [a,1]
[a] *CRMPA, Centro di Ricerca in Matematica Pura ed Applicata, Italy*
[b] *DIIMA, Università di Salerno, Italy*

Abstract. This paper is centred on the main results of the ELeGI Integrated Project with respect to formal learning approaches. The ELeGI project provided the infrastructure for convergence of the technological solutions and the pedagogical models well defined in literature. The paper first presents the theoretical learning model which allows to automatically generate a personalised Unit of Learning and to dynamically adapt it during the learning process according to the learner's behaviour, preferences and learning styles. The ELeGI formal Learning Model drives the design of the ELeGI formal learning software architecture, conceived for supporting the execution of the processes defined in the learning model. The design methodology followed results as an interesting case from the software engineering point of view. A prototype of the ELeGI formal architecture is the ELeGI formal learning software platform. The most important one is IWT-GA that is the re-engineered version of the commercial e-learning solution Intelligent Web Teacher (IWT) integrated with the GRASP middleware, a service oriented Grid middleware.

Keywords. e-learning; Learning Model, Web Services, Learning Grid, IMS-LD.

Introduction

The European Learning Grid Infrastructure (ELeGI) project [1], a EU-funded Integrated Project (23 partners from nine EU countries) has the ambitious goal to "*radically advance the effective use of technology-enhanced learning through the design, implementation and validation of a pedagogy-driven, service-oriented software architecture based on Grid technologies*".

It aims at promoting and supporting a new learning paradigm focused on the knowledge construction using experiential based and collaborative learning approaches in a ubiquitous, collaborative, experiential-based, contextualised, individualized, and personalised way and taking into account informal learning aspects as well.

In order to foster this approach toward human learning, ELeGI will create dynamic contexts and will use Grid [2] technologies to create highly realistic virtual scientific experiments and develop active learning processes with progressive abstraction levels, leading to the knowledge construction in a dynamic way, sharing knowledge and

[1] Corresponding Author: CRMPA, Centro di Ricerca in Matematica Pura ed Applicata, via Ponte Don Melillo, 84084 Fisciano (SA), Italy; E-mail: ritrovato@crmpa.unisa.it.

experiences with others. Moreover, it will allow the definition of personalised and individualised learning paths that take into account learners' skills and knowledge.

To achieve these goals, ELeGI needs a clear strategy, formalized through the definition of models (supporting formal and informal learning scenarios), methodologies, and technologies, enabling to overcome the drawbacks of traditional e-Learning solutions and to advance the effective use of technology-enhanced learning. To address the issues related to both formal and informal learning, the ELeGI project is structured according to two main Action Lines: ELeGI-f and ELeGI-i.

The ELeGI-formal (ELeGI-f) line is centred on learning taking face in formal educational scenarios; the ELeGI-informal (ELeGI-i) is focussed on collaboration and conversational processes in informal learning. This paper is centred on the main results related to the first action line.

Its purpose is to investigate the formal learning researches in terms of models and architectures in order to define new models of human learning and to implement an advanced service-oriented Grid based software architecture.

Among the current different models (behaviourism, cognitivism,...) most researchers of didactics embrace a "constructivist" vision of learning. In such a direction we have proposed, in the Section 2, a general theoretical learning model to personalise the learning on the real needs and preferences of the user.

The Section 3 is dedicated to the definition of a software architecture and infrastructure in order to deliver personalised learning experiences. A concrete case of study will demonstrate how the model and its concrete instantiation on three processes, and the service of the ELeGI formal software architecture, allow the personalisation of learning experiences. The evaluation of the performance of the model and the software architecture defined in this paper is provided. Conclusions and references will follow.

1. ELeGI Formal: General Approach

The overall approach proposed by the formal learning project line follows three main steps: 1) general model definition 2) conceptualisation of the solution and 3) realisation of the solution.

From a pedagogical point of view, a general learning model is defined. The application of the general model, in order to produce an operational process, needs its contextualisation with respect to three underlying models: Knowledge, Didactical and Learner Model, giving rise to the so-called conceptual solution.

The selection of the suitable technologies, including specific versions of the models/solutions according to concrete scenarios (SEES – Service Elicitation and Exploitation Scenario), is then the final step to achieve an applicative solution, providing also the SEES validation. Grid, Service Oriented Architecture (SOA) and standards play a central role mainly for the solution and model implementation.

The **Figure 1** shows, from a graphical point of view, the interrelationships present in ELeGI among models definition (including pedagogy as well as collaboration and enhanced presence), technology, SEES and validation and evaluation aspects (from both pedagogical and usability point of view).

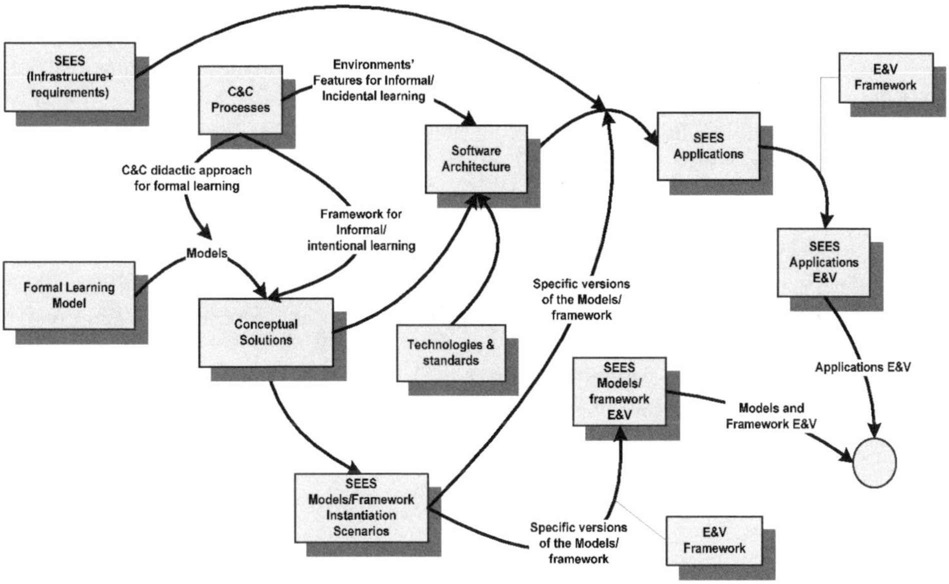

Figure 1. The overall approach followed by the ELeGI formal learning

2. Theories and Models for Formal Human Learning

In this section we describe the main results concerning the Pedagogical aspects. In brief, the main results are the ELeGI formal learning model and its didactic methods including the collaborative ones.

2.1. Theoretical Learning Model

The general learning model allows to automatically generate a "Unit of Learning" and to dynamically adapt it during the learning process according to the learner's behaviour. In the proposed model [3], a Unit of Learning (UoL) is anything delimited as an educational object, such as a course, a module or a lesson structured as a sequence of Learning Activities represented by Learning Objects and/or Learning Services. In order to produce an operational process, the learning model uses three specific models: Knowledge Model, Learner Model and Didactic Model, which interact to define the specific and personalised learning path. Such models allow taking into account the following: the knowledge that is the learning objective; the context, where the educative process occurs; the learning method and style; the learner's preferences and demands.

The Knowledge Model describes, in a way that the machine can process, the subject-matter to be attained according to the teacher's learning domain representation and acts in the system as a blackbox allowing the construction of the UoL. Besides, this process allows an automatic construction and personalisation of the student's learning path thanks to the possibility to link LOs to the concepts of the knowledge domain. The student's personal knowledge will arise from a suitable interaction (implication) of the student with the LOs.

The Learner Model (LM) allows representing, in a way that the machine can process, the learners' characteristics. The Didactic Model (DM) allows to formalise different pedagogical approaches to be used in a learning experience, both at macro-level (general structure of the UoL) and at micro-level (i.e. didactic guidelines, according to pedagogical theories, to enable the student to create some knowledge).

Before presenting the main steps of the logical workflow to produce the personalised UoL, we point out the meaning of Didactic Method and how it relates to the Didactic Model. As evidenced above, the macro level represents the general structure of a UoL while the micro-level allows to take into account both the didactic approach (e.g. the inductive-experiential, Cooperation and Conversation (C&C), problem based learning, Case-based approach, Jiigsaw model, and so) and the concrete flow of learning activities of an UoL. The flow of activities is prepared in accordance to the selected didactic approach and allows implementing it. This flow of activities is called ***Didactic Method***.

The main step of the logical workflow whose output is the UoL can be summarised as follows:

- Formalisation of the knowledge domain, taking into account the Context in which the learning experience takes place and the specific learner's characteristics.
- Specifications of the Learning Experience to build. This step requires the retrieval of the Learning Experience Model (LEM) in order to fix the whole structure of a course (e.g. if and when intermediate exams occur, test, self-evaluation, definition of general learning strategies such as collaborative or not collaborative, tutoring modalities); the retrieval of the Target of Learning (TL), consisting of a set of elementary concepts (atomic) to achieve in the course.
- Design of the Whole Learning Experience. Given a TL, the Knowledge Model allows to infer the Learning Path (LP), as a sequence of concepts to be acquired, while the Didactic Model gives the specifications of the Learning Activities, associated to each concept.
- Production of the UoL. The last step is the binding of the previous design with concrete learning material and services. The output will be a highly tailored UoL with respect to the contextualisation and personalisation features. The learner's active involvement and interaction with such a UoL allows him/her to construct his/her knowledge.
- Updating of the UoL. The UoL, produced by the previous process, is not a static object but instead a first instantiation. Indeed, according to the assessment procedures, making use of the Learner Model, the UoL can be dynamically updated. In case of failure of the "in itinere" assessment phases, an automatic procedure can be developed in order to compute a new Learning Path. Consequently, the process previously described can restart generating an updated UoL.

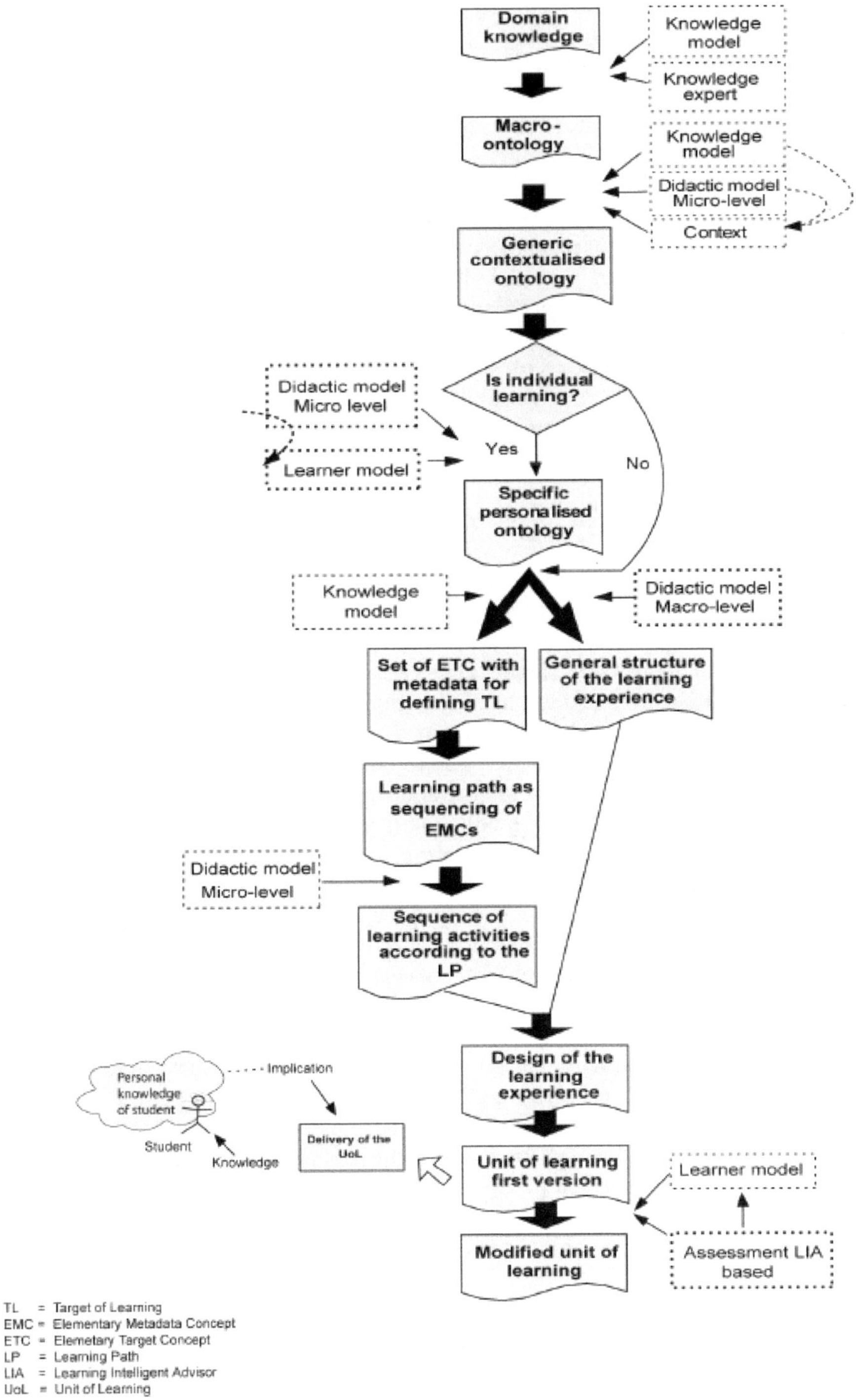

Figure 2. The overall approach followed by the ELeGI formal learning .

The Learning Model provides a high level of flexibility in terms of didactic strategies and models in order to allow the implementation of different educational approaches. In fact, different conceptual solutions may be derived from the ELeGI learning model by instantiating in different ways the three components of the learning model: Knowledge Model, Learner Model and Didactic Model.

In order to create learning experiences based on inductive and experiential approach, specific didactic methods are adopted in the general Learning Model. So, a Virtual Scientific Experiment (VSE) Model has been defined. It combines aspects of the Learning Cycle approach (Kolb) [4] and aspects of the Theory of Didactic Situations (Brousseau) [5] and it meets some fundamental aspects within a cognitivist/constructivistic approach: the importance of the situated learning (thus the specific context), and the experiential learning.

The didactic complexity of the general learning model and of the correspondent didactic methods, has allowed to acquire knowledge on the different experiential methods (like problem solving, case based teaching, simulation, and so on) that, thanks to their autonomous didactic validity, can be easily applied in other learning contexts.

2.2. Collaborative Didactic Methods

The Collaborative process can be seen as a specific didactic approach that can be realised through different collaborative didactic methods that, generally, bring to the creation and execution of learning experiences in which collaboration and communication among participants play a key role.

So, in order to consider also collaborative aspects in the theoretical model, different collaborative didactic methods have been investigated in order to define features of specific collaborative Learning Objects (e.g. collaborative writing, asynchronous collaborative discussion, and so on).

From our point of view, the collaborative learning can be considered "neutral" in the sense that it can be used both in formal and informal learning. The adoption of the collaboration process in a formal learning environment allows having a well structured model to adhere to, with precise, predefined Learning Objectives, and Target of Concepts referred to specific learning activities. So, the innovative aspect of such a method, with respect to a merely informal learning context, consists of the possibility to evaluate the acquired knowledge in the different phases of the collaborative method taken in to account.

Since the didactical models, based on an inductive- experiential approach, have been the focus of our research, in an analogous way we have put our attention on the integration of collaborative didactic methods in experiential learning design. In the specific case, for the VSE (Virtual Scientific Experiment) Method we have defined a collaborative learning micro-phase both in the Practical and in the Abstract Situation. In such a way we can apply to it a right collaborative didactic method taking into account both the learning objectives and the learner preferences.

3. ELeGI Software Architecture and Infrastructure

The purpose of this paper is to illustrate the current state of our research with respect to the ELeGI software architecture and infrastructure that allow to deliver personalised learning experiences. The architecture has been designed and developed:

- taking into account the general learning model allowing us to obtain a solution that is flexible with respect to the pedagogies
- on top of Service Oriented Grid technologies, allowing us to obtain several advantages in the process of creation and delivery of personalised learning experience like, for instance, ubiquitous and seamless access to educational services and resources.

In designing the ELeGI software architecture for formal learning, we have focused our attention on several viewpoints. Each viewpoint puts light on the design from a specific perspective. All the considered viewpoints are mainly "model driven", in the sense that we draw requirements mainly from the theoretic models and we refine them on the basis of pilots needs.

The first and the most important viewpoint is the learning model, which plays a primary role. The other viewpoints that have been inspired by the Reference Model for Open Distributed Processing (RM-ODP) framework further enrich the perception of all the aspects of the architecture, and in particular: Decomposition in subsystems (logical viewpoint); Subsystems deployment (deployment viewpoint); Re-use of existing software solutions (re-engineered applications and tools viewpoint); Architecture support for pilots (SEES viewpoint).

The first task, executed in order to design the software architecture, has been to define, starting from the learning model, the operational processes for the knowledge building, UoL building and UoL delivery, that have been the main source for our design activity.

In addition to the above mentioned three processes, other processes have been identified, for instance, a set of user related processes (knowledge representations authoring, complex learning object authoring, learning experience delivery, …) to support the previous ones and to drive a correct definition of the ELeGI formal learning service interfaces. The Figure 3 shows a layered classification of the identified processes.

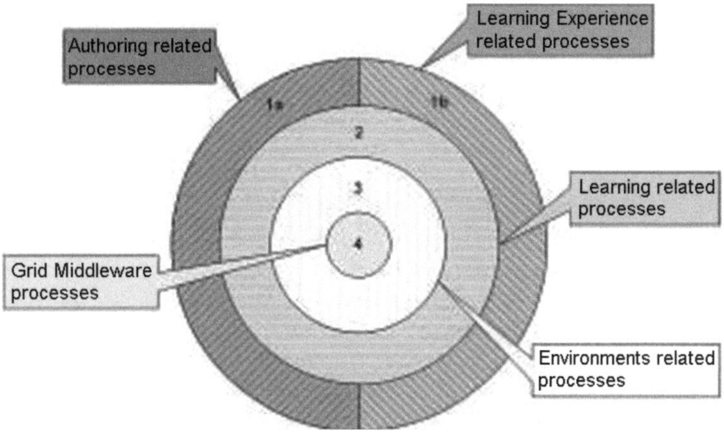

Figure 3. A layered classification of the ELeGI process .

In brief, the processes of layer 1 represent macro-functionalities provided to users through Graphical User Interfaces (GUI); the processes of layer 2 and 3 come from the defined learning model and are implemented by a services of the ELeGI formal learning architecture and, eventually, the processes of layer 4 are considered infrastructure processes provided by existing middleware. The processes can be classified as follows:

- **Authoring related processes** (layer 1a) – All the processes controlled by means of graphical user interfaces and regarding the authoring of knowledge structures (MO, GCO, Context Profile, …), learning objects (and/or content without explicit didactic value), didactic model structures.
- **Learning Experience related processes** (layer 1b) – All the processes controlled by graphical user interface and regarding the management of learning experiences. For instance, teachers can assemble learning experiences packaged as UoLs and populate them. Learners can execute a learning experience coming from a UoL.
- **Learning related processes** (layer 2) – these are the main processes of ELeGI (i.e. the ones coming directly from the learning model) and include all processes offering support for the user interactions related processes at layer 1. At layer 2 we have: i) Knowledge Building Process, ii) UoL Building Process, and iii) UoL Delivery Process.
- **Environments related processes** (layer 3) – The processes at this layer provide the environments sustaining the learning experiences (learners' enrolment, users' groups' composition, metadata based discovery of content, and so on).
- **Grid Middleware processes** (layer 4) – OGSA compliant processes for managing the Service Oriented Infrastructure (e.g. discovery, instantiation, notification, etc.)

In order to identify and design ELeGI formal learning services and their interactions, we have done an analysis of the processes at the three layers. In particular: 1) an analysis of layer 2 and layer 3, in order to identify from a functional point of view the services of the software architecture; 2) an analysis of layer 1, in order to have a clear vision of the interactions between users and the Application Layer of software architecture; 3) an analysis of services interactions, in order to define a dynamic behaviour of the designed system in contraposition to the static view defined in the phase 1 and 2.

3.1. The ELeGI Software Architecture

The ELeGI software architecture for formal learning can be defined as "*domain verticalization of the Semantic Grid improved with tools, services, standards and technologies for the Education & Training*". The main purpose of the ELeGI software architecture, depicted in the following figure, is from one side to allow the creation and the operational management of a Virtual Organisation (VO) based environment, where it is possible to execute the learning processes, and from the other side to allow the production of the appropriate operational process related to the learning model and its conceptualisation.

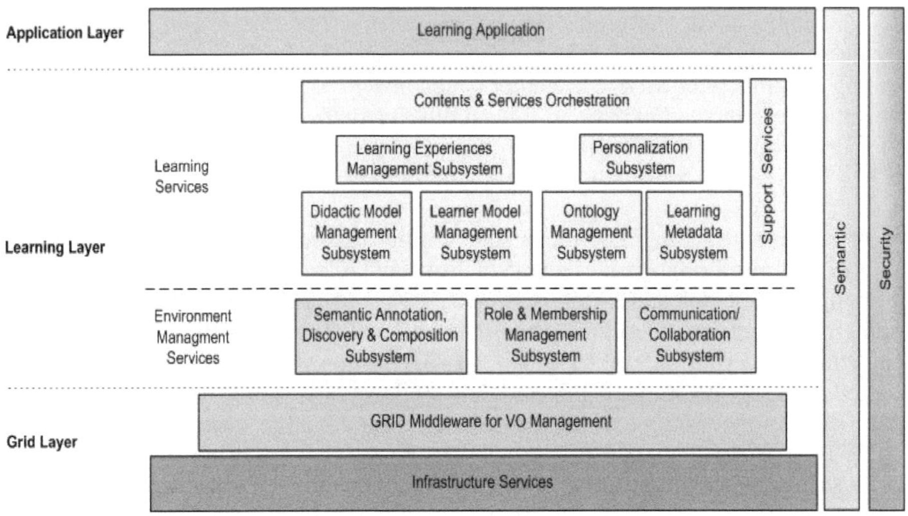

Figure 4. The ELeGI software architecture for formal learning.

It is worth mentioning that the effort in defining the architecture has been focused on the top of the Grid layer and the most relevant services belong to the Learning layer that is devoted to the execution of the processes related to the Learning Model. In particular, the Learning Services sub-layer provides services and tools to support the execution of the three processes of the Learning Model.

There are services and tools to create and manage the Ontologies (Ontology Management sub-system), the Learner's Profile (Learner Model Management sub-system) and the Didactic Model (Didactic Model Management sub-system), that represent the three basic structures of the Learning Model. The Personalization sub-system aims at dynamically adapting and delivering educational contents and services, matching the learner's needs and preferences according to his/her profile.

Our approach leads to an open solution. Instead, the software architecture provides several features of openness, extensibility and interoperability with respect to:

- *services and tools:* the adoption of standards or standards de facto like Web Service Remote Portlets (WSRP), Web Service Resource Framework (WSRF), allows to add, to the ELeGI architecture, new services and tools. The new services are indexed and annotated with metadata and can be exploited during the execution of the learning experiences. Moreover, exploiting services oriented models and technologies, we can create new functionalities/services by composition of existing ones.
- *didactic material:* the adoption of standard or standard de facto in the area of e-learning like IMS didactic material: the adoption of standard or standard de facto in the area of e-learning like IMS-LOM used to annotate learning objects allows supporting the re-use of didactic resources from and to other e-learning systems. Existing authoring tools supporting the adopted specifications can be used without difficulties in order to create learning objects which will be subsequently indexed and stored using the related ELeGI services.

- *the selection of the pedagogy:* the adoption of the Learning Model allows implementing different didactic approaches (and relating didactic methods) through the manipulation of some parameters and categories of the conceptual solution (Knowledge, Learner and Didactic Models). This aspect, together with to the adoption of an Educational Modelling Language, such as IMS-LD, (used to describe the learning scenarios) guarantees openness and extensibility with respect to the selection of the pedagogy.

A prototype of the ELeGI formal learning architecture is the ELeGI software platform. The most important one is IWT-GA. IWT-GA [17] is an e–learning platform supplying advanced features for personalisation and arises from reengineering of a commercial product named IWT (Intelligent Web Teacher) [16] on Grid technology. The Grid middleware at the base of IWT-GA is the WSRF version of the GRASP middleware a service oriented grid middleware developed in the frame of the homonym FP5 research project and providing services for operational management of a VO.

IWT-GA includes some of the sub-systems of the Learning Services layer. In detail, services providing functionalities of the Learning Management System and services providing high-level functionalities for a personalized learning experience (like learning path personalization), for learner's model evaluation and for management and delivery of learning experiences. The Personalisation service is based on the extension of LIA – Learner Intelligent Advisor- component already available in IWT.

The educational resources are retrieved from distributed repositories exploiting the functionalities of Grid Data Services with OGSA (Open Grid Services Architecture) DAI compliant interfaces.

The learning services are localised in a VO and instantiated (if they are transient services) upon a suitable host of the VO by exploiting Grid services of the GRASP Middleware. The **Figure 5** shows relationships with the overall ELeGI architecture.

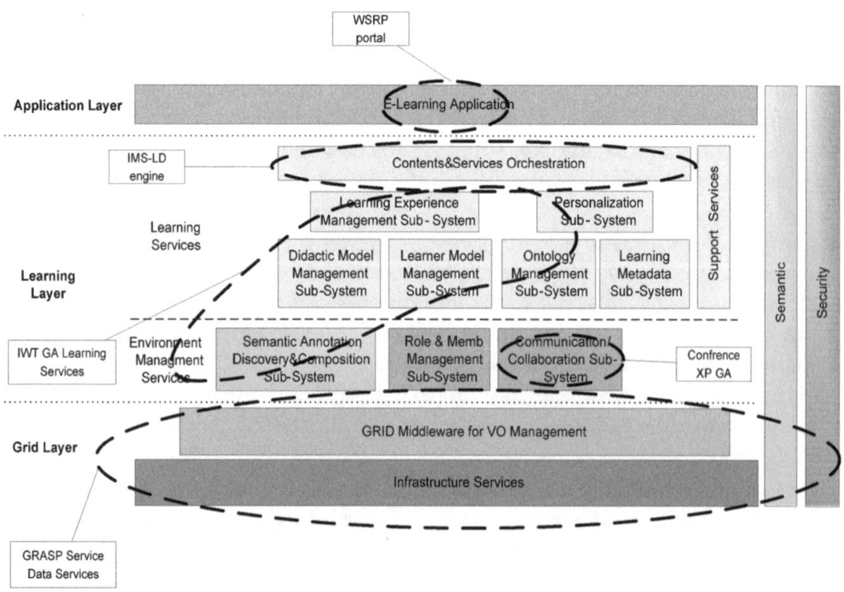

Figure 5: The architecture of the Grid environment

In the **Figure 5**, the services used for the experiment are grouped by the dashed lines. In particular, the Grasp services to localise and create services' instances and the Data Services belong to the Grid layer (i.e. the Grasp Middleware). The services used for the UoL creation and execution are the one of IWT GA. The modified engine for UoL execution is the Content and Services Orchestration service and the Conference XP GA service belongs to the Communication and Collaboration subsystem. Finally, the VSE is enjoined by the means of the IWT GA (WSRP Compliant) portal belonging to the Application Layer.

The proposed design approach can be exploited also in other domain, different from the e-learning context, where requirements do not directly come from the end-user but mainly from a set of models and processes derived from theoretical researches.

3.2. The ELeGI Software Infrastructure

The implementation of the infrastructure has concerned all the layers and related sub-systems of the ELeGI Software architecture.

The major focus on the *Application Layer* has been to pave the way for an integrated user interface in the form of a portal, exploiting the WSRP protocol to reach interoperability between the two major technology strands in the project .Net and Java.

The .Net based WSRP framework has been developed implementing the WSRP specification. In order to evaluate the WSRP.Net implementation, it was investigated different interoperability and integration aspects and the results of the different test-types were successful, evidencing in particular the interoperability between WSRP.Net Consumer and Java Stringbeans producer.

The *Learning layer* can be logically divided in two sub-layers:

- Environment Management
- Learning Services

The Environment Management sublayer provides services and tools to support the creation, operation, evolution, and maintenance of a learning community. It also provides functionalities for semantic annotation, discovery and composition of educational contents and services and tools for asynchronous and synchronous communications.

The Learning Services sub-layer provides services and tools to support the execution of the three main processes of the Learning Model.

Concerning the Semantic Annotation Subsystem an ontology support has been provided that produces learning related ontologies. We concentrate on learning experience ontologies that are based on IMS-LD and aims to model the most common entities representing the conceptualization of the learning in research and education.

By functionality, the services can be categorized into different aspects of semantic management in elearning – including ontology management, semantic annotation and semantics based knowledge reuse such as query and inference. The semantic annotation service provides functionalities that use ontological data in the selected ontology to annotate learning related resources and therefore create a repository of semantic annotations in the format of RDF triples. The knowledge reuse services include a semantic query service that can query the semantic annotations to discovery semantic facts of the annotated learning resource.

In the Table 1, Table 2 and Table 3 we shortly present the more relevant and innovative services.

Table 1. Grid Layer Services

Subsystem	Service Name	Description
Grid Layer	**Service Instantiator**	The Service Instantiatior has capabilities to select a suitable host in a Virtual Hosting Environment and to dynamically create a service instance on the selected host.
	Service Locator	This service allows to publish and search the services that virtualise the educational resources.
	RemoteFS Service	This service virtualizes the file system allowing the capability to store and retrieve file and folder.

Table 2. Learning Layer Services

Subsystem	Service Name	Description
Learner Model Management	**Learner Profile Management Service**	The Learner Profile Management Service allows the management of the Learner Profile. This service manages both the learner preferences and the cognitive state.
Personalization	**Remedial Work Service**	This service builds remedial works. On the basis of the scores obtained after an assessment phase (by a learner), it calculates a new sequencing of learning activities, in order to better explain the concepts that have not understood. The new sequence of LO will be plunged in the original UoL

Subsystem	Service Name	Description
Personalization	**Learning Path Service**	This service calculates the learning path starting from an ontology (GCO or MO) and selecting one or more target concepts. The GCO or MO can be created and uploaded on the Metadata Services using the Knowledge Representation Tool .
Learner Model Management	**Learner Profile Management Service**	This service allows the management of the Learner Profile taking into account both the learner preferences and the cognitive state
Learning Metadata	**Learning Metadata Service**	This service allows the annotation of the educational resources and provide indexing and storing capabilities. It uses the RemoteFS service to store and retrieve the files of the educational resources
Communication/ Collaboration	**Collaborative writing**	This service provides a support for a collaborative writing session, creating group of learners that should be collaborate to the realization of a common task
	Buddyspace	This service provides an access to the MSG BuddySpace instant messaging service during the UoL execution
	Matchmaking	This service provide searching functionalities to assist the learner in the finding users with a specific cognitive state.
	Wikipedia Search	This service provides searching functionalities using WikiPedia for additional material.

Table 3. Application Layer Services

Subsystem	Service Name	Description
Application Layer	**WSRP.NET Produces**	The portType implementation of WSRP Producer allows us to host our portlets and return their html to WSRP Consumers.
	Portal	IWT-GA portal is the access point for accessing the functionalities offered by EleGI formal architecture.

3.3. A Concrete Scenario

In this section we present and describe a case of study for showing all the personalisation and adaptation capabilities in terms of contents, didactic approaches and didactic methods provided by the formal learning services.

The concrete scenario is based on the Mathematician Domain and in particular for a University course of the first year about the study of Limits. It is focussed on the following topics:

- **Contextualised Unit of Learning**. The teacher selects a LEM, a GCO (Generic Contextualised Ontology) and the target concepts to create in a automatic way the UoL contextualised. The course (LEM) is structured as follow:

  - **Presentation phase.** A learning activity with a textual description prepared by the teacher to illustrate the learning experience that is starting. A chat service available, where teacher can answer to the students' doubts.
  - **Didactical material study phase.** In this phase the students study the learning objects presented to explain the concepts of the Learning Path. There are also two services available to offer an optional investigation on those concepts. One service searches for alternative didactic materials on a Web repository, the other service offers the possibility to find and contact experts on specific topics. This phase foresees a milestone with an assessment phase, in order to check the learner knowledge status, and to start a personalised remedial work.
  - **Workgroup Collaboration phase.** In order to evaluate the efficiency of the overall learning process, in the last phase, the teacher will assign to the workgroups a collaborative writing task related to the target concepts of the course. The teacher can observe and evaluate the tasks evolution and finally write a report on the results of this collaboration.

To create the UoL, the teacher interacts with specific functionalities of the ELeGI formal Learning portal provided by IWT-GA.

- **Virtual Classroom learning experience**. The teacher publishes the built UoL and assigns to it the class students. Each student of the class access to the Learning Experience and is able to navigate in the proposed learning path to learn the different concepts. In order to emphasize the classroom environment will be provided services to allow the collaboration. In particular they have access to a service for collaborative writing and for communicate (both synchronous and asynchronous communications).
- **Personalised Remedial Work**. After the assessment phase, for each student will be calculated a personalised remedial work and will be presented a list of new LOs to explain the concepts that are not learned. In this way the student can read and study the personalised list of new proposed didactical resources. After that he will execute again the tests.

3.4. The Evaluation Process

The **Evaluation** is the process to determinate the value of a service or an object or a product with respect to a predefined metric (i.e. the software quality evaluation process).

This term is somewhat versatile, but principally associated with assessing the value of any entity. For example, Trochim (1999,[18]) defines evaluation as the systematic acquisition and assessment of information to provide useful feedbacks on an object and thus, to determine the value of this object. Generally, an evaluation is goal-oriented, serving a specific purpose (e.g. use, usefulness, usability of a programme). The evaluation procedures have to meet current scientific techniques and research methods.

What is the tenor in evaluating distance education from the learning perspective? In this context, evaluation of distance education often aims in judging whether learning has been enabled, enriched or enhanced through the use of technology. This means, the pedagogical effectiveness or educational value is to be evaluated. For this purpose, the following measures are commonly used:

- student outcomes (e.g. grades, test scores);
- student attitudes (e.g. about learning through distance education, preferences);
- overall student satisfaction toward distance learning.

Aside from evaluating the educational effectiveness of distance learning, the evaluation may provide a range of useful information for future course design, planning and implementation (e.g. by identifying problems that occur when running a eLearning environment). Furthermore, as eLearning usually involves high levels of investment that need to be justified, evaluation may also address on demonstrating the cost effectiveness of such innovations. On the whole, the evaluation may serve three main purposes: the development (in terms of e.g. infrastructure, content, support services), the educational value, as well as the accountability and justification of eLearning systems.

There are two main types of evaluations, namely formative and summative evaluations. *Formative evaluation* is carried out during the design and implementation phase of a distance learning environment. Within the scope of this type of evaluation information about a prototype resource is collected to improve or strengthen it, for example, by enhancing the usability and quality of this resource.

Summative evaluation takes place at the end of the development cycle to demonstrate the effectiveness of the resulting resource. Evaluations depend on who it is being carried out for, and therefore, the different stakeholders and their concerns have to be kept in mind as well as to consider the budget that is available. Depending on the respective evaluation questions (e.g. evaluating the use of technology, cost effectiveness), suitable evaluation instruments (e.g. log-data, interviews, questionnaires) have to be determined to collect the desired data. For example, for evaluating the satisfaction of students using a new learning system, questionnaires are adequate measurement instruments. If it is to be evaluated how efficient an adaptive assessment of knowledge proceeds (e.g. the number of questions that have to be posed to the learner), system log data can provide relevant information. Well-designed evaluations make use of a mix of different techniques (quantitative as well as qualitative methods) to build up a coherent picture. After identifying appropriate data analysis methods, the collected data have to be analysed. In order to ensure that the results of the evaluation are used effectively, they need to be fed into the development process of the learning system.

In order to evaluate the process defined in this paper, we can make a comparative analysis through the user feedbacks; in other words we ca submit to the user a pre-interactive questionnaire and a post-interactive questionnaire that evaluates the user's improvement. For example, if we consider a learning system, we can make the evaluation through the feedbacks of a classroom learning both in the presence of the learning system and in its absence.

4. Achieved Results and Innovations

In this section we summarise the main results and the innovations related to the ELeGI formal learning model, software architecture and infrastructure above exposed.

The general learning model definition focuses on how to relate the learning path to the learner and to formative objectives in a dynamic intelligent way in order to allow personalized, experiential and contextualized learning processes. Innovative aspects are the following:

- Personalisation and Contextualisation with respect to:
  - **Knowledge** through the definition and use of the Generic Contextualised Ontology and/or the Specific Personalized Ontology;
  - **Pedagogy** through the selection of the more suitable Didactic Methods for different concepts;
  - **Contents** through the selection of suitable contents on the basis of the Learner Profile that includes existing knowledge and learning preferences and the Context Profile as well.
- Dynamicity and effective re-use of resources

- Real separation of roles/responsibility between didactic domain experts (ontologies), instructional designer (didactic methods), content developers, teachers, tutors (on-line, supports) and learners
- Possibility to use in the Unit of Learning any kind of services and educational resources

After that different collaborative didactic methods have been investigated and defined in order to identify features of specific collaborative Learning Objects and control the knowledge acquired by the learner during activities execution. The collaborative didactic methods allow:

- to instantiate a dynamic and collaborative workspace which allows to use traditional collaboration and communication tools in a controlled way in a learning scenario
- to have a well structured model to adhere to with precise and predefined Learning Objectives.

Like modern Enterprise software architectures are created for supporting business processes, the ELeGI formal Learning software architecture has been conceived for supporting the execution of the processes and the approach defined in the ELeGI formal Learning Model enabling the creation and execution of personalised learning experiences. The design methodology followed results as an interesting case from the software engineering point of view.

In order to shorten the gap between the technologies and the learning theories/models a prototype of the ELeGI formal learning architecture has been defined. The most important one is IWT- GA that provides an integrated set of services like:

- Grid- Aware version of an IMS-LD framework that orchestrates services for the creation and delivery of personalized learning experiences.
- Personalised Learning Path creation according to the ontology, the learner preferences.

5. Conclusions and Future Work

In this paper, we have presented our approach to the analysis and design of the ELeGI theoretical learning model and of ELeGI software architecture and infrastructure for formal learning. Our work has been mainly motivated by the difficulties we have encountered in exploiting current methodologies and tools in order to model the problem domains.

We believe that the proposed approach can be exploited also in other domain, different from the e-learning context, where requirements do not directly come from the end-user but mainly from a set of models and processes derived from theoretical researches.

With respect to the technological aspects we have experienced that traditional design methodologies are rigid and driven by functional requirements. The ELeGI software architecture has been conceived for supporting the execution of the processes defined in the general learning model. The design methodology followed results as an interesting case from the software engineering point of view.

6. Acknowledgement

This work is partially supported by the European Commission under the Information Society Technologies (IST) programme of the 6th Framework Programme for RTD, project ELeGI, contract IST-002205. We are very pleased to thank all the people involved in the Definition, Design and Implementation of the General Learning Model and Architecture.

References

[1] M. Gaeta, P. Ritrovato and S Salerno: Making e-Learning a Service Oriented Utility: The European Learning Grid Infrastructure Project. In the book Towards the Learning GRID: advances in Human Learning Services. Publisher: IOS Press in the series: "Frontiers in Artificial Intelligence and Applications", August 2005 ISBN: 1-58603-534-7, pp. 63-75

[2] I. Foster and C. Kesselman, The Grid: Blueprint for a New Computing Infrastructure, Morgan Kaufmann, 1999.

[3] G. Albano, M. Gaeta, S. Salerno: E-learning: a model and process proposal in the International Journal of Knowledge and Learning – Volume 2 issue 1/2 2006 Inderscience Publisher, ISSN (Online): 1741-1017 - ISSN (Print): 1741-1009, pp73-88.

[4] D.A. Kolb, "Experiential Learning", Englewood Cliffs, NJ.: Prentice Hall, 1984

[5] G.Brousseau: Theory of didactic situations in mathematics. Kluwer Academics Publisher, 1997

[6] I. Foster et al.: OGSA™ WSRF Basic Profile 1.0. Recommendation GWD-R GGF, OGSA WG, September, 7, 2005 Available at https://forge.gridforum.org/projects/ogsa-wg/document/draft-ggf-ogsa-wsrf-basic-profile/en/38

[7] IMS Global Learning Consortium, IMS Learning Design v1.0 Final Specification, available at http://www.imsglobal.org/learningdesign/index.cfm, 2003

[8] N. Capuano, A. Gaeta, G. Laria, F. Orciuoli and P. Ritrovato: How To Use GRID Technology for Building Next Generation Learning Environments. Published in the book "Towards the Learning GRID: advances in Human Learning Services", Volume 127 Frontiers in Artificial Intelligence and Applications. Edited by: P. Ritrovato, C. Allison, S.A. Cerri, T. Dimitrakos, M. Gaeta and S. Salerno, November 2005, 252 pp., hardcover ISBN: 1-58603-534-7, pp 182-192

[9] A. Gaeta, M. Gaeta, G. Meo, F. Orciuoli, P. Ritrovato and S. Stefanucci: How the ELeGI software architecture enables the creation and delivery of Adaptive Unit of Learning: the Implementation of the VSE Model, proceeding of the Workshop 4d: Next Generation in Technology Enhanced Learning, e-Challenges 2006, Barcelona, Spain, 25 - 27 October 2006

[10] G. Albano, M. Gaeta, P. Ritrovato, "IWT: an innovative solution for AGS e-Learning model" to appear in the in Volume 3, (double) Issue 2&3, November 2007 of the International Journal of Knowledge and Learning – Inderscience Publisher, ISSN (Online): 1741-1017 - ISSN (Print): 1741-1009.

[11] Angelo Gaeta, Matteo Gaeta, Gennaro Meo, Francesco Orciuoli, Pierluigi Ritrovato, Silvio Stefanucci "*Creation and Delivery of Adaptive Unit of Learning using the ELeGI Software Architecture: the VSE Model Implementation Case Study*" in the Exploiting the Knowledge Economy - Issues, Applications, Case Studies Book, P. Cunningham and M. Cunningham (EDS) IOS Press 2006, Vol 3, pp 1459-1466, ISBN 1-58603-682-3.

[12] P. Ritrovato, M. Gaeta, A. Gaeta "*A grid based software architecture for delivery of adaptive and personalised learning experiences*" to be appear in ACM Personal and Ubiquitous Computing Journal ISSN: 1617-4909

[13] P. Ritrovato, M. Gaeta, A. Gaeta and F. Orciuoli "*Defining a Service Oriented Architecture for e-Learning: The European Learning Grid Infrastructure Project Experience*" to be appear in International Journal on Technology Enhanced Learning – Inderscience Publisher, ISSN (Online): 1753-5263 - ISSN (Print): 1753-5255.

[14] N. Capuano, M. Gaeta, P. Ritrovato, S. Salerno, "*How to Integrate Technology Enhanced Learning with Business Process Management*" to be appear on Journal of Knowledge Management – Emerald Group Publisher ISSN: 1367-3270.

[15] Matteo Gaeta, Sergio Miranda and Pierluigi Ritrovato "ELeGI as enabling architecture for e-Learning 2.0" to be appear in International Journal of Knowledge and Learning – Inderscience Publisher, ISSN (Online): 1741-1017 - ISSN (Print): 1741-1009

[16] N. Capuano, M. Gaeta, A. Micarelli., E. Sanginetto, "An Intelligent Web Tutoring System for Learning Personalization and Semantic Web Compatibility", Proc. of PEG 2003, St. Petersburg, Russia.

[17] N. Capuano, A. Gaeta, G. Laria, F. Orciuoli, P. Ritrovato, "How To Use GRID Technology for Building Next Generation Learning Environments", in the book Towards the Learning GRID: advances in Human Learning Services. Publisher: IOS Press, Volume 127 Frontiers in Artificial Intelligence and Applications. Edited by: P. Ritrovato, C. Allison, S.A. Cerri, T. Dimitrakos, M. Gaeta and S. Salerno, November 2005, 252 pp., hardcover ISBN: 1-58603-534-7, pp 182-192

[18] Trochim, W. (1999). Knowledge Base: An Online Research Textbook: Introduction to Evaluation. Cornell University. Available: http://trochim.human.cornell.edu/kb/intreval.htm

The Learning Grid Handbook
S. Salerno et al. (Eds.)
IOS Press, 2008

Gridcole, a Tailorable System for the Realization of Scripted Collaborative Learning Situations Using Grid Service-Based Tools

Miguel L. BOTE-LORENZO [a,1], Eduardo GÓMEZ-SÁNCHEZ [a], Guillermo VEGA-GORGOJO [a], Yannis A. DIMITRIADIS [a], Juan I. ASENSIO-PÉREZ [a], Iván M. JORRÍN-ABELLÁN [b]

[a] *School of Telecommunications Engineering, University of Valladolid, Spain*

[b] *Faculty of Education, University of Valladolid, Spain*

Abstract. Gridcole is a grid service-based tailorable collaborative learning system that provides two significant features. First, it enables the possibility of integrating tools that require supercomputing capabilities or specific hardware resources in order to support the collaborative learning situations in which this type of tools is required. Furthermore, it can interpret collaboration scripts created by educators in order to guide participants during the realization of collaborative learning situations. This chapter provides an overview of the system and describes a sample collaborative learning situation that can be supported by Gridcole with the purpose of illustrating its capabilities.

Keywords. Grid services, scripted collaborative learning, tailorability

Introduction

Computer Supported Collaborative Learning (CSCL) [1] is a mature research field of increasing interest in recent years. As a result of the efforts made in this research domain, many systems have been developed to promote and support collaborative methods of learning. These systems, which are typically called collaborative learning systems, are software applications that usually include a set of tools in order to support a given collaborative learning situation. The tools may be either specifically conceived for a given learning domain (e.g. a collaborative energy chain editor may be very useful in physics education) or generic (e.g. a text editor), and either for individual use and for collaborative use.

One of the features most desired by educators in a collaborative learning system is *tailorability*. A computer application is said to be tailorable if its functionalities can be modified by end-users so as to better suit their needs [2]. In this way, tailorable collaborative learning systems typically enable easy integration of suitable tools in order to support the realization of new collaborative learning situations. Examples of

[1] Corresponding Autor: ETSI de Telecomunicación, Camino Viejo del Cementerio s/n, 47011 Valladolid, Spain; E-mail: migbot@tel.uva.es.

this kind of systems include DARE [3], Symba [4] and Cure [5]. Unfortunately, the tailorable collaborative learning systems that can be found in the literature have two important drawbacks.

On the one hand, current systems *do not enable the integration of tools requiring supercomputing capabilities or specific hardware devices*. However, this type of tools is essential to support collaborative learning scenarios in many areas such as engineering, medicine and natural sciences. This idea is supported by the fact that there is a number of non-tailorable collaborative learning systems in which this kind of tools is employed. For example, Covase [6] employs supercomputing capabilities to generate a virtual reality environment in which students can interact with 3D complex models related to fluid dynamics. Instead, Pearl [7] accesses to specific hardware devices such as signal pattern generators and oscilloscopes so that students can collaboratively work in a remote laboratory of electronics.

On the other hand, existing systems *do not support scripted collaborative learning*. A collaboration script is a set of instructions prescribing, among other things, the sequence of activities to be per-formed by students, as well as the way they should collaborate [8] in order to achieve predefined pedagogical objectives. According to [6], the realization of learning situations following well-defined collaboration scripts may increase the effectiveness of learning. With this aim, the systems that support scripted collaborative learning are capable of interpreting collaboration scripts so as to guide students through the sequence of activities to be performed in a given scenario [9] while providing suitable tools and documents to support each of them. Universanté [6] is a good example of a non-tailorable collaborative learning system that provides guidance to students participating in situations conceived with the aim of helping them to learn strategies to cope with different health problems.

Within this framework, we have proposed Gridcole (Grid-based Collaborative Learning Environment) [10], a new tailorable collaborative learning system that overcomes these drawbacks. Gridcole exploits grid service technology [11] to enable the integration of tools that are not limited in terms of supercomputing and specific hardware needs. Furthermore, it is able to interpret collaboration scripts described by educators using the IMS-LD (IMS Learning Design) [12] specification.

The rest of this chapter is organized as follows. Section 1 provides an overview of Gridcole functioning, architecture and implementation. Next, Section 2 illustrates the potential uses of Gridcole by introducing a real collaborative learning situation that can be supported with our system. Finally, conclusions and future work can be found in Section 3.

1. Overview of the System

Gridcole combines the use of the service-oriented grid with the IMS-LD specification in order to tackle the drawbacks of tailorable collaborative learning systems identified above. After showing the way both technologies are employed in Gridcole, this section describes the basic functioning of the system and its architecture. Then, the prototype of Gridcole is introduced.

1.1. Gridcole Approach

The service-oriented computational grid is employed in Gridcole as an infrastructure that allows multiple organizations to share a large pool of software tools that may be integrated with the purpose of supporting all sorts of either individual or collaborative learning scenarios. These organizations can be, for instance, educational institutions willing to share their tools in exchange for the right to access tools offered by others or companies that want to make money by letting other organizations access their tools.

The tools shared in the grid infrastructure are provided as presentation-oriented grid services. More specifically, the business logic of the tool is offered as a service that is compliant to the OGSI (Open Grid Services Infrastructure) [13] specification while the presentation logic is offered as Java-based clients that can be automatically downloaded, installed and executed according to the JNLP (Java Network Launching Protocol) [14] specification. As it will be shown later, the tools shared in this way can be integrated in Gridcole according to the "tailoring by soft integration model" defined in [2]. Furthermore, it must be noticed that tools requiring the use of supercomputing capabilities or specific resources can also be offered following this presentation-oriented service sharing approach. In this way, this type of tools can also be integrated in Gridcole for the support of collaborative learning situations.

In addition, IMS-LD documents are employed in Gridcole in two different ways. First, as collaboration scripts that can be interpreted by the system in order to provide guidance to the participants of the specified scenario. As shown in [15], collaboration scripts can be specified with IMS-LD when it is employed along with the extension proposed in [16]. Second, as tailoring scripts describing the tools that must be integrated by the system so as to properly support each activity defined in the collaboration script. In this case, the description of tools is included in collaboration scripts by using the IMS-LD and IMS-LRM (IMS Learning Resource Metadata) [17] specifications in a combined way.

IMS-LD documents can be created by educators with the help of tools such as Collage [18] or Reload [19]. Then, they can be provided to Gridcole packaged in a file called *unit of learning* along with the tools and documents that are going to be used in the collaborative learning situation described in the IMS-LD document or, alternatively, with the references that may be employed to locate such resources. This packaging is made according to the IMS-CP (IMS Content Packaging) [20] specification.

1.2. Basic Functioning

Educators can provide Gridcole with two types of units of learning: complete and incomplete. Complete units of learning are those that include all the information required by the system to integrate the actual tools to be used during the realization of a collaborative learning situation. Incomplete units of learning do not contain such information. Instead, they include a generic description of the tools required for the situation according to the IMS-LRM specification.

Gridcole can only start the realization of collaborative learning situations from complete units of learning. However, the system can be employed to generate complete units from incomplete ones. With this aim, Gridcole is capable of searching the tools offered in the service-oriented grid infrastructure that best match the descriptions included in an incomplete unit of learning. The list of tools found by the system is then provided to the educator so that he can choose the tools that he considers more suitable for the situation to be realized. Next, the system generates a complete unit of learning including the information that enables the integration of the tools selected by the educator. The complete unit of learning is then stored in the system for later use.

When the educator decides to start the realization of a scenario described in a complete unit of learning, the system provides him with the list of users registered in the system as well as of the different roles that are defined for participants in the collaboration script. The educator can then specify the users that are allowed to join the realization as well as the roles that each of them will play. Once this is done, selected users can join the system to start participating in the realization of the situation.

During the realization of a collaborative learning situation, Gridcole interprets the corresponding IMS-LD document in order to inform each participant about the activity that he should be performing in every moment according to the collaboration script as well as about the tools and documents that have been defined for the support of the activity. When a participant decides to work with one of the documents, the system automatically downloads it for him. Instead, if the participant decides to use a tool, Gridcole automatically obtains, installs, and launches its client in the user's machine so that he can start using the tool immediately. In the case of collaborative tools, Gridcole takes care of configuring them in order to transparently put in touch users that have to collaborate in a given activity.

The main interactions that take place between the users and the system, as described in this subsection, can be observed in Figure 1.

1.3. System Architecture

The different elements that make up the logical architecture of Gridcole can be seen in Figure 1 organized according to the three-tier pattern (presentation layer, business layer,

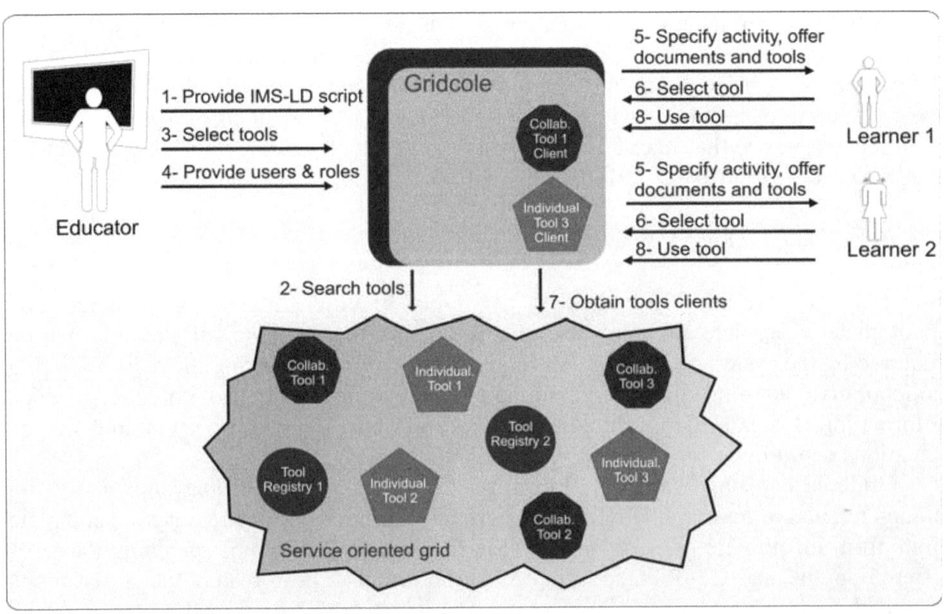

Figure 1: Summary of the main interactions that take place during in the basic functioning of Gridcole.

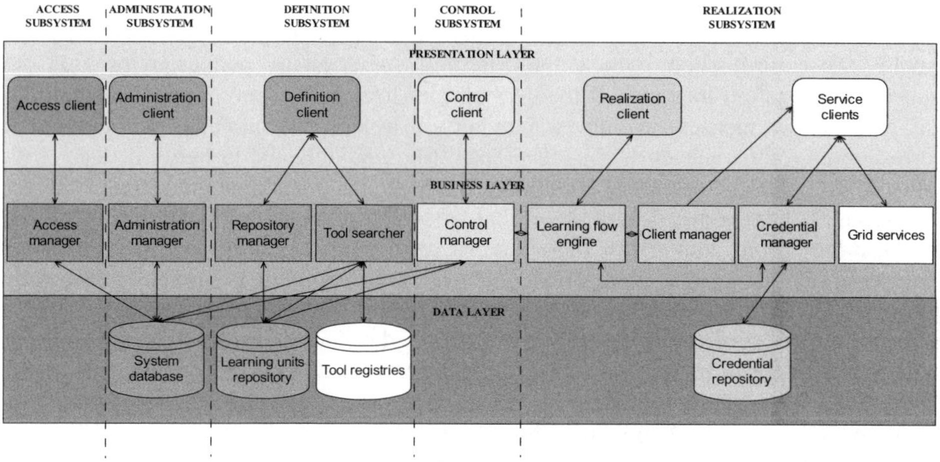

Figure 2: Logical architecture of the Gridcole system.

and data layer) typically employed for the design of distributed applications. It is important to notice that the elements represented with white background are not part of the system since they are offered by providers in the service-oriented computational grid. However, these elements are essential for the functioning of Gridcole, and have thus been included in the figure according to the role they play within the context of the system. The architecture of Gridcole can also be decomposed in five subsystems from a functional point of view, as shown in Figure 2. These subsystems as well as the elements of the most relevant ones are described next.

The access subsystem is in charge of checking the identity of users and granting access only to those that have been previously registered in the system. Access control is required in Gridcole so as to try to avoid the impersonation of participants in the realization of collaborative learning situations as well as the access to confidential data. The administration subsystem allows maintaining the list of users updated. Furthermore, it allows managing the information concerning the location of the tool registries that, as shown later, enable the discovery of tools within the context of a computational grid.

The specification subsystem allows providing the formal description of the collaborative learning situations whose realization is to be supported by Gridcole. This way, the subsystem offers three basic operations: inserting a new (complete or incomplete) unit of learning into the system, deleting a unit of learning, and generating a complete unit of learning from an incomplete one. These operations are offered to the user by the specification client, which is also responsible for obtaining the information required for each operation. The business logic of the addition and deletion operations is implemented in the repository manager. This element updates the repository in which the units of learning available in the system are stored. The tool searcher includes the business logic for the generation of complete units of learning. It is thus in charge of finding those tools available in the computational grid that best match the descriptions included in incomplete units. With this goal, the tool searcher queries the tool registries available in the computational grid in which providers publish descriptions of their tools as well as the information required to integrate them.

The control subsystem allows managing the collaborative learning situations that are realized in the system. More specifically, three operations are supported by this subsystem: start the realization of a situation, check the state of a situation being realized, and finish the realization of a situation. The user (typically an educator) can employ the control client to select the desired operation as well as to provide the information required for them. If the user decides to start the realization of a situation, the control manager carries out a number of tasks. This includes retrieving the corresponding complete unit from the repository, updating the system database with information about the users that are allowed to participate, and creating instances of the grid services corresponding to the tools that will support the situation. Once this is done, all the information required for the actual realization of the situation is passed to the realization subsystem that is described below. This subsystem is also queried by the control manager if the user wants to check the state of a situation being realized in order to retrieve such information. When the user decides to finish the realization of a situation, the control manager also performs several tasks such as notifying this event to the realization subsystem, destroying the instances of grid services created for the situation, and conveniently updating the system database.

The realization subsystem allows users to participate in the realization of situations according to the IMS-LD based collaboration scripts included in complete units of learning. The main element of this subsystem is the learning flow engine that interprets the scripts to determine the activities that must be performed by each participant in every moment during the realization of the situation, and also the tools and documents that they may employ in each activity. This information is provided to the user through the realization client. When the user decides to use one of the documents available for a given activity, the realization client retrieves from the flow engine the information required to automatically download it. Instead, if he decides to use a tool, the client manager automatically obtains and installs the grid service client of the tool so that the participant can start using it immediately. Should the client need a proxy credential to access the grid service in a secure way, it can be obtained from the credential manager. The credentials employed in the Gridcole system are stored in the credential repository.

1.4. Prototype

The current prototype of Gridcole is based on the Coppercore learning flow engine [21] and the Webplayer client that is also distributed with this engine. Both of them have been conveniently modified with the aim of enabling the use of tools offered as non-secure grid services with Java clients distributed according to the JNLP specification during the realization of IMS-LD based collaboration scripts.

This prototype can be employed to realize collaborative learning situations described in complete units of learning. As a limitation, the educator must manually perform some operations that should be carried out by the control subsystem before starting the realization of a situation. However, once this is done, the prototype provides full support for the realization of collaborative learning situations. If fact, this prototype has already been employed in experiences with real users for the realization of different situations. One these experiences is introduced in the next section.

A snapshot of the interface of Gridcole prototype can be seen in Figure 3. More specifically, the figure shows the modified Webplayer client as seen by students during the realization of a situation. This client includes three frames: a frame on the top left in which participants can see the activity to be performed in every moment, a frame on the bottom left that shows the description of the activity, and a frame on the right in which participants can see the tools and documents available for the support of the activity. In

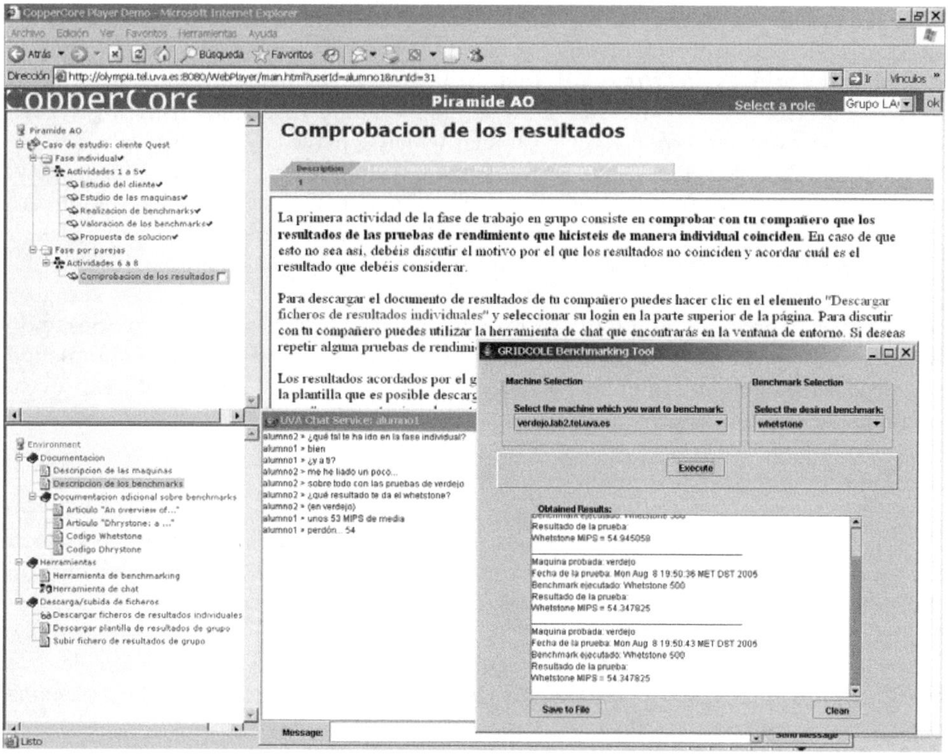

Figure 3: Snapshot of Gridcole prototype along with the clients of two grid service-based tools integrated by the system.

our prototype, grid-based tools can be selected in this frame. The clients of a two grid-based tools that were launched by the prototype can also be seen in the snapshot.

2. A Sample Collaborative Learning Situation

Gridcole can be employed to support a wide range of collaborative learning situations as long as they can be formally described in an IMS-LD based collaboration script and there are suitable tools for their support that can be integrated by the system. This section illustrates the potential uses of Gridcole by means of a sample collaborative learning situation requiring tools with special hardware needs that was actually supported by the system in an experience with real students. Next, other situations that eventually could be supported by Gridcole are outlined. Interested readers can also find the details of a situation requiring supercomputing capabilities as well as of a thorough evaluation of the system in [10].

2.1. Educational Context

The collaborative learning situation described in this section was conceived for a course on Computer Architecture for undergraduate students of the School of Telecommunications Engineering at the University of Valladolid, Spain. This course is organized around a computer architecture design and evaluation design project which in turn is divided in three subprojects (see [22] for details). In this project, students organize themselves in groups of four pairs and collaboratively play the role of consultants that have to advise on a computing solution (machine, operating system, software, network, etc.) for a given customer, which is played by the teacher.

The situation considered here concerns the first subproject, in which students get to know the client, model the customer's presumed computational load by mixing standard benchmarks, test real machines using the benchmarks, and finally make a recommendation to their client. This subproject pursues clear learning objectives. On the content side, it is expected that students learn how to use benchmarks, and get a quantitative impression on a few real machines (with different CPUs, memories, etc.). On the skills side, several abilities, such as interpreting and selecting information, arguing, and taking compromise solutions are promoted. The subproject lasts for six two-hour sessions on approximately four weeks.

2.2. Description of the situation

The collaborative learning situation was designed according to the well-known *pyramid* collaboration pattern [23]. More specifically, the participants of the situation are expected to carry out the sequence of activities that is outlined next:

1. Individually, study customer requirements and propose a workload model.
2. Individually, study the documentation on available machines and benchmarks, and propose an evaluation plan.
3. Individually benchmark available machines and propose a recommendation.
4. In pairs, discuss the workload model and propose an agreed model.
5. In pairs, discuss the evaluation plan, and propose an agreed plan.
6. In pairs, if necessary repeat experiments, or recombine results, and propose an agreed machine recommendation.

This situation requires that documents about the requirements of the customer, the features of the machines being evaluated and the description of the benchmarks are available for users. A chat tool is needed in activities 4, 5 and 6 in to enable the communication among students. Furthermore, a benchmarking tool is required in activities 3 and 6 so that participants can use it to measure the performance of the machines under study. It is noteworthy that the benchmarking tool uses specific hardware resources, which are the specific computers with different architectures that can be benchmarked by users.

2.3. Realization of the Situation

In order to realize the collaborative learning situation described in previous subsection, a benchmarking tool and a chat tool were developed following the specifications mentioned in section 1.1. Furthermore, the collaboration script corresponding to the situation was formalized using the IMS-LD specification and packaged in a complete unit of learning. Figure 4 shows an excerpt of the IMS-LD-based description of the collaboration script.

```
<manifest ...>
 <organizations>
  <imsld:learning-design identifier="LD-piramide-LAO" level="B"
uri="">
   ...
    <imsld:learning-activity identifier="LA-realizar-benchmarks">
     <imsld:title>Realizacion de benchmarks</imsld:title>
     <imsld:environment-ref ref="E-realizar-benchmarks"/>
     ...
    </imsld:learning-activity>
    ...
    <imsld:environment identifier="E-realizar-benchmarks">
     <imsld:title>Entorno de benchmarking</imsld:title>
     <imsld:learning-object identifier="LO-benchmarking-tool">
      <imsld:title>Herramienta de benchmarking</imsld:title>
      <imsld:item identifier="I-benchmarking-tool"
identifierref="RES-benchmarking-tool"/>
     </imsld:learning-object>
    </imsld:environment>
   ...
 </imsld:learning-design>
 </organizations>
 <resources>
  <resource identifier="RES-benchmarking-tool"
type="gridserviceclient"
href="http://egeo.tel.uva.es/gridserviceclients/benchmarkingtoolclient.
jnlp">
    <dependency  identifierref="RES-benchmarking-service-factory"/>
   </resource>
  <resource identifier="RES-benchmarking-service-factory"
type="gridservicefactory"
href="http://egeo.tel.uva.es:8080/ogsa/services/gridcole/services/Bench
amrkingServiceFactory"/>
 </resources>
 ...
</manifest>
```

Figure 4. Excerpt of the collaboration script showing the definition of the benchmarking activity and the specification of the tool that will be employed to support it.

The complete unit of learning and the tools were employed along with Gridcole prototype to support the realization of the situation in an experience with 8 students of the course on Computer Architecture during the spring semester of 2005. In this experience, which lasted about 4 hours, all students were in the same room but each of them used a different computer to participate in the situation. Figure 5 shows a picture of the participants taken during the realization of the collaborative learning situation.

Once the participants finished the realization of the collaborative learning situation, they were asked to fill a questionnaire about their opinion on the experience. Table 1 provides an overview of the answers that the participants gave to some of the main issues covered by the questionnaire. Furthermore, 4 participants were interviewed in order to gain further insight into their opinions. Interestingly, it was found that most volunteers considered that Gridcole had helped them to realize the situation in collaboration with their partner. According to the detailed discussion that can be found in [10], this can be attributed to several factors related to the system. First, the guidance provided by the system, which was considered helpful by most participants to realize the situation. Second, the fact that the systems allowed students to collaborate fruitfully,

Figure 5: Students of the course on Computer Architecture using Gridcole.

as it was agreed again by most of them. And third, the fact that the tools integrated by the system were considered helpful to realize the situation by most volunteers.

Table 1. Main results obtained from the questionnaires answered by the participants of the experience with Gridcole.

	Completely agree	Agree	Somewhat agree	Somewhat disagree	Disagree	Completely Disagree	NA
System helped to realize the situation in collaboration with partner	2	4	2	0	0	0	0
Guidance helped to realize the situation	5	2	1	0	0	0	0
Collaboration with partner was fruitful	6	2	0	0	0	0	0
Benchmarking tool was useful to realize the situation	5	3	0	0	0	0	0
Chat tool was useful to realize the situation	1	3	4	0	0	0	0

2.4. Other Collaborative Learning Situations

Gridcole can be employed to support many collaborative learning situations apart from the scenario introduced above. With this aim, Gridcole could integrate different tools similar to the many grid-based tools that use supercomputing capabilities or specific hardware resources that can be found in the literature. For instance, Gridcole could integrate a tool that uses supercomputing capabilities to predict the packing process of molecular crystals [24] for the support of interesting learning scenarios that could be conceived for students of Chemistry. The integration of a tool that uses supercomputing capabilities to analyze live financial data [25] would enable the realization of motivating learning situations for the students of a degree in Economics. A tool that controls a servo-hydraulic system to simulate the effect of earthquakes on the structure of buildings [26] could be integrated to enable the support of new learning situations within the context of studies on civil engineering. The integration of a tool that controls a robot [27] could also be very useful in learning situations that aim at teaching students fundamental concepts of robotics. Besides, many tools not requiring supercomputing capabilities or specific hardware resources (e.g. a conceptual map editor, a shared file repository, an asynchronous discussion forum) could also be integrated to support these or other situations. Of course, each situation should have a different collaboration script describing diverse sequences of activities that would be interpreted by Gridcole.

3. Conclusions and Future Work

This chapter provided an overview of Gridcole, a system that can be easily tailored by educators to support the realization of collaborative learning scenarios designed by themselves. To do so, educators can provide a script specifying the sequence of learning activities to be performed by students as well as the documents and tools required to support them. Gridcole can then search for these tools in a service-based grid to make them available to users whenever it is required. Significantly, these tools are not limited in terms of access to supercomputing capabilities or specific hardware resources. Furthermore, Gridcole can guide students during the realization of the collaborative learning scenario according to the sequence of activities defined in the script.

Current research work includes the completion of Gridcole prototype, the enhancement of Gridcole's tool search capabilities using ontologies [28], and the integration of the system with the Collage [18] IMS-LD editor of collaborative learning scenarios. The use of a workflow engine to handle the automatic management of the data flow between tools integrated in Gridcole [29] is also being studied currently. In the long term we plan to study the possibility of integrating tools based on P2P technology in Gridcole. Furthermore, scheduling facilities, which are usually employed in grid computing, will be studied to provide collaborative tools according to predefined Quality of Service (QoS) parameters.

Acknowledgements

This chapter is a derivative work of an article previously published by the authors in [10]. The authors would like to fully acknowledge Elsevier Science for the use of this material.

References

[1] T. Koschmann. *CSCL: theory and practice of an emerging paradigm*, Malwah, NJ, USA: Lawrence Erlbaum (1996).

[2] A. Morch. "Three levels of end-user tailoring: customization, integration and extension". Proceedings of the 3rd Decennial Aarhus Conference, Aarhus, Denmark, 1995, pp. 41-45.

[3] G. Bourguin, A. Derycke. "Integrating the CSCL activities into virtual campuses: foundations of a new infrastructure for distributed collective activities". Proceedings of the 1st European Conference on Computer Supported Collaborative Learning (EuroCSCL 2001), Maastricht, The Netherlands, 2001, pp. 123-130 .

[4] M. L. Betbeder, P. Tchounikine. "Symba, a tailorable framework to support collective activities in a learning context". Proceedings of the 9th International Workshop on Groupware (CRIWG 2003), Grenoble, France, 2003, pp. 90-98.

[5] J. M. Haake, T. Schümmer, A. Haake, M. Bourimi, B. Landgraf. "Two-level tailoring support for CSCL". Proceedings of the 9th International Workshop on Groupware (CRIWG 2003), Grenoble, France, 2003, pp. 74-81.

[6] N. Jensen, S. Seipel, W. Nejdl, S. Olbrich. "COVASE: Collaborative visualization for constructivist learning". Proceedings of the International Conference on Computer Support for Collaborative Learning (CSCL 2003) , Bergen, Norway, 2003 , pp. 249-253.

[7] L. Ferreira, F. Lucchese, T. Yasuda, C. Y. Lee, C. A. Queiroz, E. Minetto, A. Mungioli. *Grid computing in research and education*, IBM Corporation (2005).

[8] P. Dillenbourg. "Over-scripting CSCL: the risks of blending collaborative learning with instructional design". In: *Three worlds of CSCL. Can we support CSCL*, ed. P. A. Kirschner. Heerlen, Open Universiteit Nederland, pp. 61-91 (2002).

[9] P. Jermann, A. Soller, A. Lesgold. "Computer software support for collaborative learning". In: *What we know about CSCL in higher education*, eds. J. W. Strijbos, P. Kirschner, R. Martens. Amsterdam, The Netherlands: Kluwer, pp. 141-146 (2004).

[10] M. L. Bote-Lorenzo, E. Gómez-Sánchez, G. Vega-Gorgojo, Y. Dimitriadis, J. I. Asensio-Pérez, I. M. Jorrín-Abellán. "Gridcole: a tailorable grid service based system that supports scripted collaborative learning". Computers & Education (in press) (2007).

[11] I. Foster, C. Kesselman. *The Grid 2: blueprint for a future computing infrastructure*, San Francisco, CA, USA: Morgan Kaufmann Publishers (2004).

[12] IMS Global Learning Consortium. "IMS Learning Design Information Model v1.0", 2003. Available at http://www.imsglobal.org/learningdesign/ldv1p0/imsld_infov1p0.html.

[13] Global Grid Forum (GGF). "Open Grid Services Infrastructure (OGSI) version 1.0", 2003. Available at http://www.ggf.org/documents/GFD.15.pdf.

[14] Sun Microsystems. "Java Network Launching Protocol & API specification version 1.5", 2001. Available at http://www.jcp.org/en/jsr/detail?id=56.

[15] M. L. Bote-Lorenzo, D. Hernández-Leo, Y. A. Dimitriadis, J. I. Asensio-Pérez, E. Gómez-Sánchez, G. Vega-Gorgojo, L. M. Vaquero-González. "Towards reusability and tailorability in collaborative learning systems using IMS-LD and grid services". International Journal on Advanced Technology for Learning 1 (3) (2004), 129-138.

[16] D. Hernández-Leo, J. I. Asensio-Pérez, Y. Dimitriadis. "IMS Learning Design support for the formalization of collaborative learning patterns". Proceedings of the 4th International Conference on Advanced Learning Technologies (ICALT 2004), Joensuu, Finland, 2004, pp. 350-354.

[17] IMS Global Learning Consortium. "IMS Learning Resource Metadata information model v1.2.1", 2001. Available at http://www.imsglobal.org/metadata/imsmdv1p2p1/imsmd_infov1p2p1.html.

[18] D. Hernández-Leo, E. D. Villasclaras-Fernández, I. M. Jorrín-Abellán, J. I. Asensio-Pérez, Y. Dimitriadis, I. Ruiz-Requies, B. Rubia-Avi. "COLLAGE, a collaborative learning design editor based on patterns". Journal of Educational Technology & Society, Special Issue on Learning Design 9 (1) (2006), 58-71.

[19] Reusable eLearning Object Authoring & Delivery (RELOAD) editor v2.0: http://www.reload.ac.uk, last visited in November 2007.

[20] IMS Global Learning Consortium. "IMS Content Packaging Information Model v1.1.3", 2003. Available at http://www.imsglobal.org/content/packaging/cpv1p1p3/imscp_infov1p1p3.html.

[21] CopperCore Project: http://coppercore.org/, last visited in November 2007.

[22] Y. Dimitriadis, A. Martínez, B. Rubia. "Cooperative learning in Computer Architecture: an educational project and its network support". Proceedings of the Frontiers in Education Conference (FIE 2001), Reno, NV, USA, 2001, pp. 13-18.

[23] D. W. Johnson, R. T. Johnson. *Learning together and alone: cooperative, competitive and individualistic learning*, Needham Heights, MA, USA: Allyn and Bacon (1999).

[24] B. Butchart, C. Chapman, W. Emmerich. "OGSA first impressions - a case study re-engineering a scientific application with the Open Grid Services Architecture". Proceedings of UK e-Science All Hands Meeting 2003 (AHM 2003), Nottingham, UK, 2003, pp. 810-816 .

[25] L. Gillam, K. Ahmad, G. Dear. "Grid-enabling social scientists: the FINGRID infrastructure". Proceedings of the 1st International Conference on e-Social Science, Manchester, UK, 2005.

[26] L. Pearlman, C. Kesselman, S. Gullapalli, B. F. Spencer, J. Futrelle, K. Ricker, I. Foster, P. Hubbard, C. Severance. "Distributed hybrid earthquake engineering experiments: experiences with a ground-shaking grid application". Proceedings of the 13th IEEE International Symposium on High Performance Distributed Computing (HPDC 2004), Honolulu, HA, USA, 2004, pp. 14-23.

[27] S. Vialle, A. De Vivo, F. Sabatier. "A grid architecture for comfortable robot control". Proceedings of the European Grid Conference in Advances in Grid Computing (EGC 2005), Amsterdam, The Netherlands, 2005, pp. 344-353.

[28] G. Vega-Gorgojo, M. L. Bote-Lorenzo, E. Gómez-Sánchez, Y. A. Dimitriadis, J. I. Asensio-Pérez. "A semantic approach to discovering learning services in grid-based collaborative systems". Future Generation Computer Systems 22 (6) (2006), 709-719.

[29] L. Palomino-Ramírez, A. Martínez-Monés, M. L. Bote-Lorenzo, J. I. Asensio-Pérez, Y. Dimitriadis. "Flow between Tools: Towards a Composition-Based Solution for Learning Design". Proceedings of the 7th IEEE International Conference on Advanced Learning Technologies, ICALT 2007, Niigata, Japan, 2007, pp. 354-358.

The Learning Grid Handbook
S. Salerno et al. (Eds.)
IOS Press, 2008

Application Design of Learning Grid in Computer-Mediated Communication

Duska ROSENBERG [a,1], Mirja LIEVONEN [a], Pedro CONTRERAS [b], Fionn MURTAGH [b], Guido KUEHN [c] and Ralf DOERNER [d]

[a] *I-COM Research Centre, Royal Holloway, University of London*
[b] *Computer Science, Royal Holloway, University of London*
[c] *Electronic Arts, Cologne*
[d] *Wiesbaden University of Applied Sciences*

Abstract. Developing e-Learning applications concerns issues of human communication and facilitating technology. One of the key research issues in Computer-Mediated Communication (CMC) is the participation of remote audience in a communicative activity. This is particularly important in learning contexts. In the two studies reported here, we discuss systems infrastructure by presenting the concept of the Virtual Observatory through the AstroGrid project. We explore how such a Grid can be used in the future as an e-Learning service platform and as a tool for wider audiences that require access to documents and similar information resources. However, an integrated e-Learning environment has to provide access to people (teachers and students) as well. In order to explore how the two kinds of facility may be integrated, we discuss the design of communication tools that provide access to both people and information. We also present Augmented Reality (AR) applications that facilitate teacher interaction with remote student audience by increasing the interactivity of the virtual classroom. Studies of virtual classrooms have identified limitations of computer-mediated learning environments since they do not provide sufficient contextual information to support communication. The virtual information space is critically dependent on the visualization aspects of the user interface. This has been designed with additional functionality to enable the lecturer to navigate the remote information space.

Keywords. e-Learning, grid, visualization, augmented reality.

Introduction

Developing e-Learning environments requires consideration of both technical and human communication aspects. First, what kind of infrastructure is suitable for e-Learning is a wide-ranging issue of systems architecture. Grid technologies provide access points to the web-based communication tools that are needed for teachers and learners to interactively manage the learning content, such as giving feedback, participating in chat discussions and contributing to the news.

From the perspective of human communication, these facilities support indirect communication where participants use the facilities in order to jointly write documents, create news items and build communities that share the same interests and concerns. In

[1] Corresponding Author: I-COM Research Centre, Royal Holloway, University of London, Egham, Surrey TW20 0EX, United Kingdom; E-mail: d.rosenberg@rhul.ac.uk.

addition to this, e-Learning environments should support direct communication by providing facilities for conversations in the virtual classroom. Traditionally the technologies such as video-conferencing, virtual reality and other facilities for computer-mediated communication have been developed independently from web-based communication tools. In this chapter we attempt to bring the two together by exploring design issues of e-Learning environments where video-conferencing enhances the range of communication tools originally provided by the AstroGrid platform. In particular, we focus on the user interface to the integrated Learning Grid portal and discuss what kind of interface design is suitable in this context.

One of the key research issues in Computer-mediated Communication (CMC) concerns the participation of a remote audience in a communicative activity and the associated use of informational resources to support conversations in the virtual classroom. This is particularly important in learning contexts, as studies of virtual classrooms have identified strong tendencies to treat remote students as observers, rather than active participants. The key design issue of the integrated Learning Grid portal is thus to support both direct and indirect communication primarily by providing a user interface that appropriately represents people and information required for learning to take place.

In this chapter, we discuss e-Learning environments and their development first by describing two ongoing projects; AstroGrid that focuses on software architecture, and Augmented Reality that concentrates on the user interface to e-Learning applications. We then discuss usability issues and the experimental design that we have developed in order to evaluate the impact of these applications on teacher-student communication (both direct and indirect) in an integrated e-Learning environment.

1. Requirements for e-Learning environments

1.1. Continuous integration and collaborative work in AstroGrid

The AstroGrid [1] development process is an open collaboration between researchers and technologists. To allow these people to work in partnership effectively, a range of web-based tools is required. In such a collaborative software project there are different obstacles to overcome before the collaborative development can become effective. Firstly, good communication is essential in many aspects. Developers need to be aware of information regarding the project as a whole, information regarding specific sections, and they need to be able to directly communicate with other developers. The latter is of high importance in the AstroGrid case.

Developers working within the project are assigned tasks in so-called development cycles, which are specified by astronomers through the definition of science cases. Developers will work on a certain task or project module for a few months before being moved to another area. In some cases more than one cycle or iteration is necessary to achieve a goal. In any case task assignment is under constant review by the project leaders, with a view towards reallocating human resources when and where they are needed.

The benefit of an approach like this is a highly cross-trained development team. For example in the case of a member's absence, another developer who has previously worked in that area can be assigned to the task. The fact that, at some point, they would have worked in the particular area means they can quickly re-integrate themselves into the development team for the particular project modules. However, an adequate facility for communication must be in place for developers to be able to exchange ideas and to make and to respond to queries, so that the development process is as efficient as possible.

One important issue in relation to this cyclic development process is development by second parties. As well as providing communication facilities there are other ways to ensure that the collaboration is as effective as possible. Standards play an important role in facilitating code development by second and third parties. Standard forms of software design and standard coding styles all play a part in reducing development time.

1.2. Communication tool

To facilitate good communication practice, any person with expertise or simply an interest in the Virtual Observatory [2] concept, Grid technologies or e-Science is free to post or comment upon news articles, to participate in the forum exchanges or to post documents making use of the AstroGrid portal. The portal provides an access point to the various communication tools available. The **Wiki** pages provide support for relevant documents posting. Wiki is a leading-edge, web-based collaboration platform targeting the corporate Intranet world. TWiki [3] fosters information flow within an organization.

The groups deal with site-related topics, project-specific topics and general areas such as virtual organizations and Grids. A news section is also available to allow developers to be kept up to date with various information about articles posted, items of **news**, events and polls. A central portal providing access to the various communication platforms is essential to effective collaboration. There is no confusion over how to contact other members as all contacts are made through the use of one central site. Further to these web-based community-oriented communication tools, one-to-one contact is necessary in order to ensure that developers can carry out their tasks efficiently.

For example in the case of second party development, the ability to contact a previous developer to query some aspect of the work greatly reduces re-development time. To facilitate the necessary direct communications between project members, project contracted people keep close contact through **e-mail, telephone conferences, chat** programs and **regular meetings**. An extension to these facilities that is explored in this chapter concerns the use of video-conferencing enhanced with Augmented Reality applications that allow simultaneous access to people and documents they are working on. This would provide a richer, more effective and more natural channel for direct communication, thus making it possible for users to jointly author or edit the documents and solve problems in virtual meetings as well.

1.2.1. Wiki

AstroGrid's Wiki pages (http://wiki.astrogrid.org) is a web site that allows the registered user to change the pages on a browser and to add their own pages. Pages can be formatted using either simple Wiki formatting marks (like *this* to make this) or the full range of HTML markup tags. The site includes help pages, a tutorial and an experimental Wiki where users can try out adding pages, comments and other kinds of contribution.

1.2.2. Forum

The AstroGrid forum pages provide a number of grouped discussion areas. The groups deal with site-related topics, project-specific topics and general areas such as Virtual Observatories (VO) and Grids. They can browse the forums and, if registered, add comments or new topics for discussion.

1.2.3. News

AstroGrid's news pages (http://www2.astrogrid.org/news) are the central part of the AstroGrid site. Articles are posted here, as well as items of news, events and polls. Any registered user can add to any of these. The item will be checked by one of the administrators and then released to the site. Users can also comment on most items. Comments can be viewed in nested, threaded or flat form.

1.2.4. Content Management System

A content management system (CMS) is a web application designed to make it easier for non-technical users to add, edit and manage a website. Some of the most important characteristics of CMS systems are to:

- automatically generate navigation elements
- make content searchable and indexable
- keep track of users, their permissions and security settings.

AstroGrid-2 uses Plone (http://plone.org/) as CMS, but there are several others available, with implementations in a wide area of technologies, such as Java, PHP, C++, Perl, Phyton, ASP, just to name a few.

1.2.5. Other tools

A list of further available tools is presented below.

- e-mail and e-mail lists. This is essential for the day–to–day work
- Messaging. Chat rooms and messaging programs can be important when communicating with other developers. AstroGrid uses the Jabber protocol, which allows different clients to connect when registered
- Telephone. Teleconferencing is carried out often in AstroGrid
- Meetings. This includes specific working group meetings as well as conferences.

1.3. Programming tools and languages

1.3.1. Coding standards and Java

Code integration is tackled using Current Version System [4] to store, modify and keep track of code changes. This has various uses in software development practice helping returning developers to identify and understand changes that have been made since they last worked on a particular project area. JUnit [5] Test is used to prove code integrity and ensure quality of service. JUnit is a regression-testing framework for code made with Java. Usually a unit test exercises some particular method in a particular context in order to prove that a specific piece of code does what it is supposed to do. Code bugs are tracked using Bugzilla [6], a "Defect Tracking System" or "Bug-Tracking System". Defect Tracking Systems support individuals or groups of developers by keeping track effectively of outstanding bugs in their software. Once an error, misbehavior or an unexpected answer has been detected, this will be described and assigned to a developer in the form of a ticket that contains all the information related to the bug.

To provide standard coding practices a number of tools are used in the AstroGrid project. A range of free Integrated Development Environment (IDE) tools such as Eclipse [7] and JBuilder Foundation are used during the development process. These, in conjunction with code design standards (e.g. UML), are needed to establish the basis on which to allow different people in different places to modify each others' code easily, the philosophy being that if everybody is using the same tools to build a product, the components of the product can be more easily modified or enhanced.

The main programming language used in AstroGrid is Java. Different standards such as UML, XML and Web Services are used for the process design to maintain consistency. When coding in Java a standard is used, which allows different people to understand the work of each other, and maintain coding style and consistency. This leads to a cleaner and easier coding process. AstroGrid code guideline standards are described in Vermeulen et al. [8], but a good set of standards can be found easily on the Internet.

1.3.2. Documentation

Code management and documentation is addressed mainly through the use of standard Java Docs and Maven [9]. This is a Java project management and project comprehension tool. It is based on the concept of a project object model (POM) where all the Maven objects are a result of a well-defined model. Builds, documentation, source metrics, and source cross-references are all controlled by the POM. Maven aims to make the developer's life easier by providing a well-defined project structure, well-defined development processes to follow and a coherent body of documentation that keeps developers aware of what is happening within the project.

Maven alleviates a lot of what most developers consider a problem. This is essential in projects where there are not many people dedicated to the task of documenting and spreading the critical information about the project, which is necessary in order to dedicate resources to other critical tasks such as coding and code testing.

1.4. File access and security

One issue that has not been included in the above section is security and the identification of information that can be publicly accessible. Because AstroGrid is an open project, almost every document is publicly accessible through the Internet. One exception is the code, as there are restrictions in place as to who is authorised to upload and to integrate code. Here SSH [10] protocol is used to allow secure communication between developers and the server repository.

Though remote login is the primary use of SSH, the protocol can also be used as a general-purpose cryptographic tunnel, capable of copying files, encrypting e-mail connections, and triggering remote execution of programs. Currently AstroGrid uses

SSH Version 2, which operates over TCP. In its simplest mode of operation, it connects to a server, negotiates a shared secret key, and then begins encrypting the session. A username and password are passed over the encrypted session and, if authenticated, the server starts a command shell over the encrypted session.

1.4.1. Version Control System

Version control system software is a key technology when sharing code between programmers. Some important advantages are listed by Thomas and Hunt [11]:

- It gives to the project the ability to undo the code to previous versions
- It allows multiple developers to work on the same code base in a controlled manner
- It keeps a record of the changes made over time
- It support multiple software releases at the same time so the development process can continue.

The most widely used version control systems are Subversion [12] and the Concurrent Version System (CVS). AstroGrid uses CVS to manage its code. Version control system has named its processes with a common vocabulary. Some of the most important terms are the following:

- **Repository:** This is where the files are stored, often on a server.
- **Working copy:** This is the local copy of files from a repository, at a specific time or revision. All work done to the files in a repository is done to a "local" working copy.
- **Check-out:** This creates a local working copy from the repository. Either a revision is specified; a module, or the latest code is used.
- **Commit:** This happens when a copy of the changes made to the working "local" copy is written to the repository in the server side.
- **Update:** This merges the changes that have been made in the repository (e.g. by other people) into the local working copy.
- **Module:** This is a name given to a project, or project part in the repository, which can also be a branch. When checking out, a module name can be specified, and doing so simplifies the development process in a large project through support of small modules.
- **Branch:** A set of files may be branched at a point in time so that, from that time forward, two copies of those files may be developed at different speeds and in different ways independently of each other.
- **Merge:** This brings together two sets of changes to a file or set of files into a unified revision of that file or files.
- **Tag:** This refers to an important snapshot in time, consistent across many files. These files at that point may all be tagged with a user-friendly, meaningful name or revision number. This is relevant when a specific tagged version may be needed.
- **Conflict:** This occurs when two changes are made by different parties to the same document or place within a document. Since the software may not be

intelligent enough to decide which change is "correct", a user is required to resolve the conflict.

The repository is usually created in a server. In the CVS case the repository can be accessed using the *Pserver* or *external* techniques. In Pserver mode, CVS runs a server process on the repository machine, and all clients connect to it. Pserver mode has some advantages:

- It is relatively simple to set up
- It can enforce read-only users
- It supports anonymous access.

As mentioned above, the AstroGrid is a central portal that provides access to the various communication platforms and in this way it fosters information flow between users in different teams, groups and sections of the virtual organization. It is therefore essential not only to effective collaboration, but also to learning in an interactive setting. In a real-life learning environment, group contact, as well as one-to-one contact are necessary in order to ensure that users can carry out their tasks efficiently.

To facilitate the necessary direct communications between project members, project contracted personnel keep close contact through **e-mail, telephone conferences, chat** programs and **regular meetings**. In the section that follows, the support for learning through interaction in virtual meetings is described with the aim of identifying the requirements for a user interface to the central portal.

1.4.2. AstroGrid architecture

In concordance with the construction of the VO (Virtual Observatory), AstroGrid has a modular architecture [13], open to all contributions from data, services or resources. The following modules are present in AstroGrid:

- **Portal:** the portal is a server-based component, which provides an interface for accessing services in the VO. In AstroGrid all components that interact with the users will do so through a Portlet. A portlet gives a modular and flexible layer. Any developer is able to add his/her own functionality by wrapping it on a portlet.
- **Community:** this module allows a group to construct an online community. A resource centre can then assign permission to use its resources to one or more groups within a community instead of having to name the individuals themselves. Within a community, the administrator of the community can assign rights to individuals and groups, including the right to add members and create groups.
- **AstroPass:** this is a central server that stores users' credentials. Once permission has been assigned to a user, he/she decides how much information of its profile is passed to other VO portals.
- **Workflow:** this enables the construction of complex tasks such as building queries and data analysis, upload/download of data and rendering the output in a different format such as tables or images.

- **Registry:** this contains metadata descriptive information about resources available, which is based on IVOA standards. A resource can be a data set, web service, service, information on other registries, etc.
- **Common execution architecture:** this concept – also called by the initials CEA – is an abstraction of application components and the necessary parameters to run it.
- **Astronomical tools:** a number of essential astronomical tools such as object catalogue builder SExtractor and photometric redshift analyzer HyperZ (which are freely available) are incorporated into AstroGrid through a portal wrapper. Some of the tools currently included are: AstroScope, Helioscope, Aladin, and TopCat.
- **MySpace:** this defines a virtual space to allocate both temporal and long-term data, such as data sets generated by queries submitted to databases. MySpace is not necessarily in a local repository, but it will interact with the user as easily as if it were on a local machine.
- **Authorization/Authentication:** this is the component in charge of identification and granting of access to users, as well as maintaining security in AstroGrid.
- **Grid middleware**: this allows AstroGrid to integrate different astronomical data centers and to share resources in a coordinated way.
- **Data sets:** data is allocated in a distributed way in different data centers, across the United Kingdom in AstroGrid's case, and across the globe once the Virtual Observatory alliance will be fully working.

On the basis of these modules a number of tools (as mentioned above) are available to the end user. The Figure 1 shows a screenshot of workbench data discovery tools.

- **AstroScope**: this allows positioning an object in the sky along with a region. As a query is submitted a process is started looking up various catalogue and image servers, asking them for data based around the query. If results are found then information is displayed in a graphical form on the screen allowing the user to surf the result in the form of various nodes. By default objects are seen in a "radial" form, requiring a "click of the mouse" to browse up and down the various nodes. Another option is the "Hyperbolic" view which shows everything in a tree state, where by a click of the mouse the system re-

Figure 1. AstroGrid WorkBench data discovery.

centres the selected node. The user may then select a particular object to have the data (including images) saved to MySpace or their computer.

- **HelioScope**: this tool allows to query archives of images, spectra and catalogue data around a given position, visualize the results and download data files either to a local machine or to a storage space on the AstroGrid storage system MySpace.
- **Task launcher**: this executes a single task on the AstroGrid system. A task can be either querying an archive for data or running a tool that, for example, operates on data files or runs a model.

As shown in Figure 1 a number of additional user interfaces are also available (e.g. Data Analysis, System Services, Helper Application and Advanced). The relevant point here is that AstroGrid tools allow us to visualize and to interact within the context of Computer-mediated Communication applications.

1.4.3. User interface

Augmented Reality (AR) applications were originally developed in order to facilitate teacher interaction with remote student audience. The working assumption was that improving the information space of each participant will increase the interactive potential of the virtual classroom. The virtual information space is critically dependent on the visualization aspects of the user interface, which has been designed with additional functionality – to enable the lecturer to navigate the remote information space.

This is achieved by AR applications that are capable of integrating the video images of the remote audience with virtual pointers using as input technology a game console controller that allows performing natural pointing gestures. This enables the lecturer to navigate the remote information space in order to highlight individual students, thus “inviting” them to take the floor, or to use the pointer for identifying remote objects to focus audience attention.

Usability experiments have shown that such pointing helps people to naturally identify participants and establish the topic of conversation. Pointing is normally defined as a form of “deictic reference” that emphasizes a particular feature of the context in order to facilitate mutual understanding and the creation of the common ground amongst participants. Research is in progress and focuses on experiment design to investigate the usability of the hybrid interaction space, notably how visualizations can bridge the gap between the physical and virtual information space.

Use of AR in making communication for collaborative work more effective has been studied in laboratory conditions where the focus was on subject responses to different AR representations on the screen. However, in order to bring the AR interface to the real-life classroom we need to address the technology platform issues – that is, what configuration of technologies will be required to make this a learning facility. Issues of privacy also need to be addressed, not only with respect to access to information but also the visibility of people on the screen. AR applications allow for different degrees of focus on people and information, thus enabling a richer set of “privacy” setting.

2. Scenarios of Use in e-Learning Environments

We consider e-Learning as use of any electronic device to assist the education or training process, taking advantage of the Internet or any other communication channel to connect other devices to deliver information and knowledge.

The Virtual Observatory presents big challenges for the e-Learning community; the Virtual Observatory is expected to provide a data Grid platform for astronomers and the scientific community. But it can also provide an opportunity for students to experience Grid computing in a real-case scenario. Students will be able to implement experiments in areas such as image processing, algorithms and data mining in computer science related areas, just to name a few.

But e-Learning does not stop there: it will be possible for e-Learners to use this platform to implement experiments or to investigate theories. The most interesting aspect would be the interaction of these individuals doing work as a group driven by common interest. Just as research projects such as AstroGrid work as a collaboration of individual researchers, students can re-enact this by working in interdisciplinary groups, using the platform to learn to effectively share individual knowledge and expertise.

This scenario, however, needs adequate tools to coordinate, support and monitor such virtual groups. A starting point is to take Open Source software to generate an adequate bundle of software that will enable students to organize such a group. The scenario presented above is not just a challenge for teachers and students: it also presents a challenge for the scientist working in today's Virtual Observatory.

Questions such as the following are on the agenda:

- What kind of service would we like to offer to e-Learners? The findings of the AR project suggest that the key issue we need to address is how interactive the e-Learning environment should be.
- How are we going to present such information in a friendly, open way? The findings of the AR project suggest that an interactive learning environment should represent information about both people and the documents they work with in an integrated "interaction space".
- How will effectiveness and efficiency of VO e-Learning systems be evaluated? So far, the findings of the AR project suggest that usability experimentation may provide the basic framework for identifying the critical features of the interaction space in support of effective collaborative learning.

In summary, the key issues that need to be addressed concern the capability of the architectures of today to incorporate future e-Learning schemes. Essentially all Virtual Observatories are based on open standards such as XML and Web Services. This makes the architecture transparent for incorporating customized plug-ins or extensions in the case of designing e-Learning modules. The problem we find here, and must address, is that VO architectures can reach very complicated states, and the more complicated this is the more difficult it will be to incorporate additional modules that can respond adequately to the learning process.

As our starting point we can consider Gilly Salmon's model for understanding learning via CMC [14] for implementing e-Learning modules that can be on the top of AstroGrid architecture. This model, shown in Figure 2 is derived from analysis of

Computer Mediated Communication and it has become established as a course design tool. Salmon presents a five-layer process leading to knowledge construction.

The advantage presented by this model is that it is rather close to the AstroGrid philosophy, since this approach is not formally but intrinsically related to the way that AstroGrid is developing today. Also it is a non-exclusive model, for example to ensure quality of services. Learning via the CMC model can interact with Allison's [15] layers of distributed learning environments.

The Salmon model helps to understand the kind of service that we would like to offer to potential e-Learners. In a more concrete scenario we can consider the implementation of the Intelligent Web Teacher Platform (IWT) as described by Capuano et al. [16]. IWT is a distributed learning platform, which offers external plug-in connectors that can be designed specifically to connect AstroGrid Portal. Since AstroGrid supports special designed portlets to access its resources, IWT presents a potential solution that facilitates the creation of an e-Learning environment.

The effectiveness of such an e-Learning environment has been evaluated in usability experiments focused on the interactive features of the distributed learning setting. Several usability issues of the interface design for e-Learning applications were addressed when testing an Augmented Reality application. AR technologies were used to manipulate the video stream with a game controller as an input device (Wii™ Remote). The controller makes it possible to move visual representations of a pointer in 3D (up-down, left-right, back-forth) and in this way it was possible to augment the video with the visual pointer representation. Simple shapes such as a dot, a circle, an arrow, a highlighted area were used to point to people and objects on the screen.

The Wii™ game controller was connected to a PC running Windows operating system via Bluetooth. In order to calculate the target pointing position on the screen, the Wii™game console uses a sensor bar containing two IR light sources. We have replaced the sensor bar with our own hardware using infrared LEDs, which were placed on either side of the target display. Tacking these beacons in the sensors' field of view, the Wii™remote processes the captured images from the PixArtIR chip and sends the minimum information that is required to calculate the target position.

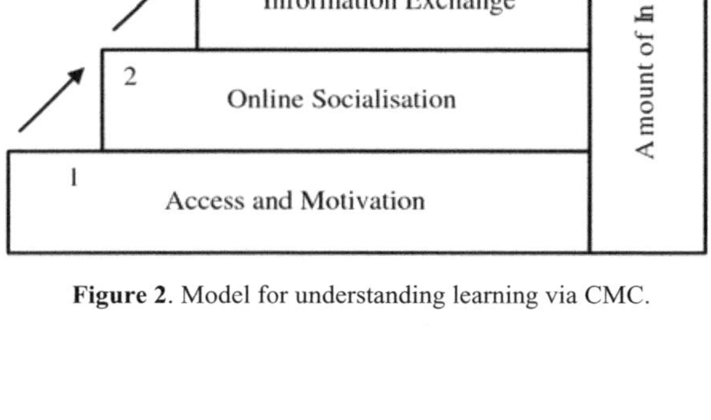

Figure 2. Model for understanding learning via CMC.

The software used to access the information from the game controller was GlovePIE (Glove Programmable Input Emulator). This provides a basic scripting language for mapping events from different devices to mouse and keyboard events. For implementing AR functionality, we used the OSGART library which extends the OpenSceneGraph framework with the functionality provided by ARToolkit. The visual representations of our pointer have been realized by writing a GLSL shader and inheriting from the OSGART class GenericVidoeShader.

The developed prototype application shows smooth runtime behavior, and there were no difficulties meeting real-time constraints. There can, however, be delays due to the distribution of the augmented video stream by the videoconferencing application (such as the commercial Polycom system). In some settings this delay can cause disruption in user communication and we have overcome this difficulty to some extent, by providing an additional monitor where users can see both the remote audience and the view of themselves as represented on the remote screen.

Our test setting was a simulation of a videoconference, where both sites had the two displays, one representing an augmented video stream from the participants at the remote site, and the other from the local site. We ran several test sessions with students and members of staff where the participants had to jointly carry out tasks, such as to decide which room of the floor plan shown at the remote site they would prefer as their office, or discussing where the problem points for pedestrians were on the road shown on a map hanging at the remote site, and making a group decision after a discussion. Three series of tests in addition to a pilot session were run, each session comprising 4-5 people. The tests were designed so that, in order on carry out the tasks, people had to rely on deictic gestures. The sessions were video-recorded for analysis and the participants were interviewed after the session.

In order to support their communication over the video link, a specific pointer controller was used to facilitate the performance of deictic gestures. In our test setting, the camera shooting the local view to the remote site was above the display where the video stream from the remote site was represented. In the videoconferencing session, it seemed as if the local end participants were looking at the people at the remote site and vice versa – which is close to natural communication, and obviously beneficial in videoconferencing. In order to link the origin of pointing, that is, who was pointing, to what was pointed at, people had to follow both screens.

This camera position gave us a good view to follow the back-and-forth gaze direction between the two displays when people kept track of possible pointing represented at the adjacent display. The two perspectives at both ends provided both of the groups with live video stream that enabled them to integrate the origo of pointing (the person using the pointer controller), with the reference of pointing (the person or the object pointed at), and thus overcome much of the fragmentation normally encountered in computer mediated communication.

Users could hold the controller in one hand in the same way as any pointing stick while they perform natural deictic gestures (pointing). The system tracks the movements and supports the collaboration over distance by providing a common context through visualizing the semantics of pointing gestures.

Multiple options of representations for pointing were mapped on the pointer controller such as highlighting an area when indicating a person, circles in three different colors, a smaller size dot and an arrow that could be turned in relevant direction and used as an alarm. In order to find out whether there are any preferences by the users between different visual representations, tests need to be run with a larger number of users than we had initially.

The way people seemed to adapt to a technical context novel for them and how they adopted a novel way of working was unexpectedly quick. The outcome of the usability test tends to suggest that increasing the shared information space by providing visual cues improves communication over distance.

Even in our test situation it turned out that people intuitively tend to point at an object at the remote site, though realizing instantly that it does not work, since the remote participants have no clue what they are pointing at. Because pointing has a powerful role in normal collocated communication and collaboration, our motivation was to find ways of improving gestural communication in videoconferencing situations. Pointing and gestures are also typical of teaching and learning situations: lecturers often point when explaining something for the class, and in any hands-on activities the role of pointing and manipulating objects is crucial.

We found out in our usability tests that the participants quite effortlessly embraced the basic functionalities of pointing with the pointer controller at objects at the remote site, fully concentrating on the task, as if they were not dealing with anything new. Secondly, they adapted to the situation where they had to follow the two displays in order to keep track on what was going on as to gestural references.

Even in a situation where the person holding the pointer controller at the local end and a person at the remote end had to coordinate their actions while marking something on a map hanging at the remote site, they managed to do it without excessive procedural utterances: the remote person turned to look at the display to check the position of arrow representing the reference of pointing on the display, and then he marked it by pen on the real map behind him.

Their coordination was surprisingly smooth taking into consideration what a complex spatial navigation was in question. It seemed that pointing at an object at the remote site was no more difficult than pointing any object with a pen, and there did not seem to be any problems of precision either. These preliminary findings encourage us to carry on our work on exploring spatial navigation in the technology mediated work settings, in particular in videoconferencing and e-Learning contexts.

Pointing at *people* was another issue, as it is the case in human communication in general. First, when introducing people at the remote site, a person in question was highlighted by an AR representation. This obviously worked well from the *indicative* point of view, but the participants found it unpleasant if they were in the spotlight for a long time. The learning from such experience is to highlight the person only momentarily, as if calling them to take the floor.

This interpretation some participants gave as the communicative meaning of being pointed at: it was a call to say something. Pointing is a sensitive issue in human communication in general, and that became clear in our usability tests as well. First, a "heavy-looking" representation such as a thick red arrow flying toward a user's face may evoke feelings as if an object be falling on the person; therefore the AR-representations should not evoke any feelings of concrete threat.

Once the communicative function of pointing is completed, the pointer representation becomes an immediate disturbance. If for instance an arrow representation of the pointer approached the head of the person, she would try to avoid it. Pointing and their representations have to obey the same social norms of appropriateness and etiquette as natural communication; for instance it is important to avoid pointing at sensitive parts of the body to avoid embarrassing situations and awkward feelings.

Our usability tests also showed the power of imitation as a strategy of learning. In the first usability test, we asked a participant to use the control after he had been given instructions and time to practice for about 10 minutes. It turned out in the test situation that managing it all after such a short briefing was an excessive cognitive load for the person as he seemed to under-perform in his main task of chairing the session. The test design was then modified so that the designer himself was in the role of the chair, controlling the pointer and thus providing best practice to follow. This design was successful: it helped us find out how people coped with AR-information in carrying out joint tasks.

Another, and even more interesting finding was that the person sitting next to the chair soon learned from the chair how to utilize the pointer and started to use it when relevant to his/her contribution. Such learning did not take much time: one participant for instance quite naturally grabbed the pointer from the chair's hand after having used it only once before, when wanting to point something next time. The more familiar the functionality became in the course of the test tasks, the less attention people paid to the tools. They were concentrating on the contents of the task and were immersed in their shared information space, communicating effortlessly and effectively. Procedural utterances such as "look at the display" were no more needed.

Using Augmented Reality made it possible for us to experiment also with markers and annotation of remote objects. In the beginning of the session, information about the names and affiliations of the participants was inserted and mapped to the markers that the participants wore during the test session. This gave the chair an option to check the name of the person and his affiliation during the session. Such a functionality might be beneficial for instance during a lecture or in a conference where the lecturer / chair might want to call a person by name instead of a long description of a-person-in-the third-row-with-a-green-cardigan.

There are also situations where it may feel embarrassing for the chair not to remember the name of a participant, and were such additional information readily available, he would save his face without needing to reveal that he has forgotten the name. That would, however, require an additional private screen as a prerequisite. If there are several people in a session, in particular in an international context, it is often difficult for the chair to know how to pronounce the name of some participants. Turning on the marker functionality would in such a situation help all participants in case the pronunciation of the name fails badly.

Augmented Reality turned out to be helpful also from the point of view of decision making: in the course of the conversation when people discussed problem points along the nearby road, represented on the map at the remote site, it was possible for the chair to take and save snapshots of the points mentioned during the discussion. When it was time to make a joint decision which of the points the group found as the most difficult, he could retrieve each of the snapshots as a reminder. The functionality seemed to support the process of making a group decision, and at least gave us an encouraging view of using AR-techniques in videoconferencing as a support of decision making as well.

The usability tests run in summer 2007 were designed for one-way pointing. In normal communication and collaboration situations, there are equal options of pointing. Therefore, we carry on our research and focus on two-way pointing in a setting that provides a pointer controller both for the local and for the remote site. This gives us a chance to examine strategies of spatial navigation and negotiation of space as well.

A tentative conclusion from the usability experiments is therefore that the user interface based on the spatial metaphor may provide an appropriate enhancement for Learning Grid. Its implementation using AR applications may form a part of the technology configuration that includes the grid infrastructure, the AstroGrid portal and the communication tools in an integrated platform. Such a platform would provide a powerful resource to support e-Learning. In the section that follows we discuss some usability issues arising from our attempt to design and implement a novel user interface that can appropriately handle the complexity of the Learning Grid applications.

3. Discussion of a Unified Conceptual Framework

A unified conceptual framework covering both human communication and technical issues was created to aid the work of developers and designers of e-Learning environments. Even shared terminology requires particular attention, as same words tend to be used in different ways depending on discourse in question. When for instance the term "information space" is discussed in a technical context, the focus is on the physical features of space, whereas in human communication we are dealing with perceived and conceived space.

Navigation not only concerns a particular physical perspective or change of place in the physical space but also change in the contents of mind such as changing intention or meaning. It would therefore be helpful to make a distinction between these two types of space, physical and cognitive, for instance using *information space* when the physical aspects of space are discussed, and *infoscape* when dealing with human perception and interpretation of space.

Computer mediated communication unavoidably fragments natural communication into streams of sound and image. Multimodality of human communication therefore poses specific requirements for developing e-Learning environments. In order to capture the differences between natural and computer mediated communication, we need a conceptual framework robust enough to cover modality particularly well. For instance keeping track on what is going on – including signal failure or misunderstanding – relies heavily on multimodal resources.

The way humans naturally navigate space includes effortless and continuous switching of communication mode: for instance turning the head in the direction of the object to focus attention; giving feedback by establishing gaze contact, or nodding, pointing to a shared object or manipulating it, or uttering, drawing or writing something as response; establishing common ground by accessing the same room, or addressing a person by phone; expressing hesitation by changing body posture during discourse or intonation or delay during a speech. In collocated situation we are normally aware of what is also peripherally going on, for instance when a person enters the room or leaves it, whereas in videoconferencing such peripheral awareness is challenged as we only see what the camera focuses on.

In computer mediated communication providing feedback relies on few channels only, such as visual, auditory or at times haptic output. From the collaboration or communication point of view, deictic references have a paramount role in the spatial "choreography" of communication as pointing and gaze direction are heavily used in natural communication. The location of the human body as the origin of experience and action is therefore a key issue in the design of tools and interfaces for computer mediated collaboration.

The position of the observer in his environment constrains the scope of information available for him/her in the physical and cognitive sense, but his/her cognitive "position", i.e. history of experiences is the origin of motivation where to focus attention. The sensory array of a human body and its functionalities constrain what is possible as information available to the observer to be perceived. At the level of interpersonal communication, mutual understanding is the crucial thing. Without such "common ground" human communication would simply fail.

A spatial access is a technically critical precondition to establish a common ground. Another critical precondition is finding a shared set of symbols in order to reach a flow of communication. At the interpersonal level, different communication modes and their role in establishing the common ground is an important issue. As to the interactions space, people also use various strategies to demarcate their mutual interaction space by guarding the confidentiality and privacy by leaving people non-relevant to the contents of communication out of their interaction space.

Cognitive level again is crucial for personal orientation, motivation, intentions and strategies. Each human perspective onto the world is a unique continuity of personal experiences and identification. Personal memory is a precondition for the process where new encounters are interpreted against previous personal experiences and included to maintain personal identity in the course of experiences. Therefore, all four levels and their interrelations are relevant for understanding human communication.

In order to cover technical and communication issues alike, the conceptual framework needs to embrace all relevant components of the human-human interface in natural and technology mediated settings, ranging from physical to cognitive phenomena, from individual perspective to multi-perspective, and from human to artefact as a node of coordination. Using a spatial approach may work well in order to interrelate/interface relevant issues/components as it allows the articulation of four different levels relevant to computer mediated communication and collaboration [17].

1. physical level - how events relate to each other
2. sensory level - how information is available to the observer in his/her location, i.e. establishing the origo of what Buehler called I-Here-Now-Origo [18]
3. level of interpersonal communication - how common ground is established and maintained among participants of communication and collaboration, and what kind of strategies people use to regulate interaction space in terms of inclusion of people relevant to ongoing communication and collaboration
4. cognitive level – how information available is interpreted in the individual mind

The two projects described in this chapter have thus provided distinct perspectives on key issues in the design of e-Learning environments. One perspective, illustrated by AstroGrid and the application of Augmented Reality in user interface design, focuses on the technology platform that makes e-Learning possible. The other perspective, that guided the usability experimentation, focuses on cognitive, social and organizational impacts on e-Learners. Both perspectives make crucial contributions to the application design of e-Learning environments.

Acknowledgements

The authors thank the German Academic Exchange Service (DAAD) and the Academic Research Collaboration of the British Council for funding this project. AstroGrid is a UK government funded project through the Particle Physics and Astronomy Research Council (PPARC, now STFC, Science and Technology Facilities Council).

References

[1] AstroGrid. AstroGrid portal, 2007. http://www. astrogrid.org.
[2] IVOA, the International Virtual Observatory Alliance. 2007. http://www.ivoa.net/
[3] TWiki, Enterprise Collaboration Platform, 2007, http://www.twiki.org/.
[4] CVS. Concurrent Versions System, 2007. https://www. cvshome.org/.
[5] JUnit. Java™ Testing Framework, 2007, http://www.junit.org/.
[6] BugZilla, Bug-tracking system, 2007, http://www.bugzilla.org/.
[7] Eclipse, Eclipse Foundation, 2007, http://www.eclipse.org/.
[8] A. Vermeulen, The Elements of Java™ Style, Cambridge University Press, Cambridge, 2000.
[9] Maven, Apache Maven Project, 2007, http://maven.apache.org/.
[10] SSH, Secure Shell, 2007, http://www.openssh.com/.
[11] D. Thomas and A. Hunt, Pragmatic version control using cvs, Pragmatic Bookshelf, Sep. 2003.
[12] Subversion, Subversion Version Control System, 2007, http://subversion.tigris.org.
[13] T. Linde, Astrogrid Architecture Thesis, 2003, http://wiki.astrogrid.org/bin/view/AstrogridArchitectureThesis#Bib3.
[14] G. Salmon. E-moderating: the Key to Teaching and Learning Online. Kogan Page, London, 2000.
[15] C. Allison. (2003) Quality of service requirement for the e-Learning grid. In 2nd International LeGE-WG Workshop on e-Learning and Grid Technologies: a Fundamental Challenge for Europe, March. http://ewic.bcs.org/conferences/2003/2ndlege/session2/paper3.htm
[16] N. Capuano, A. Gaeta, G. Laria, F. Orciuoli, and P. Ritrovato. (2003) How to use grid technology for building the next generation learning environments. In 2nd International LeGE-WG Workshop on e-Learning and Grid Technologies: a Fundamental Challenge for Europe, March. http://ewic.bcs.org/conferences/2003/2ndlege/session1/paper3.htm
[17] M. Lievonen, (2006). "Spaces of Collaboration: Place Taking for Sense Making" [online]. APROS 11: Asia-Pacific Researchers in Organisation Studies 11th International Colloquium. Pp. 268-274. Melbourne: Asia-Pacific Researchers in Organisation Studies, 2006.
[18] K. Buehler, 1934. Sprachtheorie. Fischer, Jena.

The Akogrimo Mobile Grid Framework as Enabling Technology for Next Generation eLearning Paradigms

Francesco D'ANDRIA[a,1], Josep MARTRAT[a], Sandra JIMÉNEZ[a]
Stefan WESNER[b], Pierluigi RITROVATO[c,d], Giuseppe LARIA[c]
[a] *Atos Origin Research and Innovation, Spain*
[b] *High Performance Computing Centre Stuttgart, Germany*
[c] *CRMPA, Centro di Ricerca in Matematica Pura ed Applicata, Italy*
[d] *DIIMA, Università di Salerno, Italy*

Abstract. The next generation of e-Learning will be represented by mobile learning (mLearning). This consideration is justified by the observation that the next dimension of learning and training is the development of wireless communication and wireless learning in our society over the coming years. Future is becoming ever more wireless and at the eLearning domain there is an increasing effort to put in place wireless solutions to replace the wired computer scenarios of today's eLearning. At the same time, there is a significant effort to introduce an enhanced learning approach, based on a paradigm that focuses on the learner and on new forms of learning: the learner will have an active and central role in the learning process and the learning activities will be aimed at facilitating the learner's construction of knowledge and skills. Grid technologies can have a leading role in this approach since they are able to provide, in the next generation, the suitable features to achieve this vision. Mobile and Grid Technologies provide complementary features that can address the requirements of next generation eLearning applications and therefore the merging of both Technologies is a relevant challenge to be accomplished. The result of Akogrimo project will be a platform based on both mobile and Grid technologies. This platform will be able to support different application domains and it will be validated through an eLearning application as well. This paper describes a hypothetical mLearning scenario and how Akogrimo will support it [1].

Keywords. e-Learning, Grid, Mobile Learning.

Introduction

Future societies and economies are being formed in the classrooms of today. Students need to be both educated in their chosen field and digitally literate if they want effectively to be part of tomorrow's knowledge society. eLearning achieves both aims, but not only for young students if the objective to make learning a lifelong endeavour with people of all ages continuously developing their skills is met.

[1] Corresponding Author: Atos Origin Research and Innovation Av Diagonal. 210-218, 4th, 08018 Barcelona, Spain; E-mail: francesco.dandria@atosorigin.com.

eLearning can make a significant contribution for workers and organisations transforming the way they learn, interact and work. Moreover social integration and inclusion, opening access to learning for people with special needs and those living in difficult circumstances (marginalised groups, migrants, single parents, etc.) is promoted.

The integration of advanced information and communication technologies into the education system exploiting new multimedia technologies and the Internet to improve the quality of learning is the enabler to access to resources, services in the same way as remote exchanges and collaboration. Modern eLearning solutions recognise the importance of learning as a social process offering possibilities for collaboration with other learners, their interaction on available content guided by teachers, trainers and tutors.

These learner-centred approaches put the learners back in command, with a wealth of learning resources at their fingertips, customised to their individual needs. Teachers and trainers, however, continue to play a central role, using virtual and traditional face-to-face interactions with their students in a 'blended' approach.

This paper describes the new eLearning paradigm: the integration of new technologies in eLearning scenarios poses new challenges, and provides new added values very useful for eLearning. The mobile network technology will provide new ways of eLearning usage for a mobile student, while the integration of Grid technologies will provide new applications and scalability to traditional eLearning scenarios.

The integration of these individual technologies in eLearning has already been addressed, for example in the scope of the ELeGi [2] (European Learning Grid Infrastructure) IST FP6 project and the MOBIlearn [3] (Next-generation paradigms and interfaces for technology supported learning in a mobile environment exploring the potential of ambient intelligence) IST FP5 project. The innovation raised in the Akogrimo project will be the combination of both technologies for the eLearning scenarios, with the use of the so-called "Mobile Grid" infrastructure [4].

1. A new eLearning Paradigm

Nobody really knows just how we learn! However, we do know that some characteristics and approaches are more likely to be effective in formalized and structured educational programmes. In order to advance effective learning these features must be incorporated into an educational paradigm that focuses on the learner and on new forms of learning. With this approach the learner has an active and central role in the learning process.

Learning activities are aimed at facilitating the construction of knowledge and skills in the learner, instead of the memorisation of information. Information transfer will still obviously exist in the new paradigm, but only as a simple component, not the main goal. Accordingly we can say that the new paradigm subsumes the old one in its displacement. More "complete" knowledge construction occurs through new forms of learning based on:

- The understanding of concepts through direct experience of their manifestation in realistic contexts (i.e. providing access to real world data)

which are constructed from sophisticated software interfaces and devices, and represented as services;
- "Social learning" – active collaboration with other students, teachers, tutors, experts or, in general, available human peers, by using different kinds of collaboration technologies, including enhanced presence.

In this approach collaboration is considered as a complex conversational process that goes far beyond a simple information exchange. In order to support such a "ubiquitous conversational process", one must consider the social context where the learning process occurs. Accordingly we do not consider the learner's ability in an abstract way, but relate it to a specific situation (the context). In this ambit the term "ubiquitous" does not refer simply to "anytime / anywhere", but more generally to the ability to support multiple diverse learning contexts and automatically adapt to them.

As we consider human learning as a social process, collaboration implies community membership, it means working together, providing added value, sharing and executing tasks in order to reach a common goal. ELearning is no longer an isolated activity – it implies mutual trust, shared interests, common goals, commitments, obligations, exchanging of services, a genuinely proactive, motivated behaviour.

In order to support ubiquitous, collaborative, experiential and contextualised learning in dynamic virtual communities, a learning environment should provide the following features for learners:

- Collaboration; Socio-constructivist: group working should be routinely supported as well as the more traditional model of the solitary learner – this includes support for self-organising online communities who share common educational goals
- Experiential; Active Learning: learning resources should be interactive, engaging, and responsive – active learning and knowledge formation should be emphasised above simple information transfer;
- Ubiquity and accessibility;
- Wider, more flexible access to educational resources should be provided, often referred to as "anytime/anywhere" learning;
- Multiple different types of devices, interfaces, and network connection types should be supported where possible;
- Contextualised; Adaptive: appropriate learning contexts may be naturally be short-lived, as well as the more traditional static situations such as the classroom and the library – this calls for dynamicity in the creation of contexts.

The pedagogical goals outlined above have highly demanding technical requirements, many of which are also the concerns of distributed systems research. Group working implies shared interactive services and resources, necessitating both concurrency control and awareness of others activities. Active learning requires interactive resources (services) many of which will only be engaging if they are suitably responsive – a quality of service (QoS) issue that depends on many components of a distributed system – the low-level infrastructure (hardware, OS, network), the middleware and the interface software. Concurrency control and interactive responsiveness can make conflicting demands on a system. Real world input, such as live stock market prices, or remote sensing data, makes a network connection mandatory, and this again raises QoS issues such as fault detection, masking and tolerance for the learning environment.

Accessibility, as in "anytime/anywhere", requires availability, which may be supported through replication of resources, but this creates further tensions with responsiveness and concurrency control due to the need to maintain state across replicas. Accessibility also means adapting to available capabilities. For example: can the same learning environment be delivered through low-bandwidth mobile devices and high-bandwidth multimedia workstations? Accessibility also means supporting the special needs of an individual, such as disabilities.

More generally, the individual user should be recognised and catered for, and this personalisation requires semantic tagging and profiling that can be difficult to formulate, both conceptually and in terms of machine representation. Standards efforts have been particularly slow in addressing this problem.

Contextualisation requires a move from the traditional view of an online learning environment as a stable long-lived entity (e.g. during the lifetime of a teaching module) – to one where the environment may evolve and change much more frequently, perhaps even several times a day – a dynamicity that is alien to current eLearning products.

We believe that these technical requirements can best be addressed by building on the open distributed service model that has evolved exploiting Grid and Semantic technologies.

2. From e-Learning to m-Learning

Today, Internet and World Wide Web have enhanced learning activities providing a high degree of interactivity among geographically separated learners and teachers.

It is worth mentioning that Internet doesn't provide just another way to deliver learning contents, actually the potential is there to create learning environments that fit the needs of modern, diverse learners that are placed in the centre of the process by engaging them in purposeful activity, problem solving, collaborations, interactions and conversations.

The wide diffusion of Internet allows maintaining that e-learning is today the state of art for distance learning in Europe. As technology development never stops new emerging technologies are supposed to be applied in the future in order to provide new innovative learning approaches.

A phenomenon that could be observed in the past is the expectation of a learning revolution with the availability of a new technology. Based on our past experience the next generation of distance learning will be the mobile learning (mLearning) paradigm. Never in the history of technology in education a technology with the universal penetration of mobile telephony had been available. Additionally mobile phones are a technology that citizens have accepted and are using frequently.

We have to take into account that it is estimated that today there are more than 0.5 billion data-enabled mobile handsets in use worldwide. These mobile handsets will create the first 'always on' generation of technologically enabled citizens who will spend the majority of their time in close proximity to Web access and e-applications. The purpose of next generation learning systems is to harness current and new technologies to provide new methods of learning and training that are available to all who wish to be part of the 'always on' generation.

Looking ahead, it will be crucial to achieve the merging of e-learning and m-learning providing pioneering approaches that will support new learning models based on ubiquitous, collaborative, experiential and contextualised learning. It is here that Grid and Mobile technologies enter into the picture because they are supposed to provide the missing features to enable the new forms of learning.

The next generation Grid's [5] goal is to enable as well as to facilitate the transformation of Information into Knowledge, by humans as well as – progressively – by software agents, providing the electronic underpinning for a global society in business, government, research, science, education and entertainment (semantic aspects).

Mobile technology will add ubiquitous and pervasiveness to the Grid potential, and in this vision it will not be only a medium to access the Grid, but the mobile devices will be part of the Grid itself that, in this way, will evolve towards a nomadic system.

It is worth mentioning that the environment of nomadic computing is very different from that of traditional distributed systems. In such an environment there is a variety of mobile workstations, handheld devices, and smart phones, which nomadic users use to access services in the Internet.

3. An Akogrimo Overview

The Akogrimo project is driven by the basic idea that Next Generation Grids (NGG) should be integrated with Next Generation Networks [6] [7] [8]. An Akogrimo NGG must be able to address the needs of a volatile environment with fast changing context such as bandwidth, device capabilities, location, a variety of competing access network providers and global and local service providers.

Consequently Akogrimo assumes a pure IP-based underlying net infrastructure. As a result the Akogrimo architecture can be immediately deployed in Unlicensed Mobile Access (UMA) environments such as hot-spot infrastructures. In the mid term it is the assumption that along the convergence of networks Telecom sector eventually will come to a similar network technology. The basic concepts and terms required in addressing this challenging task are summarised in this document.

The major identified research challenges are identity and security management, cross organisational accounting, the handling of context and the interrelation of signalling as basic protocol element. Akogrimo does not consider the network as a pure transport mechanism for data or control messages but aims on one hand to avoid the duplication of functionality but more important to enable a cooperation between applications, grid and network middleware and the network.

The goal is to reach a platform combining the functionality of next generation networks, service and knowledge oriented services that are able to provide a general purpose added value services provisioning platform not limited to a certain area such as conversational services. We see a general purpose and open platform enabling dynamic and ad-hoc collaboration addressing beside audio and video communication at the same level also the provision of data, knowledge and computational services as the key element of success.

The Akogrimo platform aims to provide business opportunities for different stakeholders and enable the dynamic composition of complex services. So in summary the key differentiators of Akogrimo compared to existing Grid solutions are:

- Support for Dynamic Virtual Organisations (VO) that may be even built ad-hoc e.g. by including local service providers
- Enable adaptive and context aware applications reacting on the changing conditions of the VO members such as bandwidth, device capabilities or e.g. RFID based events
- Provide a smooth integration of multimedia communication with application services
- Prevent the duplication of functionality in the Grid middleware layer by leveraging the functionality anticipated in the next generation of networks such as Identity Management or Cross-Organisational accounting.

3.1. The Generic Akogrimo Architecture

Figure 1 shows the Akogrimo Architecture on a very high and conceptual level. The figures shows basically four areas which have been named in the initial phase of the project as formal "layers", but during the evolution of the architectural design such a strict layered approach was considered as inappropriate to describe the approach and has been kept as organisational "area".

The lowest "area", the network interfaces with all the other areas, but has most interaction with the network middleware providing network services like Authentication, Authorization, Accounting, Auditing and Charging (A4C), session control and network context in conjunction with the network. Basically promoted by the traditional "Grid" community, two additional areas, the Grid Middleware Services providing an infrastructure for a service provider as well as the application support area providing Virtual Organisation (VO) infrastructure services complete the overall conceptual architecture supporting the applications running "on the Akogrimo platform".

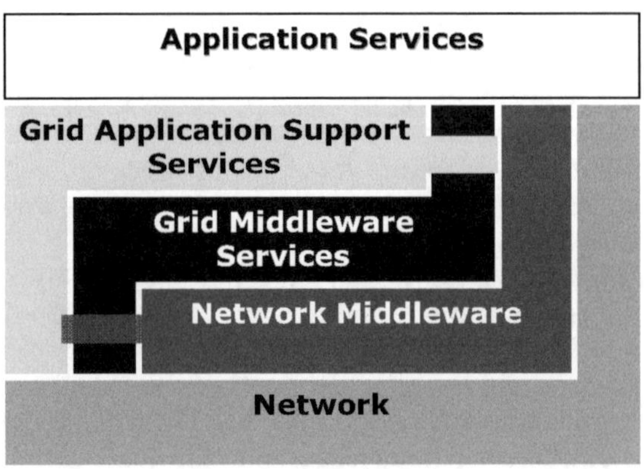

Figure 1. Akogrimo Conceptual Architecture

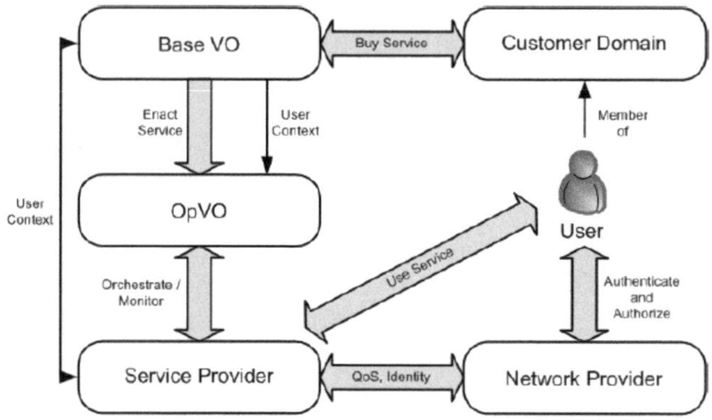

Figure 2. Akogrimo Building Blocks

Generally, in Akogrimo all services (including the traditional services offered on the network layer) are virtualised as a (web) service. And the role sharing is more function based rather than a protocol stack. A further major principle is the bi-directional exchange of all information between these "areas" such as identity, context, etc., which will be explained in more detail within this document.

Figure 2 shows the conceptual architecture and the main building blocks. Here the 5 key building blocks are the network provider, the service provider, the Operative VO (OpVO), the Base VO (BVO) and the Customer domain.

3.1.1. Base and Operative VO

In Akogrimo the term "Virtual Organization" (VO) is an organizational model describing the rules of interaction between companies not limited to IT resources. Virtual Organizations can provide services and thus participate as a single entity in the formation of further Virtual Organizations. This enables the creation of recursive structures with multiple layers of "virtual" value-added service providers.

The Base Virtual Organisation (BVO) is a central building block in the Akogrimo architecture and conceptually interacts with all the other building blocks introduced in Figure 2. The interactions with those building blocks are related to the role that the different participants can have inside the BVO. Three main roles have been identified: Network Provider (NP); Customer (C); Service Provider (SP). The following relationships are established between the BVO and the other building blocks:

- The BVO provides services to the customer domain. In detail, the user belonging to the customer domain is allowed to perform two main actions inside a BVO: searching for services and creating OpVO. Then the relation with the BVO will be oriented to manage this kind of interactions between the Customer domain and the BVO. In particular, the creation of an OpVO has relevant effects on the BVO domain due to its security implications (strong authentication, authorization, possible attacks,…)
- The SP will be allowed to publish his services inside the BVO and their use will be acquired by the customer through the BVO itself. In this case the relation with the BVO is oriented to manage the publishing phase.

- The OpVO building block is a component derived from the BVO. The BVO interacts with the OpVO creating it and configuring a dedicate subdomain for its execution.

The Operative Virtual Organisation (OpVO) is a building block that fulfils an important role at execution time when the application is actually delivered to the customer. The OpVO is the "run time environment" for Akogrimo applications. The OpVO is built from a subset of members of a BVO. Each BVO can create several, even overlapping, OpVOs. The OpVO can be seen as a particular instance of a VO. Similar to the BVO, the OpVO interacts with all the building blocks identified in Figure 2

3.1.2. Customer Domain

The customer is the entity that buys services from the Grid on behalf of a user and offers them to a user or consumes them herself (in that case the customer is also the user). That can be a hospital offering aggregated medical services to patients or a mobile user who wants to access a printer.

The Customer Domain is the Home Domain of the customer; if the customer is also a service user the terms Customer Domain and Home Domain (of the user) refer to the same domain. A trusted relationship between the Customer Domain and the BaseVO (BVO) Domain is needed as well as between the Customer Domain and the Home Domain of the user.

3.1.3. Service Provider

On the service provider domain are services that manage and supply resources and enforce policy and service level agreements. The tasks that are supported by the services located in the service provider domain include but are not limited to:

- **Execution management:** This task is decomposed into multiple tasks, all related to the execution of the services requested by the client, such as preparation, initiation and managing of the execution. These tasks are addressed by the Execution Management Service (EMS), a suite of services that appears as a single service from the client's perspective. The EMS covers these tasks and involves interactions with many other services located in the other domains.
- **Accounting and charging:** A service that supports the metering of the resources that are being consumed during the execution of a service is located in every machine that is hosting a service for sale. This service supports the accounting and charging process by sending aggregated information about the consumption of the resources.
- **Discovery**: The service provider can advertise its services and resources. This activity is supported by the EMS that is located in the specific service provider domain. The service provider can create advertisements about the services and/or resources that are for sale and register them to the index service of the EMS that serves as a SP-domain wide index service. The EMS performs discovery by querying its index service in order to find a service that satisfies the clients' criteria.

- **Identity**: All services located in the service provider domain are accompanied by a set of mechanisms for establishing identity and negotiating authentication.

3.1.4. Network Provider

On the Network provider domain there are all functions represented required to provide network services in a Grid-compliant manner. This makes this domain unique to Akogrimo as basic network functions – as currently provided in other architectures as well – are so far not described in a Grid/Web Services compliant way.

The available accounting and charging functionality in this domain is used to account and charge for Grid services in a similar and integrated way as done for the usage of network resources. This makes the network domain basically ready to commercially deploy grid services on their infrastructure in a way compliant to the current IETF approaches. This comprises an identity concept which is able to offer Single Sign On (SSO)-based services for Grid services and network services assuming the authorization and authentication of the device used by the user.

The Discovery of Services is a complex issue especially having the different bootstrap processes in mind and is considered within Akogrimo as one of the key research challenges. Finally, network management issues contribute to overall policy-based management concepts covering all "areas".

3.2. Key Akogrimo Concepts

In this section some, but not all, key concepts are introduced. A complete list is defined in [6], [7] [8] [10][12], [14]

3.2.1. Mobile Dynamic Virtual Organization

As described before a Virtual Organisation in Akogrimo is the dynamic collection of individuals and institutions which are required to share resources to achieve certain goals. Starting from this generic concept two derived concepts have been defined: the Base Virtual Organization and the Operative Virtual Organization.

3.2.2. Mobility Concepts

One of the main objectives of Akogrimo is to allow mobile users to not only use the Akogrimo net-work, but to allow the effective use of those users devices and resources as part of the whole Akogrimo network. Mobility presents several challenges; a breakdown of the types of mobility involved follows.

- **Terminal Mobility**, as the name implies, relates to the mobility of the device (or terminal) the user utilizes for accessing the network. Topology changes can occur when users move from one network access point to a new network access point. Without terminal mobility support, the change from one access point to the other will cause the terminal to lose its connection with the old access network, acquire a new connection in the new access network and a new IP address. In practice, this causes network connections to be stopped. They then have to be restarted, with a new IP address, which causes problems for most of the software that uses the network.

- **User Mobility** relates to the capability of the user to access personalised services independently of the terminal device and access network he or she is using. It is provided by a user-oriented security and authentication framework. The user has to perform his/her registration in the network – and in the Grid infrastructure – before using the network services. This registration process associates the user with the terminal.
- **Session Mobility** enables the transfer of application sessions between different devices without interruption. This is achieved with the SIP protocol. SIP can be used both by the user, and by the Grid infrastructure, to redirect communications (e.g. image display) to different devices, retaining the user association mentioned above.

3.2.3. Context Awareness

Context is any information that can be used to characterise the situation of an entity, primarily a user. Context awareness means that devices, applications and systems have information about the circum-stances under which users are operating and can adapt behaviour to be optimal for the current situation. In this way context-aware services will be an important enabler for pervasive and ubiquitous computing; allowing the user to solve his/her tasks while devices and technology fade away into the background.

The vision of Akogrimo involves context-aware mobile Grid services. Akogrimo focuses on context that describes the situation of a mobile user. While much prior Grid research has focused on batch-mode supercomputing applications, Akogrimo introduces the mobile Grid, where interactive services involving mobile and nomadic users are of key importance. The lives of humans are much more varied and dynamic than those of computational resources, so when humans are introduced as resources in the Grid, there is a need to keep track of their context. By knowing this context, the system may easier choose the right people to participate in a workflow, and better adapt service behaviour to the situation of those people.

The definition of context is open-ended; the set of data that should be monitored will depend on the application domain. Common scenarios in Akogrimo include eHealth, eLearning, and Crisis Management. For these scenarios we are interested in keeping track of user context in terms of:

- Presence: Is the user logged on? Is he idle or busy?
- Physical properties: User location, local time, body temperature etc.
- Environmental information: Temperature, humidity, weather.
- Device context: What terminals and other I/O units are available to the user and what are the hardware and software capabilities of those devices? What are the display capabilities (display resolution, screen size), and network capabilities (bandwidth, connection type).
- Local services: What services are found in the proximity of the user?

In Akogrimo context information for a user is mainly obtained via the device(s) he/she is using, but also by relating the user to local information for the place he/she is located at. A general framework for context handling is shown in Figure 3, where Context Manager (CM - part of the Akogrimo Network Middleware) is the central component. The following actions take place:

1. Applications subscribe to context information for a specific user. These applications are located in the Generic Application Services Layer or within Domain and Application Specific Services.
2. CM will request raw context data from context sources, which may be the users themselves, the user terminal, sensors, or location technologies.
3. CM will refine, filter and store current context for each user which has a pending subscription.
4. Updates are distributed to the requesting applications. Distribution may take place when the context for a person changes, or in appropriate intervals.

4. Presented Scenario: Field Trip

This scenario is based on the traditional field trip improved by appropriate use of information and communication technologies. It illustrates experiential, contextualised, collaborative and personalised learning for knowledge creation and sharing [6] [7] [8] [15].

Figure 4 illustrates the typical Grid perspective in combination with mobility: changing physical location of nodes, active building of VO and processing of context related information in distributed areas, as well as the need for timely high performance computing power. Akogrimo is the platform on top of which this scenario takes place, providing these capabilities through its infrastructure services described on section 3.

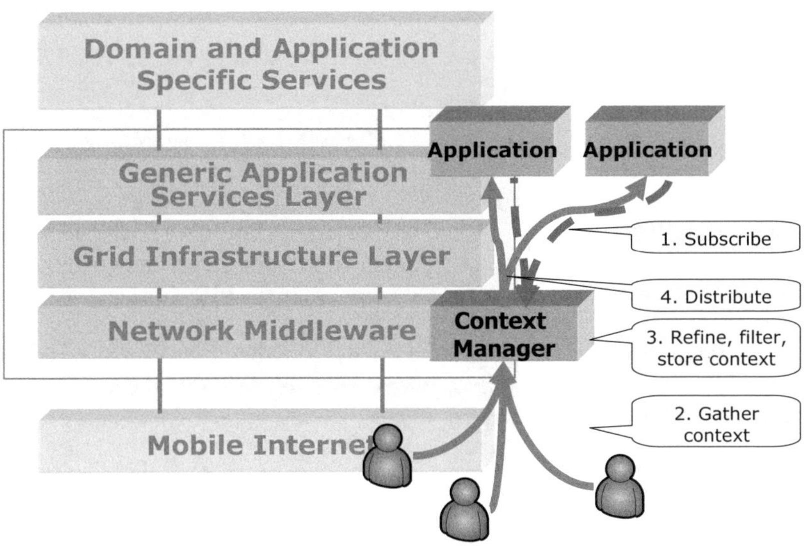

Figure 3. Context Management Concept [16]

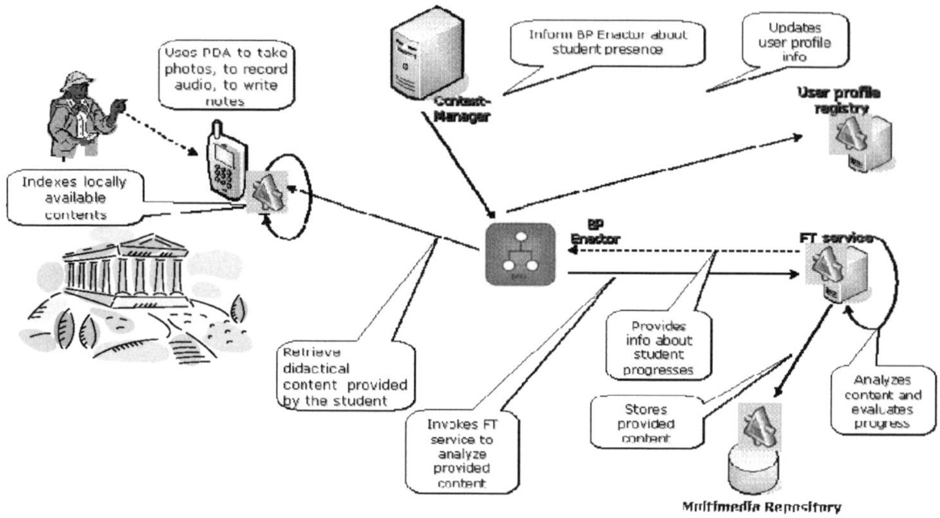

Figure 4. Presented Scenario

4.1. Description

There is a group of students, all equipped with a 4th generation PDA, which are working on a Field Trip project for their Archaeology spring exam. During their activity they store information, experience, emotion, in terms of photos, video clips, text notes, audio comments, etc. The PDA devices, using the user profile and context dependant information automatically indexed these contents using appropriate metadata. The PDA will negotiate with the network service provider operative in that zone which kind of network communication will be used according to the necessary bandwidth, the price, etc.

The information collected by all students is sent via the appropriate selected network to the Field Trip (FT) Grid service created by the teacher of the course for their project. The PDA will use user biometric data for secure access to the Grid based virtual learning organisation and for data ciphering. The FT Grid service, orchestrating speech to text Grid services (provided by Company A) and advanced semantic tool for text interpretation virtualised as Grid services (provided by Company B), will analyse the student's information comparing them with the learning objective foresees for the project experience and formalised in an ontology-based knowledge representation (concepts to be learned, goals to reach, relationships, etc.).

It summarises all data from the learning point of view in terms of progress and weaknesses to the teacher, and stores all the information in a multimedia repository Grid service. At the end of the day, the students working in the field trip meet for sharing their experiences and for consolidating the acquired knowledge. They will use the PDA speech recognition capability for sending commands to the search engine in order to retrieve some information and for its visualisation. During these sessions it is frequently necessary to consult digital libraries (provided by different organisations) in order to find new information or to check some hypothesis done and/or evaluations made about the origin of discovered objects.

During the daily work in the field trip some collaborative sessions with other students in the school are needed in order to share their experiences. To this purpose the students collect with their PDA photos of the field trip and the objects discovered and send them to the Virtual Collaboration Grid service, asking to build them in 3D. The VC Grid service invokes the high performance 3D modelling and rendering tools (provided by the High Performance Computing Centre of the University) virtualised as Grid services in order to make the 3D reconstructions and to render them.

The FT Grid service, using the context data and the information collected by each student, provides them the possibility to discuss with selected (by the teacher) experts on the field (historical period, zone, objects nature, etc.), in order to make more productive the experience. Moreover, using the semantic-based Grid service capability of searching and location, the FT Grid service will provide information about the availability of other groups in the same zone or in different zones, but with affinity with their work, and belonging to different Grid enabled virtual learning organisations to share their experience.

4.2. Field Trip Storybook [16]

Bob is a teacher of an archaeological course in the "**Ivy League Schools**". With the aim of supporting his students for their spring exam by using modern IT functionalities, Bob uses an "eLearning virtual environment" to start a "Greek civilization virtual course".

Bob, as course administrator, sets the "**Ivy League portal**" to be available for the "Greek Civilization Virtual Course". Consequently, Bob logs in the portal and asks for starting this course. Jane and Luisa attend Bob's course (Bob will use the portal to register his students) to enjoy it while traveling through Greek amphitheatres, museums and archaeological vestiges.

During their visit Jane and Luisa take and store photos, video clips and data by means of cameras and register themselves as "available" in their "Mobile Terminals".

All the gathered information will be indexed automatically using appropriate metadata standards (taking into account their user profile and the context information) and retrieved from the mobile device in order to be stored in a multimedia repository Grid service. This repository will allow sharing experiences among the students belonging to virtual learning organizations (also not directly related to FT course).

At the end of the day (while traveling back home, or whenever they prefer) the students working in the field trip course access to the e-Learning platform for consolidating the knowledge acquired. Using the data provided by Jane, Luisa and other student groups as well as using other sources (e.g. Web), Jane can visualize a 3D simulation by means of her laptop, since her PDA video is unable to visualize 3D data. Furthermore, she will consult digital libraries provided by different organizations in order to compare her experience with others. If necessary, teachers and/or experts on the field will be involved in discussions through video conference to provide a more detailed explanation on some specific topics.

The above storyboard identifies two different phases in the student's interactions with the FT course:

- The **content provision phase**: Jane and Luisa act as content providers enriching the eLearning repository with additional contents.

- The **knowledge acquisition phase**: Jane and Luisa use the eLearning platform to consolidate their learning experience.

In the **content provision phase,** the Akogrimo users (in this case the students) are able to provide contents (take photos and record short videos) via mobile devices, which interact with the "Indexing Metadata Service" to automatically index the content, using the appropriate metadata standards and considering user profiles and context information. In the **knowledge acquisition phase** the students interact with "**Ivy League portal**" that allows enjoying the FT course.

4.3. E-Learning scenario actors and administrative domains mapped on Akogrimo.

The following list reports e-Learning scenario actors and administrative domains mapped on Akogrimo.

- **Universities** will act in the Base Virtual Organization as Customer, so they can create Operative Virtual Organizations[2].
- **Universities** will host privately the on-line course (it is managed internally and it is not a matter of the Base Virtual Organization). Students and teachers of the university will be allowed to access this on-line course. The management of this access is done by the university. The on-line course will interact with the Operative Virtual Organization created by the university in the Base Virtual Organization.
- **Students**, acting as regular students, will be transparent with respect to the Base/Operative Virtual Organization. They will use the university on-line course.
- **Students** providing contents will be registered in the Base Virtual Organization with the role of Service Provider or they can be added afterwards in the Operative Virtual Organization by the Administrator or the Teacher. This is a crucial point because it implies that the service provider is unknown in the Base Virtual Organization.
- **Experts** will be registered in the Base Virtual Organization with the role of Service Providers.
- **Teachers** will not be registered in the Base Virtual Organization. They will be added in the Operative Virtual Organization by the University (instantiating a User Agent) and they will have the role of "teacher" in the Operative Virtual Organization.
- **Service Providers** will be subscribed to the Base Virtual Organization with the role of Service Provider. Each service provider will publish in the GrSDS his services (i.e. the services listed in the table).

It is worth mentioning that some of the listed services will not be published in the GrSDS:

---

[2] To create an Operative Virtual Organization means in this context to create the environment to provide the field trip course.

- The **Portal** is not a service provided in the Base Virtual Organization. It is an internal service of the University. It is hosted in the University private domain. The portal role is providing the on-line courses of the university.
- Core eLearning services: these services will be split between the University private domain and the Akogrimo infrastructure services hosted in the Base Virtual Organization domain.

4.4. Operative VO domain creation.

The Figure 5 and Figure 6 customize a general idea presented in [13] towards the eLearning storyboard.

In Figure 5 the University asks for the Field Trip Operative VO creation as shown by red arrow. This request is elaborated by Base VO services, which have to negotiate with the Service Providers the QoS for service instances (green arrows: as example here just two service providers are shown).

Negotiated service instances become members of the Operative VO and Service Agent and User Agent instances are created. In the figure just the Service Agents of the repository service and of the content provider on the student's mobile device are shown. Finally the University will create several User Agents depending on the number of the students that will attend the course. A User Agent associated to the teacher will be instantiated as well.

The Figure 6 explains how a student (or teacher), from the Customer domain, accesses to the on line course (e.g. on the university portal).

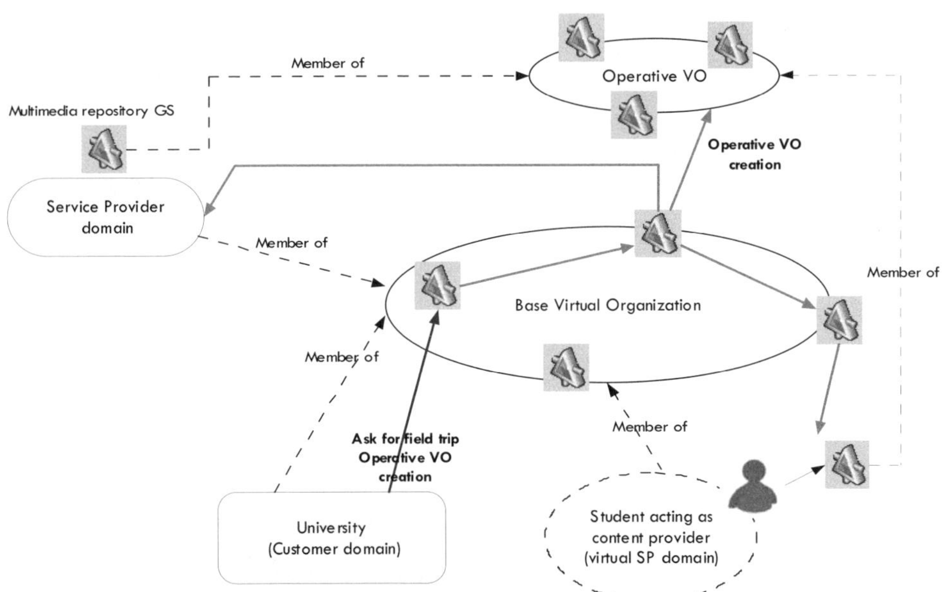

Figure 5 Operative VO domain creation

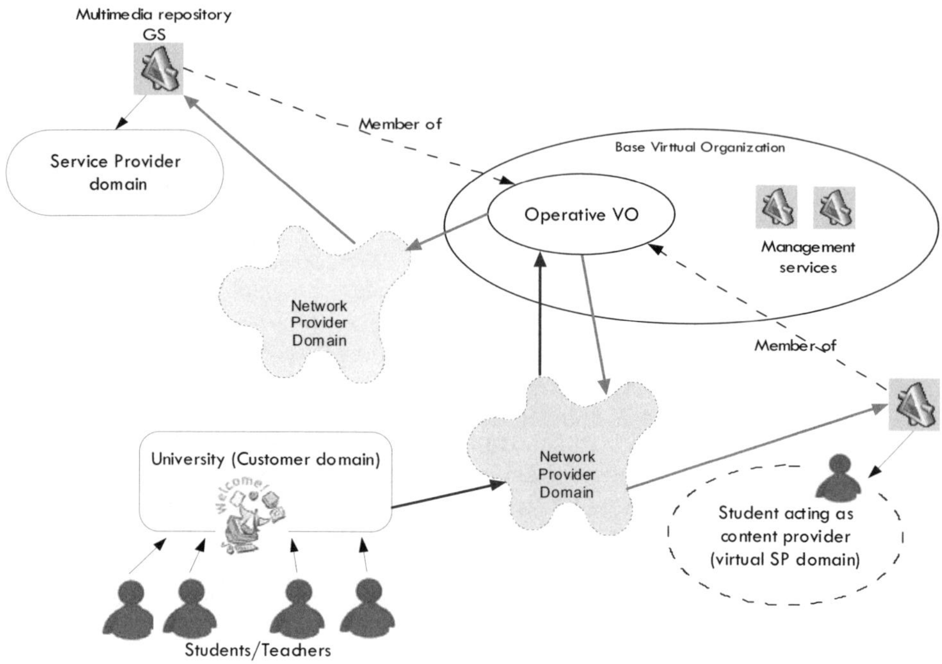

Figure 6 A student/ teacher accesses to the on-line course

Through the portal the student/teachers use the Operative VO functionalities as shown by red arrows. The Operative VO invokes services belonging to the Service Provider domains, as shown by green arrows, to orchestrate service capabilities and deliver the final service to the end user. The access to services in the Operative VO and in Service Provider domains is realized via Network Provider domains.

5. Conclusions

It has been estimated that the learning, education, and training industry is over USD 1 trillion per annum worldwide. Much effort is being spent on information technology and its integration within the learning environment. Institutional entities are spending much effort on multi-cultural learning resources and environments.

The learner includes home users, nomadic users, institutional users, children and adult users. The variety of learning environments includes standalone, classroom, networked, internet-based, nomadic, federated (groups of resources), distance, collaborative, asynchronous, synchronous, and so on. With all these environments and international participants the emerging of a new generation mobile Grid for distance learning will raise the interest of at least four different target groups and potential users:

- The telecommunications industry;
- The e-Learning industry;

- Stakeholders and decision makers in vocational and education training (VET);
- Trainers, students and training organizations.

The next generation of learning is of vital importance to stakeholders and decision makers in VET. The attractiveness of this learning vision is the capability of harnessing and sharing the almost universal availability of mobile devices to education and training. This widespread availability can be harnessed and exploited to provide access to training opportunities for those who otherwise might be at a disadvantage for geographic (wireless networks span the rural-urban divide), economic (mobile handsets are relatively inexpensive) or social reasons, but mainly to take in place innovative contextualised learning approach, where the learner "achieves" knowledge and skills in an active way instead of simply storing information. The realism will be the cornerstone of such a learning environment.

The needs, for the target groups identified above, are to be prepared for the next generation of learning and training. The development of a mobile grid infrastructure for the provision of nomadic learning will meet this need opening new scenarios for both the telecommunication industry and the developing e-learning.

The Akogrimo project addresses this need delivering a framework for the provision of IT Value Added Services, offering a reference architecture for Mobile Grids reflecting the needs of a challenging scenario such as the new mLearning paradigm. It offers network and services operators an environment to provide services in an integrated world based on Grid and Mobile communications concepts. The Akogrimo platform presents a set of components that realises the major building blocks needed to build a Grid infrastructure designed for fixed, nomadic and mobile Learning Organizations in line with the 'everywhere at every time in any context' paradigm.

References

[1] Akogrimo Project http://www.mobilegrids.org.

[2] ELeGI, European Learning Grid Infrastructure http://www.elegi.org/.

[3] MOBIlearn project http://www.mobilearn.org.

[4] m-learning project http://www.m-learning.org/.

[5] Roman Tirler (Editor), Next Generation Grid(s) – European Grid Research 2005-2010, Expert Group Report, 16 June 2003.

[6] Stefan Wesner, Towards an Architecture for the Mobile Grid, it-Information Technology, vol. 47, issue 6/2005

[7] Jürgen M. Jähnert, Stefan Wesner and Víctor A. Villagrá (Editors), The Akogrimo Mobile Grid Reference Architecture, http://www.mobilegrids.org.

[8] Jürgen M. Jähnert, Stefan Wesner, Antonio Cuevas, Víctor A. Villagrá and Vicente Olmeda, "The Akogrimo Service Provisioning Platform" in proceedings of ASWN 2007

[9] Giuseppe Laria, eLearning scenario whitepaper – "Mobile and nomadic user in e-learning: the Akogrimo case" http://www.mobilegrids.org.

[10] Akogrimo Project – D2.2.4 "Report on the State of the Art" http://www.mobilegrids.org.

[11] Akogrimo Project – D2.3.1 "Testbed Description" http://www.mobilegrids.org.

[12] Akogrimo Project – D2.3.2 "Validation Scenario" http://www.mobilegrids.org.

[13] Akogrimo Project – ID443 "Updated Grid infrastructure layer Architecture" http://www.mobilegrids.org.

[14] Akogrimo Project – D4.2.1 "Overall Network Middleware Requirements Report" http://www.mobilegrids.org.

[15] Akogrimo Project – D4.4.2 "Final Integrated Services Design and Implementation Report" http://www.akogrimo.org.

[16] P.-O. Osland, B. Viken, F- Solsvik, G. Nygreen, "Enabling context-aware applications" in proceedings of the 15th IEEE In. Workshops on Enabling Technologies.

[17] Akogrimo Project – ID5.2.1 "Testbed definition" http://www.akogrimo.org.

The Learning Grid Handbook
S. Salerno et al. (Eds.)
IOS Press, 2008

L4*All*, a Web-Service Based System for Lifelong Learners

Sara de FREITAS [a], Ian HARRISON [a], George MAGOULAS [a], George PAPAMARKOS [a], Alexandra POULOVASSILIS [a,1], Nicolas VAN LABEKE [a], Adrian MEE [b] and Martin OLIVER [b]

[a] *London Knowledge Lab, Birkbeck, University of London, UK*

[b] *London Knowledge Lab, Institute of Education, University of London, UK*

Abstract. L4*All* is a system that records and shares learning trails through educational offerings with the aim of facilitating progression of lifelong learners from Secondary Education, through to Further Education and on to Higher Education (HE). The focus is on helping those post-16 learners who have traditionally not participated in HE. L4*All* allows learners to access information and resources registered with the system by their providers, to plan their own learning, and to maintain a record of their learning. Tutors are able to register recommended learning pathways through courses and modules, thereby encouraging progression into HE. The system allows learners to share their learning plans and experiences with other learners (if they wish) in order to encourage collaborative formulation of future learning goals and aspirations.

Keywords. Lifelong Learning, Web Services.

Introduction

The **L4*All*** "LifeLong Learning in London for All" project[2] was funded under the JISC Distributed e-Learning Programme[3] and focussed on supporting the lifelong learner, particularly those 16+ learners who traditionally have not participated in higher education.

We believe, on the basis of research into life course choices, that there are two closely related issues that contribute to this non-participation: firstly, a lack of information about education opportunities, and secondly a perception that such options are 'not for me', leading to self-exclusion from such opportunities. The situation appears to be particularly acute for those who identify themselves as being from ethnic minorities or as having an impairment that may affect their participation.

L4*All* aimed to provide lifelong learners in the London region with access to information and resources facilitating their progression from Secondary Education, through to Further Education (FE) and on into Higher Education (HE). To achieve its aims, the L4*All* project brought together a diverse group of people from different disciplines and a range of institutions all of whom are committed to providing learning

---

[1] Corresponding Autor: London Knowledge Lab, Birkbeck, University of London, 23-29 Emerald Street, London WC1N 3QS, United Kingdom; E-mail: ap@dcs.bbk.ac.uk

[2] http://www.lkl.ac.uk/research/l4all/

[3] http://www.jisc.ac.uk/programme_edistributed.html

opportunities which enhance career development and widen participation across the London region. The L4*All* project was informed by other recent projects undertaken by researchers from Birkbeck and the Institute of Education at the London Knowledge Lab, including the EU SeLeNe project (Keenoy *et al.* 2005) and the EU Kaleidoscope project (Keenoy *et al.* 2004a, 2004b) as well as research reported in (Papanikolaou *et al.* 2003, Peterson and Levene, 2003, Magoulas *et al.* 2005).

The L4*All* pilot system allows learners to record their past learning, and more generally life, experiences as well as their planned future learning experiences along their "timeline", which is managed by the system. As an aid to constructing their timeline, learners are able to search through learning opportunities registered with the system by their providers. Learners are able to access the timelines of other learners (if these have been made public by their owners) and also to access recommended learning pathways through courses and modules, as provided by tutors. This gives learners a repertoire of learning possibilities that they may not have otherwise considered, allowing sharing of successful learning pathways and presenting successful learners as role models to inspire confidence and a sense of opportunity amongst those previously excluded.

The follow-on project **MyPlan**[4] **"**Personal Planning for Learning Throughout Life" is aiming to increase the value of the L4*All* pilot by researching, developing, deploying and evaluating user models for lifelong learners, and personalised functionalities for creation and search of timelines and recommended learning pathways. The following sections of the paper address the aims and objectives of the L4*All* and MyPlan projects to date, methodology, development approach and technologies used, results, outcomes and finally conclusions and directions of future work.

1. Aims and Objectives

The L4*All* project had as its aim the development of a pilot system that provides an environment for the lifelong learner to access quality-assured learning materials, personal development plans, recommended learning pathways, personalised support for planning of learning, and reflecting on learning.

The system aims to offer: (i) interaction with a Web Portal that provides information on work-based, FE and HE courses and modules available to learners in the London region; (ii) personalised support in planning and reflecting on personal development and lifelong learning activities; (iii) advice on learning and personal development; (iv) support in designing and maintaining personal learning and development plans; (v) support for learners to share information and collaborate with peers and tutors. The following objectives were identified at the outset of the L4*All* project in order to achieve these aims:

- Definition of User Requirements, Usage Scenarios and Technical Requirements;
- Metadata Generation and Provision;
- Development of the Pilot;

[4] http://www.lkl.ac.uk/research/myplan/

- Employment of a User-centred Evaluation Process that uses usability inspection methods, including user testing and heuristic evaluation, to improve the system so that the needs of learners and providers can be met.

The follow-on MyPlan system includes the following additional objectives:

- Development of User Models and a User Modelling Ontology for planning of lifelong learning;
- Specification, development, deployment and evaluation of personalised functionalities for planning of lifelong learning.

2. Methodology

The L4*All* project was structured around a number of work packages. First, the User and Technical Requirements were produced, in early 2005. For the former, we first considered previous models of learner choices in career and education. These previous models were rational and economic choice based and therefore a poor match with the target learner community.

We therefore proposed an alternative model based upon learning *trails* (Bush, 1945; Peterson and Levene, 2003). In our context, a "trail" is a sequence of learning opportunities, experienced over time by a learner. We believed at the outset of the L4*All* project that a timeline-based representation of learners' work, learning and other life experiences could provide a holistic approach to learners' life experiences and continuity between their learning episodes and work experiences.

We conducted a series of user studies which aimed to define the users' needs and requirements of the L4*All* system, including the main functionality required, how this functionality should be provided to the user, information to be solicited from users, the information to be returned by the system, and the interaction between different components of the system.

Usage scenarios for the L4*All* system were formulated by consultations with relevant stakeholders, including widening participation officers of the institutions and colleges of the consortium, groups of learners, tutors, student liaison committee members, and content providers. Among the main aims of this consultation process was to identify learners' individual educational goals and objectives, articulate expectations for the learner's performance in general education activities, and accommodate different user needs and individual differences. The outputs of these sessions provided the basis of the user requirements and specification of the system.

The L4*All* project was funded by the JISC Distributed e-Learning Programme[5], which mandated that (i) systems developed under the programme should use, as much as possible, existing e-tools and services provided by other JISC-funded projects, and (ii) systems should be compliant with the JISC E-Learning Framework and service-oriented architecture[6].

In our case, the detailed Technical Requirements were elicited by: (i) undertaking a study of candidate portal technologies and a critical evaluation of them that identified

---

[5] http://www.jisc.ac.uk/programme_edistributed.html

[6] http://www.jisc.ac.uk/index.cfm?name=elearning_framework

uPortal[7] as the most appropriate choice; (ii) undertaking a study of existing e-tools and services provided by other JISC-funded projects that could provide relevant functionality to L4*All*; (iii) specifying a system architecture that used a selection of these tools as well as uPortal, Apache Tomcat and Apache AXIS SOAP; (iv) undertaking a study of e-learning metadata standards relevant to the L4*All* application domain that identified *IMS Metadata*[8], *IMS-LIP*[9] and *eduPerson*[10] as the most appropriate standards to be used as the basis for describing the L4*All* learning resources (IMS Metadata) and the L4*All* users (IMS-LIP and eduPerson); and (v) identifying RDF and the Jena framework[11] as providing a flexible, portable solution for storing the L4*All* metadata.

The Development of the Pilot, and the Metadata Provision and Generation phases followed the specification of the User and Technical requirements. A number of extensions to the standard metadata schemas were first designed in order to fully support the L4*All* functionality, namely metadata describing learners' timelines and additional metadata for the login details, contact details and learning preferences of users.

The pilot system was developed in two phases, resulting in two versions during the lifetime of the L4*All* project. This was in order to allow an early first phase of evaluation that would allow the user requirements and usage scenarios to be validated by a range of user stakeholders. This would demonstrate the benefits of a large subset of the envisaged functionality of the pilot, detect non-compliant situations and identify possibilities for improvement. The outcomes of this first evaluation phase served as input into the development of the second, functionally complete, version of the pilot. The outcomes of the second evaluation phase were then used to make further minor adjustments to the system and also led into the follow-on MyPlan project.

The first version was produced in July 2005 and incorporated the user requirements identified earlier relating to search over courses (provided by the DELTA service[12]), creation and management of learners' timelines, searching on timelines, and user profile creation and management. Further improvements were made to this first version in parallel with the first evaluation phase during July – September 2005, relating mainly to timeline management. The second version of the pilot incorporated also a visual front-end and an automatic course sequencing service, using the ISIS sequencing engine[13], and was completed in February 2006.

The Metadata Provision and Generation work package took as input the L4*All* metadata specification produced earlier. Staff with responsibility for managing the information required for the L4*All* metadata fields were identified within the participating institutions, and they provided the necessary metadata for loading into the pilot's metadata repository via a simple loading tool.

As mentioned earlier, the Evaluation work package was organised in two phases. The first phase involved consultation with student representatives, tutors, widening

---

[7] www.uportal.org

[8] http://www.imsglobal.org/metadata/

[9] http://www.imsglobal.org/profiles/

[10] http://www.educause.edu/eduperson/

[11] http://jena.sourceforge.org

[12] http://www.essex.ac.uk/chimera/delta/index.html

[13] http://www.hull.ac.uk/esig/isis.html

participation officers and content providers, and conventional Human-Computer Interaction methods were adopted.

The second phase adopted heuristic evaluation methods focusing upon usability issues, as defined by Nielsen (2006) and Nielsen and Loranger (2006). This second evaluation round took the form of remote usage of the system in conjunction with an online survey, face-to-face interviews with learners, and discussions held using the Blackboard virtual learning environment.

The evaluation centred upon three main user groups: FE learners from Community College Hackney (6 users), professional learners on the Certificate/Diploma in IT Applications at Birkbeck (16 users), and Teacher Education learners from the Institute of Education (12 users). The evaluation activities were designed to inform both design parameters (are these the right tools to develop?) and usability issues and concerns, including accessibility (can learners use these tools?). The feedback from this second phase was used as the basis for undertaking further minor improvements to the pilot, and also led into the follow-on MyPlan project.

On the basis of the original user requirements from the L4*All* project, from its evaluation, and from other lifelong learning applications, we have now conducted initial work within the MyPlan project to produce a first version of user models, covering user preferences and characteristics in planning their lifelong learning, and a first version of a user modelling ontology.

We have also produced a specification of the personalised functionalities for planning of lifelong learning, which are currently under development within a new "personalisation engine". The personalisation engine is providing personalised search of timelines from "people like me", personalised recommendation of which course(s) to study next; and customisation of the delivery and presentation of content. Its development is currently reaching completion and it is under internal testing before being transferred to the server that will be used for the online evaluation and user testing towards the end of 2007/early 2008.

The personalisation engine incorporates a set of similarity measures for comparing learners' timelines, based on converting timelines into strings of comparable tokens and using string metrics for ranking them. For the recommendation functionality, we are planning that tutors' recommended learning pathways entered into the system will be encoded similarly and will be compared with learners' timelines to propose matches. Several customisation features have also been developed to date (colour/shapes used in the timeline visualisation, bookmarks for interesting timelines, etc.).

The MyPlan project has also redesigned the original Flash-based user interface of the L4*All* pilot system using DHTML and javascript-powered widgets to deploy users' timelines. This decision is allowing us to improve the possibilities of learners' interaction with their timeline (such as maintenance of their own timeline and also comparison between their timeline and someone else's) and therefore to better support personalisation of timeline-based functionalities.

3. Development approach and technologies

The L4*All* system consists of a set of components and services. The architecture comprises two parts: (a) the backend and (b) the user interface. In the current version of the system, the user interface is a Web portal deploying several DHTML pages that interact with the backend and present to the user the L4*All* functionality relating to the

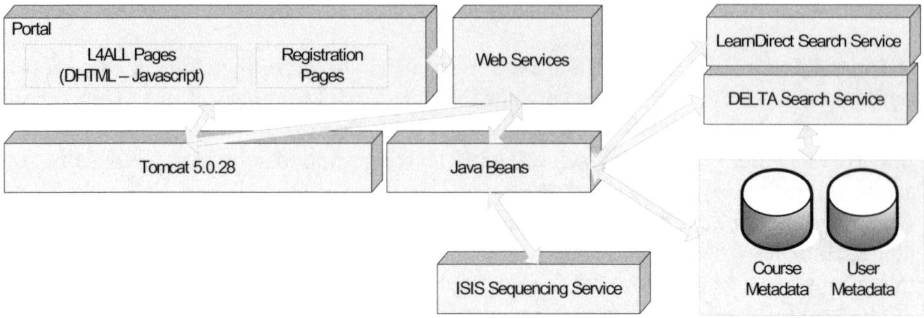

Figure 1. L4*All* system components

creation of personal timelines, searching the available courses metadata, searching for other users and other timelines, and obtaining recommendations regarding future learning. The backend connects with the underlying RDF repositories for storing, retrieving and modifying metadata describing users, courses and timelines. It also integrates three external services: DELTA, ISIS (see Section 2) and a service for search and retrieving information about courses in the LearnDirect database[14].

Figure 1 illustrates the overall architecture and its major components. The Web Services component consists of a set of web services which we have developed in order to wrap the backend functionality into a set of services that can be called by the user interface. These web services are implemented as Java servlets over Apache Tomcat. They accept GET and POST requests from the user interface components and dispatch them to the appropriate Java Bean for processing. The results of processing are passed from the Java Beans back to the called service where they are formatted into XML and passed back to the calling user interface component. The Java Beans are a set of Java classes providing the core backend functionality. This is where the three external services are integrated with the system and where communication with the metadata repositories is handled, including all actions relating to storing, retrieving and modifying the course and user metadata.

4. Results to Date

The L4*All* pilot has achieved almost all of the user requirements identified in the early part of the L4*All* project, successfully integrating a set of external services, tools and resources exhibiting high heterogeneity. The user interface provides screens for: user registration and login; a home page providing links to the main L4*All* functionality; a screen for entering personal details relating to past and present occupation, skills, qualifications, interests, future learning goals and preferred study type (full-time or part-time); screens for creating personal timelines incorporating past and future episodes of learning and work; and screens for searching over courses, timelines and other users based on a variety of search criteria.

[14] http://www.learndirect.co.uk/

Figure 2. The main interface of the L4All web portal.

Figure 2 shows the main screen for the creation and visualisation of timelines, the central access point of the portal. In the top right-hand box appears a brief description of the user's details. On the left-hand side of the screen is where the various functionalities of L4*All* are available: modifying the user's profile and preferences, searching for courses, people or timelines, exploring learning pathway recommendations, etc. In the middle of the screen, the user timeline is accessible through a dynamic multi-stripe. On top of it, a popup menu ("Add Episodes") provides a rich set of predefined episodes (e.g. courses, university, work, travel, marriage) that can be chosen to be placed within the user's timeline. The user can choose from this set of episodes, create a new custom episode, or include courses resulting from his/her searches.

The visualisation of the timeline is currently provided by a DHTML widget (the SIMILE timeline[15]) which displays time-based events in a scalable and scrollable fashion. Each event in the timeline is materialised by a rectangular shape spreading from the start date to the end date of the event. Clicking on an event displays popup balloon dialog which presents a short summary of the event (see Figure 2). By clicking on the edit button in that balloon, the user accesses a new dialog box (see Figure 4) for the user to modify the details of the episode. Saving the episode in the timeline initiates (transparently to the user) a synchronisation of the visual front-end with the databases at the backend.

15 http://simile.mit.edu/timeline/

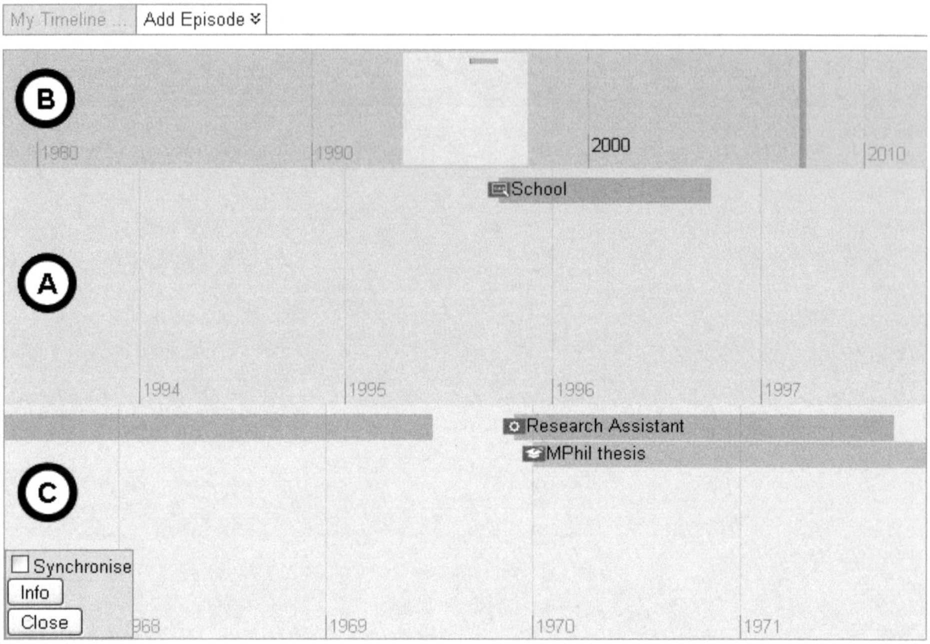

Figure 3. Synchronised visualisation of two timelines, the current user's one (top and middle) and that of a second user (bottom).

The middle stripe (labelled A in Figure 3) is the user's timeline, presenting episodes that have been added over the user's repeated usage of L4*All*. The top stripe (labelled B) is a reduced version of the main stripe, with a different time scale (usually a decade), allowing an overview of the whole timeline and a quicker scroll-across time. Both timelines can be dragged forward and backward in time and remain synchronised (the time frame visible in the user main timeline is indicated in the summary by a lighter zone).

The bottom stripe (labelled C) is an optional timeline that is activated on demand by the user, usually by searching for other people in the L4*All* system and displaying their timelines. This timeline only displays episodes that have been made public by the owner. Both timelines (the user's and the friend's) can be synchronised by date (scrolling the user's timeline will modify the friend's accordingly) or allowed to be independent, hence allowing the user to explore the friend's timeline and extract information, inspiration or examples of learning activities to plan.

The user can search for courses by clicking on the SEARCH COURSES link in Figure 2. A search dialog pops up that allows the user to specify the search parameters, ranging from a general keyword, to the distance the user is willing to travel in order to attend a course, the postcode of the course, the level of the course, the institution providing it, the subject covered and the type of the course (full-time or part-time). The search mode can be chosen so as to set matching to all of the specified criteria (AND) or any of the specified criteria (OR). The search results appear in a pop-up window, from where they can be explored in detail and added to the timeline.

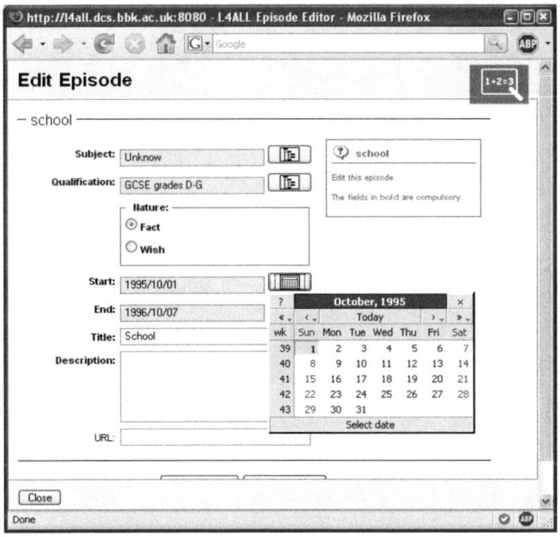

Figure 4. Editing an episode of the timeline.

Clicking on SEARCH TIMELINES in Figure 2 opens a new window for searching for timelines by providing a keyword or the title of an episode within a timeline. The results are presented in a list, from which a timeline can be selected to be viewed in more detail. Clicking on SEARCH PEOPLE in Figure 2 again opens a window for search for users via a set of search criteria including skills, qualifications, interests, age and occupation.

More interestingly, clicking on SEARCH SIMILAR TIMELINES allows users to perform a personalised search in the L4*All* system by looking for 'people like me'. The definition of 'people like me' being a highly subjective concept, users are presented with an interface for specifying their own criteria (see Figure 6).

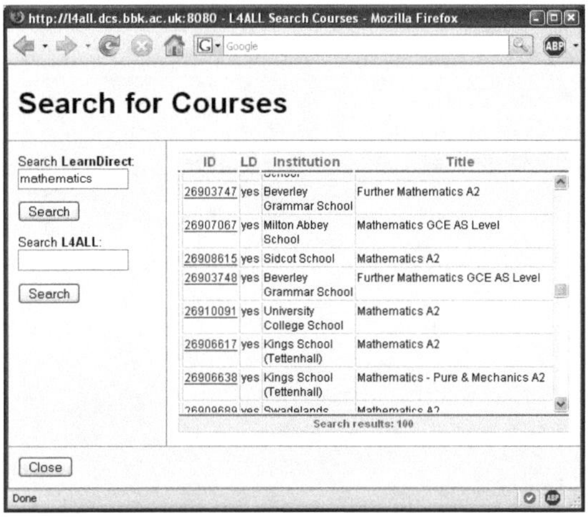

Figure 5. Searching for courses in L4*All*.

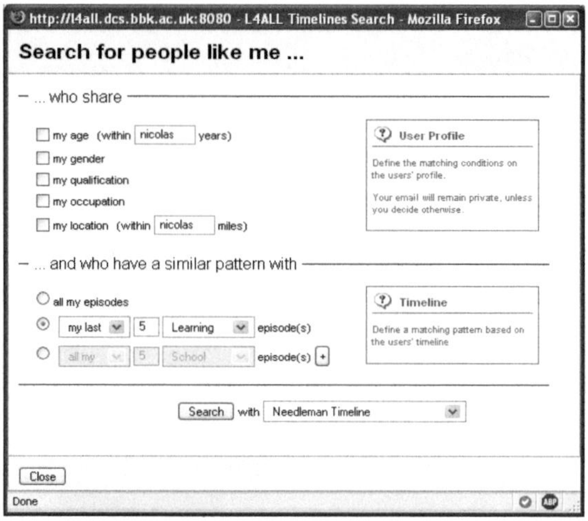

Figure 6. Searching for similar timelines.

By specifying matching criteria on their user profile (e.g. age within a certain range, gender, current occupation, etc.) and matching patterns on their timelines (e.g. considering all episodes, considering only educational or professional episodes, considering only the last 5 professional episodes, etc.), users can define a personalised search space that is matched against all the timelines and users stored in the system. The results, ranked according to their relevance by using string-based similarity measure techniques, are presented to the user, who has the possibility to display appropriate timelines in the main visualisation screen and explore them.

Finally, Figure 7 illustrates the screen for entering or modifying the user's profile and learning preferences while Figure 8 illustrates the screen for customising the display of a user's timeline.

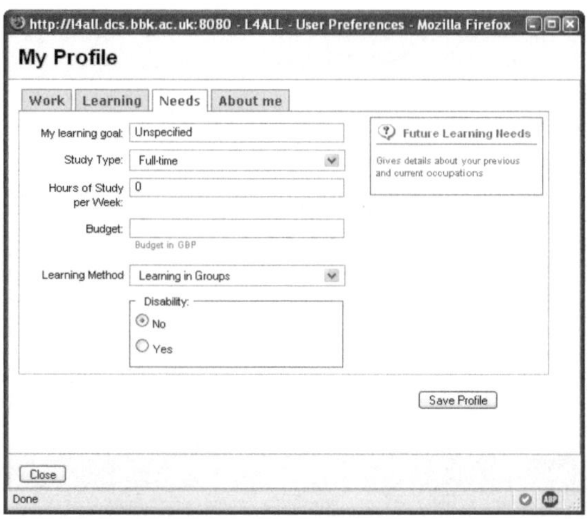

Figure 7. Editing the user's profile.

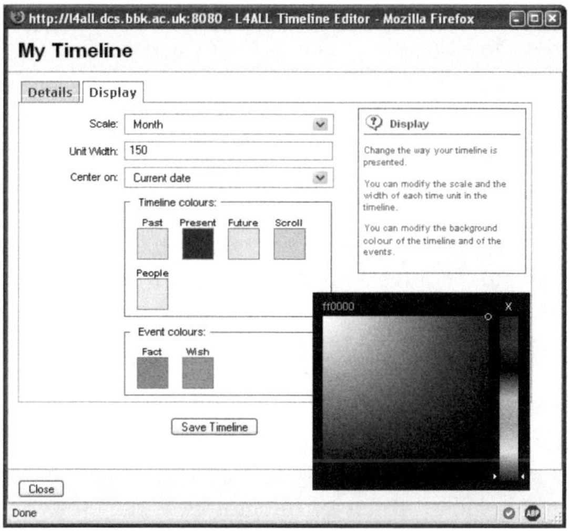

Figure 8. Customisation of the timeline visualisation

5. Outcomes and Conclusions

The second evaluation phase (of version 2 of the L4*All* system) centred upon usage of the functionality provided by the system. Users were invited to complete a range of tasks and after completing these tasks to reflect upon these activities in an online survey structured around (i) aesthetics, navigation and general user experience, (ii) timeline creation, (iii) search and expectations, and (iv) quality of user support. The main finding of the second evaluation phase has been the overall endorsement of the L4*All* pilot. There was agreement across all user groups of the potential of the approach to support otherwise excluded learners. Particularly positive was the response of FE learners suggesting that this might be a group that will benefit particularly from L4*All*. The evaluation study was also useful in identifying areas of further technical refinement and development that are required in the future e.g. differentiating the needs of different learner groups and developing strategies for differentiated interaction with the system; extension with e-portfolio and online journal capabilities; and extension with a 'live chat' facility. Another interesting observation was the way in which visualisation of learning and work choices prompted users to rethink their own identity as a learner and potential employee.

A key conclusion of the project centres upon the methodology adopted, including the use of the *trails* concept and the adoption of a user-centred approach to development. The provision of a system based specifically upon usage scenarios has proved popular with its intended users. The methodology enables a significant input into the development of the system from major stakeholders throughout the lifetime of the project (learners, instructors, institutional representatives and others).

To our knowledge, the holistic approach to life and learning experiences provided by L4*All* is novel and unique. The services-oriented approach has allowed several existing services to be incorporated into the system's functionality to date, with the possibility of further extensions in the future, for example with e-portfolio and social networking services, and this is part of ongoing research within the follow-on MyPlan project. This is the chief advantage of a services-oriented as opposed to a monolithic development approach, namely the possibility of reuse, aggregation and extension of existing services within the broader sphere of lifelong-learning support.

The potential educational significance of the system is a long-term one, involving the identification and sharing of successful educational experiences and the impact of this on learner choice. Such impact can only be studied longitudinally, and our evaluative studies will continue in the coming years in the context of the HEFCE-funded Linking London Lifelong Learning Network (L4N) led by Birkbeck, in order to provide more longitudinal findings as to the impact of the system upon career choices and education decisions. Our objectives for the next phases of the ongoing MyPlan project include:

- validating the design of the first version of the personalisation engine through its evaluation with small groups of lifelong learners selected via partner institutions in the L4N;
- investigating the possibilities of integrating a game-based tutorial for lifelong learners with the system.

The L4N has created new drivers for change to accommodate the needs of learners moving between various groups and institutions. A MyPlan project workshop took place in May 2007 and brought together several key stakeholders in lifelong learning. The workshop identified, in confirmation of previous outputs of the L4*All* user evaluation, the need for supporting user engagement and participation in lifelong learning, and stressed the importance of facilitating collaboration among lifelong learners for community building. So lifelong learners require support not only at the level of the individual user but also at the level of a group or team, and of the community. The results of deploying the system within the L4N and of its evaluation with different groups of users will in the longer term be able to inform the formulation of policies for engaging the interest of lifelong learners.

References

[1] Bush, V. (1945). As we may think. Atlantic Monthly, 176, 101-108.

[2] Keenoy, K., Levene, M., de Freitas, S., Montandon, L., Pernin, J-P., Eyssautier, C., Jones, A., Brasher, A. and Waycott, J. (2004a). Personalised trails and learner profiling in an e-learning environment. EU Kaleidoscope Trails Deliverable 22.4.1. See: http://www-kaleidoscope.imag.fr/pub/trails/ .

[3] Keenoy, K., Levene, M., de Freitas, S., Montandon, L., Emans, B., Schoonenboom, J., Pernin, J-P., Eyssautier, C., Jones, A., Brasher, A., Waycott, J., Turcsanyi-Szabo, M. and Bodnar, E. (2004b). Collaborative trails and group profiling within an e-learning environment. EU Kaleidoscope Trails Deliverable 22.4.2. See: http://www-kaleidoscope.imag.fr/pub/trails/

[4] Keenoy , K., Poulovassilis A., Christophides V., Rigaux P., Papamarkos G., Magkanaraki A., Stratakis M., Spyratos N., Wood P., (2005). Adaptive Personalisation in Self e-Learning Networks, 1st International Workshop on Distributed e-Learning Environments (held in conjunction with the 1st International ELeGI Conference on Advanced Technology for Enhanced Learning), Naples, March 14, 2005.

[5] Magoulas G.D. and Dimakopoulos D.N. (2005) Designing Personalised Information Access to Structured Information Spaces, Proceedings of the Workshop on New Technologies for Personalized

Information Access, 10th International conference on User Modeling, July 24-29, 2005, Edinburgh, Scotland, UK, 64-73.

[6] Nielsen, J. (2006) .Ten usability points. Last accessed10th March 2006 online at: http://www.useit.com/.

[7] Nielsen, J and Loranger , H. (2006) Prioritizing Web Usability. New Riders Press, Berkeley.

[8] Papanikolaou, K., Grigoriadou, M., Kornilakis, H., and Magoulas, G.D., (2003). Personalising the Interaction in a Web-based Educational Hypermedia System: the case of INSPIRE, User-Modeling and User-Adapted Interaction, vol. 13, 213-267.

[9] Peterson, D. and Levene, M. (2003). Trail records and navigational learning. London Review of Education, 1, 207-216.

The Learning Grid Handbook
S. Salerno et al. (Eds.)
IOS Press, 2008

Personalisation Services for Self e-Learning Networks

Kevin KEENOY [a, 1], Vassilis CHRISTOPHIDES [b], George PAPAMARKOS [a], Alexandra POULOVASSILIS [a], Dimitris KOTZINOS[b], Philippe RIGAUX [c], Nicolas SPYRATOS [c], and Peter WOOD [a]

[a] *School of Computer Science and Information Systems, Birkbeck, University of London*
[b] *Institute of Computer Science, Foundation for Research and Technology - Hellas*
[c] *Laboratoire de Recherche en Informatique, Universite Paris-Sud*

Abstract. This chapter describes personalisation services for *self e-learning networks*. A self e-learning network consists of web-based learning objects that have been made available to the network by its users, along with metadata descriptions of these learning objects and of the network's users. The proposed personalisation facilities include: querying learning object descriptions to return results tailored towards users' individual goals and preferences; the ability to define views over the learning object metadata; facilities for defining new composite learning objects and automatically deriving their descriptions; and facilities for subscribing to personalised event and change notification services. The personalisation facilities are realised using a combination of Semantic Web technologies including RDF/S, RQL, RVL, and RDF ECA rules.

Keywords. E-Learning, personalisation, metadata management, Semantic Web

Introduction

Life-long learning and the knowledge economy have brought about the need to support diverse communities of learners throughout their lifetimes. These learners are geographically distributed and may have heterogeneous educational backgrounds and learning needs. In the most general case, learners organise themselves into communities according to their own criteria, such as having common interests. We envisage a *self e-learning network* (SeLeNe) as existing to support a specific community of providers and learners. Learning communities can occur in an educational institution, in a workplace, or on the web.

The SeLeNe EU FP5 [1] project ran from November 2002 to January 2004 and investigated the feasibility and design of tools to support learning communities by matching learners' needs with educational resources potentially available on the Web. Our proposed personalisation services relied on the availability of semantic metadata describing educational material and learners, and included services for the discovery, sharing, and collaborative creation of learning objects (LOs), aiming to facilitate syndicated and personalised access to such resources.

[1] Corresponding Author: London Knowledge Lab, Birkbeck, University of London, 23-29 Emerald Street, London WC1N 3QS, United Kingdom; E-mail: kevin@dcs.bbk.ac.uk.

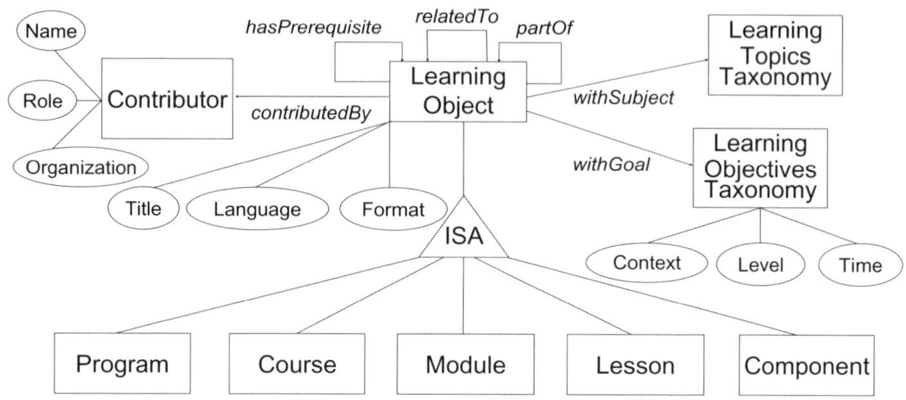

Figure 1. Overview of the SeLeNe Information Space

LOs capture any chunk of learning resource regardless of its form, granularity and functionality. By definition, LOs encapsulate both learning content and appropriate descriptive information (i.e. metadata). LOs aim to provide self-describing learning material that once developed can subsequently be exchanged, retrieved and reused. LOs are uniquely identified via their Uniform Resource Identifier (URI) [2] while their metadata are *submitted* to the *SeLeNe* with which they are registered.

The key factor for supporting large scale interoperability, portability and reusability of LOs is the quality of the semantic description of LOs i.e., its metadata specification. The LO metadata and the schemas to which these conform form the SeLeNe *LO information space* (see Figure 1). Users need to be able to query the LO information space in order to locate LOs appropriate for their specific learning or teaching needs, and also need to be able to define personalised views over this potentially large number of heterogeneous resources.

Following the open tradition of the Web, LOs may be physically stored in the web site of an organisation (educational or corporate) or in the web pages of individual users. A SeLeNe will not manage the LOs themselves, but will instead facilitate access to them by managing their metadata descriptions. In order to enable effective search for LOs in a SeLeNe, we assume that LO descriptions conform to e-learning standards such as IEEE/LOM (Learning Object Metadata) [3], and also employ topic-specific taxonomies of scientific domains such as ACM/CCS (Computing Classification System) [4] or taxonomies of detailed learning objectives. LO schemas and descriptions are represented in the Resource Description Framework/Schema Language (RDF/S) [5], which offers appropriate modelling primitives for the SeLeNe information space.

Figure 1 illustrates the main concepts and properties of the RDFS schemas we employed in the SeLeNe project to capture the semantics of existing e-learning standards. The information content of a LO can be described using attributes such as *title*, *language*, *format*, etc., or one or more terms from a topic-specific taxonomy like ACM/CCS, e.g. a LO about C++ could have a *withSubject* property referencing the ACM/CCS classification *D.3.2.11*, which is the taxonomic path representing *Software.ProgrammingLanguages.LanguageClassifications.ObjectOrientedLanguages*.

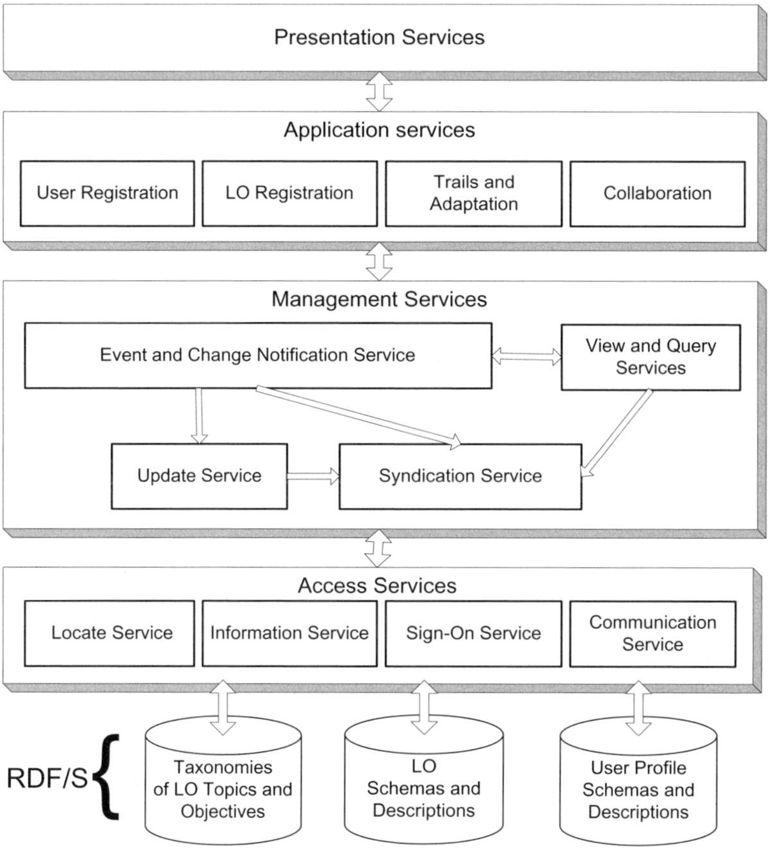

Figure 2. SeLeNe Service Architecture

The schema also allows description of the granularity of a LO (e.g., *Course*, *Lesson*), its relationships with other LOs (e.g., *hasPrerequisite*, *partOf*), and its relationships with other classes of resource (e.g., *contributedBy*). A taxonomy such as Bloom's *Taxonomy of Educational Objectives*, combined with a topics taxonomy, can be used to describe the desired learning outcomes of a LO. For example, a LO *withGoal Application.Use* (from Bloom's taxonomy) [6] and *withSubject D.3.2.11* (from ACM/CCS) is thereby described as having the educational objective "to be able to use an Object-Oriented language".

The diversity and heterogeneity of the learning communities we envisage using SeLeNes means that no single architectural design is suitable to support all of them. We thus defined a service-based architecture that can be deployed in a peer-to-peer, mediation-based or centralised fashion (which is a special case of peer-to-peer); so the deployment option best addressing the needs of any particular learning community can be chosen. We envisage each SeLeNe network as consisting of a number of peers, each of which will support some subset of the full set of SeLeNe services. Figure 2 illustrates the architecture of a SeLeNe. The facilities that are the focus of this chapter are provided by the User Registration, LO Registration, Trails and Adaptation, Event and Change Notification, and View services. We refer the reader to [7] for further discussion of the architecture and other services.

The users of a SeLeNe will include *instructors*, *learners* and *providers* of LOs – a single person could play each of these roles at different times. New users will be able to join a SeLeNe by contacting any peer of the SeLeNe that provides the User Registration service. When registering, users will supply information about themselves and their educational objectives in using this SeLeNe. This information is stored in their *personal profile*.

Providers of LOs will maintain control of the content they create and will be free to use any tools they wish to create their LO content before registering it. We call such LOs, created externally to SeLeNe, *atomic LOs*. Users will also be able to register new *composite LOs* – LOs that have been created as assemblies of LOs already registered with the SeLeNe, for example a course LO which has been created by assembling several module LOs. The SeLeNe will be able to automatically derive the taxonomical description of a composite LO from the taxonomical descriptions of its constituent LOs. The LO registration process and automatic derivation of taxonomical descriptions are discussed in Section 1.

The SeLeNe will provide facilities for defining personalised *views* over the LO information space, which we discuss in Section 2. The SeLeNe will also provide browsing and searching facilities over the LO information space, which return results tailored towards users' individual goals and preferences. This is discussed in Section 3. A user may wish to be notified of changes made to a LO's description. SeLeNe can provide automatic change detection and notification facilities by comparing the new and old descriptions of a LO. More generally, SeLeNe can support personalised notification services depending on users' profiles. Provision of such facilities is discussed in Section 4. Finally, our conclusions are presented in Section 5.

1. Registration of LOs

Registration of a LO with a SeLeNe consists of providing a metadata description including the URI of the LO. Here we focus on the *taxonomical* part of a LO's description.

A taxonomy (T, $\preccurlyeq$) consists of a set of terms *T* together with a subsumption relation $\preccurlyeq$ between terms. It can be represented as a graph, where the nodes are the terms and there is an arrow from term *s* to term *t* iff *s* subsumes *t*. Figure 3 shows a taxonomy, which is used by all examples in this section.

A *taxonomical description* is a set of terms from a taxonomy. For example, if a LO contains the Quicksort algorithm written in Java then the terms `QuickSort` and `Java` can be chosen by the LO's provider to describe its content. We call the set of terms `{QuickSort,Java}` the *publisher taxonomical description* (PTD) of the LO.

An important feature of the registration process will be the ability to automatically infer a taxonomical description for a composite LO *o*, from the taxonomical descriptions of the LOs $o_1,\ldots,o_n$ it has been assembled from. This description, which 'summarises' the taxonomical descriptions of the parts of *o*, is called the *implied taxonomical description* (ITD) of *o*.

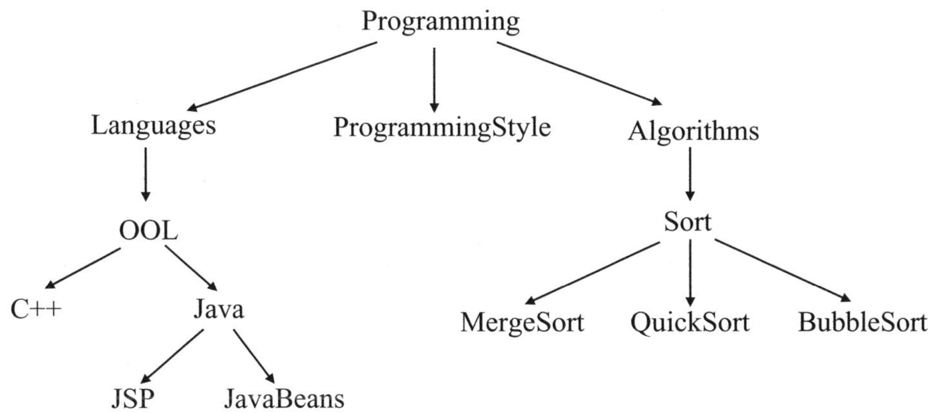

Figure 3. An example Taxonomy showing a set of terms that could be used when describing the topics of LOs in the area of computer programming. The arrows show the subsumption relationship that exists between the terms, for example the terms *MergeSort*, *QuickSort* and *BubbleSort* are subsumed by the term *Sort*, and *Sort* is subsumed by *Algorithms*.

A SeLeNe will automatically derive the taxonomical description D of a composite LO from its PTD augmented by its ITD, removing any redundant terms (i.e., terms that are subsumed by other terms). Consider LOs $o_1, \ldots, o_4$ with the following taxonomical descriptions:

$D(o_1)$ = `{QuickSort,Java}`; $D(o_2)$ = `{BubbleSort}`;
$D(o_3)$ = `{BubbleSort, C++}`; $D(o_4)$ = `{C++}`.

Intuitively, the ITD of a composite LO o expresses what its parts have in common – a composite LO o composed from o_1 and o_2 will have the ITD `{Sort}`. Intuitively, both o_1 and o_2 concern sorting algorithms, and the fact that one of them is written in Java is considered to be irrelevant as far as the composite LO is concerned. Thus, the term `Java` is not reflected in o's ITD as it is not something that both parts share. However, this does not mean a loss of information: if a user searches the SeLeNe for objects related to Java, o_1 will be in the answer set and o will not.

The ITD of a composite LO retains what its parts have in common, while subsuming the taxonomical descriptions of each part. Consider the composite LO o' with parts o_1 and o_3 – in this case the common part would be `{Sort,OOL}`. This result for the ITD should be interpreted as meaning that each part of o' concerns both sorting and object-oriented languages.

Note that a LO may generate different ITDs depending on what its 'companion' parts are. Consider the composite LO o'' with parts o_1 and o_4.The ITD of o'' is `{OOL}` – o_1 is part of each of the composite LOs o, o' and o'', but each time with a different 'companion' part. It is interesting to note that, depending on the companion part, either the 'sort-aspect' of o_1 or its 'OOL-aspect', or both, appear in the ITD.

One may wonder why the PTD of a composite LO is not sufficient and why we need to augment it by its ITD. The answer is that the provider of a composite LO *o* may not describe the parts of *o* in the same way as the providers of these parts have done. For example, suppose that the two LOs, o_1 and o_3, have been created by two different providers, with the PTDs as above. Assume now that a third provider considers these LOs as examples of good programming style, and decides to use them as parts of the new composite LO o'. The provider of o' provides the PTD `{ProgrammingStyle}`. Although this PTD might be accurate for the provider's own purposes, the LO *o* still can serve to teach, or learn, Java and sorting algorithms. This information will certainly be of interest to users searching for LOs containing material on Java and sorting algorithms. Therefore, the PTD `{ProgrammingStyle}` is augmented by the ITD `{OOL, Sort}` to obtain `{ProgrammingStyle,OOL,Sort}` as the overall taxonomical description for o'.

The ITD of a composite LO *o* composed of parts $o_1,\ldots, o_n$ with descriptions $D_1,\ldots, D_n$ is computed by a simple algorithm, which takes the Cartesian product of $D_1,\ldots, D_n$, computes the least upper bound of each *n*-tuple and then 'reduces' the resulting set of terms by removing all but the minimal terms according to the subsumption relation $\preccurlyeq$. The overall taxonomical description of a LO *o* is computed by another simple algorithm: if *o* is atomic then its taxonomical description is just its PTD. Otherwise its taxonomical description is recursively computed from its PTD and the taxonomical descriptions of its constituent parts. Readers are referred to [8] for more details of both algorithms.

2. Declarative Queries and Views

One of the novel features of SeLeNe is its ability to exploit the available semantic relationships (see Figure 1) defined among the RDF/S classes of LOs in order to implement conceptual navigation and retrieval. We believe that the semantic relationships of LOs play a crucial role especially in peer-to-peer learning environments, where users have the ability to freely insert or modify LOs and their descriptions while at the same time they are striving for a contextual access to learning material available to a SeLeNe.

Finding LOs and exploring their semantic relationships relies on the RDF/S Query Language (RQL) [10], a declarative language for browsing and querying RDF/S schemas and descriptions. For instance, consider the following RQL query, which retrieves all *Course*s about Object Oriented Languages (*OOL*) that have been *contributedBy* someone having a *name* attribute:

```
SELECT Y, X, W
FROM{Y;ns1:Course}ns1:contributedBy{X}.ns1:name{W},ns2:OOL{Y}
USING NAMESPACE ns1=&www.ieee.org/lom.rdfs#
                ns2=&www.acm.org/class/1998ccs.rdfs#
```

An RQL `FROM` clause consists of path expressions, which provide a navigation through schemas and description bases and bind the introduced variables. The first RQL path expression

```
{Y;ns1:Course}ns1:contributedBy{X}.ns1:name{W}
```

will match instances of class *Course* and their associated *contributedBy* properties, which link them to some instance of *Contributor* and its *name* value. For each such match, we get a binding that maps Y to the *Course* resource, X to the *Contributor* and W to the *name* value. The second path expression

```
ns2:OOL{Y}
```

is evaluated for each binding of Y, and filters *Course* instances by checking whether they are classified under the topic *OOL*. Note that in this query several schemas are used, identified by the corresponding namespaces `n1` and `n2` defined in the `USING NAMESPACE` clause.

Using RQL, more complex scenarios of conceptual navigation and retrieval can be implemented using appropriate Graphical User Interfaces (GUI). In particular, RQL queries can be automatically generated from the browsing actions of learners both at the level of LO schemas and their descriptions in the SeLeNe information space [11]. For example, starting from a *Course* a learner can navigate through the *prerequisite* relationship and retrieve LOs belonging to the target course(s). Alternatively, a learner can choose to visit a *Lecture*, where (s)he can discover whether another *Lecture* or a *Module* of a *Course* is required to fully understand the content of this lecture. Additionaly, (s)he can also find out whether this *Lecture* is *required* for any *Assignment*s that (s)he has to fulfill in order to successfully assimilate *Course* material. In this context, we can consider *prerequisite* and *requires* as "strong" relationships, literally forcing a learner to follow a specific learning path while *partOf* and *SeeAlso* are rather "weaker" relationships suggesting a path but not forcing learners to follow it.

These are few examples of **query-based personalization** techniques, which are based on the RDF/S schemas employed to semantically describe LOs. However, despite our efforts for a modular, extensible and intuitive RDF/S schema design, the SeLeNe information space one has to master still remains incredibly rich. Hence, LOs' providers may encounter difficulties when querying or updating LOs' descriptions due to a misleading or even erroneous understanding of the LOs' semantics. Moreover, LOs' consumers may also need to consider LO descriptions according to their educational level and current subject of study rather than the RDF/S schemas employed to register LOs in a SeLeNe. For these reasons, we need additional support to specify and visualise appropriate **semantic views** of LO descriptions and schemas. The RDF/S View Language (RVL*)* [9] provides this ability by introducing virtual RDF/S schemas and descriptions on top of the SeLeNe information space.

To illustrate the RVL functionality we will consider a simple virtual schema (view) for instructors, which represents only OOL course material and its authors. This schema can be specified by a set of RVL statements whose output is an RDF/S virtual schema and resource descriptions. In RDF/S the uniqueness of (meta) schema labels and the ability to describe resources using labels from several schemas is ensured by the XML namespace facility. In our example this RVL statement defines a unique namespace:

```
CREATE NAMESPACE myview=&http://www.selene.org/LO.rdf#
```

The following RVL statement specifies the virtual classes `Author` and `OOLCourse` and the virtual properties `creates` and `name`:

```
VIEW rdfs:Class("OOLCourse"),rdfs:Class("Author"),
     rdf:Property("creates", Author, OOLCourse),
     rdf:Property("name", Author, xsd:string);
```

where *rdfs:Class* and *rdf:Property* are two core metaclasses provided in the default RDF/S namespaces. As in RQL, the `USING NAMESPACE` clause declares the namespaces used in view statements. The following statement 'populates' the virtual classes and properties defined in the view:

```
VIEW OOLCourse(Y),Author(X),creates(X,Y),name(X,W)
FROM {Y;ns1:Course}ns1:contributedBy{X;ns1:Author}.
       ns1:name{W}, ns2:OOL{Y}
USING NAMESPACE ns1=&www.ieee.org/lom.rdfs#
                ns2=&www.acm.org/class/1998ccs.rdfs#
```

It is worth mentioning that although the input of both RQL and RVL in the `FROM` clause is an RDF/S graph, only the latter produces virtual schemas and resource descriptions rather than the simple variable bindings returned by the former. This functionality is ensured by the `VIEW` clause, where appropriate population functions are used, taking as parameters the variable bindings produced by the `FROM` clause (and optionally a `WHERE` clause). For instance, the virtual class `OOLCourse` is populated with instances (bound to variable Y) of the base class *Course*, also classified under the topic *OOL*. The virtual class `Author` is populated with instances (bound to variable X) of the base class *Contributor*, which are the range values of the property *contributedBy* applied to *Course* resources. In other words, `Author` is populated with all the contributors who have created an OOL course. Virtual properties are populated with pairs of resources (e.g., `creates` is populated with authors having created OOL courses) or resource-value pairs (e.g., `name` is populated with the names of OOL course authors).

One of the most significant features of RVL is its ability to create virtual schemas by simply populating the two core RDF/S metaclasses *Class* (e.g., with schema classes `Author` and `OOLCourse`) and *Property* (e.g., with schema properties `creates` and `name`). A SeLeNe user could then easily formulate queries *on the view* (using a user-friendly graphical interface), such as the following RQL query retrieving the OOL courses created by the author named "Christophides":

```
SELECT Y
FROM {X}myview:creates{Y}, {X}myview:name{Z}
WHERE Z = "Christophides"
USING NAMESPACE myview=&http://www.selene.org/LO.rdf#
```

A concrete implementation of the personalization techniques presented in this section is available at the Online Curriculum Portal of the Computer Science Department of the Univeristy of Crete [12].

3. Trails and Query Adaptation

Personalisation of query results relies on the *personal profile*, which is an RDF description of the user conforming to a number of RDFS schemas, created when a user registers with a SeLeNe. Figure 4 shows a simplified version of SeLeNe's personal profile schema.

To avoid proposing yet another schema for demographic and other information that is already adequately catered for by existing profile schemes, we included elements from the IEEE LTSC's Personal and Private Information (PAPI) Standard [13] and the IMS Learner Information Package (LIP) [14], extending the data model with our own elements where existing specifications fail to be expressive enough.

The shortcomings of existing learner profile specifications were generally in the recording of competencies, learning goals and preferred learning styles, and we developed RDF schemas that allow the expression of all three of these. For competencies and learning goals, we adopted the same topic and learning objectives taxonomies as those used for learning object descriptions, (i.e. the taxonomies shown in Figure 1). Other customised sections of the SeLeNe profile are related to the active functionality of SeLeNe – a history of user activity (accesses to LOs) is included, which allows the profile to adapt to take account of the user's behaviour over time, for example by automatically updating the information in it by means of Event-Condition-Action rules (see Section 4). The learner also has a *messages* property with a *Notifications* class as its target. This can store personal notifications (of new users and new or updated LOs) for the user.

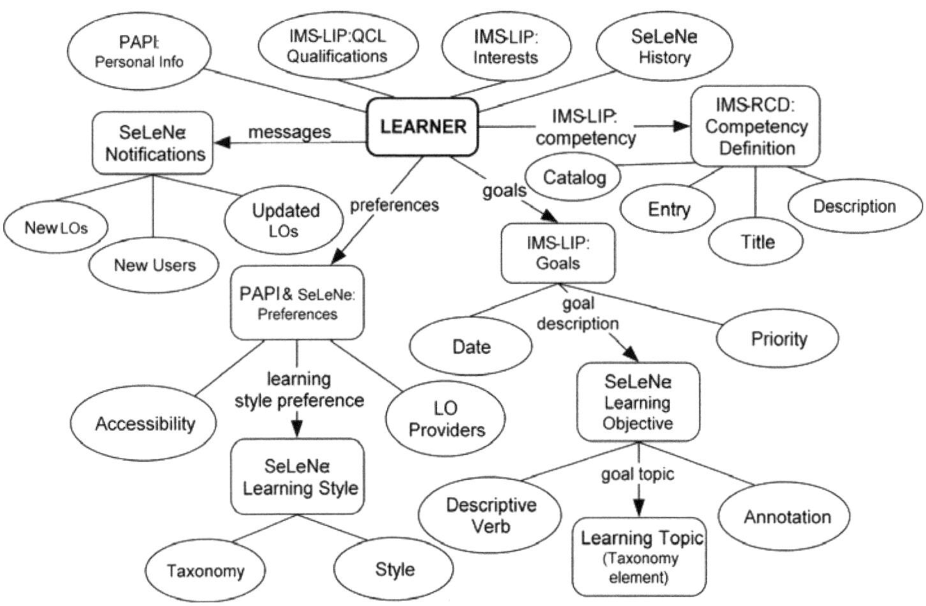

Figure 4. SeLeNe's Personal Profile Schema

Although the underlying query mechanism in SeLeNe is RQL, we envisage that users will generally search for LOs using simple keyword-based queries (possibly augmented with attribute information). Search results will then be personalised by *filtering* and *ranking* the LOs returned according to the information contained in the user's personal profile.

Filtering will take place before a query is evaluated: all keyword-based queries submitted to the SeLeNe will be routed through the Trails and Adaptation service, which will construct corresponding personalised queries. The user's original query will then be re-formulated and/or annotated to reflect elements of their personal profile. For example, if the profile records that the user only speaks English, all searches they enter can be augmented with the annotation *lang:en*, ensuring that all returned LOs will be in English. The augmented keyword query will then be translated into an appropriate RQL query and executed by the Query service. The reader is referred to [15] for the full SeLeNe profile schema and for discussion of the translation of keyword-based queries into structured queries in SeLeNe.

The next step is to rank the filtered set of LO descriptions in order of relevance to the user. Relevance of a LO to the user will be judged by matching the LO's metadata description against the combination of the personal profile and the original query. The information contained in the SeLeNe personal profile allows the following factors to be taken into consideration when judging relevance, and a combination of weighted scores for each of these factors can be used to provide an overall relevance score for each candidate LO:

- relevance of the LO to the query (judged using techniques such as those described in [16], [17]);
- whether the user has the prerequisite knowledge and experience to be able to tackle the LO;
- how well the learning objectives of the LO match the user's learning goals;
- if the user's learning styles are those catered for by the LO; if the user is likely to prefer it for other reasons (e.g., it is by a preferred provider);
- how well the LO caters for the user's accessibility requirements;
- the user's most recent activity (as contained in the history section of their profile).

The different sections of the personal profile can be matched in a focussed way against relevant sections of the LO descriptions. For one LO to be more relevant to the user than another it must meet more of the user's different preferences, or match preferences to a greater degree. For example, if the user has OOL as one of their *goal_topic*'s then a LO including OOL in its taxonomical description will score well on relevance to the user. If the LO description additionally includes the information that it caters for one of the user's learning styles then it will be considered a better match again. The best algorithm and weightings to use for this ranking needs to be determined empirically, and may well need to be adaptive.

Once a personalised ranking of the remaining LOs has been generated, the search results will then be returned to the user. SeLeNe can give the user the option of having their query results presented not as a simple list of individual LOs, but rather as a list of *trails* of LOs, where a trail is a suggested sequence of interaction with the LOs [18]. We have defined an RDF representation of trails whereby they are defined as a subclass of the RDF *Sequence* (a sequence of LOs) with two associated properties, *name* and *annotation*, that provide additional information about the pedagogic use of the trail.

These trails will be automatically generated. Algorithms for the automatic generation of trails in hypertext systems already exist [19], but in SeLeNe's case the links between LOs are not explicit hyperlinks – links will be derived from information contained in the LO descriptions about the semantic relationships between LOs. For example, by inspecting the *LOM:Relation* fields in a collection of LO descriptions (in this case a set of results), trails of LOs with early LOs in the trail being prerequisites for later LOs can easily be derived and annotated with the term "prerequisites".

4. Event and Change Notification

Many applications on the web need to be *reactive* i.e., to be able to detect the occurrence of specific events or changes in information content, and to respond by automatically executing the appropriate application logic. *Event-condition-action* (ECA) rules are one way to implement this kind of functionality. An ECA rule has the general syntax: `on` *event* `if` *condition* `do` *actions*. The event part specifies when the rule is *triggered*. The condition part is a query that determines if the information space is in a particular state, in which case the rule *fires*. The action part states the actions to be performed if the rule fires. These actions may in turn cause further events to occur, which may in turn cause more ECA rules to fire.

There are several advantages in using ECA rules to implement this kind of functionality: management of an application's reactive functionality within a single rule base; analysis and optimisation techniques for ECA rules that cannot be applied if the same functionality is expressed directly in application code; and provision of a generic mechanism that can abstract a wide variety of reactive behaviours.

Motivated by these advantages of ECA rules, we proposed providing SeLeNe's reactive functionality by means of ECA rules over RDF/S metadata. This reactive functionality includes features such as automatic propagation of changes in the description of one resource to the descriptions of other, related resources (e.g., propagation of changes in the taxonomical description of a LO to the taxonomical description of any composite LOs depending on it, or updating a user's personal profile based on changes in their history of accesses to LOs), automatic notification to users of the registration of new LOs of interest to them and of changes in the description of resources of interest to them.

SeLeNe peers that support the Event and Change Notification service will have installed an *ECA Engine* consisting of three main components: an *Event Detector*, *Condition Evaluator* and *Action Scheduler*. The Event Detector determines which rules have been triggered by the most recent update to the local description base, by invoking the Query service to evaluate the event queries of rules that may have been triggered. The Condition Evaluator then calls the Query service to determine which of the triggered rules should fire. The Action Scheduler generates from the action parts of these rules a list of updates, which are then passed to the Update service for execution.

Our RDF ECA rule language, RDFTL [20], is implemented over FORTH's RDFSuite query and update API [21]. In RDFTL, the event part of a rule is an expression of one of the following three forms:

(i) (INSERT | DELETE) *e* [AS INSTANCE OF *class*]

This detects insertions or deletions of resources described by the expression *e*, which is a path expression evaluating to a set of nodes, optionally followed by a clause `AS INSTANCE OF` *`class`*. The rule is triggered if the set of nodes returned by *e* includes any new node (in the case of an insertion) or any deleted node (in the case of a deletion) that is an instance of the *`class`*, if specified. A system-defined variable `$delta` is available for use within the condition and actions parts of the rule, and its set of instantiations is the set of new or deleted nodes that have triggered the rule.

(ii) (INSERT | DELETE) *triple*

This detects insertions or deletions of arcs specified by *triple*, which has the form *(source, arc_name, target)*. The wildcard '_' is allowed in the place of any of a triple's components. The rule is triggered if an arc labelled *arc_name* from the *source* node to the *target* node is inserted/deleted. The variable `$delta` has as its set of instantiations the triples which have triggered the rule. The individual components of one of these triples can be referenced by `$delta`.source, `$delta`.arc_name, `$delta`.target.

(iii) UPDATE *upd_triple*

This detects updates of arcs, where *upd_triple* has the form *(source, arc_name, old → new)*. Here, *old* is the target node of arc *arc_name* from the *source* node before the update, and new is its target node after the update. Again, the wildcard '_' is allowed in the place of any of these components. The rule is triggered if an arc labelled *arc_name* from *source* changes its target from *old* to *new*. The variable `$delta` has as its set of instantiations the triples which have triggered the rule. The individual components of one of these triples can be obtained by `$delta`.source, `$delta`.arc_name, `$delta`.old_target, `$delta`.new_target.

The condition part of a rule is a query consisting of conjunctions, disjunctions and negations of path expressions. The actions part of a rule is a sequence of one or more actions. Actions can `INSERT` or `DELETE` a resource – specified by its URI – and `INSERT`, `DELETE` or `UPDATE` an arc. The actions language has the following form for each one of these cases:

```
INSERT e AS INSTANCE OF class
DELETE e [AS INSTANCE OF class]
```

for inserting or deleting a resource;

```
(INSERT | DELETE) triple (',' triple)*
```

for inserting or deleting the specified arcs(s); and

```
UPDATE upd_triple (',' upd_triple)*
```

for updating arcs by changing their target node. Wildcards are allowed in place of some of the components of triples, with the obvious semantics. We give two examples of

RDFTL rules below, which refer to the LO schema illustrated in Figure 1 and the personal profile schema illustrated in Figure 4.

Firstly, if a LO is inserted whose subject (OOL, say) is the same as one of user 128's goal topics, then the following rule adds a new arc linking the newly inserted LO into the `new_LOs` collection in user 128's personal messages:

```
ON INSERT resource() AS INSTANCE OF LearningObject
IF $delta/target(rdf:type)
   = resource(http://www.dcs.bbk.ac.uk/users/128)
     /target(ims-lip:goal)
     /target(ims-lip:goaldescription)
     /target(selene:goaltopic)
DO LET $new_los :=
   resource(http://www.dcs.bbk.ac.uk/users/128)
   /target(selene:messages)/target(selene:new_LOs)
   IN INSERT ($new_los,seq++,$delta);;
```

Here, the event part checks if a new resource belonging to the `LearningObject` class has been inserted. The condition part checks if the inserted LO has a subject which is the same as one of user 128's goal topics. The `LET` clause defines the variable `$new_los` to be user 128's collection of new LOs. Finally, the `INSERT` clause inserts a new arc from `$new_los` to the newly inserted LO (the syntax `seq++` indicates an increment in the collection's element count).

As a second example, if any property of a LO whose subject is the same as one of user 128's goal topics is updated, then the following rule adds a new arc linking user 128's `updated_LOs` collection to the modified LO:

```
ON UPDATE (resource()AS INSTANCE OF LearningObject,_,_->_)
IF $delta/target(rdf:type)
   = resource(http://www.dcs.bbk.ac.uk/users/128)
     /target(ims-lip:goal)
     /target(ims-lip:goaldescription)
     /target(selene:goaltopic)
DO LET $updated_los :=
   resource(http://www.dcs.bbk.ac.uk/users/128)
   /target(selene:messages)
   /target(selene:updated_LOs)
   IN INSERT ($updated_los,seq++,$delta);;
```

We refer the reader to [20,22] for an overview of related work in ECA rule languages, the syntax and semantics of RDFTL, conservative tests for determining the termination and confluence of sets of RDFTL rules, and architecture, implementation and performance details.

5. Concluding Remarks

This chapter has described several techniques for providing personalisation services in *self e-learning networks*. Our use of RDF/S for representing the descriptions of educational material and users within a SeLeNe has allowed us to reuse and extend as necessary a number of existing metadata standards for learning objects and learners. It has also allowed us to adopt a uniform approach to manipulating information about learning objects and learners in the RQL, RVL and RDFTL languages, and a uniform approach underpinning the SeLeNe personalisation services.

The novel aspects of the SeLeNe project compared with other peer-to-peer, RDF-based systems for supporting e-learning (e.g. UNIVERSAL, Edutella, Elena[2]) included:

- the use of Semantic Web technologies to support the collaborative creation and semi-automatic description of new composite LOs, which does not seem to be addressed specifically by any other system and which gives users flexibility in the generation of learning resources tailored to their needs;
- declarative views over combined RDFS/RDF descriptions (i.e. over both the LO descriptions and their schemas) that ensure compositionality of queries with views and mappings, giving users the power to narrow their view of a rich information space to see only the parts of relevance to them;
- personalised event and change notification services, operating at the level of LO or user RDF/S descriptions, allowing users to be kept up-to-date with relevant changes and additions to a SeLeNe as it evolves;
- automatic generation of trails of LOs from their descriptions assists users in planning individual learning paths.

Many open issues still remain. As the SeLeNe project was a feasibility study, the complete architecture designed in the project and illustrated in Figure 2 was not implemented, and therefore it was not possible to undertake a usability evaluation. The facilities described in Sections 1, 2 and 4 were fully implemented and those in Section 3 partially implemented. The algorithms for personalised ranking of query results remain to be empirically evaluated. This evaluation would need to include a study of the comparative usefulness, for personalisation purposes, of the different cognitive models included in our taxonomy of learning and cognitive styles.

There is still no standard query or update language for RDF, although we believe that the RQL, RVL and RDFTL languages we have developed provide sound and expressive foundations for the development of such standards, and also for development of optimisation techniques for query, update and view languages over RDF. Whatever standards eventually emerge for such RDF languages, if ECA rules are to be supported on RDF repositories then the event sub-language for RDF ECA rules needs to be designed so that it matches up with the actions sub-language. In general, the ability to analyse and optimise ECA rules needs to be balanced against their complexity and expressiveness. Another important open area is combining ECA rules with transactions and consistency maintenance in RDF repositories.

Finally, in implementing a system such as this, the design of user interfaces enabling easy and intuitive access to SeLeNe's advanced personalisation services is crucial – end-users will need to be shielded from the complexities of RDF and the RQL,

[2] http://www.ist-universal.org, http://edutella.jxta.org, http://www.elena-project.org.

RVL and ECA languages, and also from the complex taxonomies of topics, competencies and goals in use by the system.

References

[1] The European Commission: CORDIS FP5web. See http://cordis.europa.eu/fp5/ (2002)

[2] Berners-Lee, T., Fielding, R., Masinter, L.: Request for Comments 2396: Uniform Resource Identifiers (URI) Generic Syntax. See http://www.ietf.org/rfc/rfc2396.txt (1998)

[3] IEEE: Draft Standard For Learning Object Metadata. See http://ltsc.ieee.org/wg12/files/LOM_1484_12_1_v1_Final_Draft.pdf (2002)

[4] Association for Computing Machinery: The ACM Computing Classification System (1998 Version). See http://www.acm.org/class/1998/ (1998)

[5] Brickley, D., Guha, R.V.: RDF Vocabulary Description Language 1.0: RDF Schema. W3C Recommendation 10 February 2004. See www.w3.org/TR/rdf-schema (2004)

[6] Bloom, B. S., Krathwohl D. R. (Eds.): Taxonomy of educational objectives: The classification of educational goals: Handbook I, cognitive domain. Longman, New York. (1956)

[7] Samaras, G., Karenos, K., Christodoulou, E.: A Grid service framework for Self e-Learning Networks. See http://www.dcs.bbk.ac.uk/selene/reports/Del3.pdf (2003)

[8] Rigaux, P., Spyratos, N.: Generation and syndication of learning object metadata. See http://www.dcs.bbk.ac.uk/selene/reports/Del4.1-2.2.pdf (2004)

[9] Magkanaraki, A., Tannen, V., Christophides, V., Plexousakis, D.: Viewing the Semantic Web Through RVL Lenses. In: Web Semantics: Science, Services and Agents on the World Wide Web, Vol. 1(4), 2004, pp. 359-375

[10] Karvounarakis, G., Magkanaraki, A., Alexaki, S., Christophides, V., Plexousakis, D., Scholl, M., Tolle, K.: RQL: A Functional Query Language for RDF. In: The Functional Approach to Data Management: Modelling, Analyzing and Integrating Heterogeneous Data, P.M.D.Gray, L.Kerschberg, P.J.H.King, A.Poulovassilis (Eds.), LNCS Series, Springer-Verlag, (2004)

[11] Athanasis, N., Christophides, V., Kotzinos D.: Generating On the Fly Queries for the Semantic Web: The ICS-FORTH Graphical RQL Interface (GRQL). In: Proceedings of the Third International Semantic Web Conference, Hiroshima, Japan, November 7-11, 2004. (2004)

[12] Kotzinos, D., Pediaditaki, S., Apostolidis, A., Athanasis, N., Christophides, V.: Online Curriculum on the Semantic Web: The CSD-UoC Portal for Peer-to-peer e-learning. In: Proceedings of the 14th International World Wide Web Conference (WWW'05), Chiba, Japan, May 10-14, 2005. (2005)

[13] LTSC Learner Model Working Group of the IEEE: IEEE P1484.2/D7, 2000-11-28 Draft Standard for Learning Technology - Public and Private Information (PAPI) for Learners (PAPI Learner). IEEE, (2000)

[14] Smythe, C., Tansey, F., Robson, R.: IMS Learner Information Package Information Model Specification. See http://www.imsproject.org/profiles/lipinfo01.html (2001)

[15] Keenoy, K., Levene, M., Peterson, D.: Personalisation and trails in Self e-Learning Networks. See http://www.dcs.bbk.ac.uk/selene/reports/Del4.2-1.4.pdf (2003)

[16] Anyanwu, K., Sheth, A. P.: Rho queries: enabling querying for semantic associations on the semantic web. In: Proceedings of the Twelfth International World Wide Web Conference, WWW2003, pages 690-699, Budapest, Hungary, May 2003. ACM, (2003)

[17] Stojanovic, N., Studer, R., Stojanovic, L.: An approach for the ranking of query results in the Semantic Web. In: Proceedings of ISWC 2003, Sanibel Island, Florida, USA, October 2003. LNCS 2870, Springer (2003)

[18] Peterson, D., Levene, M.: Trail Records and Navigational Learning. London Review of Education, 1, pp 207-216, (2003)

[19] Wheeldon, R., Levene, M.: The Best Trail algorithm for assisted navigation of web sites. In: Proceedings of the 1st Latin American Web Congress (LA-WEB'03), Santiago, Chile (2003)

[20] Papamarkos, G., Poulovassilis, A., Wood, P.: Event-Condition-Action rules on RDF metadata in P2P environments. Computer Networks 50(10), pp 1513-1532 (2006)

[21] Alexaki, S., Christophides, V., Karvounarakis, G., Plexousakis, D., Tolle, K.: The ICS-FORTH RDFSuite: Managing Voluminous RDF Description Bases. In: Proceedings of the 2nd International Workshop on the Semantic Web (SemWeb 2001) (2001)

[22] Papamarkos, G., Event-Condition-Action Rule Languages over Semi-Structured Data, PhD Thesis, University of London (2007).

The Learning Grid Handbook
S. Salerno et al. (Eds.)
IOS Press, 2008

A Grid Approach to Efficiently Embed Information and Knowledge about Group Activity into Collaborative Learning Applications

Santi CABALLE [a, 1], Fatos XHAFA [b] and Thanasis DARADOUMIS [a]
[a] *Open University of Catalonia, Spain*
[b] *Polytechnic University of Catalonia, Spain*

Abstract. Constantly embedding information and knowledge about group activity into on-line collaborative learning is a challenging yet one of the latest and most attractive issues to influence learning experience in a positive manner. The possibility to enhance learning group's participation by means of providing appropriate knowledge is rapidly gaining popularity due to its great impact on group performance and outcomes. Indeed, by storing parameters of interaction such as participation behaviour and giving constant awareness and feedback of these parameters to the group may influence group's motivation and emotional state as well as enhance the learners' and groups' problem solving abilities. This implies a need to capture and structure the information generated by group activity and then to extract the relevant knowledge in order to provide learners and tutors with efficient awareness and feedback as regards group performance and collaboration. To that end, we first identify and define the main types of information generated in on-line group activity and then we propose a process for efficiently embedding this information and the knowledge extracted into collaborative learning applications. However, in order to provide learners with effective knowledge, it is necessary to process large and complex event log files from group activity in a constant manner, and thus it may require computational capacity beyond that of a single computer. To that end, in this chapter we show how a Grid approach can considerably decrease the time of processing group activity log files and thus allow group learners to receive selected knowledge even in real time.

Keywords. Grid, parallel applications, collaborative learning, interaction analysis, knowledge management, CSCL.

1. Introduction

The provision of effective knowledge extracted from the information collected in Computer-Supported Collaborative Learning (CSCL) environments is essential for any form of cooperation, namely coordination, communication and collaboration [1]. It allows implicit coordination of collaborative learning, opportunities for informal, spontaneous communication, and gives users awareness [2] and feedback [3] about

[1] Corresponding Author: Open University of Catalonia, Department of Computer Science, Multimedia and Telecommunication. Rambla Poblenou, 156, 08018 Barcelona, Spain; E-mail: scaballe@uoc.edu.

what is happening during collaboration. Indeed, it is crucial for group members to be aware of others' participation in the collaborative process as this may enhance the collaboration a great deal in terms of decision-making, group organization, social engagement, support, monitoring and so on [1], [2]. Moreover, providing appropriate feedback about the collaborative activities may impact positively on the motivation, emotional state, and groups' well-being in on-line collaborative learning [1], [3] by means of a steady tracking of parameters related to group functioning, task performance and scaffolding [4] and by giving a constant feedback of these parameters to the group. Note that in this context information refers to quantitative and qualitative data generated by the learning group whereas knowledge refers to the result of the treatment of this information in terms of analysis techniques and interpretations that will be presented to the same group that generated it.

Therefore, participants in a collaborative learning experience may greatly enhance their abilities by increasing their knowledge about others in terms of cognitive processes and skills of the students and the group as a whole in solving problems, individual and group effectiveness regarding participation and interaction behavior, social support and help and so on. As a result, the success of CSCL applications depends to a great extent on the capability of such applications to embed information and knowledge of group activity and use it to achieve a more effective group monitoring [1], [4] as well as constantly provide group members with as much awareness and feedback as possible. Awareness [2], [6] refers to the knowledge provided to participants about both what other participants are doing at the same time and what they did in the past, whereas feedback [3], [7] goes one step further than awareness by providing exhaustive and elaborated information and knowledge of what is going on in the group over a long period of time. Furthermore, the persistent storage of the knowledge extracted as group memory [5] is essential for both students and tutors since, on the one hand, it allows participants not to access only the latest documents and data, which are commonly stored for later retrieval, but also the context in which they were created, and, on the other hand, it allows tutors to track the collaborative learning process for several purposes such as scaffolding and assessment of the learning outcome.

In all cases, the provision of effective knowledge implies receiving knowledge simultaneously both synchronously and asynchronously since the current and history interaction data shown are continuously updated. Therefore, on the one hand, users should be aware of the current activity in the group (the contribution of other members, their location and availability, the users working on a shared document at the same time and so on) and should know what other co-participants are doing in real time (e.g. during a multi-user editor session, who is editing and what is being shown). In an asynchronous context, on the other hand, users must know the activities performed by receiving deferred information of who, when, how and where others' interactions have been performed, and also why these interactions have been performed, which implies receiving complex knowledge of the interaction history. However, the supply of efficient and transparent feedback to users in both synchronous and asynchronous modes is a significant challenge. Users are continuously interacting with the system (creating documents, reading others' contributions, etc.) thus generating a lot of events, which, once collected, they must be classified, processed, structured and analyzed [6], [7]. As a consequence of the complex knowledge provided to participants (e.g., constant and automatic learner's assessment according to quantitative and qualitative parameters of the interaction) we need to capture all and each type of possible data that could result in a huge amount of information that is generated and gathered in data log files.

CSCL applications are characterized by a high degree of user-user and user-system interaction and hence generate a huge amount of information usually maintained in the form of event type information. In order to capture the interaction correctly, this event information can be classified into different categories such as work sessions, messages, workspaces, documents and many other objects and thus may generate large size of information, especially, in real online collaborative learning that comprise complex learning activities to be carried out during a rather long period of time and involve a considerable number of participants. This information may include a great variety of types and formats and hence tends to be large in size [7]. Indeed, at a first level of classification, we can find group activity log files of CSCL applications associated with synchronous (e.g. multi-user editors) and asynchronous collaboration (e.g. discussion forums). These applications generate different types of information depending on their specific needs and functions (e.g. a discussion forum can generate event-type information so as to capture the participants' contributions). This information can be then stored in different formats.

Our experience at the Open University of Catalonia(UOC)[2] has shown the need to monitor and evaluate real, long-term, complex, collaborative problem-solving situations through data-intensive applications that provide efficient data access, management and analysis. As a result, there is a strong need for powerful tools that record the large volume of interaction data and can be used to perform an efficient interaction analysis and knowledge extraction. Given the real needs of any online collaborative learning situation, in order to provide different types of awareness and feedback, we need to capture all and each type of possible data that could result to a huge amount of information that is generated and gathered in data log files. Moreover, the need to make the analyzed information available in real time entails that we may come across with processing requirements beyond those of a single computer.

As a matter of fact, most of the existing approaches in the literature consider a sequential approach mainly due to three reasons: (i) processing for a specific purpose (i.e. limiting the quantity of information needed for that purpose); (ii) processing the information afterwards (i.e. not in real time) and (iii) processing of small data samples, usually for research and testing purposes (i.e. not for real learning needs). Yet, the lack of sufficient computational resources is the main obstacle for processing large amounts of data log files in real time. In real situations this processing tends to be done later, after the completion of the learning activity, thus having less impact on it [8].

Recently, Grid technology is increasingly being used to reduce the overall, censored time in processing data by taking advantage of its large computing support. The concept of a computational Grid [9] has emerged as a way of capturing the vision of a networked computing system that provides broad access not only to massive information resources, but to massive computational resources as well. Thus, in this chapter, we show how a Grid approach can be used to match the time processing requirements.

Several studies have been conducted at the UOC [7], [10], [11], [12], [13] to show that a Grid approach can increase the efficiency of processing a large amount of

[2] The Open University of Catalonia (UOC) is located in Barcelona, Spain. The UOC offers distance education through the Internet since 1994. About 40,000 students, lecturers and tutors are involved in 600 on-line official courses from 23 official degrees and other PhD and post-graduate programs. The UOC is found at http://www.uoc.edu

information from group activity log files [6]. These studies have involved the interaction data collected from the log files of both the BSCW system [14] used at the UOC to support Problem-Based Learning practices in small groups and the own virtual campus of the UOC. The experimental results allow us to show first the gain provided by the Grid approach in terms of relative processing time and, second, the benefits of using the inherent scalable nature of Grid while the input log files are growing up in both number and large size. In this chapter we report the different experiments carried out at the UOC that show the feasibility of the Grid approach to achieve an effective embedding of the appropriate knowledge into collaborative learning practices.

The rest of the chapter is organized as follows. In Section 2 we give the context that motivated this research and make some reference to other studies in the field. In Section 3 we show the process of creating effective knowledge and exemplify a real situation. Section 4 presents the performance problems found in processing large and complex amounts of event information while Section 5 and 6 show several Grid-based approaches that help overcome this inconvenience. We conclude in Section 7 and 8 by analysing further the results obtained and outlining ongoing work.

2. Related Work

In a real context, the Open University of Catalonia provides several on-line courses involving hundreds of undergraduate students and a dozen of tutors in a collaborative learning environment. The complexity of the learning practices entails intensive collaboration activity generating a great amount of group activity information. To implement the collaborative learning activities and capture the group interaction we use the Basic Support for Cooperative Work (BSCW) [14] as a shared workspace system which enables collaboration over the Web by supporting document upload, group management and event service among others features. BSCW event service provides awareness information to allow users to coordinate their work [15]. Events are triggered whenever a user performs an action in a workspace, such as uploading a new document, downloading (i.e. reading) an existing document, renaming a document and so on. The system records the interaction data into large daily log files and presents the recent events to each user. In addition, users can request immediate email messages whenever an event occurs and the daily activity reports which are sent to them daily and inform them about the events within the last 24 hours.

BSCW and its extension to the learning domain called Synergeia [16] provides neither log file processing nor tools for analyzing the processed information, thus it can not provide enriched awareness to users to support collaboration and learning (e.g., model the users' behavior, and track and assess the collaborative learning process). Moreover, BSCW records the interaction as line-structured text files which are scarcely commented while they produce a high degree of redundancy. As a result, the processing and analysis of this huge amount of ill-structured information requires an efficient data processing system.

There exist several approaches in the literature that deal with the processing and analysis of data for awareness purposes so that to keep track of the collaborative learning activities. In [17] a tool for processing event logs of the BSCW is presented using a social network analysis method. Other approaches [18], focus on processing event log files for analyzing the dialogue and interaction, or for using them in query systems to increase awareness [19]. On the one hand, these approaches consider the processing of the data just for a specific purpose, limiting thus the scope of the developed tools. On the other hand, they do not address the issue of processing time requirements that might result from the huge amount of data that are to be processed, which is a common issue in collaborative learning environments.

3. The Process of Creating Effective Knowledge

Creating useful, effective, heterogeneous, yet structured knowledge is a complex process. As part of the process of embedding information and knowledge about group activity into CSCL applications (see Figure 1 and [6]), this consists of four separate, indispensable stages: collection of information, processing, analysis and presentation. The entire process fails if one of these stages is omitted.

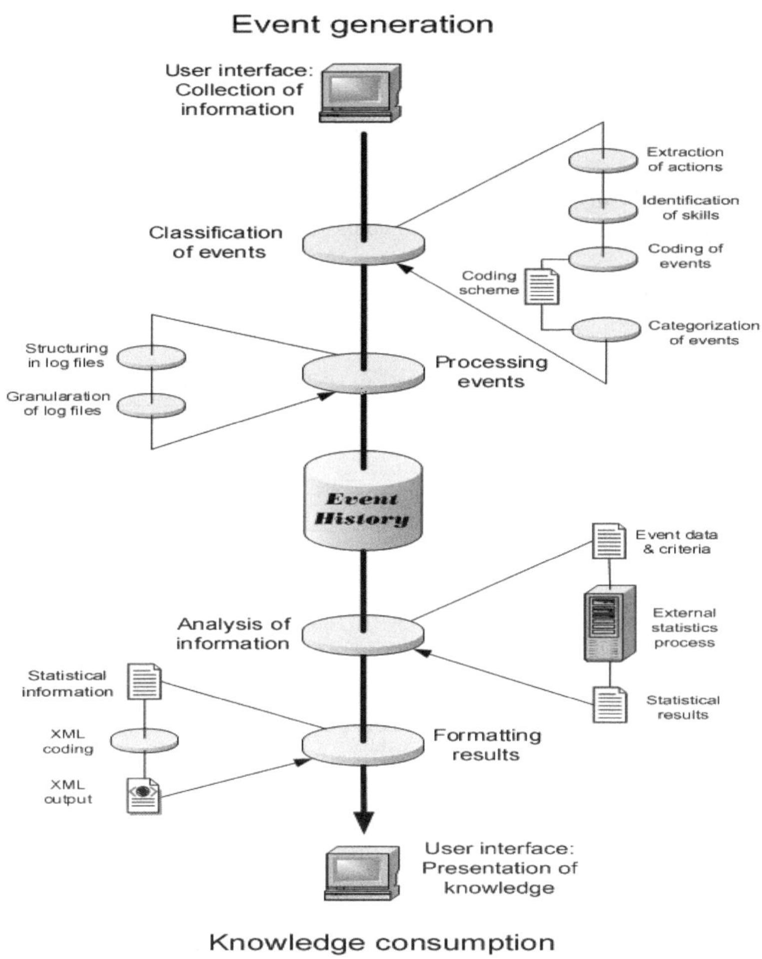

Figure 1. The embedding of information and knowledge about group activity into CSCL applications.

During the first stage, the information is collected from the collaborative actions triggered by the students and is classified in terms of specific events. Due to its conceptual importance, we now describe this stage in more detail. In particular, during the information collection, the objective is to gather as much information as possible generated during group activity to use it as a basis for the next three stages. To this end, we propose a solution consisting of classifying information by means of three generic group activity parameters, namely collaborative learning product, group functioning, and scaffolding (social support and task or group functioning help oriented services), which represent high-level collaborative learning processes [4], [20].

To measure each indicator (or skill) forming each mentioned parameter, we associate it with the actions that students perform and which represent each indicator in the best possible manner. We employ a similar terminology to the one usually used in the BSCW system [14] to refer to the actions that can be carried out in any groupware platform. Even so, they are general enough to be independent from BSCW and represent all the typical and basic actions encountered in every groupware platform.

The collaborative learning product parameter (see Table 1) features the production function and task performance of on-line groups. It is characterized by the type of actions (events) that capture and describe the functional knowledge, cognitive processes and skills of the students and the group as a whole in solving problems and producing learning outcomes in a collaborative learning practice. It is used to analyze and evaluate the individual and group effectiveness as far as task achievement concerns. It can be measured as a qualitative and quantitative parameter by the type of user task-based actions that represent contributions which express basic and supporting active learning skills as well as perception skills.

Table 1. Indicators (skills) that model *task performance*

Skills	**Sub-skills (Learning outcome contribution)**	**Actions (&objects) involved**
Basic active learning skills	Information generation	Create doc/note
Supporting active learning skills	Information refinement	Edit doc
	Information elaboration	Version/Replace doc
	Information revision	Revise/Branch doc
	Information reinforcement	Create_Noteboard doc/URL /Notes (as an attachment)
Information processing (perception) skills	Information acknowledgement	Read event

The group functioning parameter (see Table 2) is made up of the type of actions (events) that represent and are used to measure and analyze the individual and group effectiveness regarding participation and interaction behavior that facilitate the group's well-being function. As a quantitative parameter, it enables us to measure important participant contributions (in terms of specific types of user actions) which indicate skills related to: active or passive participation, well-balanced contributions and role playing, participation quality and communication flow among group members, as well as the necessary skills that facilitate and enhance group interaction, namely active processing skills (such as task, workspace and communication processing skills). In addition, interaction behavior can also be measured as a qualitative parameter by group reflection (i.e. group and individual self-evaluation).

Table 2. Indicators (skills) that model *group functioning*

Skills	**Sub-skills (Group functioning contribution)**	**Actions (&objects) involved**
Active participation behavior and peer involve-ment skills	Participation in managing (generating, expanding and processing) information	Create Event, Change Event, Read Event
Social grounding skills	Well-balanced contributions, adequate reaction attitudes, and role playing	Create Event, Change Event, Read Event, Move Event
Task processing skills	Task planning	Create/Link Appointment Create/ChangeAccess WSCalendar
	Task (and knowledge) management	Create Folder Create Notes (as a contribution in a bulletin board)
Workspace processing skills	Workspace organisation and maintenance	Move event (cut, drop, copy, delete, forget)
Communication processing skills	Clarification	Change Description/ Change Event doc Change Description url
	Evaluation	Rate document/url
	Description (illustration)	Edit/Change Description Folder Change Description Notes
	Communication improvement	Edit Note Chvinfo/Chvno/Checkin/Checkout doc Rename Folder/Notes/doc/url/
	Meeting accommodation	ChangeDesc/ChangeDate /ChangeLocation Appointment

The scaffolding parameter (see Table 3) is specified by the type of events that refer to social support among members as well as to task- or group functioning-oriented help provided to a participant who is not quite able or ready to achieve a task on his or her own. As for the former, we look at event information that includes actions which support and promote group cohesion, such as motivational and emotional support, conflict resolution, etc. As for the latter, we focus on those specific actions designated to provide effective help to the peers when they need it during the collaborative learning activities. The participants' actions aiming at getting or providing help are classified and measured according to whether they refer to the task or group functioning.

In the next stage of processing, a tight structuring of the generated event information is performed and stored in log files. During the analysis stage, this information is analyzed and interpreted in order to extract knowledge according to different criteria. The final stage, presentation, is to show the students the knowledge obtained, thus providing them appropriate awareness and meta-cognition.

Table 3. Indicators that model *scaffolding*

Social support
Members' commitment toward collaboration, joint learning and accomplishment of the common group goal
Level of peer involvement and their influential contribution to the involvement of the others
Members' contribution to the achievement of mutual trust
Members' motivational and emotional support to their peers
Participation and contribution to conflict resolution
Help Services
Help is timely
Help is relevant to the student's needs
Help is qualitative
Help is understood by the student
Help can readily be applied by the student

Therefore, in order to provide users with continuous awareness, once the event information generated in group activity is correctly collected and classified, this information needs to be structured in a way that facilitates its later processing and analysis and can be addressed in a distributed environment such as a Grid [7], [8], [10].

To that end, during the processing stage, we propose the following generic steps so as to structure the event information correctly for later processing [8]: we first classify the event information collected from the collaborative actions and turn it into persistent data; then we store it in the system as structured log files. Next, we structure the files according to appropriate criteria (such as time and workspace) depending on the desired knowledge to be presented. For each of these criteria these files represent as great a degree of granularity as possible so that we can concatenate several log files and obtain the appropriate degree of granularity during data processing. This makes it possible for a distributed system such as Grid to parallelize data processing efficiently according to the characteristics of its computational resources.

Thereby, CSCL applications can take a great advantage of the inherent parallelism of a Grid environment to process several files (e.g. all the groups in a classroom) at the same time and thus considerably reduce the overall computational time. As a result, it is possible for these applications to process a large volume of collaboration activity data and make the results available in real time. The aim is to process large amounts of information efficiently enabling the constant presentation of both single awareness information in (almost) real-time and complex, in-depth deferred awareness.

At this point, in order to clarify the process of creating complex and useful awareness in a real situation, we briefly exemplify the case of monitoring the users' behavior by processing BSCW log file information involving time and workspaces. Note that the case of the UOC virtual campus and other collaborative learning systems are very similar.

We first take all the daily single BSCW log files as a starting point within the desired period of time that are to be analyzed. Each of these log files records all the event information generated each day and thus they collect all the users' activity in the system. This information is first classified according to users, time and workspaces so that it is only related to the user who generated events, the time when they occurred and the workspace where they took place. Then, the resulting log file is partitioned into multiple log files of a finer grain, each one storing all the workspaces that a certain user has visited during the shortest time interval. Consequently, several of these log files will be concatenated so as to obtain the appropriate degree of granularity and thus fit their size to the characteristics of the computational resources of Grid's nodes. The aim is to distribute the workload among the Grid's nodes correctly and as a result to parallelize the data processing efficiently. Finally, the processed results are stored in a database in a way that they can be easily analyzed by statistical packages so as to extract knowledge about the user's behavior: usual time to enter and leave a certain workspace, time average staying in each workspace and number of times per day entering the same workspace are, among others, some analysis needs. At the end of the process, this obtained knowledge can be presented to the user as structured data.

4. A Sequential Approach

In this section, we report how to deal with the problem of extracting useful information from the event logs generated by both the BSCW system and the UOC's virtual campus.

4.1. The Problem of Processing log files of the BSCW

For the case of the BSCW, we developed a simple application in Java, called *EventExtractor*. This application runs offline on the same machine as the BSCW server and uses the daily log files generated by the BSCW server as input so as to: (i) identify the event boundaries inside the log file, (ii) map specific information contained in these events about users, objects, sessions, etc. to typed data structures, and (iii) store these data structures in a persistent support. Note that as the processing is done offline there is no need for a sensor component. In order to analyze the performance of this sequential application, we designed a specific test battery in which we used both large amounts of event information and well-stratified short samples consisting of all the existing daily log files making up the whole group activity generated during an academic term in the computer science subject "Software Development Techniques" at the Open University of Catalonia. This course involved two classrooms, with a total of 140 students arranged in groups of 5 students and 2 tutors. On the other hand, other tests involved a few log files with selected file size and event complexity forming a sample of each representative stratum. This allowed us to obtain reliable statistical results using an input data size easy to use.

All our test batteries were processed by this application on single-processor machines involving usual configurations. The test batteries were executed several times with different workload in order to have more reliable results in statistical terms involving file size, number of events processed and execution time along with other basic statistics. As an example, the experimental results from the sequential processing of the *EventExtractor* application are summarized in Figure 2, where for each event log file we show the relative comparison scale for the file size, number of events and the processing time. In a similar way, Figure 3 presents the processing results of over one hundred event log files involving file size and processing time showing that the processing time is linear on the size of the log file processed.

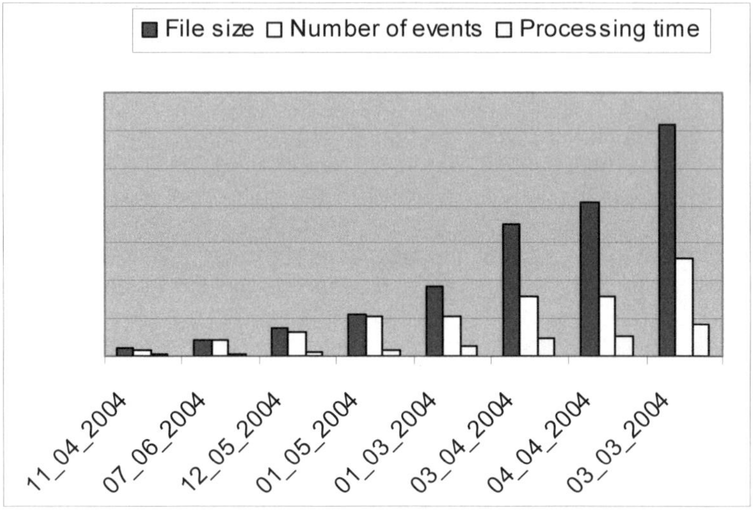

Figure 2. Relative comparison scale of a sample of selected log files with the group activity occurring in 8 certain days of the spring academic term of 2004. Note that due to the different event complexity, the number of events does not increase linearly with the file size.

However, when executing sequentially in a single machine, this application needs a lot of time and resources to process such amount of information and hence it is not feasible to constantly process data log files in real time. Therefore, these statistical results make evident the lack of computational resources as the main obstacle to constantly present knowledge to users in terms of awareness and feedback in real time.

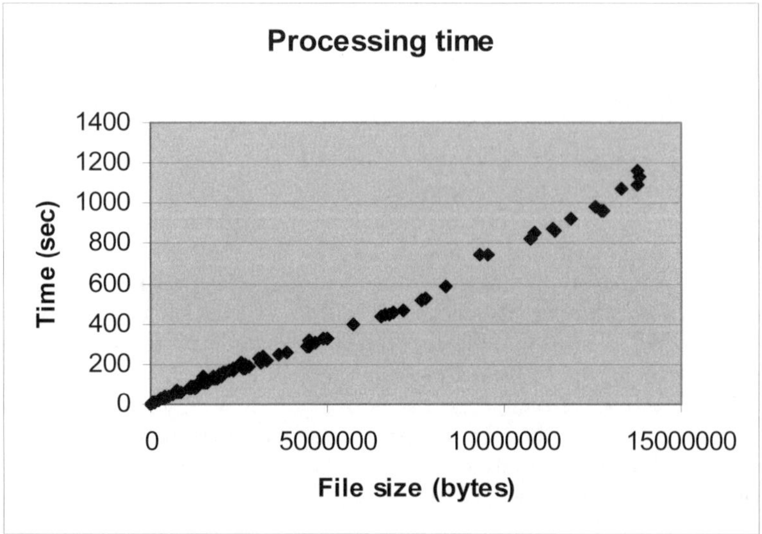

Figure 3. Sequential processing time for every event log file size.

4.2. The Problem of Processing log files of the Virtual Campus of the UOC

The on-line web-based campus of the UOC is made up of individual and community virtual areas such as mailbox, agenda, classrooms, library, secretary's office, and so on. Students and other users (lecturers, tutors, administrative staff, etc.) continuously browse these areas where they request for services to satisfy their particular needs and interests. For instance, students make strong use of email service so as to communicate with other students and lecturers as part of their learning process.

All users' requests are chiefly processed by a collection of Apache [21] web servers as well as database servers and other secondary applications, all of which provide service to the whole community and thus satisfy a great deal of users' requests. For load balance purposes, all HTTP traffic is smartly distributed among the different Apache web servers available. Each web server stores in a log file all users' requests received in this specific server and the information generated from processing the requests. Once a day (namely, at 01:00 a.m.), all web servers in a daily rotation merge their logs producing a single very large log file containing the whole user interaction with the campus performed in the last 24 hours.

A typical daily log file size may be up to 10 GB. This great amount of information is first pre-processed using filtering techniques in order to remove a lot of futile, non relevant information (e.g. information coming from automatic control processes, the uploading of graphical and format elements, etc.). However, after this pre-processing, about 1.8 GB of potentially useful information corresponding to 3,500,000 of log entries in average still remains [22].

Log file entries are structured following a type of format known as Common Log Format (CLF) [23] which is produced by most of web servers including Apache and is fairly configurable. For the purpose of registering the campus activity, log files entries were set up with the purpose of capturing the following information: who performed a request (i.e. user's IP address along with a session key that uniquely identifies a user session); when the request was processed (i.e. timestamp); what type of service was requested (a URL string format description of the server application providing the service requested along with the input values) and where (i.e. an absolute URL containing the full path to the server application providing the service requested).

At this point, we point out some problems which arise when dealing with these log files. Each explicit user request generates at least an entry in the log file and after being processed by a web server, other log entries are generated from the response of this user request; certain non-trivial requests (e.g. user login) involve in turn requesting others and hence they may implicitly trigger new log entries; the what and where fields contain very similar information regarding the URL strings that describe the service requested and the parameters with the input values; certain information is found in a very primitive form and is represented as long text strings (e.g. user session key is a long 128-character string). Therefore, there is a high degree of redundancy, tedious and ill-formatted information as well as incomplete as at some cases certain user actions do not generate any log entry (e.g. user may leave the campus by either closing or readdressing the browser) and have to be inferred. As a consequence, treating this information is very costly in terms of time and space needing a great processing effort.

In order to deal with the above mentioned problems and inconveniences, we developed a simple application in Java, called *UOCLogsProcessing* that processes log files of the UOC. In particular, this application runs offline on the same machine as the logging application server. It uses, as an input, the daily log files obtained as a result of merging all web servers' log files. The following process is run: (i) identify the log entries boundaries and extract the fields that make up each entry, (ii) capture the specific information contained in the fields about users, time, sessions, areas, etc., (iii) infer the missing information, (iv) map the information obtained to typed data structures, and (v) store these data structures in a persistent support.

However, after running similar test batteries as those for the BDCW case, the repercussions of processing UOC's log file data sequentially are very similar to those mentioned for the case of BSCW log file processing. Thus, the sequential processing of the *UOCLogsProcessing* also takes too long to complete the work and it has to be done after the completion of the learning activity, which impedes from providing complex feedback to users in real time.

In the next section, we present an improved version of the processing of log files to parallelize the processing of information and the main experimental results achieved. Although our approach is generic and is valid for both types of log files (i.e., the BSCW system and the UOC virtual campus), for testing purposes we use the type of log file which most fits and can take advantage of characteristics of each resulting prototype.

5. Parallel Grid-based Approaches

In this section, we present improved versions of the sequential-execution applications to process log files. To this end, we first describe a general Grid-based approach to process log files. Then, we will show different Grid middleware approaches to realize our approach in order to efficiently parallelize the processing of log files. The next section will show the main experimental results achieved.

5.1. A Grid-based approach to process log files

Over the last few years, Grid computing has become a real alternative for developing parallel applications that employ its great computational power. However, due to the complexity of the Computational Grid, the difficulty encountered in developing parallel applications is higher than in traditional parallel computing environments. Thus, in order to simplify the development of Grid-aware applications several high-level programming frameworks have been proposed, among which is the Master-Worker Framework (MWF) [24].

The Master-Worker (MW) [25] model (also known as Master-Slave or Task Farming model) has been widely used for developing parallel applications in traditional supercomputing environments such as parallel machines and clusters of machines. In the MW model there are two distinct types of processors: master and workers. The master processor performs the control and coordination and assigns tasks to the workers. It also decides what data will be sent to the workers. The workers typically perform most of the computational work. The MW model has proved to be efficient in developing applications using different degrees of granularity of parallelism. Indeed, it has several advantages such as flexibility and scalability (the worker processors can be implemented in many different ways and they can be easily added if needed) as well as separation of concerns (the master performs coordination tasks and the worker processors carry out specific tasks). This paradigm is particularly useful when the definition of the tasks to be completed by the workers can be done easily and the communication load between the master and workers is low.

MWF allows users to easily parallelize scientific computations through the master-worker paradigm on the computational Grid. On the one hand, MWF provides a top level interface that helps the programming tasks to distribute large computations in a Grid computing environment; on the other hand, it offers a bottom level interface to existing Grid computing toolkits, for instance, using the Condor system to provide Grid services. The target applications of MWF are parallel applications with weak synchronization and reasonably large granularity. As we show next, this framework is appropriate for processing log files of group activity since we have different degrees of granularity available so as to guarantee efficiency and, furthermore, there is no need for synchronization or communication between the worker processors. Moreover, in our application, the communication load between the master and workers is very low.

The architecture of the application (see Figure 4) is made up of three parts: (1) the Collaborative Learning Application Server, which is in charge of maintaining the log files and storing them in specified locations; (2) the MW application for processing log files and, (3) the application that uses the resulting information in the data bases to compute statistical results and present them to the final user.

Next subsection introduces two different realizations based on this architecture in the form of Grid middleware to efficiently parallelize the processing of logs files from both the *EventExtractor* and *UOCLogsProcessing* routines described in Section 4.

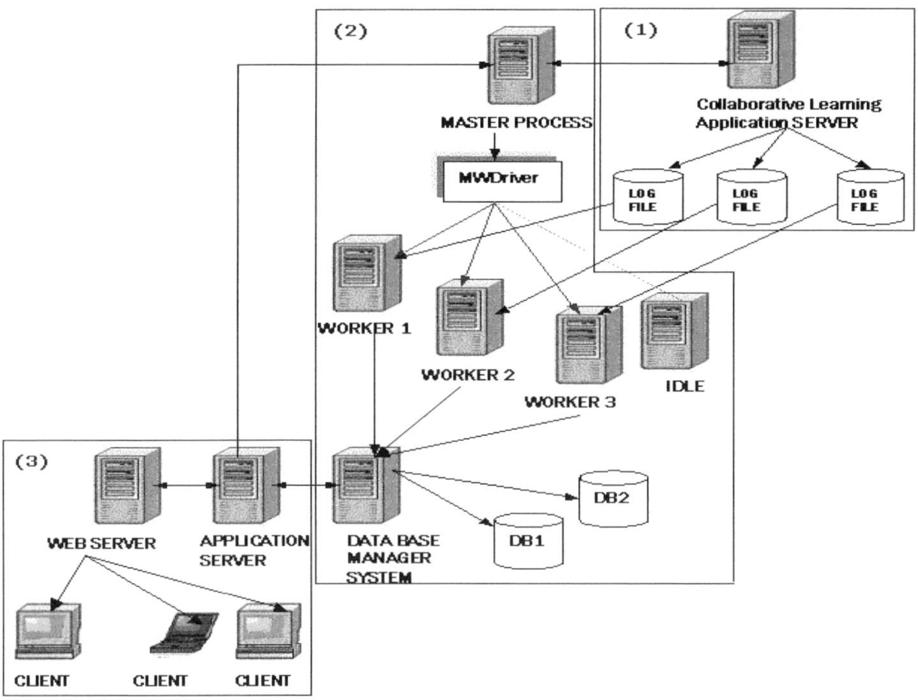

Figure 4. Generic architecture of the application for processing log files

5.2. Using Grid infrastructure to Parallelize theProcessing of Log Files

We show here how the MW paradigm is appropriate for processing log files of group activity in a Grid environment, since we have different degrees of granularity available and, moreover, there is no need for synchronization between the worker processors as tasks are completely independent from one another. To this end, we have written a minimal Grid implementation prototype using both the standard Globus Toolkit (GT) [26] middleware and an ad hoc middleware called Juxta-CAT [28] and have deployed it on the Planetlab [29] platform. The latter is first described next.

Planetlab [10], [29] is an open platform for developing, deploying and accessing planetary-scale services. It is, at the time of this writing, composed up of 825 nodes hosted in 406 different sites. Each Planetlab node runs the same base software, basically a modified Linux operating system offering services to create virtual isolated partitions in the node, which look to users as the real machine. The next subsection introduces two different realizations based on this architecture in the form of Grid middleware to efficiently parallelize the processing of logs files.

5.2.1. Using standard Grid middleware

The Globus Toolkit (GT) [6], [10], [26] is the actual de facto Grid middleware standard. Version 3 of GT (GT3) is a refactoring of version 2 in which every functionality is exposed to the world via a Grid service (i.e. basically, stateful web services). The core of the GT is a Grid service container implemented in Java that leverages and extends the Apache's AXIS [30] web services container.

In order to test this Grid prototype we used log files of the BSCW system due to their relatively small size and relatively low occurrence of complex events but with high variability of file size, which fits well in this case. To this end, we turned Planetlab into a Grid fabric by installing the GT3's Grid service container. Moreover, we implemented the worker as a simple Grid service that we deployed on the GT3's container. Then, we wrote a simple Java client that plays the role of the master by dispatching tasks just by calling the operations exposed by the worker Grid services, as follows:

- The worker Grid service publishes an interface with only one operation that the master calls in order to dispatch a task to the worker. This operation, which is implemented by wrapping the Java code of the mentioned *EventExtractor* routine (see Section 4), passes as an input a textual representation of the events to be processed by that task and returns a data structure containing performance information about the task executed (i.e. elapsed time, number of events processed and number of bytes processed).
- The master is just a simple Java application that reads from a configuration file (1) the folder that contains the event log files to process, (2) the available workers, (3) the number of workers to use, and (4) the size of the task to be dispatched to each worker expressed in number of events. The master then proceeds as follows: it picks as much workers as needed from the configuration file and puts them all in a queue of idle workers. Then it enters a loop reading the events from the event log files and, each time it has read a number of events, it either waits for a worker if the queue is empty or calls the worker's operation. Once the call to the worker returns, the worker is put back

into the queue of idle workers. The master exits the loop when all events in the event log files have been read and all the tasks that were dispatched have finalized.

As we have stated, this is not a real GT3 Grid implementation of the MW paradigm but a proof-of-concept prototype, thus important features in a real environment such as fault-tolerance and dynamic discovery of available workers, are missing. Finally, the experimental results of processing log files using GT middleware are shown in Section 6.

5.2.2. Using ad hoc JXTA-based Grid middleware

In this section, we briefly introduce the main aspects of the Grid platform, called Juxta-CAT [28], which we have used for the processing of log files. The Juxta-CAT platform has been developed using the JXTA protocols [31] and offers a shared Grid where client peers can submit their tasks in the form of java programs stored on signed jar files and are remotely solved on the nodes of the platform. Juxta-CAT Project and its official web site have been hosted in Java.NET community [28]. In order to test this Grid prototype we used the very large and ill-structured log files of the UOC virtual campus due to the great flexibility provided by the JXTA protocols, which allowed us to split the large log files into many short samples consisting of representative daily periods with different activity degrees.

The architecture of Juxta-CAT platform is made up of two types of peers: common *client peers* and *broker peers*.

- Client peers create and submit their requests using a GUI-based application (see Figure 5) and are the end users of the Juxta-CAT, which are obtained by downloading and installing the application from the official page of Juxta-CAT. Once the machine is converted into a client peer, the user will connect to the peer-to-peer network and can submit execution requests to their peer group nodes. Also, client peers will be able to process received requests sent to them by other nodes through the brokering and notify them the result of the requests, once they are completed.
- Broker peers are the administrators of the Grid, which are in charge of efficiently assigning client requests to the Grid nodes and notify the results to the owner's requests. Whenever a broker receives a request, it explores the state of the rest of nodes currently connected to the network, examining their working and connection statistics. Then, it uses this historical/statistical data to select, according to a price-based economic model, the best candidate peer for processing that request. To assure an efficient use of resources, brokers use an allocation algorithm, which can be viewed as a price-based economic model, to determine the best candidate node to process each new received petition.

The implementation and design of peers, groups, job and presence discovery, pipe-based messaging, etc. are developed using the latest updated JXTA libraries (currently release 2.3.7) and JDK 1.5 version.

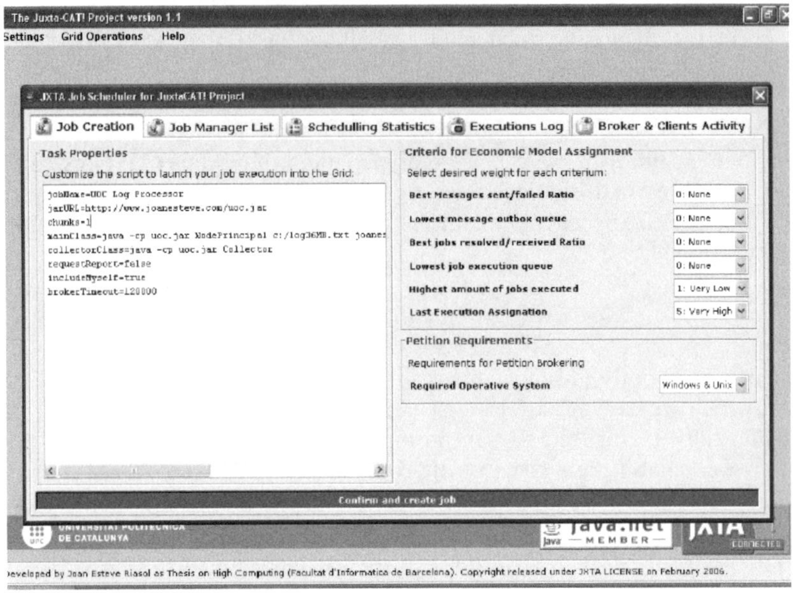

Figure 5: GUI view of submitting the processing of a log file to the Juxta-CAT.

We explain now how the processing of log files is done in the Juxta-CAT platform. The implementation follows the well-known Master-Worker paradigm. We note first that the sequential java class of the *UOCLogsProcessing* routine described in Section 4 also encapsulates functionalities to provide the division of the log file into as many equal parts as Grid nodes will be used for processing them; these parts will be later on submitted for processing to the Juxta-CAT. The main steps that would follow the user (the master node) to process a log file in the Juxta-CAT are as follows:

1. [**Preparation phase**]: Provide the necessary information (to the Master) for the preparation of the petitions to submit to the Juxta-CAT:
    a. Indicate the path to the log file and its name and the number of nodes participating in the processing. Log processor routines count the total number of lines of the log file, totalNbLines, and knowing the number of Grid nodes to be used, nbNodes, each node will read and process a totalNbLines/nbNodes of lines from the file.
    b. Indicate an FTP server, a user name and a password as well as a public address where the parts of the file will be uploaded. The implementation of FTP for Java, known as PureFTP, is included in the Jakarta Apache *commons-net-1.4.1.jar* library [32].
2. [**Master Loop**]: Repeat
    a. Read totalNbLines/nbNodes lines
    b. Upload the file to the indicated public address via FTP
    c. Create a petition and submit it to Juxta-CAT

   Until the original log file has been completely scanned.
3. [**Juxta-cat processing**]:

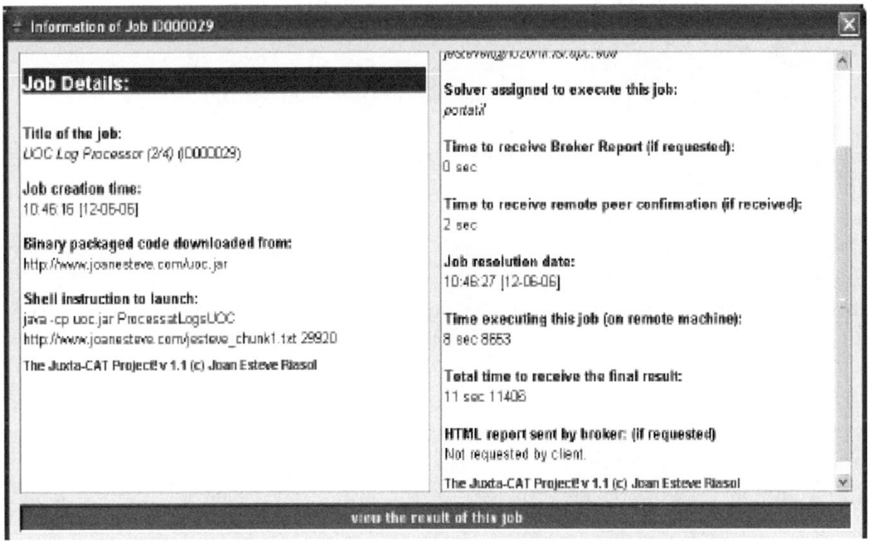

Figure 6. State information of a petition once it is processed.

a. Each time a petition is received by brokers of Juxta-CAT, it is assigned to a peer node of the platform.
b. The peer node, upon receiving the petition, reads according to the petition's description, the part of the file it has to read via HTTP. The peer runs *UOCLogProcessing* functionality for processing the lines of the file, one at a time, and stores the results of the processing in a buffer.
c. The peer node, once the processing of the petition is done, sends back to the master node the content of the buffer.

4. [**Master's final phase**]: Receive messages from peers and append the new received resulting file to the final file containing the information extracted from the original log file.

The *UOCLogsProcessing* routine is compiled in a unique java jar packages, which includes the library developed by Jakarta Apache needed for the FTP transfer. The code has been optimized using Java Proguard 3.5 so that the final jar file size is 28.7 KB. Figures 5 and 6 show the submission of a petition to Juxta-CAT and the state information once it is processed. Note that the user has to just provide the in formation needed in Step 1 (see above); the rest is automatically done by Juxta-CAT. The experimental results using Juxta-CAT are shown in Sub-Section 6.2.

6. Experimental Results

In order to carry out a comparative study between the sequential and Grid approaches, we designed a specific test battery in which we used both large amounts of event information and well-stratified short samples. In this section, we present the experimental results achieved of our Grid prototypes while next section analyzes certain important aspects of these results to be considered.

6.1. Results from Paralleizing the Processing of BSCW Log Files

In order to test our GT-based prototype and compare the results to the sequential approach, we run the *EventExtractor* routine for processing log files from the BSCW system on this Grid platform in the Planetlab nodes. To this end, as mentioned in Section 4, we used the existing daily log files making up the whole group activity generated during a whole academic term in the course "Software Development Techniques" at the Open University of Catalonia. Other tests involved a few log files with selected file size and event complexity forming a sample of each representative stratum.

The linearity found in processing time in the sequential approach (see Figure 3) allowed us to greatly simplify the experiment by using the same event log file as input for all the Grid tests in the experiment. Then, we left to vary the parameters regarding both the number of workers and the size of the tasks (expressed in number of events) which were to be executed by the workers. We ran tests for a different number of workers with different task sizes.

Parallel speed-up is used to measure the performance gain from a parallelized execution over its serial execution and defined as `S(s,p) = Ts (s) / Tp(s,p)`, where s is the size of the log file, `Ts(s)` is the total running time of the sequential execution for a log file of size s and `Tp(s,p)` is the total running time of the parallel execution for a log file of size s, using p processors.

Figure 7 shows the maximum speed-ups achieved for the observed bandwidth between our master processor and the Planetlab nodes at the time of running the experiment and for the different number of workers we tested.

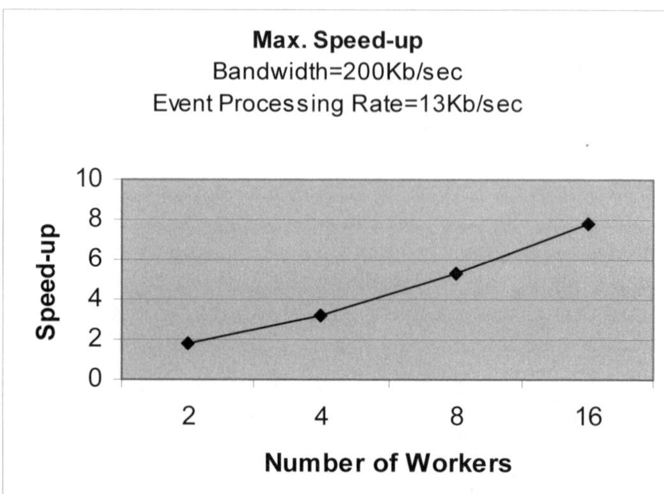

Figure 7. Maximum speed-up vs. number of workers

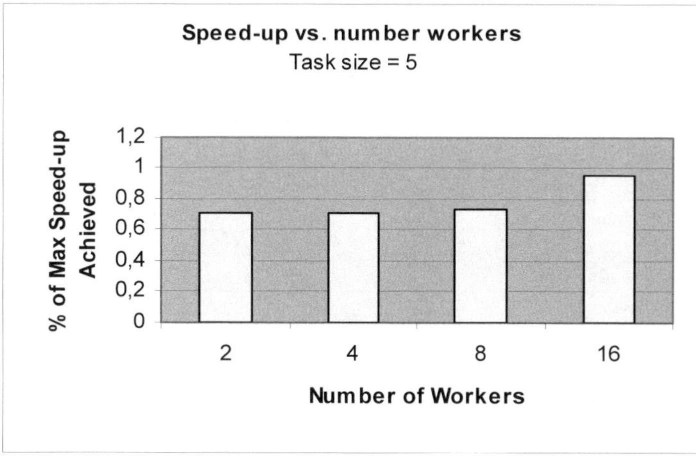

Figure 8. Relative speed-up vs. number of workers for a task size of 5 events

As mentioned before, the worker returns the elapsed time of its execution, whereas the master executes all the events found up to the input event log files have been completely parsed and all dispatched tasks have been completed. We computed the observed speed-up for the test by dividing (1) the sum of all the elapsed times returned by each invocation of the worker into (2) the elapsed time the master run multiplied by a normalization factor to compensate the different speed between the machine running the master and the Planetlab nodes running the workers.

Therefore, the main experimental results from the parallel processing of log files are given in terms of how much close each set of workers is to achieve its theoretic maximum speed-up (see Figure 7) for different task size processed and, thus, providing the best processing time possible while parallelizing the data processing. To this end, Figure 8 shows the graphical representation of an extract of these results in relative terms for a sample of a specific 5-event size task.

6.2. Results from Paralleizing the Processing of UOC Log Files

In this sub-section, we present the experimental results obtained after running our JXTA-based Grid platform Juxta-CAT in the Planetlab nodes on a test battery made up of the log files from the UOC virtual campus showing the speedup achieved.

This test battery uses both large amounts of log information (i.e. daily log files) and well-stratified short samples consisting of representative daily periods with different activity degrees (e.g. from 7 p.m. to 1 a.m. as the most active lecturing period and from 1 a.m. to 7 a.m. as the period with least activity in the campus). In addition, other tests involved a few log files with selected file size forming a sample of each representative stratum. This allowed us to obtain reliable statistical results using an input data size easy to use.

Table 4. PlanetLab nodes used to run the experiment.

Host	Description
planet1.manchester.ac.uk	University of Manchester
lsirextpc01.epfl.ch	École Fédérale de Lausanne
planetlab1.polito.it	Politecnico di Torino
planetlab1.info.ucl.ac.be	University of Louivain
planetlab2.upc.es	Universitat Politècnica de Catalunya
planetlab1.sics.se	Swedish Institute of Computer Sci.
planetlab1.ifi.uio.no	University of Oslo
planetlab3.upc.es	Universitat Politècnica de Catalunya
planetlab1.ls.fi.upm.es	Universidad Politécnica de Madrid
planetlab1.hiit.fi	Technology Institute of Helsinki
planetlab-1.cs.ucy.ac.cy	University of Cyprus
planetlab1.ru.is	University of Reykjavik
planetlab2.sics.se	Swedish Institute of Computer Sci.
planetlab1.mini.pw.edu.pl	Telekomunikacja Polska Warsaw
planetlab1.cs.uit.no	University of Tromso
planetlab-02.ipv6.lip6.fr	Laboratoire d'Informatique de Paris

The battery test was processed by the *UOCLogsProcessing* application described in Sub-Section 4.2 and executed several times first on single-processor machines involving usual configurations and with different workload in order to have more reliable results in statistical terms involving file size, number of log entries processed and execution time along with other basic statistics. Then, the same battery test was processed in a parallel fashion by Juxta-CAT using different number of nodes, specifically, 2, 4, 8, and 16 nodes, using the PlanetLab nodes appearing in Table 4.

Parallel efficiency measures the degree of utilization of the computing resources involved in the parallel computation and is defined as the parallel speed up (defined in Sub-Section 6.1) divided by the number of computing resources (i.e. processors): `E(s,p) = S(s) / p.`

From the execution times (see Figure 9) and the formulas previously introduced, we show in Table 5 the gain in terms of parallel speed-up and efficiency we achieved.

7. Analysis of the results

Analyzing the experimental results obtained from our Grid prototypes, we found that, on the one hand, from certain values of the task size, the speed-up observed was very close to the theoretic maximum achievable. This allows us to conclude that only for a very small value of the task size the impact on the speed-up can be great due to the cost of the transmission overhead. However, we also observed that the more workers we used in our tests the closer to the theoretic maximum was the speed-up achieved by the small tasks, and this increased quickly up to the point that, given a sufficient number of workers, even the smallest tasks (i.e. one-event task size) achieved considerable speed-up.

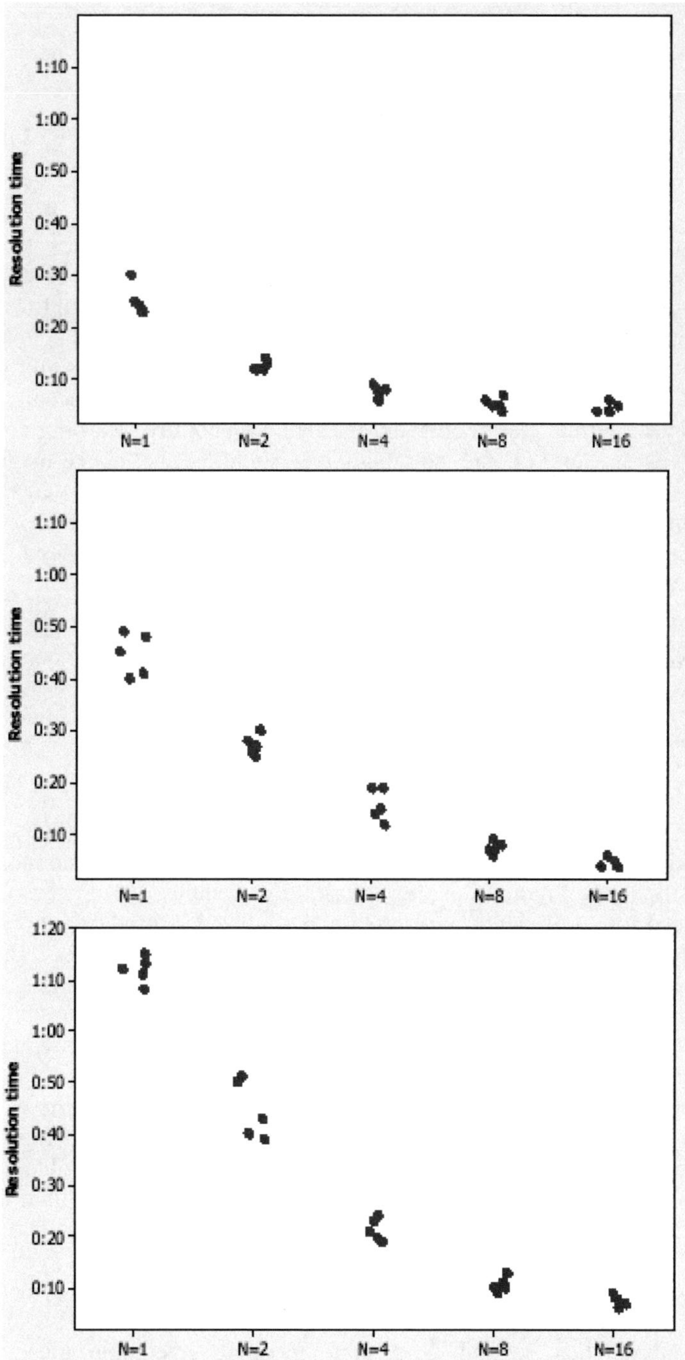

Figure 9. Three execution time results for log files with sizes of 12MB, 24MB and 36MB respectively; x-axis indicates the number of processors and y-axis the processing time (mm:ss).

Table 5. Parallel speed-up and efficiency.

Log file size	Speed-up	Efficiency
12 MB	6.1	38.2 %
24 MB	7.4	46,2 %
36 MB	9.1	56.8 %

On the other hand, the homogenous behavior observed in Planetlab nodes justified our decision of testing with the same task size for all workers. However, in a real Grid environment, task sizes should be adjusted per worker node case to fit the dynamically changing workloads the nodes may be experimenting and to account for different machine speeds.

We note, however, that although the results of this experiment are promising, a deeper and more precise analysis on both the primary interaction occurring between participants in the virtual classrooms and the real collaborative learning activity based on complex parameters of the collaboration, such as the above-mentioned task performance, group functioning and scaffolding, it is expected to generate a much larger amount and more complex events than those used for our experiments . This scenario will take much more advantage of the benefits provided by a Grid environment and will provide a more useful knowledge about the actual performance occurring in the on-line learning activity and will help monitor and support learning participants more conveniently.

8. Conclusions and Future Work

In this chapter, we have first argued how the provision of continuous knowledge to on-line teams in CSCL environments can greatly improve the group activity in terms of decision-making, group organization, social engagement, support, monitoring and so on. As a result, large amounts of log information generated from the collaborative interaction need to be efficiently processed and analyzed. Moreover, in order to make the knowledge extracted from the analysis be useful for awareness and feedback purposes (see Figure 10), users should be provided with both single information delivered fast in (almost) real-time and complex, exhaustive, yet structured deferred information thus stressing even more the processing requirements beyond those of a single computer.

We proposed then several Grid approaches to overcome these demanding requirements by improving the processing time of a large amount of log files storing complex event information from the group activity. The results obtained and the experience achieved in our studies allows us to eventually conclude that the question whether the Grid is beneficial or not will heavily depend on the volume and structure of information being processed. Therefore, these results encourage us to keep up working on the development of a real working Grid implementation to address the problem of processing group activity event log files.

We proposed then several Grid approaches to overcome these demanding requirements by improving the processing time of a large amount of log files storing complex event information from the group activity. The results obtained and the experience achieved in our studies allows us to eventually conclude that the question whether the Grid is beneficial or not will heavily depend on the volume and structure of information being processed. Therefore, these results encourage us to keep up working on the development of a real working Grid implementation to address the problem of processing group activity event log files.

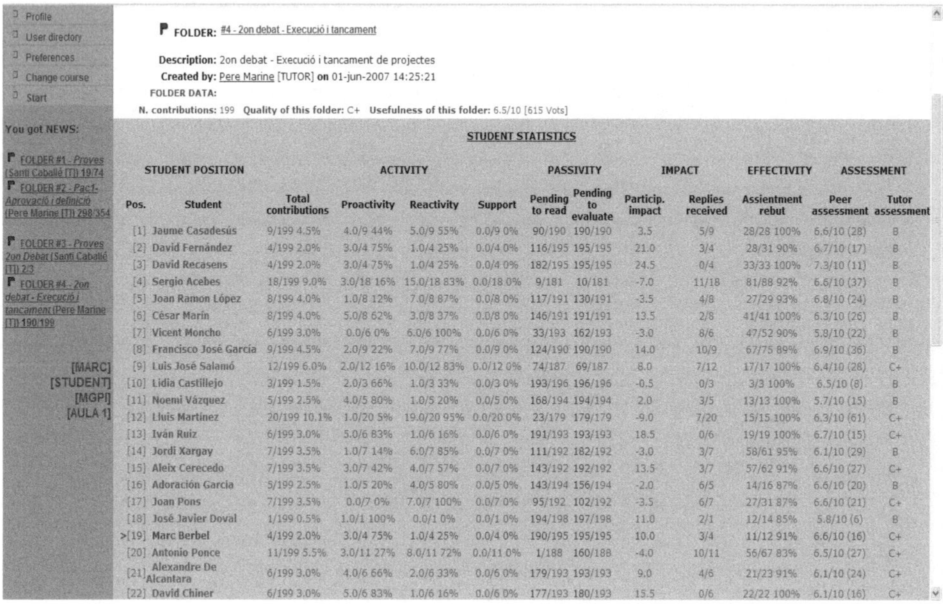

Profile
User directory
Preferences
Change course
Start

You got NEWS:

FOLDER #1 - Proves (Santi Caballé [T]) 19/74
FOLDER #2 - Pac1- Aprovació i definició (Pere Marine [T]) 298/354
FOLDER #3 - Proves 2on Debat (Santi Caballé [T]) 2/3
FOLDER #4 - 2on debat - Execució i tancament (Pere Marine [T]) 190/199

[MARC] [STUDENT] [MGPI] [AULA 1]

FOLDER: #4 - 2on debat - Execució i tancament

Description: 2on debat - Execució i tancament de projectes
Created by: Pere Marine [TUTOR] **on** 01-jun-2007 14:25:21
FOLDER DATA:
N. contributions: 199 **Quality of this folder:** C+ **Usefulness of this folder:** 6.5/10 [615 Vots]

STUDENT STATISTICS

STUDENT POSITION		ACTIVITY				PASSIVITY		IMPACT		EFFECTIVITY	ASSESSMENT	
Pos.	Student	Total contributions	Proactivity	Reactivity	Support	Pending to read	Pending to evaluate	Particip. impact	Replies received	Assientment rebut	Peer assessment	Tutor assessment
[1]	Jaume Casadesús	9/199 4.5%	4.0/9 44%	5.0/9 55%	0.0/9 0%	90/190	190/190	3.5	5/9	28/28 100%	6.6/10 (28)	B
[2]	David Fernández	4/199 2.0%	3.0/4 75%	1.0/4 25%	0.0/4 0%	116/195	195/195	21.0	3/4	28/31 90%	6.7/10 (17)	B
[3]	David Recasens	4/199 2.0%	3.0/4 75%	1.0/4 25%	0.0/4 0%	182/195	195/195	24.5	0/4	33/33 100%	7.3/10 (11)	B
[4]	Sergio Acebes	18/199 9.0%	3.0/18 16%	15.0/18 83%	0.0/18 0%	9/181	10/181	-7.0	11/18	81/88 92%	6.6/10 (37)	B
[5]	Joan Ramon López	8/199 4.0%	1.0/8 12%	7.0/8 87%	0.0/8 0%	117/191	130/191	-3.5	4/8	27/29 93%	6.8/10 (24)	B
[6]	César Marín	8/199 4.0%	5.0/8 62%	3.0/8 37%	0.0/8 0%	146/191	191/191	13.5	2/8	41/41 100%	6.3/10 (26)	B
[7]	Vicent Moncho	6/199 3.0%	0.0/6 0%	6.0/6 100%	0.0/6 0%	33/193	162/193	-3.0	8/6	47/52 90%	5.8/10 (22)	B
[8]	Francisco José García	9/199 4.5%	2.0/9 22%	7.0/9 77%	0.0/9 0%	124/190	190/190	14.0	10/9	67/75 89%	6.9/10 (36)	B
[9]	Luis José Salamó	12/199 6.0%	2.0/12 16%	10.0/12 83%	0.0/12 0%	74/187	69/187	8.0	7/12	17/17 100%	6.4/10 (28)	C+
[10]	Lidia Castillejo	3/199 1.5%	2.0/3 66%	1.0/3 33%	0.0/3 0%	193/196	196/196	-0.5	0/3	3/3 100%	6.5/10 (8)	B
[11]	Noemi Vázquez	5/199 2.5%	4.0/5 80%	1.0/5 20%	0.0/5 0%	168/194	194/194	2.0	3/5	13/13 100%	5.7/10 (15)	B
[12]	Lluis Martínez	20/199 10.1%	1.0/20 5%	19.0/20 95%	0.0/20 0%	23/179	179/179	-9.0	7/20	15/15 100%	6.3/10 (61)	C+
[13]	Iván Ruiz	6/199 3.0%	5.0/6 83%	1.0/6 16%	0.0/6 0%	191/193	193/193	18.5	0/6	19/19 100%	6.7/10 (15)	C+
[14]	Jordi Xargay	7/199 3.5%	1.0/7 14%	6.0/7 85%	0.0/7 0%	111/192	182/192	-3.0	3/7	58/61 95%	6.1/10 (29)	B
[15]	Aleix Cerecedo	7/199 3.5%	3.0/7 42%	4.0/7 57%	0.0/7 0%	143/192	192/192	13.5	3/7	57/62 91%	6.6/10 (27)	C+
[16]	Adoración Garcia	5/199 2.5%	1.0/5 20%	4.0/5 80%	0.0/5 0%	143/194	156/194	-2.0	6/5	14/16 87%	6.6/10 (20)	B
[17]	Joan Pons	7/199 3.5%	0.0/7 0%	7.0/7 100%	0.0/7 0%	95/192	102/192	-3.5	6/7	27/31 87%	6.6/10 (21)	C+
[18]	José Javier Doval	1/199 0.5%	1.0/1 100%	0.0/1 0%	0.0/1 0%	194/198	197/198	11.0	2/1	12/14 85%	5.8/10 (6)	B
>[19]	Marc Berbel	4/199 2.0%	3.0/4 75%	1.0/4 25%	0.0/4 0%	190/195	195/195	10.0	3/4	11/12 91%	6.6/10 (16)	C+
[20]	Antonio Ponce	11/199 5.5%	3.0/11 27%	8.0/11 72%	0.0/11 0%	1/188	160/188	-4.0	10/11	56/67 83%	6.5/10 (27)	C+
[21]	Alexandre De Alcantara	6/199 3.0%	4.0/6 66%	2.0/6 33%	0.0/6 0%	179/193	193/193	9.0	4/6	21/23 91%	6.1/10 (24)	C+
[22]	David Chiner	6/199 3.0%	5.0/6 83%	1.0/6 16%	0.0/6 0%	177/193	180/193	15.5	0/6	22/22 100%	6.1/10 (16)	C+

Figure 10. An example of awareness (in the form of flags) and complex feedback (statistics information) constantly presented to students from the interaction information collected, processed and analyzed during a discussion process.

As ongoing work, we plan to improve the implementation of our Grid prototypes by including a more thorough mining process that provides detailed information and deeper knowledge about the learning activity. This, in turn, will require more processing time in comparison to the log processors used and will take more advantage of the high-throughput performance offered by our prototypes.

Acknowledgements

This work has been partially supported by the Spanish MCYT project TSI2005-08225-C07-05.

References

[1] Dillenbourg, P. (ed.) (1999): Collaborative Learning. Cognitive and Computational Approaches. Elsevier Science Ltd. 1-19.

[2] Gutwin, C., Stark, G. and Greenberg, S., Support for Workspace Awareness in Educational Groupware. in Proceedings of the ACM Conference on Computer Supported Collaborative Learning, Bloomington, Indiana, USA October 17-20, 1995.

[3] Zumbach, J., Hillers, A. & Reimann, P. (2003). Supporting Distributed Problem-Based Learning: The Use of Feedback in Online Learning. In T. Roberts (Ed.), Online Collaborative Learning: Theory and Practice pp. 86-103. Hershey, PA: Idea.

[4] Daradoumis, T., Martínez, A. & Xhafa, F. (2006). A Layered Framework for Evaluating Online Collaborative Learning Interactions. International Journal of Human-Computer Studies. Special Issue on "Theoretical and Empirical Advances in Groupware Research", 64 (7), 622-635.

[5] Conklin, J. "Capturing Organization Memory". Groupware 92. David D. Coleman (editor). San Mateo, CA: Morgan Kaufmann Pub. 1992.

[6] Caballé, S., Daradoumis, T., Paniagua, C. and Xhafa, F. (2005) A Grid Approach to Provide Effective Awareness to On-line Collaborative Learning Teams. In: Proc. of the 1st International Kaleidoscope Learning GRID Special Interest Group Workshop on Distributed e-Learning Environments (DLE'05). Napoli (Italy).

[7] Caballé, S., Paniagua, C., Xhafa, F., and Daradoumis, Th., 2005. A Grid-aware Implementation for Providing Effective Feedback to On-line Learning Groups. In: proc. of the GADA'05, Cyprus.

[8] Xhafa, F., Caballé, S., Daradoumis, Th. and Zhou, N. (2004). A Grid-Based Approach for Processing Group Activity Log Files. In: proc. of the GADA'04, Agya Napa, Cyprus.

[9] Foster, I. and Kesselman, C. The Grid: Blueprint for a Future Computing Infrastructure. pp. 15-52. Morgan Kaufmann, San Francisco, CA, 1998.

[10] Paniagua, C., Xhafa, F., Caballé, S., & Daradoumis, T. (2005). A Grid Prototype Implementation for Real Time Processing of Group Activity Log Data in Collaborative Applications. In: proceedings of the 2005 International Conference on Parallel and Distributed Processing Techniques and Applications, Las Vegas, Nevada, USA (pp. 1177-1183). CSREA Press. ISBN: 1-932415-60-2.

[11] Caballé, S., Daradoumis, Th., Xhafa, F., Esteve J. (2007). Supporting Effective and Useful Web-based Distance Learning. In: proceedings of the Third International Conference on Web Information Systems and Technologies (WEBIST 2007), Barcelona, Spain. INSTICC Press. ISBN: 978-972-8865-79-5. pp. 536-539.

[12] Caballé, S., Daradoumis, Th., Xhafa, F., Esteve J., Barolli, L., Durresi, A., (2007). Using a Grid Platform for Enabling Real Time User Modeling in On-line Campus Proceedings of the CISIS 2007. IEEE Computer Society.

[13] Caballé, S., Xhafa, F., Fernández, R., Daradoumis, Th., (2007). Efficient Enabling of Real Time User Modeling in On-line Campus Proceedings of the UM 2007.LNCS.

[14] Bentley, R., Appelt, W., Busbach. U., Hinrichs, E., Kerr, D., Sikkel, S., Trevor, J. and Woetzel, G. (1997) Basic Support for Cooperative Work on the World Wide Web. Int. J. of Human-Computer Studies 46(6) 827-846.

[15] Appelt, W. (2001): What Groupware Functionality do Users Really Use? In Proceedings of the 9th Euromicro Workshop on PDP 2001, Mantua, February 7-9, 2001. IEEE Computer Society, LosAlamitos.

[16] Stahl, G. (2002) Groupware Goes to School, 8th Int. Workshop on Groupware, CRIWG'02, La Sirena Chile, LNCS, Vol. 2440, pp. 7-24. ISBN: 3-540-44112-3.

[17] Martínez, A., Dimitriadis, Y., Rubia, B., Gómez, E., Garrachón, I. and Marcos, J. A. (2003) Combining qualitative evaluation and social network analysis for the study of classroom social interactions. Workshop "Documenting collaborative interactions" in Computers and Education.

[18] Avouris, N., Komis, V., Fiotakis, F., Margaritis, M., Tselios, N. (2003) On tools for analysis of collaborative problem solving. Proceedings of the 3rd IEEE International Conference on Advanced Learning Technologies (ICALT'03).

[19] Hardings, J. (2003) An XML-based Query Mechanism to Augment Awareness in Computer-integrated classrooms. 11th International Conference on Artificial Intelligence in Education, Australia.

[20] T. Daradoumis, A. Martinez and F. Xhafa: An Integrated Approach for Analysing and Assessing the Performance of Virtual Learning Groups, 10th Int. Workshop on Groupware, CRIWG'04, San Carlos, Costa Rica. Lecture Notes in Computer Science, Vol. 3198, pp. 289-304.

[21] Apache HTTP Server Project: http://httpd.apache.org/ (web page as of November 2007).

[22] Carbó, JM., Mor, E., Minguillón, J. (2005). User Navigational Behavior in e-Learning Virtual Environments. The 2005 IEEE/WIC/ACM International Conference on Web Intel-ligence (WI'05), pp. 243-249.

[23] Common Log Format: http://httpd.apache.org/docs/1.3/logs.html#common (web page as of November 2007).

[24] Goux, J.P., Kulkarni, S., Linderoth, J. and Yoder, M. (2000): An enabling framework for master-worker applications on the computational Grid. In 9th IEEE International Symposium on High Performance Distributed Computing (HPDC'00). IEEE Computer Society.

[25] Master-Worker: http://www.cs.wisc.edu/condor/mw/ (web page as of November 2007).

[26] Globus: http://www.globus.org (web page as of November 2007).

[27] Esteve J., Xhafa F. (2006). Juxta-CAT: A JXTA-based Platform for Distributed Computing. The ACM International Conference on Principles and Practice of Programming in Java'06.

[28] Juxta-CAT: https://juxtacat.dev.java.net/ (web page as of November 2007).

[29] Planetlab: http://www.planet-lab.org (web page as of November 2007).

[30] Apache Axis: http://ws.apache.org/axis/ (web page as of November 2007).

[31] JXTA: http://www.jxta.org/ (web page as of November 2007).

[32] Jakarta Project: http://jakarta.apache.org/ (web page as of November 2007).

The Learning Grid Handbook
S. Salerno et al. (Eds.)
IOS Press, 2008

Grid-based Interactive Virtual Scientific Experiments for Distributed Virtual Communities

Ioannis T. CHRISTOU[1,a], Thanassis TIROPANIS[a], Sofia TSEKERIDOU[a] and Konstantinos ROUSSOS[b]
[a] *Athens Information Technology, Greece*
[b] *INFOTE S.A, Greece*

Abstract. E-learning technologies have matured to a point where distance learning classes are commonly offered from many leading Universities around the world. A major challenge in such distributed classrooms is the formation of virtual communities among the participating students, enhancing the overall learning experience. *Shared* virtual laboratories offer the possibility of forming such virtual communities as students form lab teams to run the same interactive simulation and in the course of such experiments learn to interact and understand each other better. We have designed and implemented a Virtual Scientific Experiment architectural framework on top of a Grid infrastructure for running interactive virtual laboratory experiments for such distributed student communities with visualization capabilities. The architecture is based on Web Services standard protocols such as WSDL and WS-Notification as implemented in the WSRF specification. For the first concrete instantiation of this architecture, we ported a stand-alone Wireless Sensor Network simulator written in Java in our Grid-based architecture and extended it to allow for initial collaborative parameter setup and on-the-fly visualization of the simulation execution and interaction with it, a capability not present in the original simulator. We report on results from running such simulations on a local Grid infrastructure. System evaluation results from a distributed pool of students show the added value of our system in enhancing distance-learning programs and Virtual Classes with extensible collaborative and interactive Virtual Laboratories sessions.

Keywords: Virtual Scientific Experiments, Virtual Communities, GRID-based Shared Virtual Laboratories, Distance Learning, Collaborative Learning, Distributed Computing, Network Simulations, Web Services.

Introduction

The emergence of broadband communications as a commodity combined with advances in computer hardware and specialized video-conferencing software has allowed for a significant growth in life-long learning, distance learning and e-learning technologies, products and services in general. As a result, some of the top Universities in the world are offering degree-granting programs with geographically dispersed campuses (virtual campuses) around the globe. Students from all these campuses form

[1] Corresponding Author: Athens Information Technology, 19Km Markopoulou Ave., P.O. Box 68, Peania 19002, Greece; E-mail: ichr@ait.edu.gr.

one virtual class and community to attend the lectures of the institutions' instructors in real-time. The MSIN program (www.ini.cmu.edu) is such a graduate program in Information Networking offered jointly by the Carnegie Mellon University in Pittsburgh, PA, USA and the Athens Information Technology (www.ait.edu.gr) operating as the CMU campus in Athens, Greece. Several courses are offered as distance-learning courses through e-learning technology. Such courses are taught in auditoriums equipped with large high definition video-walls and cameras' transmitting between the auditoriums what is happening in the other class in real-time. As a result, instructors and students at both auditoriums participate in an essentially unified but distributed virtual classroom where they enjoy full interactivity with every participant in the auditoriums at all times. Real-time audio-visual interaction is achieved through several dedicated high-speed communications links between the two campuses. The educational process is complemented with the use of an appropriately configured document repository where course related documents are placed and discussion forums for course related subjects are supported. Several courses expect students to do their coursework in teams in a laboratory environment. These teams are formed locally, meaning that students at the A.I.T. campus form their own teams and students at the CMU campus form their own teams but teams across the two campuses can not be easily formed because of lack of support of a distributed laboratory infrastructure that would enable closer student interaction and collaboration (Christou et. al. 2007).

Interactive virtual laboratory experiments run together by teams of students unrestricted by geographic location would enhance the formation of community ties between all members of the same class independent of their location. For these reasons, within the context of the ELeGI project (European Learning GRID Infrastructure) we have designed and implemented a prototype architecture for running such virtual scientific experiments, and demonstrated its power by plugging-in the SENSASIM simulation engine (Rayess et. al. 2006), a Wireless Sensor Network simulator written in Java that has been used locally in Athens Information Technology for a graduate course on Wireless Sensor Networks that is offered in the MSIN program. The tool was appropriately modified so as to allow users to alter the execution of the simulator in real time.

The deployed virtual laboratory architecture has been designed to be both *scalable* and *extensible*. Scalable in terms of enabling a large number of participants to collaboratively setup, execute and discuss about virtual scientific experiments and extensible in terms of enabling the addition of virtual scientific experiments that make use of the deployed collaborative parameter setup and GRID infrastructure by mainly customizing existing generic components and converting them to Web Services.

This is achieved by decoupling computationally intensive parts of a simulation from the non-intensive parts. The intensive parts involve the simulation logic and the visualization of the results both of which are undertaken by the GRID or the user browsers. The non-intensive parts involve the collaborative setup and execution of simulations by users of learner communities which are undertaken by customizable web applications.

In the rest of the paper, we first describe some recent related work in the field of Virtual Laboratories for educational purposes. We then proceed to describe the proposed GRID-based system architecture, which allows for the necessary scalability to tackle the computational demands of heavy engineering or scientific computing experiments with a focus on network simulations ranging from Wireless Sensor Networks to Wi-Fi (and many other types of networks). We describe in particular detail our *generic collaborative simulation management architecture* which lies at the heart of the whole system and enables teams of students and researchers logged-on via a web-based interface to the application, to collaborate in setting up the virtual experiment. Then we describe the *real-time interaction capabilities of our architecture*, and after that, we proceed with details of the first prototype implementation using SENSASIM as the core simulation engine. We provide some initial results from running a number of experiments with this tool, and then discuss our conclusions and some future directions this research might take.

1. Related Work

Even though Virtual Scientific Experiments have been studied thoroughly and very extensively over the past 15-20 years within fields such as simulation software, scientific computing and visualization or even Virtual Reality, the use of Virtual Laboratories as a means for enhancing education with particular emphasis on team-formation and students community building has not received much attention until recently. This situation is rapidly changing though, with the advent of distance learning technologies and the formation of distributed virtual University classrooms. Within the ELeGI project, the use of Virtual Reality tools and simulations was studied in order to provide GRID-enabled physics simulations (Szczytowski, 2005). Simulations of physical phenomena can be written VCLab and be visualized in the learner's browser using these technologies. While it is possible that two or more students share the same simulation session, the focus is on individual learning and not so much on team-formation or community building. Community building –albeit without focus on formal learning environments- takes a more prominent role in the work described in (Eisenstadt et. al., 2005) where the authors advocate a "light" approach to learning through peer-interactions. Tzafestas (2000) presents a stand-alone simulation software for educational purposes, and in particular for engineering education, however no distributed or GRID infrastructure is utilized in any way. Our work is different in that we place heavy emphasis on the optimal utilization of GRID infrastructure so as to support multiple collaborative lab sessions of geographically separated student teams. Mikropoulos (2003) describes in detail requirements for educational software for elementary school-children, with emphasis on the user interface mechanisms that enhance and ease the learning process. In the same context of elementary education, Kfir (2001) discusses how children can benefit from using an interactive Computer Graphics application. That paper presents a project that attempts to produce a generic tool to advance the educational use of virtual laboratories, but the focus is on school children whereas our work focuses on advanced learner groups such as electrical and computer engineering graduate students. In (Ferry et. al., 2006) an online simulation tool is described that was developed to enhance the pre-service teacher practicum experience in the area of literacy teaching. And in (Wong et. al. 2006), the authors present an edutainment approach to the problem of online life-long learning, with the introduction of a Role-Playing-Game that is designed to sharpen players' skills in management and banking. The game uses Rich Internet Application technologies, but without any focus on GRID technologies. We envisage that the infrastructure for Virtual Laboratories that we have built and which is based on turn-taking order, will be easily extended to provide management experiments in role-playing management games, which will simulate the course of a virtual business under the control of the students playing the roles of prospective executives.

2. System Architecture

Simulation based experiments that are collaboratively setup, executed and discussed in a group share certain functionality that is not particular to the simulation itself but to the workflow of a Virtual Scientific Experiment (VSE). This very functionality can be decoupled from simulation-specific features and made available in a generic component for the collaborative execution of VSEs.

2.1. Collaborative Simulation Management Generic Architecture

It has been possible to provide an architecture for the collaborative parameter setup as well as the visualization and the interaction management of simulation-oriented VSEs that includes:

1. a number of simulation components, which can be computation-intensive and can be executed using a GRID infrastructure;
2. a generic component to support the collaboration mechanisms of VSEs that is not computation-intensive and can be executed as a Web application;
3. support for the addition of simulation specific components on the Web application for parameter setup, visualization and the communication between the Web application and the computation-intensive GRID services that perform the simulations.

As shown in Figure 1, this architecture considers three distinct domains: the Web Services/GRID domain with the computation-intensive simulation GRID services, the VSE Web Server domain with the shared Web application for collaborative parameter setup and simulation visualization and the VSE client domain with the browsers of the users of the VSE applications including the necessary visualization plug-ins.

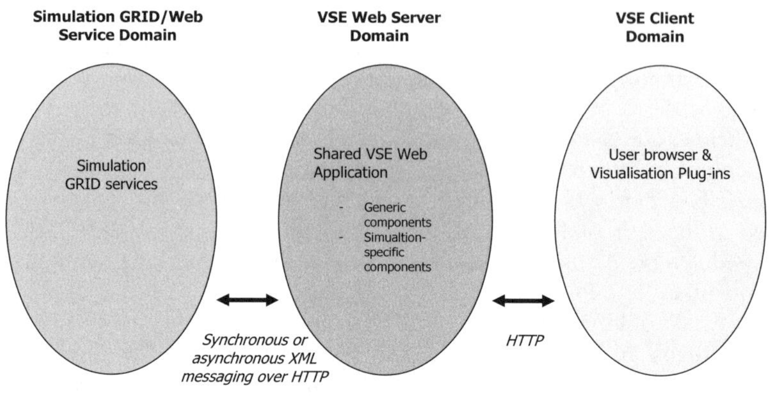

Figure 1. Collaborative simulation-based VSE domains

The requirements for this architecture have been:

- To enable learning communities to collaboratively setup and execute VSEs taking into consideration learning community roles, authentication and authorization.
- To allow for collaborative interaction and visualization of experiments in real-time.
- To provide flexible access to VSEs over the Web.
- To leverage the flexibility of GRID and Web Service technologies for the efficient execution of VSEs.
- To enable extensibility of the framework by supporting different types of simulation-based VSEs.
- To enable scalability of the framework in terms of participating community members, number of communities and number of supported simulation VSEs.

A more detailed diagram of the architecture is shown in Figure 2. It illustrates a *Collaborative Simulation Management Component (CSMC)* that enables the collaborative as well as private setup, execution and presentation of different types of VSEs to virtual communities or individual users, which is hosted on a Web server.

The CSMC implements functionality allowing a virtual community to collaboratively setup generic and specific parameters of simulation-based VSEs and the mechanisms for the communication between the CSMC and the simulation GRID services as well as the users. In addition, it enables the management of users and GRID nodes that can be used to host simulation GRID services. The CSMC provides the means to extend the repertoire of the simulations it supports by enabling a flexible addition of simulation GRID services and configuration of the visualization mechanisms and of the simulation-specific parameters for these services.

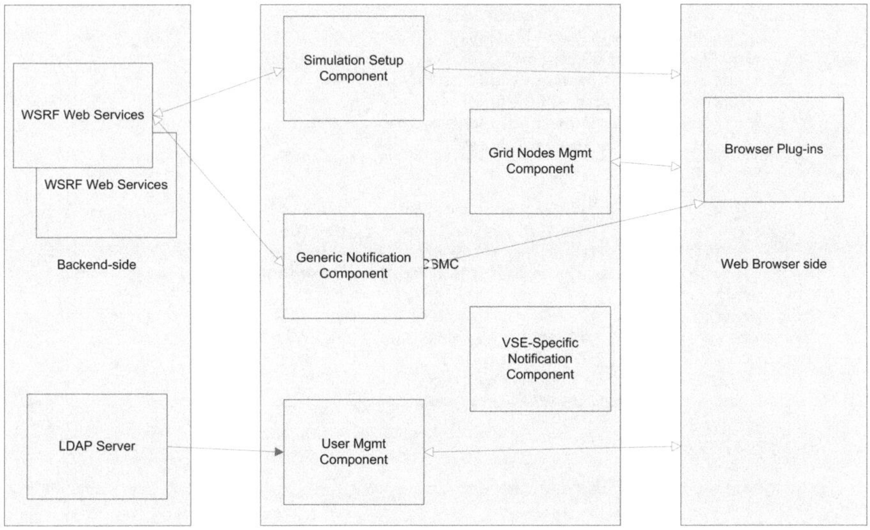

Figure 2. Collaborative Simulation Management Component Architecture

The architecture of the *CSMC* itself as depicted in Figure 2 includes the following components:

Generic Notification Component; which is able to receive notifications regarding the status of a simulation from the GRID-based simulation services, to process them and to forward them to the Browser-side visualization plug-ins.

Simulation Setup Component; which sets-up the appropriate GRID-based simulation services given a set of collaboratively determined parameters. The parameters are used to populate an XML Settings file that describes a set of attribute-value pairs. This set of attribute-value pairs (see Figure 3) describes the values given to each VSE-specific parameter by the users from the GUI rendered in their browser. Accordingly, the defined WSDL for the back-end simulation engine web service defines an XML file that must be passed in as input to the initialization of a service execution. In this way, the front-end component remains completely agnostic of the settings themselves or the way they should be organized and rendered in the GUI.

User Management Component; which allows the initial authentication of users (in collaboration with LDAP servers), and is also responsible for enabling the administrator to add/delete/enable/disable users from running simulations. It also allows the administrator to force token-passing from a slow user to any user that they choose, which can be useful in cases of users that are un-decided or un-responsive during collaborative parameter set-up.

GRID-nodes Management Component; which allows the management of the available GRID nodes.

VSE-specific Notification Component; it is optional and allows handling of notifications from legacy GRID-based simulation services to the VSE Parameter Setup Application.

```
<?xml version="1.0" encoding="UTF-8" ?>
- <settings>
  - <group id="general" label="General" folded="false">
    - <setting id="scenario" type="Integer" value="7">
      - <htmlRender label="Scenario" displayAs="comboBox">
          <option label="Broadcast Flooding" value="1" />
          <option label="Normal Flooding" value="2" />
          <option label="Bidirectional Flooding" value="3" />
          <option label="Speed Broadcast" value="4" />
        </htmlRender>
      </setting>
    - <setting id="thetaTheshold" type="Double" value="130.0">
      - <htmlRender label="Theta threshold" displayAs="textbox">
          <validation min="100.0" max="200.0" required="true" />
          <helpTooltip>This a help tooltip for the Theta threshold setting</helpTooltip>
        </htmlRender>
      </setting>
    - <setting id="broadcastMode" type="Boolean" value="false">
      - <htmlRender label="Broadcast mode" displayAs="radioButtons">
          <option label="Enabled" value="true" />
          <option label="Disabled" value="false" />
        </htmlRender>
      </setting>
    </group>
    <setting id="bpsymbol" type="Integer" value="8" />
  </settings>
```

Figure 3. VSE Settings.xml instance. Each VSE has its own settings, but each VSE type adheres to the same schema, which is used to render the parameter setup part of the GUI

The CSMC architecture is highly reusable for different web-based applications for collaborative setup of VSE simulations. The only programming that may be required when this framework is to be used for a specific simulation VSE is to provide a visualization plug-in for the browser-side part of the application and/or a VSE-specific notification component if necessary. Of course, providing a Web Service that adheres to the WSDL defined by the architecture is a must, otherwise, a plug-in component that invokes the WSRF service that does not comply to the proposed WSDL definition is required.

In addition to the visualization plug-in the setup of a simulation-specific configuration file is required. Specifically, the whole system can therefore be configured by means of two configuration files:

- **Generic Configuration File**; there is a single instance of this file. The schema of the configuration file provides for the identification of:

  - The role/community/authentication services with which the application will be able to communicate.
  - The directory in which VSE-specific Configuration files can be found.
  - Other parameters concerning the look and feel as well as configuration of the component.

- **VSE-specific Configuration File**; see Figure 3. There is one instance for *each type* of VSE supported by the framework. The schema of the VSE-specific configuration file provides for elements such as:

  - A unique identifier of the VSE (URI)
  - Short Description of the VSE
  - The names of the tabs that will be presented for parameter setup. A 'General' Tab that will enable Submitting, Saving, Deleting Parameter Sets will be available for all VSEs. Additional (optional) tabs for setting up will be identified and described by additional elements.
  - The URL(s) of the Simulation Web Service(s) to which parameters will be submitted for execution.
  - A pointer to an application function that will invoke the Simulation Web Service(s) using the values in the parameter setup tab(s) when parameter submission is selected.

2.2. User Access Control

The users of the virtual community participating in such an experiment have different access levels. These levels depend on the role that each member has in the community. Typically, instructors and administrators have full privileges to modify parameters, start simulation jobs, and/or modify simulation execution in real-time. Students on the other hand can be granted or denied modify and submit privileges on the fly by the administrator-instructor of the session. The user-interface of this tool is shown in Figure 4.

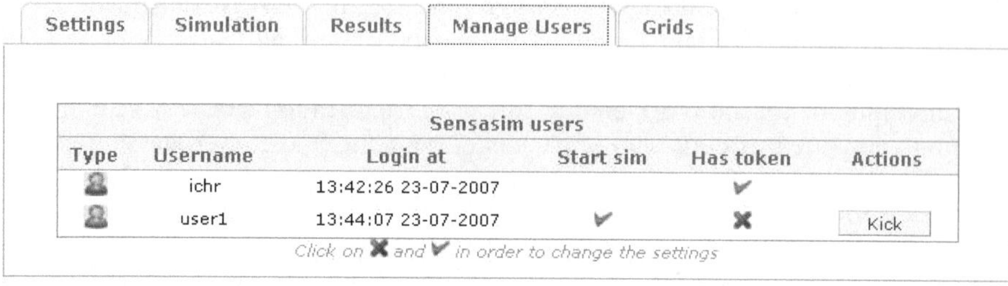

Figure 4. System Administrative Interface for User Management.

The Administrator can perform the following actions:

- Enable/Disable the ability of a simple user to start a private simulation.
- Pass the Token of the public shared simulation to the next user or give the Token to a specific user in order to by-pass turn-taking.

2.3. Using the Collaborative Simulation Management Component

The *CSMC* is the entry point of virtual community users to a variety of virtual scientific experiments that may be available. The steps that need to be followed when a virtual community member accesses this application can be outlined as follows:

The user is prompted to login and select the *type* of VSE they wish to run. The CSMC may subsequently communicate with role/community services to determine the access rights of the user to different simulations. A number of VSEs may be available for access.

The user is prompted to select the *instance* of a VSE type they want to join (collaborative public simulation) or to *create a new instance* (run a private experiment). A VSE instance is a running VSE simulation of a specific kind with a specific number of participants and a particular state. Users are also allowed to leave a VSE instance or (given they have the rights) to delete VSE instances.

For a selected instance of a VSE type and subject to rights a user can:

- Setup parameters shared by all the users joining the same instance of the VSE type *in a turn-taking manner* simulated by a token-passing scheme.
- Submit parameters for execution to the Simulation Web Service(s).
- Save parameter sets for future use.
- Delete previously saved parameter sets.
- Be alerted when simulation results are available.
- View and interact with simulation progress (making use of a browser-side plug-ins).
- Kick a user out of the simulation.

2.4. User Interaction with the Running Simulation

Besides allowing users to collaboratively set-up the initial parameters of the experiments, the system also allows for the on-the-fly collaborative modification of simulation state so as to allow for true interaction with the system and better understanding of system dynamics and underlying principles. This is accomplished via WS-Notification mechanisms.

WS-Notification is fully supported in GT4 WS-core (Sotomayor & Childers, 2005). The simulation engine was implemented as a NotificationProducer grid web service that is part of the WS-Notification standard implemented by GT4, so that it can spread the information to the clients that sent subscribing request messages without having a prior knowledge about them. The service can then accept a subscribe request which will contain the reference for the NotificationConsumer which is the endpoint designated to receive the Notify message that will actually represent an event of the simulation so whenever events for the running simulation are produced all the consumers – participants of the virtual experiment – will get notified automatically.

In the rest of this section, we describe in detail the interactions of the users with the system. Figure 5 shows the overall Graphical User Interface, which consists of 5 major areas.

1. **User panel:** Provides user information and actions. The user can **Start**, **Stop**, **Reset** the simulation (for the Administrator user the public simulation, for simple user the private one) or **Logout**
2. **Online users:** Displays the Online users status. The Administrator user/tutor is displayed in red color. The simple users/students are displayed using blue color except for the user who has the token (can enter settings) which is displayed in green color.
3. **Application tabs:** Displays the Application tabs. These are **Settings**, **Simulation** and **Results** for the student users. The Administrator user also has access to the **Manage users** (and **Manage Grids**) tab.

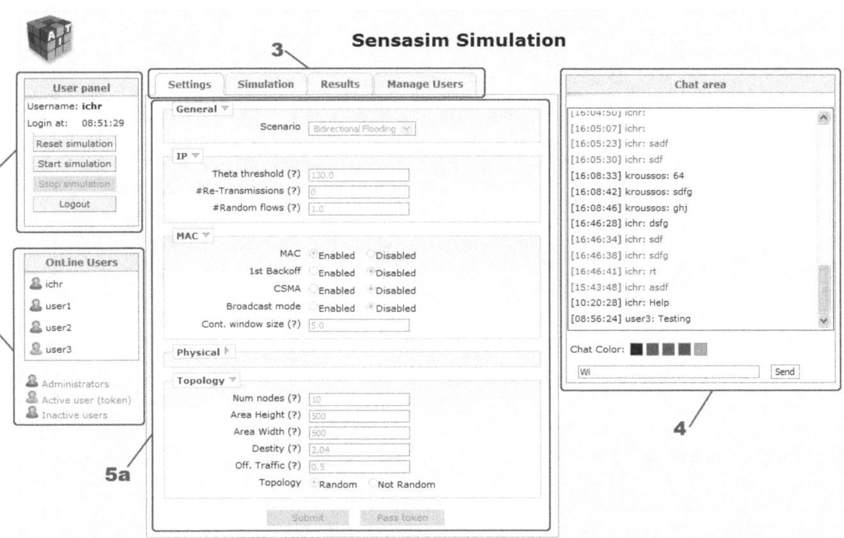

Figure 5. Overall System Graphical User Interface.

4. **Chat area:** Provides a simple global broadcasting chat. The user can change his/her displayed message color.

5a. **Settings tab:** This is the area where the users can enter settings for the simulation. Only one user at any given time can enter settings as the system implements a turn-taking approach similar to many other major collaborative internet-based tools. When a user gets the token (based on a Round-Robin, first-come-first-serve manner) the settings fields and buttons are enabled. Then the user can either **Pass token** to the next user or change and **Submit** the settings. The token can passed many rounds and it is upon the decision of Administrator when the simulation can be started.

5b. **Simulation tab:** This tab is enabled when the Administrator starts the simulation. In this type of experiment, the user can click on a node in order to simulate a random event that causes the particular node to go off-line.

5c. **Results tab:** Once a simulation finishes, statistics can be collected from the Results tab of the GUI, as shown on Figure 7.

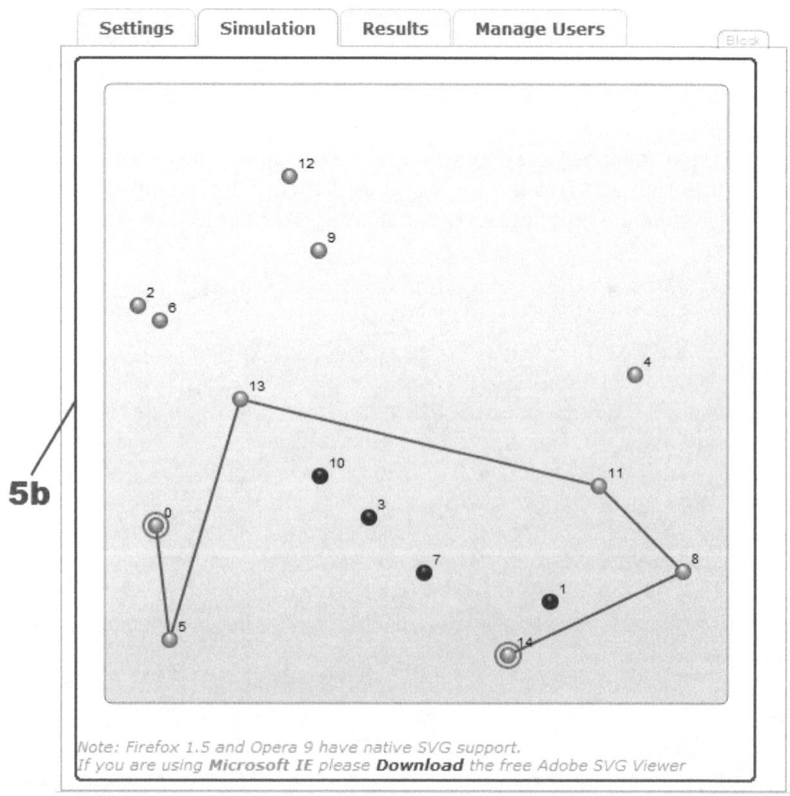

Figure 6. Simulation Area where the user can visualize the state of the simulation and also interact with the running simulation

Figure 7. Results Area of the GUI. The results can be copied to the clipboard for further processing.

3. Implementation and Deployment of the Generic VSE Infrastructure

A high-level diagram illustrating the deployment of the implemented system architecture is depicted in Figure 8. As can be seen, access to the application is provided via a web browser interface. A user logs in to the web-site and after she/he is authenticated via LDAP authentication, she/he may choose to join a collaborative simulation session (default choice) or, assuming there is an idle GRID node, she/he may choose to enter a "private simulation session" to which no other common user will have access.

A front-end Apache Tomcat server runs a J2EE application that sends a JSP with a number of components in it to the user browser. The user browser establishes a connection back to the front-end server for real-time synchronized communication with the system via AJAX technology. The user interface includes a presence window showing the team members that are currently on-line, a chat interface for instant messaging between all team members, and the main window showing the simulation environment. These built-in instant messaging and presence mechanisms offer a significant advantage for the virtual community members that have to interact heavily during the experiment. Usually during such an experiment other videoconferencing tools are also running in each user's machine in order to enhance communication between team members.

The actual simulation engine runs on any of a number of Grid nodes running the Globus Toolkit 4 (GT4) WS-core package which is platform independent as it is completely written in Java (Sotomayor & Childers, 2005). Each Grid node is connected to a Grid Server Wrapper that distributes simulation jobs between the Grid nodes.

The simulation engine itself is implemented as a WSRF Web Service with a simple Web Services Description Language (WSDL) file associated with it, allowing remote clients to call the service (Joseph & Fellenstein, 2004), and to also interact with it, changing its state on-the-fly.

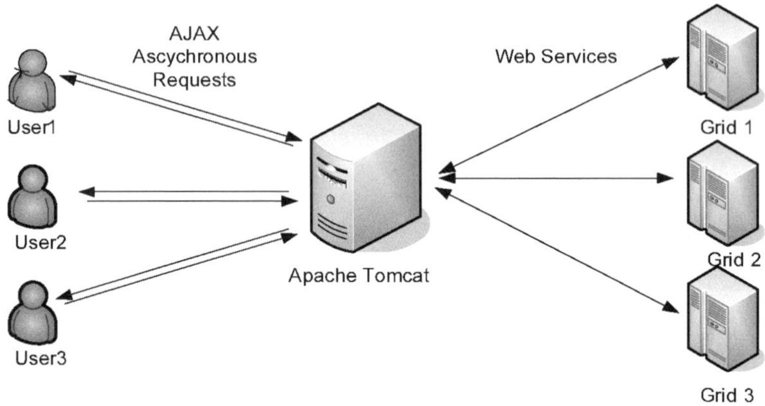

Figure 8. Collaborative Interactive Virtual Scientific Experiments Architecture.

As shown in Figure 8, the CSMC co-operates with Browser-side plug-ins via AJAX technology for the collaborative set-up of the simulation parameters and forwards them to the GRID-domain Simulation Web Services that perform the simulation logic. It also connects to a number of Grid Services to enable Authentication, Virtual Community Management and Role-based access control to VSE resources. It also communicates with other Browser-side plug-ins – such as Adobe SVGViewer for the Internet Explorer – in order to forward the state of the experiment to the browser-side renderer that renders the simulation progress via standard WS-Notification mechanisms in a callback fashion. Conversely, it also accepts user interactions indicating a request for a change in the state of the simulation and relays them back to the Web service. It is an event-driven model that is employed for the submission of the simulation setup parameters and state notification. Thus, after simulation parameters have been submitted for processing to the GRID-based simulation services, notifications are sent back to the CSMC as the component has subscribed itself as a listener for the execution of the Web services; these notifications, in turn, are forwarded to the Browser-side for display by the appropriate plug-ins.

Communication between the different components is over SOAP/HTTP or XML/HTTP.

4. Prototype Implementation of Sensor Network Simulation Service (SENSASIM)

As a first proof-of-concept of our architecture for Grid-based interactive collaborative virtual scientific experiments for virtual communities, we chose as our simulation engine an Open-Source tool for Wireless Sensor Networks that is written entirely in Java and that can support up to thousands of sensor nodes in the network topology. The tool, called SENSASIM (Rayess et. al., 2006) as already mentioned is a simulator for wireless multi-hop networks with multiple directional antennas. The simulator can be used for any ad hoc wireless network, but the focus is on the more energy-limited and constrained sensor networks. The supported physical model includes use of directional antennas, enabling the switching of the antennas' lobe at will and the finding of direction of arrival (DoA) of the signal. Two variants of Aloha and one CSMA (Carrier Sense Multiple Access) are the major MAC (Medium Access Control) protocols implemented. At the network layer, emphasis was given on SPEED (Scalable Protocols for Efficient Event Delivery in Sensor Networks) (Dimitriou et. al., 2004) and its enhancements.

The support for all these layers of the network with detailed models is a good fit for a successful laboratory experiment in the form of a VSE (Virtual Scientific Experiment) for a course in Wireless Sensor Networks that is offered in the MSIN program. The simulation engine architecture is shown in Figure 9.

We modified the simulation engine to allow for on-the-fly modifications of the simulation state and sending/receiving and responding to events such as users clicking on sensor nodes visualized on their browser to activate/deactivate them. The engine simulates the process of an event generated in a random node in the sensor network – such as a measurement reading of a quantity- and the propagation of this event to a final "aggregator" node (Rayess et. al. 2006).

The static structure of the design of CSMC is shown in Figure 10. This figure shows the major classes used to build the main module.

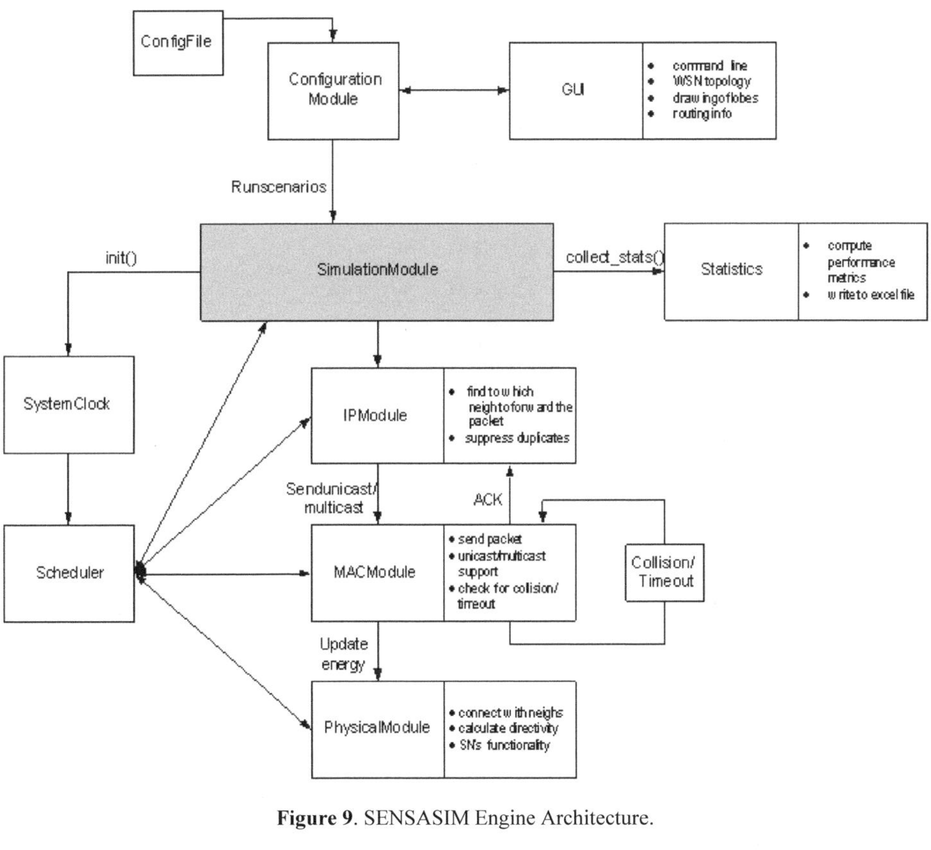

Figure 9. SENSASIM Engine Architecture.

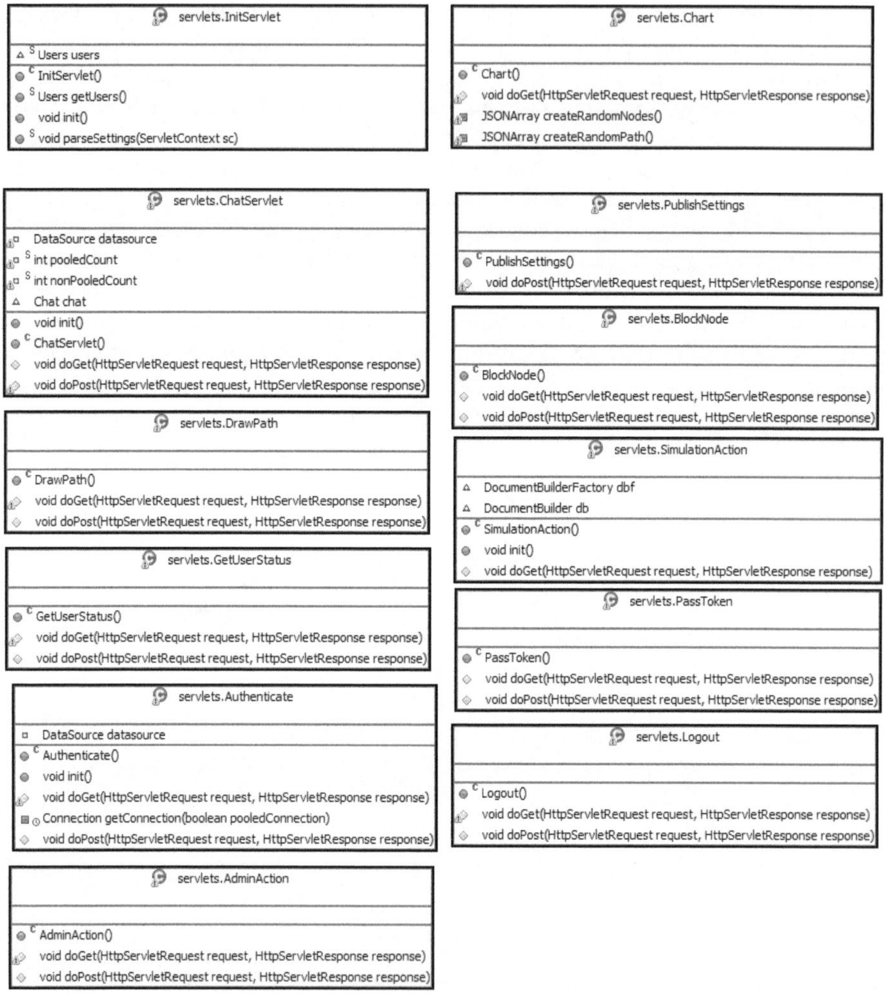

Figure 10. UML Class Diagram produced by the Eclipse IDE ® showing most of the major classes in CSMC module.

A grid cluster of three SUN/Solaris nodes running GT4's "globus-start-container" and another cluster of two Windows nodes running the WS-Core component of GT4 were created. Each Windows node is equipped with dual Pentium4 processors running at 3.2 GHz , 1GB of RAM and 120GB disk drives. These clusters are located, respectively, in the Software Systems and Web Applications Laboratory and in the Wireless Networks Lab of AIT. Another cluster located at CMU that will connect to create a single even more powerful distributed laboratory is under way, but this extra power is needed mainly for research purposes. For the educational aspects of the virtual lab, five grid nodes were found to be more than adequate. Each of the GRID nodes may start a simulation instance upon request from the front-end node of the architecture assuming it is idle at the time of the request.

5. System Evaluation

An iterative approach was adopted for the evaluation and assessment of the deployed Grid-based VSE solution, which involved two major iterations: (i) the deployment and evaluation of the first prototype and (ii) the deployment and evaluation of the second prototype, further developed and enhanced based on user feedback during the first prototype evaluation. The results of each iteration cycle are presented in the following sections. Although further iterations are envisaged in the future, the evaluation results of the second iteration already showcase increased acceptance of the Grid-based interactive SENSASIM VSE by the participating students from remote collaborating institutions.

The Grid-based VSE for Sensor networks was deployed locally at Athens Information Technology (AIT), Athens, Greece and was available for evaluation to groups of students located at AIT and at the CyLab Japan site of the Information Networking Institute of Carnegie Mellon University in Kobe, Japan, during the first prototype evaluation, and to a single group of students located at AIT during the second prototype evaluation.

5.1. First prototype evaluation

The evaluation of the first prototype of the VSE was organized in two stages (Christou et. al, 2007). The first stage involved the evaluation of the prototype by a group of 25 students following a demonstration of the VSE to the group and a Q&A session following that. Subsequently, the students filled out questionnaires detailing their evaluation of the first prototype. The results of this evaluation showed that almost two in three students appreciated the availability of communications facilities during the VSE session and they considered them a very important element of the VSE. Over eighty percent of the students preferred Web-based access to the VSE and voice and text based facilities for communication with each other and with the tutor during the setup or execution of simulations. From this first stage of the evaluation of the first prototype there was clear demand for three additional features in the Sensasim VSE: (i) interactivity with the VSE in progress by modifying running simulations, (ii) real-time graphical interfaces showing the simulation progress and (iii) turn-taking for the setup and modification of the simulation parameters. The students were content with the performance of the simulation over Grid.

A second stage of the initial evaluation involved a geographically distributed session between graduate students at AIT in Athens, Greece and graduate students at CyLab, Kobe, Japan. During the deployment of the Virtual Lab Course on Wireless Sensor Networks involving the execution of the first prototype of the SENSASIM-based Virtual Scientific Experiment (VSE) over Grid nodes, A.I.T. and CyLab Japan students were given the opportunity to form remote laboratory teams attending a common lab course, perform virtual scientific experiments in Wireless Sensor Networks to observe their simulated behaviour after changing a number of varying parameters and collaborate via chat mechanisms to exchange opinions on parameter values and justify the obtained results. During the virtual lab session, the responsible teacher presented the required theoretical concepts of Wireless Sensor Networks and explained the entire process of the simulation using the SENSASIM simulator, setting the values of the varying parameters and justifying the behaviour to students.

The trial involved initially students and tutors (1 teacher at A.I.T., 1 teacher at CyLab Japan and a number of assisting tutors) from both A.I.T. and CyLab Japan gathering at their local lab classes at a prescheduled time for the virtual lab course – announcements for this event were made well in advance to interested students. All participants were equipped with PCs, web cameras, speakers and microphones. All participants connected to the indicated Flash Meeting Booking URL (http://flashmeeting.open.ac.uk/) to enter the virtual meeting room and thus initiate communication and collaboration among remote lab classes via videoconferencing facilities. In this way students were able to ask questions and receive answers from teachers/tutors during the hands-on exercises. At the prescheduled time, the virtual lab course was initiated by the teachers at A.I.T. and CyLab Japan. The teacher at CyLab Japan made a 30 minute introduction focusing on challenges. Then the teacher at A.I.T. presented the networking challenges and introduced the SENSASIM simulator. Access to the slides of presentations was possible prior to the event from a web site where teachers uploaded them. Then, students were asked to access the SENSASIM server from their PCs through a specified URL from a Web page. Students had the chance to download the stand-alone version of SENSASIM prior to the event from an indicated Web site in order to get acquainted with it. As soon as students logged in to SENSASIM, the demonstration started by a tutor at A.I.T. A number of hands-on exercises were run to demonstrate the simulated behavior of wireless sensor networks under varying parameters of its model. Students asked questions and received answers during that part.

After the session ended, the participants were asked to complete an appropriately formatted Questionnaire that included questions both on system usability as well as on the collaboration and learning added value of the VSE prototype and its usefulness in allowing for efficient execution of virtual lab sessions and collaborative interactive simulations. The evaluation results provided a rating of 2.71 for the collaboration process in a scale 1 (process worked very well) to 5 (process did not work at all). The rating for the interest of the VSE was 2.0 in a scale 1 (very interesting) to 5 (not interesting at all), while the rating for the communication tools was 2.28 in a scale 1 (appropriate) to 5 (not appropriate). The overall rating of the system was 2.4 as far as the integration of its components was concerned in a scale 1 (strongly agree) to 5 (strongly disagree).

In addition to the evaluation of the Grid-based VSE simulator in terms of learning and collaboration, a properly structured questionnaire aimed to allow for the calculation of the system usability score (SUS) of the SENSASIM VSE simulator. Due to network congestion problems during the execution of the lab session among the remote collaborating institutions, communication and collaboration among the remote sites was bad, a fact that affected the evaluation result. The SUS score was almost 70% (in a scale 0-100).

An analysis of the evaluation results of the above two stages indicated that *the additional features enabling interactivity, turn-taking and real-time graphics would improve the performance of the VSE in terms of supporting collaboration processes, while the communication facilities could be improved, despite the fact that Internet congestion that was experienced during the second stage of the evaluation may have been the prime cause for the low rating of the communication tools rather than the functionality of the tools themselves.*

5.2. Second prototype evaluation

Taking into account the user feedback during the evaluation of the first prototype, a second Grid-based SENSASIM prototype was developed as detailed in the previous sections. The second prototype addressed the issues that were identified during the analysis of the evaluation results of the first prototype. The initial version of this second prototype had a functional but less pleasing Graphical User Interface and it was loosely integrated with the Grid-aware Intelligent Web Teacher learning portal IWT-GA, in order to provide an integrated approach to management of learning resources within the context of the ELeGI project. IWT-GA is available at http://elearning.diima.unisa.it/iwtportal/DesktopDefault.aspx. With this integration, the students actually obtained a more holistic laboratory experience since from one portal, they could first access related Units of Learning (UoL) and study the required theoretical material and then join the Virtual Laboratory without leaving the learning portal. Access to the initial version of our second prototype through the IWT-GA portal is shown in Figure 11.

A group of five students who were attending an elective course on wireless sensor networks at AIT were asked to participate in an in-depth evaluation of the second prototype, following similar deployment details of the 1st evaluation stage, and to fill out properly constructed questionnaires to evaluate both system usability and learning and collaboration potential of the simulator.

Based on the evaluation results, the SUS score of the second prototype was 80%, which was considered encouraging and was increased with respect to its initial value for the first prototype. The rating of the appropriateness of the communication tools was 2.00 in a scale of 1 (appropriate) to 5 (inappropriate). The improvement of this rating can be explained by the better performance of the local network for voice and text based communication and certain improvements in the deployed tools.

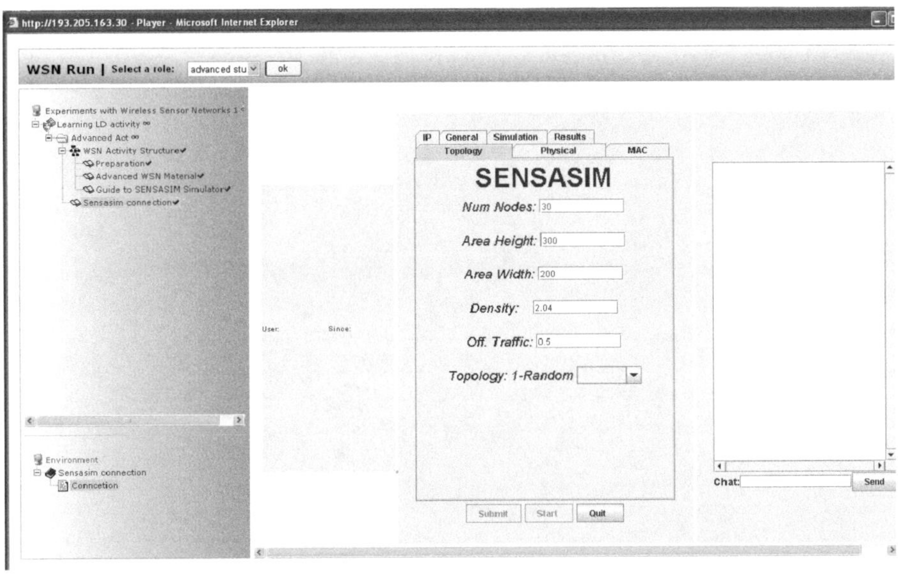

Figure 11. GRID-SENSASIM Access Through IWT-GA Learning Portal.

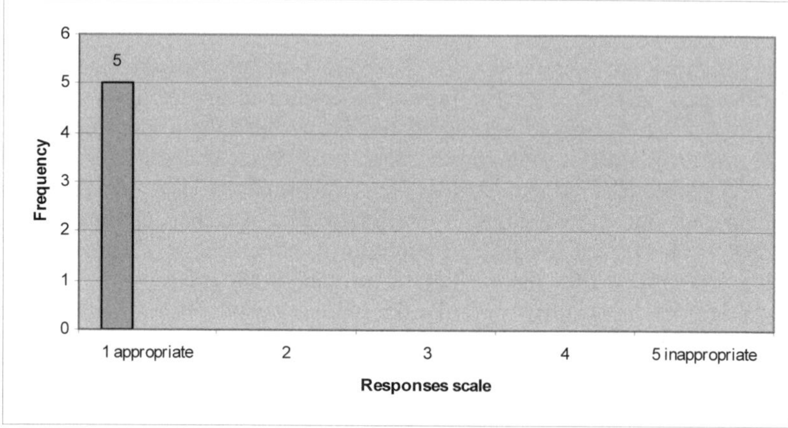

Figure 12. Evaluation of the appropriateness of media presentation in the second prototype.

The evaluation group was asked, among others, to evaluate the appropriateness of media presentation of the VSE providing feedback on the new features enabling interactivity and real-time graphics presentation. The responses, which are illustrated in Figure 12, provide a rating of media appropriateness of 1.00 in a scale of 1 (appropriate) to 5 (inappropriate), which indicates that the improvements in the second prototype were well received.

In addition, students were asked to evaluate the collaboration process as implemented in the second prototype with increased interactivity and turn taking. The evaluation results, as illustrated in Figure 11, provide a rating of 1.80 in a scale of 1 (worked well) to 5 (did not work well at all), which is a clear improvement of the rating of the first prototype.

The comprehensibility of the VSE was rated 1.40 in a scale 1 (easy to understand) to 5 (difficult to understand), while the clarity of the learning experience to the students was rated 1.60 in a scale 1 (strongly agree) to 5 (strongly disagree).

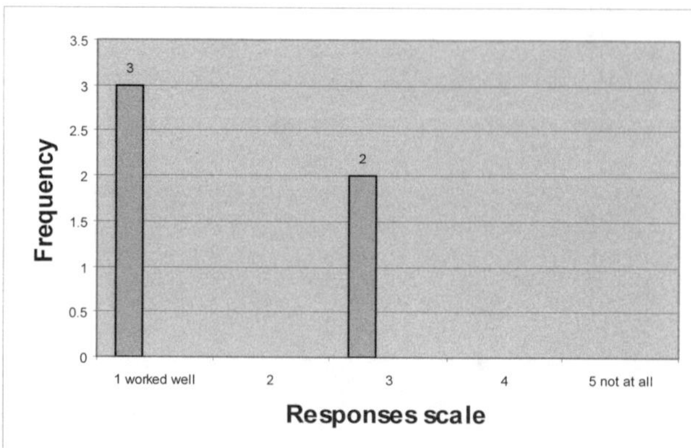

Figure 13. Evaluation of the degree of collaboration process performance in the second prototype.

Since the evaluation of the second prototype, further improvements were applied on the SENSASIM VSE regarding text-based communication (improved chatting features, color-coding of the text of each participant) and media presentation (use of scalable vector graphics – SVG) to further improve the usability, performance and interoperability of the SENSASIM VSE with different browsers as well as the reuse of the collaborative parameter setup component with different VSEs. The current Graphical User Interface of the system is shown in Figures 4 through 7.

6. Conclusions & Future Directions

We have described a generic Grid-based architecture that enables distributed learner communities to conduct virtual laboratory experiments via the web in a fully collaborative manner, thus enhancing community building among participants and resulting in overall better learning experiences. Team members interact with each other via integrated instant messaging and complementary standard video-conferencing facilities. More significantly however, the architecture allows team members to participate in the setup of the laboratory experiment's parameter set-up, and then to fully visualize the simulated lab experiment progress in real-time and interact with it modifying its execution path while it is actually running. The added value and even necessity of this interaction feature was anticipated even before the first prototype assessment phase by Prof. Takeshi Utsumi in private communications within the ELeGI project, and indeed it proved to be so, as it enables students to gain much deeper understanding of the principles being demonstrated by the experiment, by taking full advantage of the built-in notification mechanisms of Grid Web Services.

The architecture has been instantiated in a first proof-of-concept with a Wireless Sensor Network simulation engine and was well appreciated by teams of students that evaluated its features and performance in Athens Information Technology. We are working towards instantiating the same architecture with a Wireless Networks simulator based on the ns2 engine (ns2, 2007) that will allow labs to complement theoretical lecture material in courses on Wi-Fi Networks (Sturgeon et. al. 2006). The current version of our Virtual Laboratory is available in http://palantir.ait.gr:8888/ Sensasim. Users can log in with the guest login "`user1`" and password "`user1`".

Currently, the power of the Grid is used to run simultaneously different simulation sessions. We are also working towards parallelizing the two simulators to take advantage of the Grid so as to distribute a single large-scale simulation among the Grid nodes to achieve near-linear speedup in simulation execution.

References

[1] I. T. Christou, S. Efremidis, T. Tiropanis and A. Kalis, 2007: "Grid-based Virtual Laboratory Experiments for a Graduate Course on Sensor Networks", IEEE Transactions on Education, Volume 50, Issue 1, pp:17 – 26.

[2] G. Rayess, I. Tsirilakis, C. Kakogiannis, A. Kalis, A. G. Kanatas, Ph. Constantinou, 2006: "Java-based simulator for wireless multi-hop networks using directional antennas", European Wireless Conference 2006, Athens, April 2-5, 2006

[3] B. Sotomayor, L. Childers, 2005: "Globus Toolkit 4: Programming Java Services", Morgan-Kaufmann, San Francisco, CA.

[4] J. Joseph, and C. Fellenstein, 2004: "Grid Computing", Prentice-Hall, Upper Saddle River, NJ.

[5] T. Dimitriou, I. Krontiris, F. Nikakis and P. Spirakis, 2004: "SPEED: Scalable Protocols for Efficient Event Delivery in Sensor Networks", Networking 2004, Athens, Greece

[6] ns2. 2007: "The Network Simulator ns-2". [cited 2007 January]; Available from: http://www.isi.edu/nsnam/ns/index.html.

[7] T. C. Sturgeon, C. Allison, and A. Miller. 2006: "A WiFi Virtual Laboratory". in 7th Annual Conference of the Subject Centre for Information and Computer Sciences. 2006. Dublin, Ireland: HE Academy.

[8] E.S.Tzafestas, 2000: "Experiences from the Development and Use of Simulation Software for Complex Systems Education", Proceedings of the World Conference on the WWW and Internet (WebNet-2000), November 2000, San Antonio, TX.

[9] T.A. Mikropoulos, 2003: "Educational Software", Klidarithmos, Athens, Greece, (In Greek)

[10] R. Eli Kfir, 2001: "Virtual Laboratories in Education", Proceedings of ACM 1st Intl. Conference on Computer Graphics, Virtual Reality and Visualization (AFRIGRAPH), Cape-town, South Africa, pp. 27-31.

[11] P. Szczytowski, 2005: "VCLab as an Example of GRIDifying Virtual Scientific Experiments", Proceedings of ELeGI 1st Intl. Conference on Advanced Technology for Enhanced Learning, March 2005, Vico Equense, Italy.

[12] M. Eisenstad, J. Komzak, & S. A. Cerri, 2005: "Peer Conversations for e-Learning in the Grid", Proceedings of ELeGI 1st Intl. Conference on Advanced Technology for Enhanced Learning, March 2005, Vico Equense, Italy.

[13] B. Ferry, L. Kervin, & K. Rudd, 2006: "Use of Rich Internet Applications to develop an online classroom-based simulation", International Journal of Continuing Engineering Education and Life-Long Learning - Vol. 16, No.3/4 pp. 200 – 214.

[14] W.-C. Wong, M. Sheu, E. Moy, 2006: "A Rich Internet Application edutainment training system", International Journal of Continuing Engineering Education and Life-Long Learning - Vol. 16, No.3/4 pp. 280 – 296.

The Learning Grid Handbook
S. Salerno et al. (Eds.)
IOS Press, 2008

Educational Services in the ACTIVEMATH Learning Environment

Carsten ULLRICH [a] and Paul LIBBRECHT [1,b]
[a] *Shanghai Jiaotong University, Shanghai, China*
[b] *DFKI GmbH, Saarbrücken, Germany,*

Abstract. ACTIVEMATH is a Web-based learning environment for mathematics. In this article, we discuss ACTIVEMATH from a service and semantics perspective. We describe the service-oriented technologies of ACTIVEMATH and how the services interplay with the domain semantics (mathematics) and the pedagogical semantics used, e. g., for course generation. More specifically, we provide details on the knowledge representation for mathematics we use in ACTIVEMATH and how it is used to represent learning materials. We also elaborate on the representation of learning objects from a pedagogical point-of-view, that is, how we capture the instructional semantics. We then show how learning goals are represented and how a course generator assembles sequences of learning objects to fulfil these goals. Some tools in ACTIVEMATH are client-based and require different techniques. We use our assembly tool as an example to illustrate how ACTIVEMATH integrates client-based tools.

Keywords. service-oriented-architecture, web-based, learning-environment, semantics, education

Introduction

Service oriented architectures are becoming increasingly popular [19]. Their basic paradigm is convincingly straightforward: encapsulate specific functionality that is of common interest into a single service which is available to third-parties. In this chapter, we will discuss the service architecture of ActiveMath, a Web-based learning environment. In the FP6 project Le ActiveMath, we used the service paradigm to tackle a number of issues arising in distributed or grid-based learning environments. Service-orientation in ActiveMath takes place on different levels and involves different technology, ranging from XLM-RPC to WSDL. In the following, we will first introduce ActiveMath (Section 1) and basic service- techniques used in ActiveMath (Section 2). Then, we will describe the different services and motivate our decisions for the specific protocols. We will provide details on the different semantics used in ActiveMath: the mathematical and educational semantics and show how the main components operate on these semantics (Section 3). We close this chapter by a discussing of related work (Section 4) and the lessons we learned from the application of services in the LeActiveMath project.

---

[1] Corresponding Author: DFKI, Deutsche Forschungszentrum für Künstliche Intelligenz GmbH, Stuhlsatzenhausweg 3 (Building D3 2), D-66123 Saarbruecken; E-mail: paul@activemath.org.

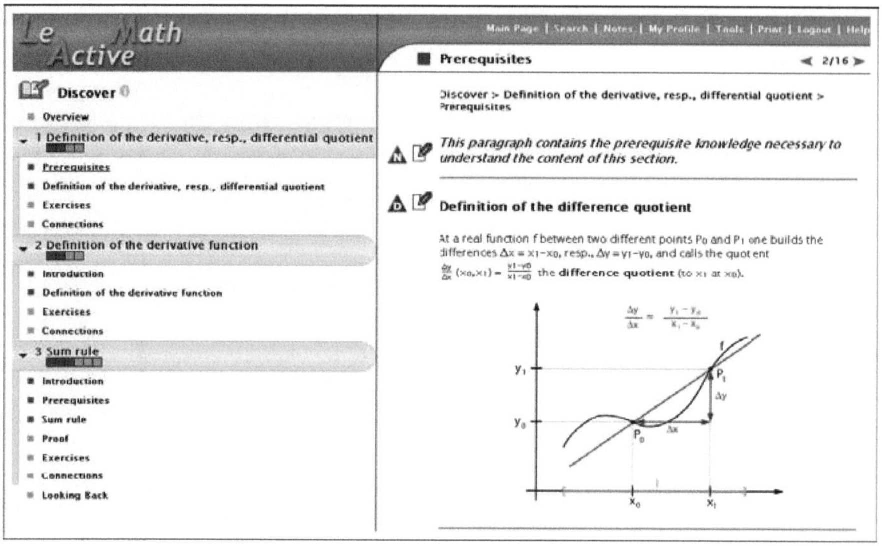

Figure 1. A course presented in ACTIVEMATH

1. The Learning Environment ActiveMath

ActiveMath [21,23] is a Web-based intelligent learning environment for mathematics that has been developed since the year 2000 at the Saarland University and at the German Research Center of Artificial Intelligence (DFKI).[2]

ActiveMath uses an extension of OMDoc [16, 22] to encode its educational resources. In addition to presenting pre-defined interactive materials, it uses a course generator (called Paigos) for the dynamic and adaptive assembly of structured sequences of learning objects. Figure 1 contains a screenshot of a course presented in ActiveMath.

A presentation component transforms the OMDoc documents represented in xml to the desired output format, e. g., html, xhtml +MathML, and pdf. A learner model stores the learning history, the user's profile and preferences, and a set of beliefs that the systems holds about the cognitive and meta-cognitive competencies and the motivational state of the learner. The domain model that underlies the structure of the learner model is inferred from the content for that domain and its metadata.

A complex subsystem in its own right is ActiveMath's exercise subsystem [9] that plays interactive exercises, computes diagnoses and provides feedback to the learner in a highly personalized way. It reports events to inform the other components about the users' actions.

In 2007, at the time of this writing, a significant amount of educational resources exists in ActiveMath's repositories for Fractions (German), Differential Calculus (German, English, Spanish) at high school and first year university level, Operations Research (Russian, English), Methods of Optimization (Russian), Statistics and Probability Calculus (German), Matheführerschein (German), and a Calculus course from University of Westminster in London.

[2] http://www.activemath.org/.

To realize a smooth and efficient cooperation of all components and in order to integrate further internal and external services, ActiveMath has a modular service-oriented architecture. It includes the XLM-RPC Web communication protocol for simplicity and remote support. In addition, an event framework enables asynchronous messaging between system components. Communication with third-parties components is done by Web-services using WSDL and SOAP. We will now discuss these service technologies.

2. Service Technologies Used in ActiveMath

In this section we first survey the basic needs of a Web-service architecture for ActiveMath then focus on the technologies we used.

The internal communication within the server is governed by pragmatic requirements, mostly targeting at an efficient communication between different components. ActiveMath components can be distributed, e. g., the domain knowledge base can run on a different machine than the course generator. On this level, communication happens via direct Java calls or XLM-RPC for efficiency reasons (see the lessons learned, in the final section).

If one leaves the restricted view of a single server-based environment, the picture changes. For instance, the generic integration of third-party repositories is much easier to achieve if standard Web-service techniques are employed. Similarly, making functionality such as course generation available to other learning environment makes more sense if the interfaces follow standards, otherwise they will rarely be used.

It is thus of great importance to provide standards-based methods, using communication interfaces that expose their documentations both to for other machines to use or for humans to use. The usage of SOAP, WSDL, XML-schema, and re-use of widespread schema parts forms an important requirement for a greater acceptance.

For the interfaces to the client used by the learner, beyond the simple browser-content delivery, a less principled approach was chosen because each client tool was customized for the ActiveMath usage and because we tried to keep the requirements on the client side fairly low, in terms of available software components and resource. Our requirement for rich-client tools were the following:

- full contextualization resulting in the start of a tool at a single click.
- privacy enforcement: individual tools launched on the client may have the ability to notify the server following an action of the user; more generally, the tools may read or write information that pertain to learner's activities: by means of an appropriate contextualization, they will have channels to write or read information about the user; these channels should only provide access to the user's own information so as to prevent even maliciously manipulated client tools to effect other user's activity.
- usage of the same communication channel as the browser since in several cases, security concerns on corporate networks allow only basic forms of http communication (generally served through a proxy).
- consistent user-experience: at a higher level, the integrated platform should be felt as such. For instance, tools that allow input of mathematical formulæ or content-item references can receive pasted content copied from the

presentation. Similarly, the language should be integrated and reference to particular learning concepts should be linked to it as much as possible.

As a consequence of these various requirements, ActiveMath uses several service oriented technologies, which we will describe in the following.

2.1. XML-RPC

Several of ActiveMath services are based on the XLM-RPC communication protocol because of its web-based nature, its simplicity, and very broad platform support. XLM-RPC is a simple http POST based encoding of remote-procedure call, similar to SOAP's RPC profile but with a much stricter encoding format which has, as consequence, for example, that xml content needs an extra packaging (for example be delivered as strings).

XLM-RPC was chosen early in the project which has allowed us to start a distributed architecture quickly. The performance of XLM-RPC was always quite good. Since then, further service-technologies have been investigated as can be seen below but all basic remote-procedure-calls still use this standard.

2.2. Event Model

For many situations and applications however, a remote procedure call (ie, synchronous communication) is inappropriate. In particular, some components need just a quick notification when events of interest occur in another service or component. Moreover, the sending component may not be aware of all services which need to be informed.

The components interested in such messages may not be known in advance or can change over time or depending on configuration. To simplify a flexible integration and reuse of Web-services, a mechanism for registering interest and for propagating events is needed. Therefore, the XLM-RPC approach is complemented by an event framework in ActiveMath now.

Events are a mechanism for a powerful and flexible, yet rather loose integration of components. The event paradigm is especially useful for state update notifications and reactions to them. Similar messaging and notification frameworks exist for SOAP. Since we use XLM-RPC rather than SOAP for simplicity and performance reasons, we devised a new lightweight event framework.

An example for event "publication" is the following: when the learner finished working on an exercise, the exercise subsystem issues an event. The event carries information describing the learner, the identifier of the exercise, the success rate, a diagnosis about the learner's mastery, the time stamp of the event, etc. Listeners to such an event can be the learner model as well as the suggestor of the tutorial component.

A component that publishes events is an event source. A component that subscribes to the events published by an event source is called a listener which receives event messages from the event source.

In contrast to a full-fledged messaging model, events are not sent from a specific sender to a specific recipient but remain anonymous: when publishing an event, the component is usually not aware who is listening to the events (only the module managing the subscriptions is). Also, usually the listener does not care which component or module created the event, it only knows where to subscribe to the events it is interested in.

Each event message object consists of attributes. The attributes common to all ActiveMath events are:

- a type, indicating what happened (eg, "user X has logged in", "new content available"). Depending on the type, the event may carry additional data for further describing the event.
- a timestamp, indicating when it happened: Events happen at a single point in time (and space). The timestamp indicates the wall-clock time of the event source when the event took place.
- a source, indicating where happened. This is typically the name of the producer, ie, the class name of the component that produced the event.

Other attributes are specific to the type of events.

It is often desirable to group event types across several dimensions, eg, for filtering ("I want all event concerning a user", "Give me all events related to the Dictionary"). However, events don't fit well into a rigid type hierarchy: For instance, consider the even "user logged in". What would be the "natural" group of such an event? An application event? An user event? An interaction event? What's needed is a flexible, non-hierarchical type framework that allows for a mixing of characteristics such as "is associated to a user". Therefore, Active-Math uses event tags. Tags are labels for event types. Each event type can be associated to zero or more tags. Tag definitions can be nested, that is, a tag can inherit from another one. Multiple inheritance is allowed.

Tags can add attributes to an event. For example, the "user" event tag adds the attribute userId to an event. Tags defined without attributes (such as "application") just serve as marker tags. The following attributes are found in event tags, among others: user event tag (identifier of the user that caused this event, empty if user is anonymous); session event tag; item event tag (the identifier of the item, interaction and application event tag.

Remote eventing based on XLM-RPC has been implemented for both server-to-server and rich-client-to-server communication. A special case is the event exchange with the browser client. Our solution is based on asynchronous client-server communication using the browser's XMLHttpRequest object. For XLM-RPC, the attribute values are simple XLM-RPC datatypes. Therefore, attribute names or an event type must be unique across the event type's class, the event tags, and the event base class.

2.3. Web-Services

A Web service can be defined as follows [3]: "a software system identified by a URI, whose public interfaces and bindings are defined and described using XML. Its definition can be discovered by other software systems. These systems may then interact with the Web service in a manner prescribed by its definition, using XML based messages conveyed by Internet protocols."

Standards for each of the given properties exists: WSDL describes a service independent from its underlying implementation by specifying the interfaces and their bindings. SOAP defines the structure and types of messages that are exchanged between server and client. Service discovery is supported by UDDI.

We will now describe educational services in ActiveMath that use the above technologies.

3. Semantic Services in ActiveMath

ActiveMath uses semantics to represent the domain knowledge, that is the subject domain, namely mathematics, and to represent the pedagogical knowledge involved in course generation (the assembling of learning objects that make up the domain knowledge to form courses). Different services operate on these semantics.

We will first discuss semantics and services from the domain point of view (mathematics): the knowledge base (Section 3.1), followed by the representation of the domain knowledge (Section 3.2). Then, we concentrate on the use from the pedagogical point of view: how to represent the pedagogical purpose of a learning object (Section 3.3) and how to use this semantic to make content from different repositories accessible to a learning environment (Section 3.4). The subsequent sections investigate learning goals, namely how to represent them (Section 3.5) and how to generate sequences of learning objects that fulfill them (Section 3.6). Finally, we discuss a client-rich tool that exemplifies how to client applications can use the above semantics (Section 3.7).

3.1. Knowledge Base Services

ActiveMath clearly separates the content from the functionalities working on it (such as course generation and presentation). Our knowledge base serves as a generic storage for the OMDoc-documents in ActiveMath. Queries include the retrieval of xml-content/items based on identifiers and search based on relations between items in both directions. Currently, fuzzy and semantic search are supported by this database.

At load time, the knowledge base resolves references relative to the mathematical theory and collection the element is in, into absolute references that include the theory and collection explicitly. This makes the structuring more flexible, integration more robust, and eases modifications. For communication, the knowledge base service provides an XLM-RPC protocol. This was chosen to balance expressivity and performance.

3.2. OMDOC and OPENMATH

One objective of using a generic semantic markup language is to keep the encoded content reusable and interoperable by other, even non-educational, mathematical applications. ActiveMath uses the semantic xml-markup language for mathematical documents, OMDoc [16, 22], for its content encoding. OMDoc has evolved as an extension of the OpenMath (European) standard for mathematical symbols and expressions [6]. ActiveMath uses these representations for the following reasons: they provide a semantic for mathematical expressions and a standardized structure of the content. Especially OpenMath is used for a variety of mathematical services, from mathematical evaluation until presentation, and thus, all applications can take advantage of each other's advances in tools and implementations.

ActiveMath's content is represented by a collection of typed items called "learning objects" annotated with metadata. The semantic information includes types, relations, and other mathematical and educational metadata. The type indicates a characterization of the items as collection, theory, concept or satellite items: an OpenMath symbol defines a mathematical concept abstractly; a theory assembles concepts and it can import other theories; concepts (definitions, algorithms, and assertions/theorems) are the main items of mathematical contents, whereas satellites (exercises, examples, explanations, introductions) are additional items of the content which are related to one or several concepts. All items are accessible via a unique identifier. The content (including the OpenMath symbols) induces an ontology.

For ActiveMath, we have extended the primarily mathematical OMDoc to serve educational purposes. For this, the metadata characterize not only mathematical, organizational, and intellectual property rights properties such as Dublin Core[3], but also educational annotations. These LOM compatible metadata [36] include properties such as difficulty, learning context, and field.

Moreover, items can be linked by relations. The `domain_prerequisite` relation expresses a mathematical dependency between concepts, ie, it describes which concepts are mathematically necessary in order to define the current one. The `for` relation links satellite items to concepts and definitions to symbols. For instance, an example or exercise may illustrate or train a related definition. The `against` relation describes an item as a counter example or misconception of the related concept. The `is-a` relation serves to represent mathematical hierarchies and special cases, eg, a "function" `is-a` specific "relation".

Note that several (mathematically equivalent) definitions may exist for one symbol, eg, the convergence of a function can be defined via epsilon-delta fomulae or via sequences. Definitions and theorems can be different for different learning-contexts or fields too. That is, only the OpenMath/symbol layer of the induced ontology is abstract in the sense that it represents concepts uniquely as required in certain ITS applications. ActiveMath items are multilingual but the system does not yet handle different versions of one and the same element which have the same metadata (e. g., learning context).

As we shall see in the following, the types and metadata properties and relations of the learning objects can be exploited to perform very advanced dynamic adaptation of the learning material, sequencing and presentation to the learner's needs and the context. Why is the semantic representation of symbols, ie, OpenMath, then needed in addition?

In ActiveMath the evaluation of the learner's input for questions and exercises can "subcontract" Computer Algebra Services, CAS, (possibly different CAS, whichever is suitable). For this, any of the CAS service has to "understand" the meaning of mathematical expressions, which is realized via the standardized semantic representation OpenMath. The language of a specific CAS or presentation MathML is not sufficient for that purpose.

Based on the OpenMath semantic representation, ActiveMath' presentation component can render mathematical formulæ appropriately for the needs and context of the learner, e. g., country-dependent notation and various output formats (html, xhtml +MathML, pdf). This is a feature unique to ActiveMath currently.

---

[3] http://dublincore.org/

In ActiveMath, copy& paste of formulæ is possible based on references to formulæ semantics hidden in the presentation. This is a feature which is unique for ActiveMath. More details about usages of this encoding in input and output of mathematical formulæ are provided in the section 3.7.

3.3. An Ontology of Instructional Objects

A first step towards intelligent services is to define the terms used in the application domain [28]. For educational services the terms need to describe the educational resources (or learning objects) as well as the learning goals. We designed an ontology of instructional objects (OIO) that was developed to characterize educational resources [37]. Although originally developed for mathematical resources, it can also be used for describing other subject domains, as long as the domain can be structured in distinct elements with relations (e. g., physics). The OIO describes resources sufficiently precise for a pedagogically complex functionality such as course generation.

Seminal work on using ontologies for e-learning was done in the ISIR lab, headed by Mizoguchi: they sketched out how ontologies can help to overcome problems in artificial intelligence in education [28]; and described how an assistant layer uses an ontology to support the complete authoring process, for instance by giving hints on the course structure [2,11].

The OIO has a more specific scope; instead of describing the authoring process during which the educational resources are developed, the ontology is focused on describing the resources. It thus defines a set of types (or classes) that is used to annotate educational resources. The ontology is described in detail elsewhere [37]. Central to the ontology (shown in Figure 2) is the distinction between the classes "fundamental" and "auxiliary". The class "fundamental" subsumes instructional objects that describe the central pieces of domain knowledge (concepts). Auxiliary elements include instructional objects which contain additional information about the fundamentals as well as training and learning experience.

3.4. A Mediator for Repository Integration

The ontology described in the previous section allows specifying the instructional function of educational resources and contains necessary information required for automatic, intelligent course generation. However, as a matter of fact, most of the repositories available today use their own metadata schema rather than the terms defined in the OIO. Yet, the pedagogical knowledge formalized in the course generator should be independent of the concrete metadata used in the repositories, as one wants to avoid designing separate knowledge for each repository.

The challenge of providing uniform access to resources has been recognized since long. Mediation information systems are a well-known solution to this challenge [41]. Its main component, called mediator, offers a uniform interface for accessing multiple heterogeneous data stores (e. g., file systems, different databases,...). The mediator uses mappings between the data representation used in the mediator and those used in the repository to translate queries. Each repository is enhanced with a wrapper, which can be integrated into the repository itself or into the mediator. This way, the query component does not have to know the specification of the data sources and their query languages.

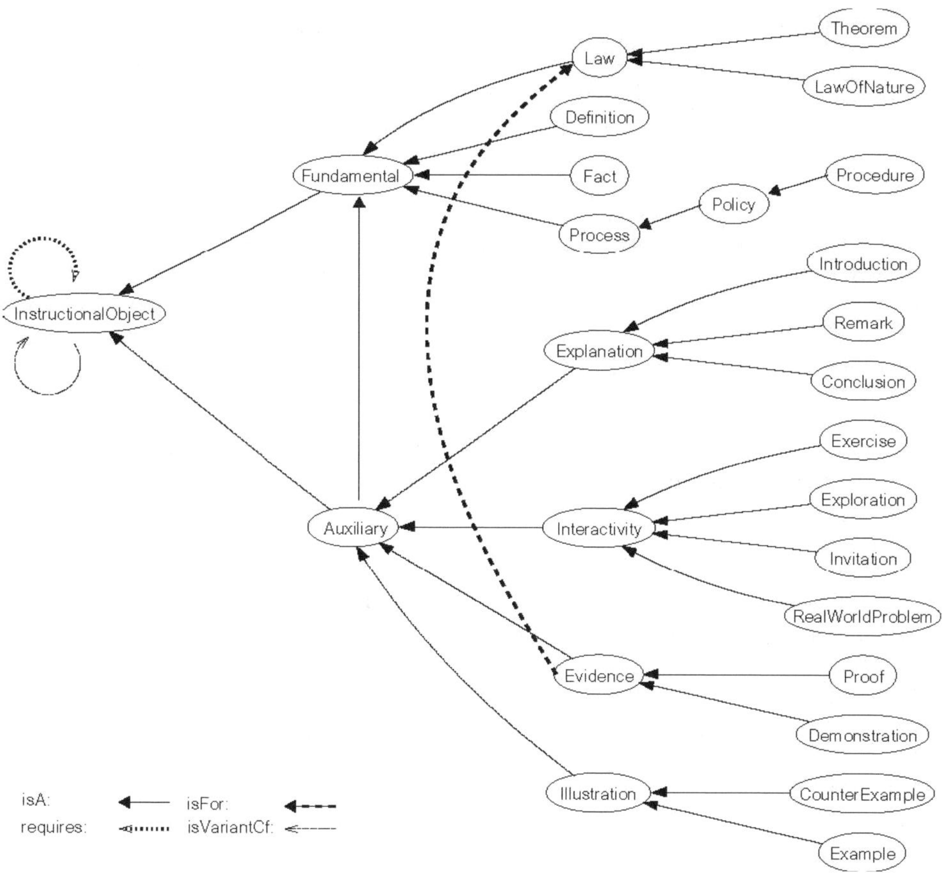

Figure 2. Overview of the Ontology of Instructional Objects

Any mediator used for course generation needs to answer queries extremely quickly: as our evaluations have shown generating an expanded course for a single concept results in about 1 500 mediator queries that are expanded to more than 11 000 queries to the repository.

Existing ontology-based query rewriting approaches [8] are very expressive, but, in consequence, complicated to use and not optimized for efficiency. Therefore, we decided to develop a query rewriting approach which is less powerful than other systems but expressive enough for our translation purposes. This specialization allows for optimizations, e. g., during query processing.

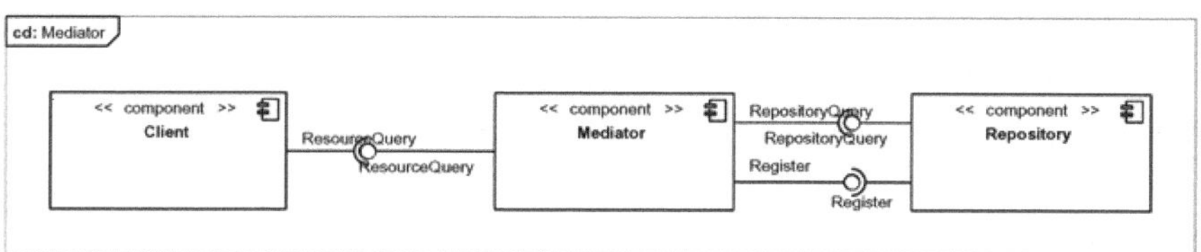

Figure 3. Overview of the mediator

Additionally, in the developed framework it is easy to integrate new repositories, by specifying a mapping between the OIO and the representation used in the repositories and implementing a small set of interfaces.

The mediator described in this section answers queries about the existence of specific educational resources. It is illustrated in Figure 3. Its interfaces[4] are Web-service interfaces. A repository can register (interface `Register`), passing an owl representation of its metadata structure as well as a mapping of the OIO onto this representation to the mediator. Additionally, each repository needs to implement the interface `RepositoryQuery` that allows the mediator to query the existence of educational resources. Clients access the mediator using the interface `ResourceQuery`.

3.4.1. Querying the Mediator

The interface `ResourceQuery` takes a partial metadata description as input and returns the set of identifiers of the educational resources that meet the description. The metadata used in a query sent to the mediator must comply to the OIO. It can consist of three parts:

Class queries specify the classes the educational resources have to belong to. They consist of a set of tuples (`class` *c*) in which *c* denotes the class of the OIO the returned educational resources must belong to.

Property queries specify property metadata. They consist of a set of triples (`property` *prop val*), where *prop* and *val* are property and value names from the OIO. Retrieved educational resources have to satisfy each given property-value pair.

Relation queries specify the relational metadata the educational resources have to meet. They consist of a set of triples (`relation` *rel id*) in which *rel* specifies the relation that must hold between the resource referenced by the identifier *id* and the educational resources to be retrieved. *rel* is a relation name of the OIO.

A query asking for all resources with an easy difficulty level illustrating the definition def slope looks as follows:

```
(relation isFor def_slope) (class illustration)
(property hasDifficulty easy)
```

While processing a query, the mediator uses the information of the OIO to expand a query to subclasses. Hence, if asked for class c, the mediator returns resources belonging to *c* and to its subclasses.

3.4.2. Ontology Mapping and Query Rewriting

A repository that registers itself using the interface Register must provide sufficient information to enable the mediator to translate the metadata of an incoming query to the metadata used by the repository.

The translation is performed by an ontology-based query-rewriting mechanism. The mechanism requires an ontological representation *O* of the metadata structure used by the repository and an ontology mapping *M*. It uses *O* and *M* to compute the rewriting steps for translating the queries it receives. A registration time, a repository

[4] The figure uses UML ball-and-socket icons. A ball represents a provided interface, a socket a required interface.

passes both the ontology and the mapping to the mediator. The mappings currently used by the mediator were produced beforehand by the developers.

We designed an xml-based ontology mapping language that represents the mappings between the OIO and the target ontologies.

An ontology mapping contains a set of mapping patterns, where each mapping pattern m consists of a matching pattern mp and a set of replacement patterns *RP* = *{rp1..., rpn}*. *mp* and *RP* consist of terms of the OIO and the ontology of the repository, respectively. A mapping pattern *m1* = *(mp1, RP1)* is more specific than a pattern *m2* =*(mp2, RP2)* if $mp2 \subset mp1$.

The idea of the ontology mapping is that every part of a query that matches a matching pattern is replaced by the replacement patterns. More formally, we say a mapping pattern *m* =*(mp, {rp1,... , rpn})* matches a query *q* if *q* contains each term specified in mp. Applying *m* to *q* results in new queries *q1,...,qn,* which are derived by replacing each term of *mp* by the terms of *rp1,..., rpn*, respectively.

The ontology mapping procedure applies the most specific mapping pattern to a query *q*. Currently, the author of an ontology mapping has to ensure manually that there is only one such pattern; future work will investigate how to support this automatically. A term for which no matching pattern is found is left as it is. This approach avoids writing mapping patterns that express the identity of terms (the use cases have shown that this is the most frequently occurring case).

3.4.3. Repository interface and caching

In order to be accessible from the mediator, a repository must implement the following interface that provides information about each of the above query types:

- `public Set queryClass(String id)` returns the classes a given resource belongs to.
- `public Set queryRelation(String rel, String id)` returns the set of identifiers of those educational resources the resource id is related to via the relation rel.
- `public Set queryProperty(String id)` returns the set of property-value pairs the given resource has.

In real use, performance matters and query processing is often time consuming mostly because of latency of the Web. For instance, course generation involves a significant amount of queries (about 100 000 expanded queries for a course for 20 concepts). Therefore, the amount of processed queries has to be reduced. We tackled this problem by integrating a caching mechanism into the mediator. If the same query (or sub-query) is sent repeatedly, the mediator does not query each connected repository again. Instead, it returns the cached set of identifiers, which increases run-time performance dramatically. The results of partial queries are cached, too.

Please note that our approach focuses on mapping of pedagogical concepts and not on mapping of instances of the subject domain. Thus, the mediator cannot yet use the information that fundamental *c1* in repository *r1* represents the same domain entity as fundamental *c2* in repository *r2*, say *def_group* in *r1* and *definition_gruppe* in *r2* both define the same mathematical concept group. In future work, we will integrate an instance mapping technology that maps domain ontologies.

3.4.4. Limitations of the Mediator as an Educational Service

The mediator allows access to resources based on their instructional function: a service generates partial metadata, and the mediator retrieves a list of corresponding educational resources. However, this is a basic service, which has some limitations:

- How to come up with the metadata? Determining the appropriate metadata for finding educational resources is not trivial. Assume a service wants to present an example of "average slope" to the learner. Is the learning context relevant? Should it be an easy or a difficult example? These decisions depend on the current learning goal, i. e., the current pedagogical task.
- Which precise educational resources to select? Typically, the mediator returns a list of resources. Which one is the most appropriate? Are they all equivalent? A too large set might indicate that the metadata was too general. However, narrowing it down might result in an over-specification an hence in an empty set.
- A single educational resource might not be sufficient to achieve learning progress. For instance, understanding content in depth requires a sequence of carefully selected educational resources. Again, the precise resources to select depend on the learning goal.

These limitations motivate the need for a course generator, i. e., a component that operationalizes the educational knowledge and provides services on a higher level of abstraction. The following sections describe the course generator.

3.5. Representing Learning Goals

The mediator architecture allows finding educational resources that fulfill given criteria. Typically, an agent (a learner or a machine) searches for the resources in order to achieve a learning goal. We designed an explicit and declarative representation that can be used to encode such learning goals.

A declarative representation of goals offers several advantages. First of all, it allows a system to autonomously generate actions to achieve the goal if the system uses an appropriate framework. Secondly, it provides an abstract layer that can be used for communication between systems. Instead of only being able to talk about the resources used in the learning process, systems can communicate about the purposes of the learning process. Third, it can be used to describe precisely the functionalities that the course generator offers: for each learning goal, Paigos can calculate a sequence of educational resources (if available) that help the learner to achieve this goal.

Existing course generators often use the domain concepts to represent learning goals. There, the generated course provides a sequence of educational resources that leads to these concepts and includes prerequisites and other resources. However, such an approach that restricts goals to resources is too limited. Depending on their current situation, learners want to achieve different objectives with the same target fundamentals, and a course should reflect the different needs associated with the objectives. For instance, a course that helps students to discover new content should differ different from a course that supports rehearsal.

Van Marcke [38] introduced the concept of an instructional tasks, which helps to define learning goals in more details: an instructional task represents an activity that can be accomplished during the learning process.

Both, the content and the instructional task are essential aspects of a learning goal. Therefore, we define learning goals as a combination of the two dimensions content and task. We call instructional tasks pedagogical objectives, in order to distinguish them from the declarative representation of learning goals, which we call pedagogical tasks:

A pedagogical task is a tuple $t = (p, L)$, where p is an identifier of the pedagogical objective and L is a list of educational resource identifiers. L specifies the course's target fundamentals, and p influences the structure of the course and the educational resources selected. The order of the resources in L is relevant and the same task with L's elements ordered differently can result in a different course.

As an example, the educational objective to discover and understand content in depth is called *discover*. Let's assume that *def_slope* and *def_diff* are the identifiers of the educational resources that contain the definition of the mathematical fundamental "average slope of a function" and "definition of the derivative, resp., differential quotient", respectively. We can now write the learning goal of a learner who wants to discover and understand these two fundamentals as the educational task *t =(discover,(def slope, def diff))*. The fundamentals are processed in the given order: first *def_slope*, followed by *def_diff*.

Table 1 contains a selection of pedagogical tasks formalized within Active-Math, partly designed in cooperation with pedagogical experts.

Table 1. A selection of pedagogical objectives used in ActiveMath.

Identifier	**Description**
discover	Discover and understand fundamentals in depth
rehearse	Address weak points
trainSet	Increase mastery of a set of fundamentals by training
guidedTour	Detailed information, including prerequisites
trainWithSingleExercice	Increase mastery using a single exercise
illustrate	Improve understanding by a sequence of examples
illustrateWithSingleExample	Improve understanding using a single example

Pedagogical tasks can be "internal" tasks, used for internal course generation purposes only, or tasks that are of potential interest for other services. The second category of tasks is called public tasks. Public tasks need to be described sufficiently precise in order to enable a communication between components as described above. The description designed for Paigos contains the following information:

- the identifier of the pedagogical objective;

- the number of concepts the pedagogical objective can be applied to. A task can either be applied to a single concept (cardinality 1) or multiple concepts (cardinality n).
- the type of educational resource (as defined in the OIO) that the task can be applied to;
- the type of course to expect as a result. Possible values are either course in case a complete course is generated or section in case a single section is returned. Even in case the course generator selects only a single educational resource, the resource is included in a section. This is due to requirements from standards like IMS CP which is used by the course generator Web-service.
- an optional element condition that is evaluated in order to determine whether a task can be achieved. In some situations, a service only needs to know whether a task can be achieved but not by which educational resources. In that case, the condition can be passed to the mediator, and if the return value is different from null, the task can be achieved.
- a concise natural language description of the purpose that is used for display in menus.

Educational tasks together with the ontology of instructional objects allow representing learning goals and the instructionally relevant aspects of resources used to achieve those goals. In the next section, we describe how the course generator Paigos uses these representations in order to assemble personalized sequences of educational resources that support the learner in achieving her learning goals.

3.6. Course Generator

Course generation has long been a research topic [32]. It uses pedagogical knowledge to generate a structured sequence of learning objects that is adapted to the learners' competencies, individual variables, and learning goals [5]. This generation happens upon request of a client (a learner or a software system). Ideally, the sequence is not a flat list of learning objects but is structured in sections and subsections. This structure can convey additional information relevant to the learning process. In course generation, the course is generated completely before it is presented to the learner. This early generation has the advantage that the course can be visualized to the learner, thereby informing her about the structure. In addition, the student can navigate freely through the course.

Early work on course generation [38] emphasized the value of the teaching knowledge used by the course generator. Today's course generators (see the section on related work) often use rather simplified pedagogical knowledge that guides the assembly, most of the time the "prerequisite"-relation that represents that understanding resource B depends on having understood resource A is used. One reason for using only very simple pedagogical knowledge is that pedagogical knowledge is hard to assess and expensive to model. Systems that aim at modeling pedagogically knowledge require a large teaching model: for instance, the instructional knowledge base of the system GTE encompasses about a hundred tasks and methods; the instructional ontology proposed in [11] consists of about 530 classes. Paigos, the course generator of ActiveMath contains about 300 rules that determine the selection, ordering and structuring of learning objects. This "expensive" functionality lends itself to being "outsourced": if the course generator is available as a service then other learning environments can access the functionality without having to re-implement it. However, none of the previously developed course generators allowed the integration of new repositories and the accessible content was restricted to the local repositories. Paigos in contrast is a Web service where clients can register their repositories and subsequently use Paigos for course generation (see Section 3.6.3).

Paigos is used to generate courses that support a learner in achieving a number of learning goals, such as discovering new content ("discover" in short), training specific competencies and simulating exams. For these learning goals, Paigos generates complete courses which contain all the learning material required by a learner to achieve the goals. Paigos is also used to retrieve single elements that specifically fulfill a given purpose, such as presenting an example or exercise adequate for the current the learner. This functionality is important for remedial, e. g., if a learner fails to solve an exercise, then the presentation of an example might help the learner to overcome the difficulty.

Paigos was developed in a moderate constructivist context. Moderate constructivism emphasizes the active engagement of the learner and stresses that knowledge cannot be transferred from the teacher to the learner but is the result of cognitive processes in the learner's mind. A moderate constructivist learning environment has to stimulate and create opportunities for these processes. Paigos is also based on the concept of "competencies", which advocates that different competencies together build up mathematical literacy [31]. In the following, we describe the Artificial Intelligence framework employed by Paigos and how it is used to describe two scenarios ("discover" and "guided tour"). In total, ActiveMath comprises seven different course generation scenarios.

3.6.1. Hierarchical Task Network Planning

Paigos uses AI planning as a framework for implementing the pedagogical knowledge of how to generate a course. In Hierarchical Task Network planning (HTN) [29], the goal of the planner is to achieve a list of tasks, where each task is a symbolic representation of an activity to be performed. The planner formulates a plan by using methods to decompose these top tasks into smaller subtasks until primitive tasks are reached that can be carried out directly using operators. The planning operators describe various actions that can be performed directly. Methods describe various possible ways of decomposing non-primitive tasks into subtasks. These are the "standard operating procedures" that one would normally use to perform tasks in the domain. Each method may have constraints that must be satisfied in order to be applicable. Planning is done by applying methods to non-primitive tasks to decompose them into sub-tasks, and applying operators to primitive tasks to produce actions. If this is done in such a way that all of the constraints are satisfied, then the planner has found a solution plan; otherwise the planner will need to backtrack and try other methods and actions.

For course generation, Paigos takes a goal task as input and returns a structured sequence of learning object identifiers (basically a table of contents) as a result [37]. The goal task consists of an educational objective that represents the type of learning goal and of learning objects identifiers for which this learning goal should be achieved. As an example, the goal task "discover average slope" represents the goal of a learner who want to reach an in-depth under-standing of the mathematical concept average slope. We now take a closer look on the knowledge that formalizes how to achieve such a learning goal.

3.6.2. Course Generation Scenarios

The scenario "discover" generates courses that contain those Learning objects that support the learner in reaching an in-depth understanding of the concepts given in the goal task. The basic structure of the scenario follows a course of action in a classroom that consists of several stages that typically occur when learning a new concept [42]. For each stage, the course contains a corresponding section. The following sections are created:

- Description: describes the aim and structure of a course. Then, for each concept given in the goal task, the following additional sections are created:
- Motivation: motivates the usefulness of the concept using adequate LOs (the precise meaning of an "adequate" LOs is formalized in methods like described below). It also contains the unknown prerequisites.
- Develop: presents the concept and illustrates how it can be applied.
- Train: provides opportunities to train the concept.
- Connections: illustrates the connections between the current and related concepts.
- Reflection: each course closes with a reflection section, which provides the learner with opportunity to reflect on the content presented in the course.

For this scenario, the course generation is started with the single goal task *(discover (c1 ...cn))* with *c1 ... cn* representing the goal concepts the student wants to learn. A first method, not shown here, inserts a subtask *(learnConceptDiscover (cn))* for each of the concepts. This task is decomposed by the following method:

```
(:method (learnFundamentalDiscover ?c)
    ()
    ((!startSection)
    (introduceWithPrereqSection ?c)
    (developFundamental ?c)
    (proveSection ?c)
    (practiceSection ?c)
    (showConnectionsSection ?c)
    (!endSection)))
```

The keyword *:method* starts the definition of a new method. The subsequent expression *(learnConceptDiscover ?c)* represent the task the method is applied on (expressions starting with "?" stand for variables and are instantiated at run-time). The task is decomposed into 7 subtasks *(!startSection) ... (!endSection)*: first, a new section is started, in this case the course itself. Then, several subtasks are inserted that mimic the informal description above. The last subtask closes the course. Similar methods exist for the other tasks.

About 30 methods encode the pedagogical knowledge how to select exercises that are "appropriate" for the learner. The exact meaning of "appropriate" differs depending on the individual learner. The most relevant factors determining exercise selection are the educational level of the learners and their current competency level. In general, the learning context of each learning object should correspond to the educational level of the learner. Otherwise it may be inadequate, that is, either too simple or too difficult (think of a second year university student being presented a definition for elementary school). In addition, in most cases, resources presented to the learner should be of a competency level that corresponds to the learner's since these are the resources he is able to master. In some situations resources with a higher competency level need to be selected, e.g., when aiming at increasing the competency level. The methods also take information about motivation and anxiety into account (assed using the performance in exercises). A similar complex set of methods determines the selection of examples.

The scenario "discover" is based on competencies and competency levels. Since competency-based pedagogy is a relatively novel approach, it is not yet widespread and most of the existing learning environments follow the traditional mastery-based paradigm. With this in mind, we developed the scenario "guided tour" based on Merrill's "First principles of instruction" [26]. In this scenario, for each concept given in the goal task, and for each unknown prerequisite concepts, the following sections are created: An introduction that arises a learner's interest by presenting LOs of the type introduction; a section that presents the concept itself, a section that provides explaining and deepening information about the concept; a section that provides opportunities for the learner to examine demonstrations of applications of the concepts; a section that enables a student to actively apply what he has learned; and finally a section that contains concluding information about the concept.

3.6.3. Course Generation as a Web-Service

The course generator is available as a Web-service (CGWS). The CGWS provides two main kinds of interfaces: the core interface that provides the methods for the course generation, and the repository integration interface that allows a client to register a repository at the CGWS. The core interface consists of the following methods:

- The method `getTaskDefinitions` is used to retrieve the pedagogical tasks which the course generator can process.
- The method `generateCourse` starts the course generation on a given task.

The client can make information about the learner available in two ways: if the learner model contains information about the specific learner, then the client passes the respective learner identifier as a parameter. In case no learner model exists, a client gives a list of property-value pairs that is used by the CGWS to construct a temporary "learner model". The course generator performs the planning in the same way as with a real learner model, however its access of learner properties is diverted by the CGWS and answered using the map. Properties not contained in the map are answered with a default value.

The result of the course generation is a structured sequence of educational resources represented in an IMS Manifest. Since the returned result does not contain the resources but only references, the return result is not an IMS CP.

The interface for repository registration consists of the following methods:

- The method `getMetadataOntology` informs the client about the metadata structure used in CGWS. It returns the ontology of instructional objects described in Section 3.4.
- The method `registerRepository` registers the repository that the client wants the course generator to use. The client has to provide the name and the location (url) of the repository. Additional parameters include the ontology that describes the metadata structure used in the repository and the mapping of the OIO onto the repository ontology.
- The method `unregisterRepository` unregisters the given repository.

3.6.4. Client Interfaces

A client that wants to use the CGWS needs to provide information about the educational resources as well as about the learner (if available).

The interface `ResourceQuery` is used by the mediator to query the repository about properties of educational resources. The interface consists of the following methods (the same as described in Section 3.4.3):

- `queryClass` returns the classes a given resource belongs to.
- `queryRelation` returns the set of identifiers of those educational resources the given resource is related to via the given relation.
- `queryProperty` returns the set of property-value pairs the given resource has.

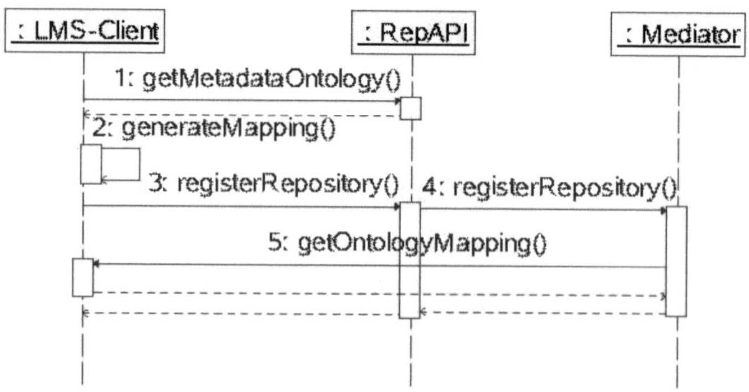

Figure 4. A sequence diagram illustrating the repository registration

The `LearnerPropertyAPI` makes the learners' properties accessible to the CGWS in case the client contains a learner model and wants the course generator to use it. In the current version of the CGWS, this interface is not yet implemented. It would require a mediator architecture similar to the one used for repository integration.

3.6.5. Interaction between Client and Server

In this section we describe the communication between client and server performed when registering a repository and for course generation.

A repository is registered in the following way (for a sequence diagram il lustrating the registration, see Figure 4): in a first step, the client (LMS-Client in the figure) retrieves the metadata ontology used in the CGWS (i. e., the OIO). The ontology is then used to generate a mapping between the OIO and the ontology representing the client metadata (Step 2) (the currently existing mappings were manually authored). Then, the repository is registered using the method `registerRepository` (Step 3). The repository is added to the list of available repositories and made known to the mediator (Step 4). Subsequently, the mediator fetches the ontology mapping from the client and automatically generates a wrapper for querying the `contentAPI` of the client.

A client starts the course generation using the service method `generateCourse`. In a first step, the CGWS checks whether the task is valid. If so, the course is generated by the course generator. During the generation process, Paigos sends queries to the mediator, which passes the queries to the repository. Like in ActiveMath, the results are cached. After the course is generated, the course generated by Paigos is transformed into an IMS manifest and sent to the client.

The CGWS is still in an early stage of development and further work is necessary to realize a mediator-like architecture for the generic integration of learner models. Yet, despite being a prototype, the CGWS was successfully used by several third-party systems, e. g., MathCoach (a learning tool for statistics [10]) and Teal (workflow embedded e-learning at the workplace [33]).

3.7. Rich Client Access to ActiveMath

In this section, we will give an example of rich client applications in ActiveMath that uses several of the service described above (the knowledge base and the course generator).

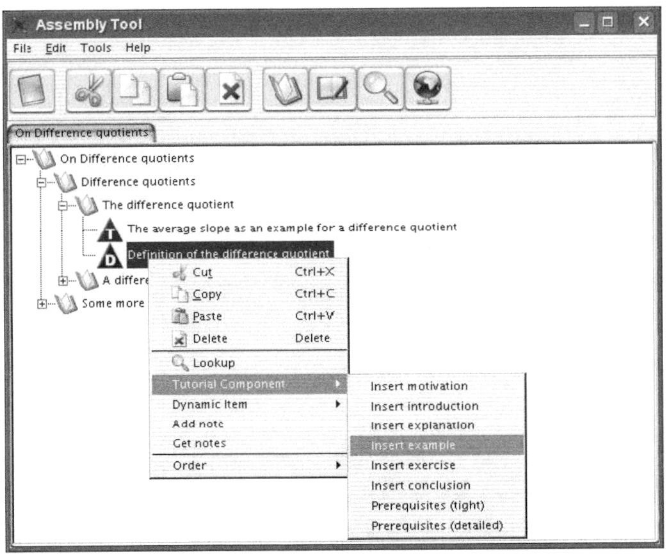

Figure 5. Screenshot of the assembly tool

3.7.1. ActiveMath's Assembly Tool

ActiveMath's assembly tool allows a learner to create a book on her own by dragging educational resources from ActiveMath (but also any other resource addressable by an uri). The tool was designed to support the learner's metacognitive reasoning, self-regulated learning and active engagement with the content.

The principal actions supported by the assembly tool are the creation of structured courses by adding chapters and drag-and-drop of resources into a table of contents. In addition, a learner has access to Paigos's functionality using a context menu. She can select the direct insertion of resources that fulfill a pedagogical task specified by the learner or insert a dynamic task that is achieved at a later time. Figure 5 contains a screenshot that illustrates the integration. In the example, the learner uses the course generator to select an example for "the definition of the difference quotient".

The Assembly Tool is started via Java WebStart. Upon clicking on a link to the Assembly Tool ActiveMath generates dynamically a JNLP [12] file and sends it back to the browser. The browser invokes Java WebStart and passes it the file. It retrieves them and starts a new Assembly Tool process. The file contains information where to locate the assembly tool's binaries, general information about the application as well as context-specific information supplied by the ActiveMath server.

Since ActiveMath is a user-adaptive system, the Assembly Tool receives context-dependant information in the JNLP file properties. The information is provided at launch time by instantiating service wrappers and providing their URLs as properties at launch time.

Both the URL to the content base and to the user manager are secured by a random number. This way, malicious alterations, in particular of the user model, are prevented. In addition, the URL to the ActiveMath server is provided. For the Assembly Tool to address the current user, the ActiveMath server includes the current user's identifier, name, and default language. If the user intends to edit an own book a book identifier is added.

The Assembly Tool is able to interoperate with other ActiveMath components. Messages are transported via XLM-RPC.

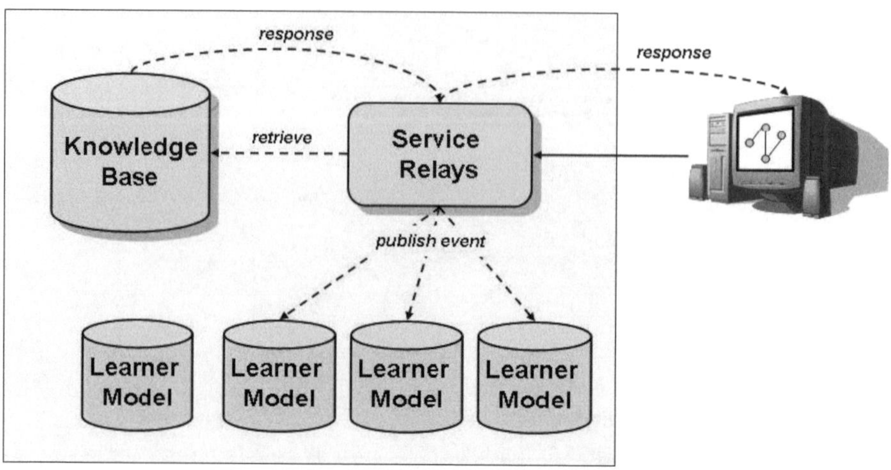

Figure 6. Assembly Tool communication with ActiveMath

Communication between Assembly Tool and LeActiveMath is twofold (see Figure 6). Requests to the content knowledge base are synchronous while client- events are issued asynchronously and they are distributed via ActiveMath's event framework.

Any action in the Assembly Tool that alters a book the student is currently working with triggers an event that is sent to the ActiveMath server. Also, actions that call service methods as well as upload/save/open/new actions cause an event.

Finally, the claim for consistency of appearance and language sketched above is achieved by the following interoperability result. Each item presented in the web-browser (e.g. within a book) can have its title dragged and dropped into the assembly tool so that the corresponding item is included in the designated page. This usage relies on the semantics of web-links which uniquely identified the rendered content items. Dropping such an item in the assembly tool triggers the insertion of the item in the table-of-contents but also a call to the knowledge base to determine the type and title of the item thus yielding almost the same rendering of the item's title in a completely different setting.

3.7.2. Integrated Semantic Mathematical Input and Output

A similar principle has been approached for the mathematical output (that is, the rendering of formulæ) and input (that is, where the user inputs formulæ): the OpenMath representation is used as lingua franca of any exchange between the components, clients and servers. Its rendering produces consistent notations which adapt to the local context (e.g. language, domain-tradition, for example the presentation of the binomial coefficient being C_a^b, C_b^a or $\binom{a}{b}$ in France, Russia, or Great Britain).

This rendering is specified by authorable notations which are the main source of knowledge for the conversion of OpenMath expressions to presentation languages. The presentation of mathematics is consistent throughout ActiveMath, regardless of whether a formula is rendered in the ActiveMath itself or other tools such as the input editor. This editor [20] is run as a Java applet and allows writing of formulæ within the interactive exercises, the free computer-algebrasystem, and the mathematical search tool. It also enables drag-and-drop of formulæ into a graph plotter.

The input-editor, at time of launch, is allocated a server-side-storage, i.e., a URL where it can read from and post to. This allows its content to be drag-and-droppable to other input-editor-instances, prevents the usage of the fragile JavaScript↔Java communication, and avoids the OpenMath expression to clutter the URL.

Copy&paste is an important help for learners to input mathematical formulæ. Thus, in ActiveMath every term of a mathematical expression can be dragged-and-dropped into an input-editor applet. Behind the scenes, a URL is drag-and-dropped. This URL is a clip-URL which provides the source OpenMath representation, or reformulations of them. The input editor then requests such a URL and inserts the OpenMath representation thus obtained in the formula where the drop occurred. See [17] for more details about the transfer facility of ActiveMath.

The integrated nature of the mathematical input-and-output was evaluated positively by students. Due to technical constraints, initiating the drag-and-drop required a slightly more complicated interaction than traditional drag-and-drop. This was criticized as being unconventional and unexpected. The web-nature of our ActiveMath system could, however, not do more than a browser showing untrusted pages could. A standardization at the level of browser is thus needed, the W3C WebAPI working group may address it.[5]

3.7.3. Other Client Tools

Several other client tools are running using a similar architecture as the assembly tool. They all are contextualized at launch time with service wrappers either using JNLP or applets. One of them is the Interactive Concept Mapping Tool iCMaP [24]. This tool allows learners to drop item references and organize them in concept-maps which can be validated against the knowledge base.

Other tools are used in exercise situations and send exercise events to the event dispatcher which allows the learner model to be kept up-to-date. Finally, a desktop based exercise system for combinatorics is currently being investigated for integration. Such a system would not be launched by an applet or JNLP file but by the download of an exercise file whose type is associated to the application.

4. Related Work

A large number of research groups investigate educational services based on semantics in an educational context. However, to our knowledge, no other system covers such a broad and complete set of functionalities as ActiveMath.

For instance, only few systems (e.g., [7]) offer a semantic representation of the content, hence loosing the possibility of rendering different output format or using the content as input for tools such as Computer Algebra Systems. To our knowledge, semantic-based copy-and-paste of formulæ is still an exclusivity of ActiveMath.

However, most systems use xml-based metadata, based on and extending IEEE LOM. Several groups, unsatisfied by the limited pedagogical coverage of LOM worked on metadata expressive enough for pedagogically mature systems (e. g., [18]). The ontology of instructional objects described in Section 3.3 draws on these approaches and represents the minimal pedagogical information necessary for pedagogically founded learner support.

Adaptive Hypermedia (AH, see [4]) covers techniques of adapting hypermedia objects with respect to the user. Well known systems are ELM-ART [40] and AHA [1]. ActiveMath offers several AH techniques but is more flexible as complete courses can be generated based on pedagogical knowledge. Course Generation (or Adaptive Trail Generation) has been investigated since long [39,38,35,34] and is still an active area of research. For instance, [25,15,13,14] focus on the generation of learning trails and courses. However, these approaches do not allow for such detailed representation of pedagogical knowledge as done in ActiveMath. Most rely on the sequencing of full pages which is a crucial loss of re-usability: typically, a definition can be shared among several learning-contexts but it is important for learning purposes to differentiate the introductory, example, and exercise material (for example relying on real world examples for the given audience).

In the last years, semantics and services their relevance for education was investigated by several groups. [30] describe an rdf-based peer to peer networking infrastructure. [27] describe an approach to query Semantic Web resources by querying

[5] http://www.w3.org/2006/webapi/.

and transforming RDF models using a rule language based on Horn logic. Their focus lies on the general approach, thus the e-learning scenario provided as an example in their paper is limited to querying exercises and it appears that such a performance as we expect is not to be expected in a near future.

5. Lessons Learned and Conclusions

In this chapter, we described educational services in ActiveMath and the underlying service-oriented technologies we are using. During the development of ActiveMath, we experimented with different technologies. The lesson we have learned is that being generic and abstract is nice, but speed matters more. More specifically this means that we used the most primitive but efficient technology that was available and appropriate to the specific service (e. g., XLM-RPC or Java for internal communication and Web services for interaction with external components). In early versions of ActiveMath, we made extensive use of its distribution features: the learner model ran on server a, the knowledge base on server b, etc. While this lowered the load on each single machine, the overall overhead increased dramatically. In real usage, that is, in a classroom setting involving several dozens of students (as done for the evaluation performed in the LeActiveMath project), the distribution was simply too inefficient and eventually we moved all internal ActiveMath components back into a single server.

One example that illustrates the load during real application is course generation. Generating a expanded course for a single concept (the course consists of a total of 40 resources) results in about 1 500 mediator queries that are expanded to more than 11 000 queries to the repository. On the other end of the spectrum, generating an expanded course for 20 fundamentals (the course consists of a total of 370 resources) results in 21 500 mediator queries and more than 100 000 expanded queries. While the amount of queries can be reduced to 150/1 200 and 2 700/14 100 by expanding some goals on-demand-only [37], the numbers remain significant. As a consequence, the course generator's performance considerably depends on the repositories and the learner model. In case the components reside on different servers, the very network latency alone reduces the overall performance: the LeActiveMath exercise repository is located in Eindhoven, the Netherlands. When accessed from Saarbrücken, Germany, it answers a single query in about 80 milliseconds. As a consequence, the generation of a 4 concepts course that requires 3 300 queries requires 4:30 minutes instead of 290 milliseconds. On the Web, four minutes are an eternity. Few learners will wait patiently for the course to appear

We think that while service-and grid-oriented educational computing has its benefits, we need to be aware of the short-comings that it still exhibits today hence should only use it where the benefits pay off.

References

[1] Ad Aerts, David Smits, Natalia Stash, and Paul De Bra. AHA! Version 2.0, more adaptation flexibility for authors. In Griff Richards, editor, Proceedings of World Conference on E-Learning in Corporate, Government, Healthcare, and Higher Education 2002, pages 240–246, Montreal, Canada, 2002. AACE.

[2] L. Aroyo and R. Mizoguchi. Authoring support framework for intelligent educational systems. In U. Hoppe, F. Verdejo, and J. Kay, editors, Proccedings of AI in Education, AIED-2003, pages 362–364. IOS Press, 2003.

[3] Daniel Austin, Abbie Barbir, Christopher Ferris, and Sharad Garg. Web Services Architecture Requirements. Online: http://www.w3.org/TR/wsa-reqs/, 2004.

[4] Peter Brusilovsky. Adaptive hypermedia. User Modeling and User Adapted Interaction, 11(1/2):87–110, 2001.

[5] Peter Brusilovsky and Julita Vassileva. Course sequencing techniques for large-scale web-based education. International Journal of Continuing Engineering Education and Lifelong Learning, 13(1/2):75–94, 2003.

[6] Stephen Buswell, Olga Caprotti, David Carlisle, Mike Dewar, Marc Ga¨etano, and Michael Kohlhase. The openmath standard, version 2.0. Technical report, The OpenMath Society, June 2004. Available at http://www.openmath.org/.

[7] Hans Cuypers and Hans Sterk. Mathbook, web-technology for mathematical documents. In Proceedings of the BITE 2001 conference, Eindhoven, The Netherlands, 22-24 November, 2001. See also from http://www.riaca.win.tue.nl/.

[8] J. de Bruijn, D. Foxvog, and K. Zimmermann. Ontology Mediation Patterns Library V1. D4.3.1, SEKT-project, February 2005.

[9] G. Goguadze, A. Gonz´alez Palomo, and E. Melis. Interactivity of Exercises in ActiveMath. In In Proceedings of the 13th International Conference on Computers in Education (ICCE 2005), pages 107–113, Singapore, 2005.

[10] Barbara L. Grabowski, Susanne G¨ang, J¨org Herter, and Thomas K¨oppen. MathCoach und LaplaceSkript: Ein programmierbarer interaktiver Mathematiktutor mit XML-basierter Skriptsprache. In Klaus P. Jantke, Klaus-Peter F¨ahnrich, and Wolfgang S. Wittig, editors, Leipziger Informatik-Tage, volume 72 of LNI, pages 211–218. GI, 2005.

[11] Yusuke Hayashi, Jacqueline Bourdeau, and Riichiro Mizoguchi. Ontological support for a theory-eclectic approach to instructional and learning design. In Wolfgang Nejdl and Klaus Tochtermann, editors, Innovative Approaches for Learning and Knowledge Sharing, First European Conference on Technology Enhanced Learning, EC-TEL 2006, Crete, Greece, October 1-4, 2006, Proceedings, volume 4227 of LNCS, pages 155–169. Springer, 2006.

[12] Java Software (Sun MicroSystems, Inc.). Java (tm) network launching protocol & api specification (jsr-56), 2004. Available at http://java.sun.com/products/javawebstart/ download-spec.html.

[13] Pythagoras Karampiperis and Demetrios Sampson. Automatic learning object selection and sequencing in web-based intelligent learning systems. In Zongmin Ma, editor, Web-Based Intelligent e-Learning Systems: Technologies and Applications, chapter III, pages 56–71. Information Science Publishing, 2005.

[14] Ian O. Keeffe, Aoife Brady, Owen Conlan, and Vincent Wade. Just-in-time generation of pedagogically sound, context sensitive personalized learning experiences. International Journal on E-Learning, 5(1):113–127, 2006.

[15] K. Keenoy, A. Poulovassilis, G. Papamarkos, P.T. Wood, Vassilis Christophides, Aimilia Maganaraki, Miltiadis Stratakis, P. Rigaux, and N. Spyratos. Adaptive personalisation in self e-learning networks. In Proceedings of First International Kaleidoscope Learning Grid SIG Workshop on Distributed e-Learning Environments, Napoly, Italy, 2005.

[16] Michael Kohlhase. OMDoc – An Open Markup Format for Mathematical Documents. Springer Verlag, 2006.

[17] Paul Libbrecht and Dominik Jednoralski. Drag and Drop of Formulae from a Browser. In Proceedings of MathUI'06, August 2006. Available from http://www.activemath.org/ ~paul/MathUI06/.

[18] Ulrike Lucke, Djamshid Tavangarian, and Denny Voigt. Multidimensional educational multimedia with ml3. In Griff Richards, editor, Proceedings of World Conference on E-Learning in Corporate, Government, Healthcare, and Higher Education 2003, pages 101–104, Phoenix, Arizona, USA, 2003. AACE.

[19] Tiziana Margaria. Service is in the eyes of the beholder. Computer, 40(11):33–37, 2007.

[20] Daniel Marqu`es, Ramon Eixarch, Gl`oria Casanellas, Bruno Mart´ınez, and Tim Smith. WIRIS OM Tools a Semantic Formula Editor. In Proceedings of MathUI'06, August 2006. Available from http://www.activemath.org/~paul/MathUI06/.

[21] E. Melis, E. Andr`es, J. Büdenbender, A. Frischauf, G. Goguadze, P. Libbrecht, M. Pollet, and C. Ullrich. ActiveMath: A Generic and Adaptive Web-Based Learning Environment. International Journal of Artificial Intelligence in Education, 12(4):385–407, 2001.

[22] E. Melis, J. Büdenbender, G. Goguadze, P. Libbrecht, M. Pollet, and C. Ullrich. Knowledge representation and management in activemath. Annals of Mathematics and Artificial Intelligence, Special Issue on Management of Mathematical Knowledge, 38(1-3):47–64, 2003. Volume is accessible from http://monet.nag.co.uk/mkm/amai/index.html.

[23] E. Melis, G. Goguadze, M. Homik, P. Libbrecht, C. Ullrich, and S. Winterstein. Semantic-Aware Components and Services of ActiveMath. British Journal of Educational Technology, 37(3):405–423, may 2006.

[24] E. Melis, P. K¨arger, and M. Homik. Interactive Concept Mapping in ActiveMath (iCMap). In J¨org M. Haake, Ulrich Lucke, and Djamshid Tavangarian, editors, Delfi 2005: 3. Deutsche eLearning Fachtagung Informatik, volume 66 of LNI, pages 247–258, Rostock, Germany, sep 2005. Gesellschaft für Informatik e.V. (GI).

[25] N´estor Dar´ıo Duque M´endez, Claudia Jim´enez Ram´ırez, and Jaime Alberto Guzm´an Luna. IA planning for automatic generation of customized virtual courses. In Frontiers In Artificial Intelligence And Applications, Proceedings of ECAI 2004, volume 117, pages 138–147, Valencia (Spain), 2004. IOS Press.

[26] M. D. Merrill. First principles of instruction. Educational Technology Research & Development, 50(3):43–59, 2002.

[27] Z. Miklos, G. Neumann, U. Zdun, and M. Sintek. Querying semantic web resources using TRIPLE views. In The SemanticWeb -ISWC 2003, Sanibel Island, USA, volume 2870 of Lecture Notes in Computer Science, pages 517–532, Heidelberg, Germany, 2003. Springer.

[28] R. Mizoguchi and J. Bourdeau. Using ontological engineering to overcome AI-ED problems. International Journal of Artificial Intelligence in Education, 11(2):107–121, 2000.

[29] Dana S. Nau, Tsz-Chiu Au, Okhtay Ilghami, Ugur Kuter, J. William Murdock, Dan Wu, and Fusun Yaman. SHOP2: An HTN Planning System. Journal of Artificial Intelligence Research, 20:379–404, 2003.

[30] W. Nejdl, B. Wolf, C. Qu, S. Decker, M. Sintek, A. Naeve, M. Nilsson, M. Palm´er, and T. Risch. Edutella: a P2P networking infrastructure based on RDF. In WWW '02: Proceedings of the 11th international conference on World Wide Web, pages 604–615, New York, NY, USA, 2002. ACM Press.

[31] OECD, editor. Learning for Tomorrows World — First Results from PISA 2003. Organisation for Economic Co-operation and Development (OECD) Publishing, 2004.

[32] Darwyn R. Peachy and Gordon I. McCalla. Using planning techniques in intelligent tutoring systems. International Journal of Man-Machine Studies, 24(1):77–98, 1986.

[33] Oleg Rostanin, Carsten Ullrich, Harald Holz, and Shenwei Song. Project teal: Add adaptive e-learning to your workflows. In Klaus Tochtermann and Hermann Maurer, editors, Proceedings: I-KNOW'06, 6th International Conference on Knowledge Management, pages 395–402, Graz, Austria, Sep 2006.

[34] Cornelia Seeberg, Klaus Reichenberger, Stephan Fischer, Ralf Steinmetz, and Achim Steinacker. Dynamically generated tables of contents as guided tours in adaptive hypermedia systems. In Piet Kommers and Griff Richards, editors, Proceedings of World Conference on Educational Multimedia, Hypermedia and Telecommunications 1999, pages 640–645, Chesapeake, VA, 1999. AACE.

[35] M. Specht and R. Oppermann. ACE -adaptive courseware environment. The New Review of Hypermedia and Multimedia, 4:141–162, 1998.

[36] IEEE Learning Technology Standards Committee. 1484.12.1-2002 IEEE standard for Learning Object Metadata, 2002.

[37] Carsten Ullrich. Course Generation as a Hierarchical Task Network Planning Problem. PhD thesis, Computer Science Department, Saarland University, Saarbrücken, 2007.

[38] Kris Van Marcke. GTE: An epistemological approach to instructional modelling. Instructional Science, 26:147–191, 1998.

[39] Julita Vassileva. Dynamic Courseware Generation: at the Cross Point of CAL, ITS and Authoring. In Proceedings International Conference on Computers in Education, ICCE'95, pages 290–297, Singapore, 1995.

[40] G. Weber and Peter Brusilovsky. ELM-ART: An adaptive versatile system for web-based instruction. International Journal of Artificial Intelligence in Education, 12(4):351–384, 2001.

[41] G. Wiederhold. Mediators in the architeture of future information systems. The IEEE Computer Magazine, March 1992.

[42] Friedrich Zech. Grundkurs Mathematikdidaktik. Beltz Verlag, Weinheim, 2002.

Author Index